Hegel on Tragedy and Comedy

Hegel on Tragedy and Comedy

New Essays

Edited by **Mark Alznauer**

Published by State University of New York Press, Albany

©2021 State University of New York Press
All rights reserved

Printed in the United States of America

No part of this book may be used or reproduced in any manner whatsoever without written permission. No part of this book may be stored in a retrieval system or transmitted in any form or by any means including electronic, electrostatic, magnetic tape, mechanical, photocopying, recording, or otherwise without the prior permission in writing of the publisher.

For information, contact State University of New York Press, Albany, NY
www.sunypress.edu

Library of Congress Cataloging-in-Publication Data

Names: Alznauer, Mark, editor.
Title: Hegel on tragedy and comedy : new essays / [editor:] Mark Alznauer.
Description: Albany : State University of New York Press, [2021] | Includes bibliographical references and index.
Identifiers: LCCN 2020048646 | ISBN 9781438483375 (hardcover) | ISBN 9781438483382 (ebook) | ISBN (pbk. 9781438483368 : alk. paper)
Subjects: LCSH: Hegel, Georg Wilhelm Friedrich, 1770–1831. | Greek drama (Tragedy)—History and criticism—Theory, etc. | Greek drama (Comedy)—History and criticism—Theory, etc.
Classification: LCC B2949.T64 H44 2021 | DDC 882.009—dc23
LC record available at https://lccn.loc.gov/2020048646

10 9 8 7 6 5 4 3 2 1

Contents

1   **Introduction** Mark Alznauer

I. Tragedy

15   1 **The Beauty of Fate and Its Reconciliation. Hegel's *The Spirit of Christianity and Its Fate* and Goethe's *Iphigenia in Tauris***
Douglas Finn (Villanova University)

43   2 **Two Early Interpretations of Hegel's Theory of Greek Tragedy. Hinrichs and Goethe** Eric v. d. Luft (Gegensatz Press)

57   3 **Hegel and the Origins of Critical Theory. Aeschylus and Tragedy in Hegel's *Natural Law* Essay** Wes Furlotte (Thompson Rivers University)

79   4 **The Tragedy of Sex (for Hegel)**
Antón Barba-Kay (Catholic University of America)

97   5 **Substantial Ends and Choices without a Will. Greek Tragedy as Archetype of Tragic Drama** Allegra de Laurentiis (SUNY Stony Brook)

117   6 **Freedom and Fixity in Shakespeare's Tragic Heroes**
Rachel Falkenstern (St. Francis College)

II. Comedy

137   7 **Taking the Ladder Down. Hegel on Comedy and Religious Experience** Peter Wake (St. Edward's University)

157 **8 From Comedy to Christianity. The Nihilism of Aristophanic Laughter** Paul T. Wilford (Boston College)

185 **9 Hegel and "the Other Comedy"**
Martin Donougho (University of South Carolina)

207 **10 The Comedy of Public Opinion in Hegel**
Jeffrey Church (University of Houston)

III. History

225 **11 Hegel's Tragic Conception of World History**
Fiacha D. Heneghan (Vanderbilt University)

241 **12 Hegel on Tragedy and the World-Historical Individual's Right of Revolutionary Action** Jason M. Yonover (Johns Hopkins University)

263 **13 Philosophy, Comedy, and History. Hegel's Aristophanic Modernity** C. Allen Speight (Boston University)

281 **Contributors**
283 **Index**

Editor's Introduction

THE FAMOUS ENGLISH LITERARY CRITIC A. C. Bradley once remarked that, in the time since Aristotle first delineated the main features of the subject of tragedy in Ancient Greece, no philosopher had treated the subject in as original and searching a manner as Georg Wilhelm Friedrich Hegel (1770–1831).[1] Similar praise could be given of Hegel's treatment of comedy—though here Hegel worked without as much guidance from Aristotle, whose own discussion of comedy is incomplete in the text of the *Poetics* that has come down to us. Certainly, Hegel's concern with the genres of tragedy and comedy was no passing one; it is evident in his early theological writings, it plays an important role in his Jena masterwork, the *Phenomenology of Spirit*, and it recurs throughout the writings and lectures of his mature period, most prominently in his lectures on aesthetics, which were given repeatedly in the last decade of his life. The scholarly literature on tragedy and comedy has grown exponentially since Bradley's comments, but the sheer extensiveness of Hegel's treatment of these genres still stands unsurpassed among philosophical treatments.

In one important respect, however, the comparison of Hegel with Aristotle is misleading, for it underestimates the striking differences between their different ways of understanding drama. Prior to the period in which Hegel wrote, most studies of tragedy and comedy followed Aristotle in restricting themselves to discussions of poetic form, that is, to the description of the formal properties of successful drama: its constituent parts and structure. But although Hegel provides his own account of the elements of poetic form, his interest extends well beyond narrowly aesthetic issues. For Hegel, drama plays an essential role in the historical transformation of political society and the deepening of human subjectivity; it embodies religious worldviews and experience, sometimes leading to their dissolution and reformulation; and it serves as a way of unveiling fundamental metaphysical truths. By allowing drama to raise these political, religious, and metaphysical issues, Hegel treats tragedy and comedy as full participants in the human conversation about what we are and what our place in the world is and ought to be. Although he did not think drama was ultimately equal to philosophy as a medium for such self-reflection, he saw it as sharing the same end or purpose, which is to express the deepest truths of human life.

Hegel was not the first thinker to see the potential for this kind of philosophical engagement with drama, and his influence would help ensure that he was not the last.[2] His specific interest in the philosophical significance of tragedy was anticipated by several of the leading figures of German romanticism, like the poet Friedrich Hölderlin and the philosopher Karl Solger, and he was undoubtedly influenced by pioneering work on the subject by his initially more illustrious friend, F. W. J. von Schelling.[3] His analysis of comedy follows in the wake of philosophical treatments of comedy by August Schlegel and the by comic novelist Jean Paul Richter (whom Hegel nominated for an honorary doctorate after a night of carousing in 1817).[4] But although Hegel might have been comparatively late to try his hand at this, he had unequaled follow-through; he was the only one among his contemporaries who developed this new intuition about the philosophical significance of art into a truly comprehensive theory of tragedy and comedy. His philosophy not only places tragedy and comedy within a systematic hierarchy of the arts, it also includes a comprehensive treatment of their most influential historical forms and integrates them into a philosophy of human activity as a whole. Although theories of this kind of art would continue to attract powerful proponents throughout the nineteenth and twentieth centuries—one thinks of Schopenhauer, Nietzsche, Heidegger, and Adorno as among the most notable figures in this tradition—none of Hegel's major philosophical successors would treat both tragedy and comedy with as much systematic thoroughness or historical detail.

Despite the prominence of these genres in Hegel's thought, this is the first volume to explore the full extent of Hegel's interest in tragedy and comedy.[5] The thirteen new essays included here range from Hegel's early works on theology and politics to his later philosophy of fine art. They cover his treatments of both ancient and modern writers and pursue his reflections of these genres beyond his aesthetics into his political, religious, and historical writings. Although there are still omissions to make up for in the future, this volume provides the reader with a better idea of the scope and breadth of Hegel's reflections on these genres than any other existing book or collection of essays.

Hegel's lectures on aesthetics offer a useful vantage point from which we can see why tragedy and comedy are so important to his philosophy in general and why it is useful to consider them together.[6] In those lectures, Hegel argues that poetry is the most perfect of the fine arts and that drama is the highest form of poetry. These claims entail that tragedy and comedy—the two primary forms of drama on his account—are to be placed at the very pinnacle of the fine arts.[7] Given Hegel's long history of engaging with these genres throughout his writings, it is perhaps unsurprising that they end up in this exalted position. But it is worth asking why they occupy this important place in his final thoughts on art.

Hegel's argument for the supremacy of drama over other forms of art and poetry is impossible to fully extricate from the rest of his system, but it is easy to state the basic standard he uses to arrive at his judgment, for he is very explicit that every artwork and every genre is to be evaluated in terms of its capacity to reveal the deepest and most comprehensive truths. "Art has no other mission [*keinen anderen Beruf*]," he says, "but to bring before sensuous contemplation the truth as it in the spirit."[8] So when he claims that tragedy and comedy are the *highest* forms of art this is because he thinks they are forms that best realize this end, forms that are most capable of revealing the deepest truths of spirit.

We can get some idea of the kind of truth he is concerned with through an understanding of why he thinks drama is so well suited to convey it. The feature of drama that he singles out in this context is its capacity to render the inner lives of human beings, particularly their aims and passions, fully visible in external actions and events. For Hegel, nonlinguistic arts inevitably fail to express the full depths of human spiritual life, and other literary genres fail because they overemphasize either the internal and subjective side of life (as in lyric poetry) or the external and objective side (as in epic poetry). The fine balance between the inner and outer experience that is characteristic of drama is crucial for Hegel because it allows tragedy and comedy to fully represent the process through which the collisions and conflicts that occur between individuals with different aims and passions reach their ultimate resolution.

Tragedy and comedy are superior to any other form of art, then, precisely because they are best at depicting the way human strife and conflict necessarily point toward a final resolution. They give us a vision of complete reconciliation (*Versöhnung*) between spirit and the natural and social world in which it finds itself. Hegel's emphasis on reconciliation already raises many difficult questions about whether reconciliation is the right standard to use in judging artworks, whether it is true that the contradictions and conflicts of spirit and nature are ultimately reconciled, and whether drama in fact reveals this truth. But there is, further, a more obvious problem, which is that even on Hegel's own account, tragedy and comedy seem to present us with what he himself calls "completely opposed" ideas as to what the reconciliation of spirit and nature might amount to.[9]

For tragedy, reconciliation occurs in the social world itself. This is easiest to illustrate with Hegel's famous reading of Sophocles's *Antigone*. For Hegel, the tragic conflict between Antigone and Creon over whether Antigone's brother should receive funeral rites embodies a collision in the social order between independently justified ethical spheres or powers: here, the family and the state. The resolution of this conflict, even when it leads to the destruction of the individual or his or her interests—as it does with Antigone and Creon, respectively—vindicates the eternal justice of the social order itself, which requires these independent but equally necessary powers in order to realize itself in the world. In tragedy, the eternal substance of the ethical order thus emerges as victorious. The experience of tragedy is an experience of the divine not as the object of religious contemplation but as a power that manifests itself in the world of human action.

But in comedy, reconciliation takes a very different form. It does not occur in the social world at all but rather within the individual subject who proves him or herself to be superior to the objective world in its entirety. The conflicts between striving individuals in comedy are ultimately misunderstandings, or they are trivial or absurd. They are self-dissolving or can be resolved merely by coming to our senses or by coming to know ourselves better. In these contexts, it is not the eternal justice of the social order that emerges as victorious but rather the individual subject who shows her superiority to all conflict, to be the "overlord of whatever happens in the real world."[10] Comedy thus provides us with an experience of infinite lightheartedness and gives us the confidence to bear even the frustration of our aims and achievements without misery.[11] For Hegel, all drama is a depiction of the divine as it manifests itself in human activity, but here the divine is encountered not as a power in the world that reestablishes the ethical order but as a power of transcending the world of finite human aims; the experience of comedy is thus very close to one of world-dissolving religious ecstasy.

Although this contrast might risk exaggerating the difference between tragedy and comedy in Hegel's overall account, it helps explain some of the characteristic associations that he makes with each genre. Tragedy is more closely aligned to the political realm, to the ancient world, and to objectivity more generally. Comedy is more closely connected with religious experience, to the prosaic modern world, and to human subjectivity. The problem is that these two genres appear to point us in different directions to find reconciliation with life—one points outward to the political and social world, and the other points inward to a new spiritual disposition. The obvious question this opposition raises is whether we should accept Hegel's way of understanding it. Does one of these genres better explain the ultimate truth of human life than the other, or (as one might expect with Hegel) are they both aspects of some higher truth? Since reconciliation is arguably the central aim of Hegel's philosophy, this is a question that goes to the heart of Hegel's project. To answer it, we need to deepen our understanding of the philosophical significance of tragedy and comedy. The following essays will address this issue.

This volume is grouped into three major sections: one on tragedy, one on comedy, and one on history.

The first two essays in the first section address the complicated relationship between Hegel and the greatest living writer of his time, Johann Wolfgang von Goethe. Goethe was more than a decade older than Hegel and had already established himself as a literary celebrity while Hegel was still in gymnasium, but they would come to know each other as Hegel's star rose in the academy. These essays approach the relationship between these great figures of the *Goethezeit* from opposite directions: Douglas Finn from the point of view of Hegel's early reception of Goethean tragedy and Eric v. d. Luft from the point of view of Goethe's late reception of Hegel's mature theory of tragedy.

Douglas Finn's essay examines the influence of Goethe's drama on Hegel's early theological writings. He carefully considers Walter Kaufmann's provocative claim that Goethe's *Iphigenie auf Tauris* (a reworking of the famous Euripidean play) first alerted Hegel to the possibility that Greek ethical life might show us how to overcome divisions and dichotomies in modern life. For Kaufman, Goethe's *Iphigenie* was the hidden model of Hegel's Jesus in *The Spirit of Christianity and Its Fate* and thus the original source of Hegel's critique of Kantian morality. Finn shows, however, that although both figures share many features—most importantly, they are both what would have been called at the time "beautiful souls"—they respond very differently to the impasses of the circumstances in which they find themselves. Jesus withdraws from society into inwardness, whereas Iphigenia offers forgiveness and the promise of political reconciliation. Over the course of Hegel's philosophical development, the insufficiencies of the former model of the "beautiful soul" become increasingly prominent, and the ideal of forgiveness comes to take on a more central role in his thinking. Finn thus argues that although Goethe's great drama certainly influenced Hegel's early writings, as Kaufmann suggested, it also anticipates insights into the danger of spiritual withdrawal that Hegel himself would not fully understand or express until his later period.

Eric v. d. Luft looks at this same relationship from the other direction: from the point of view of Goethe. Luft shows that Goethe's understanding of Hegel's theory of tragedy was not firsthand but was mediated through the work of Hermann Friedrich Wilhelm Hinrichs, who studied with Hegel at Heidelberg and who might count as Hegel's first major convert. Hinrichs wrote a deeply Hegelian treatise on Sophoclean tragedy, one that Goethe and Johann Peter Eckermann discussed extensively in 1827 (as recounted in Eckermann's famous *Gespräche mit Goethe*). Luft offers an extensive comparison of Hinrichs's interpretation of tragedy and Goethe's own conception. He explores the grounds of Goethe's summary judgment that the Hegelian interpretation of tragedy reduces the conflicts of Greek drama to a mere expression of ideas and is guilty of excessive moralizing. But Luft also shows that Hegel's theory (as interpreted by Hinrichs) offers something that Goethe's own more purely dramaturgical approach lacks: an attention to the subtle philosophical issues raised by Greek tragedy.

The next three essays show exactly what kind of philosophical themes Hegel found in Greek tragedies of the classical age.

For Wes Furlotte, Hegel's reading of *Eumenides* by Aeschylus in his "Natural Law" essay is best understood as inaugurating a kind of critical social theory that Hegel was never able to follow through on. His analysis of the "tragedy of the ethical" enables an innovative dialectical approach to critical social theory that pays attention to the contradictions of modern European social life, but it also ends up short-circuiting the potential of such a theory by heralding the availability of a kind of suprapolitical reconciliation that would obviate the need for political reform or revolution. Furlotte carefully identifies where Hegel's attempt to use tragedy as a means for analyzing historical contradictions is diverted into an attempt to provide a spuriously philosophical or metaphysical resolution of these contradictions, ultimately aestheticizing the political. Furlotte's essay thus attempts to rescue the critical kernel from the reactionary metaphysical shell of Hegel's revolutionary new manner of reading drama.

For Antón Barba-Kay, it is Hegel's famous reading of Sophocles's *Antigone* that is at issue, and the philosophical theme that is raised concerns the significance of sexual difference—the division of humans into men and women. Barba-Kay points out that a striking feature of the *Antigone* (as opposed to, say, *Oedipus Rex*) is that the central conflict of the play is sexualized—the contradiction between the city and the home is made concrete as a difference between men and women. He argues that this feature is essential to Hegel's interest in the play, which Hegel considered the single greatest work of tragedy. This was not because Hegel regarded the conflict between the sexes as of eternal metaphysical significance (as it was sometimes treated by his contemporaries like Schelling and Hölderlin) but because he thought that it is only when sexual difference takes on ethical significance that the question of the role of nature in ethical life can be properly raised. *Antigone* is especially interesting, then, because it documents the very moment in history where human nature became a problem for human culture, something that helps to explain why Hegel's treatment of *Antigone* occurs at the very beginning of his history of spirit in the Jena *Phenomenology*.

Allegra de Laurentiis offers a more general account of why Hegel took ancient tragedy as the exemplary form of tragedy itself, one that does not focus on any particular tragedian. She agrees with Furlotte and Barba-Kay that the importance of Greek tragedy for Hegel stems from the insight it gives us into the history of spirit, and like Barba-Kay, she thinks the crucial insight it gives us is into an early and unrepeatable moment in that history, one that she thinks involved for Hegel a transformation of human nature. For de Laurentiis's Hegel, Greek tragedy reenacts the moment that humanity entered into political life; that is, the historical moment when the irreconcilable but seemingly equally justified claims of conflicting individuals in the state of nature were first made commensurable and adjudicable by being subsumed under the rule of law. The perennial importance of these tragedies is that they serve as a reminder of this transformation, which forestalls a relapse into prepolitical forms of life and their correspondingly inadequate forms of self-consciousness.

In the final essay in this section, Rachel Falkenstern offers a complementary account of Hegel's theory of modern tragedy—particularly Shakespearean tragedy—one that emphasizes the distinct gains in self-consciousness that modern tragic heroes display but that also points to the limits of their self-consciousness. The puzzle she sets out to resolve has to do with the problem of reconciling Hegel's claim that all tragic heroes must be one-sidedly fixed on their aims and his claim that modern life is characterized precisely by a greater degree of subjective depth and freedom, which seems flatly incompatible with such one-sidedness. What she shows is that Shakespearean heroes are one-sided in a different way than ancient heroes, a way that is compatible with Hegel's account of the deepening of subjectivity. For example, though we might think of Hamlet as the epitome of vacillation and thus a counterexample to Hegel's claims about the importance of one-sidedness, Hegel emphasized that Hamlet was never doubtful about what he was to do—only *how* he was to do it. Although figures like Hamlet show a clear advance over the self-consciousness of the ancient tragic hero, this advance is not the end of the story. It is only another stage on the road to true or complete freedom for Hegel (the sort of freedom that is only on display in later tragedies, like those of Schiller).

The next group of essays concerns the comparatively neglected topic of Hegel's theory of comedy. Comedy plays a particularly prominent role in Hegel's *Phenomenology of Spirit*; in the penultimate chapter of that book, comedy (particularly Aristophanic comedy) is cast as the final form of "art religion," the form that follows tragedy and prepares the way for the transition to revealed religion. The first two essays on Hegel's theory of comedy, by Peter Wake and Paul Wilford, respectively, offer contrasting views on what comedy is doing in these sections of the *Phenomenology*.

For Wake, Greek tragedy and comedy offer different means for contemplating the diminution and flight of the gods at the end of the classical period. Tragedy represents the beginning of this process, for in tragedy the gods show themselves to be subject to fate, an eternal justice that asserts itself through the downfall of any individual who oversteps his or her bounds. But comedy completes the secularization of Greek consciousness: for the laughter and ridicule of comedy liberate us from *all* authority, even that of fate, thus providing us with an experience of the individual self as the negative power through which the gods themselves vanish. According to Wake, comedy represents the complete triumph and elevation of the human subject over all external limits, thus amounting to a kind of secular self-transcendence. He concludes with a suggestion that comedy's primary defect is that the liberation it offers us is both fleeting and ultimately empty—leaving us with nothing but grief at the death of the God.

Wilford's essay picks up at this very point. According to Wilford, Hegel's presentation of Aristophanic comedy in the *Phenomenology of Spirit* teaches that Aristophanic comedy is not just irreverent and iconoclastic but ultimately nihilistic. It reveals a form of self-consciousness that exalts itself above any determinate norms, over any sense of something higher than self-dissolving subjectivity. Its propensity to lightness thus leads ultimately to despair, an unhappy consciousness, and a sense that there is nothing worth taking seriously. Wilford argues that the transition from comedy to revealed religion is supposed to show that overcoming the nihilistic effects of Aristophanic comedy requires the advent of a form of religion in which the divine is not incompatible with such subjective inwardness but in fact incarnated in a single, self-conscious individual. This is a sense of the divine that is finally adequate to the new depths of subjectivity that comedy has revealed, a "divinity equal to the power of self-consciousness." This, of course, is Christianity.

In the next essay, Martin Donougho offers a general history of Hegel's reflections on comedy, one that returns to the question of the nature of the experience of comedy and provides a new answer as to the kind of truth of spirit that it is supposed to reveal. On Donougho's reading, the experience of the comic is not one of simple negation—the death of God, or nihilism in Wilford's sense—but negation balanced with sympathetic identification with the characters in the comedy. Donougho shows that Hegel's later lectures on aesthetics continue to view Aristophanes both as the very paradigm of comedy and as the end of the classical ideal of art, but he offers a more complex picture of his accomplishment than we get in the *Phenomenology*—one where Aristophanes's critical, satirical edge is counterbalanced with seriousness and true patriotism. And even though Hegel never retracted his admiration for Aristophanes, Donougho points to moments in his lectures where Hegel entertained a more positive view of modern comedy, one alive to its own specific virtues. For example, Hegel showed an unusual and surprising enthusiasm for *Lustspiel*, a form of contemporary light comedy, writing a long review of a now obscure comedy by Ernst Raupach. And he showed great admiration for the stories of T. G. Hippel. These examples, Donoguho argues, suggest that Hegel appreciated the capacity of modern comic art, alongside other seemingly minor artistic genres, to spiritualize the ordinary and quotidian and that he considered these virtues to be specific to modern comedy.

Jeffrey Church shows that Hegel's remarks on comedy are not limited to his aesthetic and religious contexts. Church's essay offers a provocative and original meditation on Hegel's theory of public opinion as involving important comic elements. It is well known that Hegel had deeply ambivalent feelings about the prominence of public opinion in modern societies, claiming that public opinion deserves to both be respected (as to its being the public's opinion) and despised (as to its content). Hegel hoped that the poor judgment of the public would be improved to some degree by the public's exposure to the arguments offered in the Estates Assembly. Church shows how the relationship between these bodies can be usefully modeled on the relationship between an audience and a performed drama. One might imagine that the drama in question is a tragedy in the Hegelian sense—a conflict between two equally justified but one-sided arguments—but he argues that Hegel himself treats it as comedic in nature, as a collision that comes to nothing. By seeing how poorly the public's own complaints fare against the educated insights expressed in the Assembly, the people learn that their own objections to the government are self-dissolving and self-undermining. They are not so much educated to better opinions as they are brought to take their own opinions less seriously. Church concludes with some interesting reflections on the role of comic cheerfulness in our own more democratic political condition.

Although all of the previous essays touch on the historical dimension of Hegel's theory of tragedy and comedy, the third and final section of the volume looks at the tragic and comic dimensions of Hegel's theory of history.

Fiacha Heneghan's essay considers whether Hegel's philosophy of world history can be defended against the common accusation that it is too optimistic by emphasizing its tragic aspects. Heneghan argues that Hegel's treatment of history explicitly incorporates two features from his treatment of tragedy. The first of these is Hegel's claim that the tragic hero's one-sided dedication to her ethical principle leads her into an experience of conflict with something that appears alien to her but that is in reality a part of the hero, a fact that she is able to recognize only in her self-destruction (if then). The second feature is the structural logic of tragic situations, which involves not the conflict between right and wrong but conflict between two ethical spheres that, in history, takes the form of the conflict between states embodying lower and higher principles of freedom. Though both of these elements go some distance in addressing worries that Hegel's philosophy of history is excessively optimistic or theodicean, Heneghan concludes that they do not go far enough; Hegel's theory of history is, despite these elements, still indefensibly optimistic.

Jason M. Yonover's essay focuses on the tragedy of the world-historical individual. We have already seen that Hegel claims that tragedy in the world involves not a conflict between right and wrong but between two rights. Since, as Yonover emphasizes, world-historical individuals take part in just such tragic conflicts, it is natural to ask whether such individuals—individuals who collide with existing ethical orders and who represent new and higher principles—are ultimately justified in contravening what their contemporaries take as right and just. Yonover argues that Hegel's view on this is quite complex—Hegel does not think such individuals are simply in the wrong, nor are they simply in the right. Yonover argues that, on Hegel's account, world-historical individuals have an absolute right that in the final analysis outdoes any wrong they may do, though this is only properly understood after the fact. Yonover holds that Hegel's retrospective justification of such figures is crucial to his vindication of the legitimacy of revolutionary action and so of great importance to any contemporary appropriation of Hegel's ethical thought.

In the final essay in this volume, Allen Speight turns to comic dimensions of history. He draws attention to a striking claim in Hegel's *Lectures on Fine Art*, a claim that the same principle that gives us the basis of our distinction between tragedy and comedy also provides the basis for the distinction between the ancient and the modern. This suggests the somewhat paradoxical claim that Hegel's treatment of Aristophanes (Hegel's paradigm of the comic art form) might offer us a key to understanding his theory of modernity. Speight points to three possible ways in which this might be so. First, Aristophanes anticipates the theatricality of modern life. Second, Aristophanic comedy represents the very endpoint of all artistic practice: the triumph of the subjective. And, finally, his comedies show us how art can reflect on its own role in life, dissolving not into nihilism or an unambiguous affirmation of life but into a genuinely philosophic meditation on the conditions of human existence.

Notes

1. A. C. Bradley, *Oxford Lectures on Poetry* (London: Macmillan, 1959), 69. Bradley's essay on Hegel is reproduced in *Hegel on Tragedy*, ed. Anne and Henry Paolucci (Garden City, NY: Doubleday, 1962).

2. Jean-Marie Schaeffer has aptly characterized this philosophical approach to art as the "speculative theory of Art" in his important monograph *Art of the Modern Age*, trans. Steven Rendell (Princeton, NJ: Princeton University, 2000). For Schaeffer the attempt to offer deep philosophical readings of art has been a catastrophe for any sane appreciation of the arts, which is better served by the traditional approach that limits itself to the labor of formal description. For a general defense of the speculative theory against these criticisms, see Sebastian Gardner, "The Romantic-Metaphysical Theory of Art," *European Journal of Philosophy* 10, no. 3 (2002), 275–301.

3. See Martin Thibodeau, *Hegel and Greek Tragedy*, trans. Jans-Jakob Wilhelm (Lanham, MD: Lexington, 2011), 1–22, which offers a helpful explanation as to why this sort of interest in tragedy became so common in the post-Kantian tradition.

4. The wonderful story of how this came about is told by Terry Pinkard in *Hegel: A Biography* (Cambridge: Cambridge University Press, 2000), 378–81.

5. The best general treatment of Hegel's theory of tragedy and comedy as dramatic genres remains Mark Roche's *Tragedy and Comedy: A Systematic Study and a Critique of Hegel* (Albany: State University Press of New York, 1998). Needless to say, there are many valuable studies of Hegel's treatment of tragedy and comedy as individual genres.

6. Hegel treats dramatic poetry at the conclusion of his lectures. The following summary is drawn from *Hegel's Aesthetics: Lectures on Fine Art*, trans. T. M. Knox, vol. 2 (Oxford: Oxford University, 1975), 1158–1237 (cited as *HA*). The corresponding German text is *Ästhetik*, Band II (Berlin: Aufbau, 1965), 512–86 (cited as *Ä*).

7. As anyone familiar with Hegel's passion for triplicity might have surmised, Hegel actually identifies *three* forms of drama: tragedy, comedy, and a third genre that mixes the two ("drama in the narrower sense"). See *HA* 1194; *Ä* 547. He treats this last form, whose great exemplars are Aeschylus's *Eumenides* and Goethe's *Iphigenie auf Tauris*, as a somewhat hybrid form, one whose defining features are not easily identifiable. Although this third form of drama is not of central interest in the following essays, it does come in for some consideration in the essays by Douglas Finn, Allegra de Laurentiis, and Martin Donougho.

8. *HA*, II: 623; *Ä* 2:17.

9. *HA* 1158; *Ä* 513.

10. *HA*, 1202; *Ä* 555.

11. *HA*, 1200; *Ä* 553.

I
Tragedy

Chapter One

The Beauty of Fate and Its Reconciliation

Hegel's *The Spirit of Christianity and Its Fate* and Goethe's *Iphigenia in Tauris*[1]

Douglas Finn

Oh! the grievous necessity of such violations of the holy! The deepest, holiest, sorrow of a beautiful soul, its most incomprehensible riddle, is that its nature has to be disrupted, its holiness sullied.[2]—FRIEDRICH HEGEL

OVER THE COURSE OF MANY YEARS and several publications, Walter Kaufmann analyzed Hegel's early writings with a view toward better understanding the philosopher's mature thought. While scholars searching for the sources of Hegel's philosophy tend to emphasize Kant's influence, Kaufmann highlights the impact of poets like Goethe and Schiller—but especially Goethe—on Hegel's thought. Kaufmann sees that influence manifested in several ways. He credits Goethe with leading Hegel to think more holistically and dynamically. With Goethe's help, that is, Hegel comes to recognize that one cannot understand theory apart from practice or thinking subject apart from thought object. Opposing positions, moreover, must be grasped in their relation to each other so that the limitations of each stance on its own might be made known and thereby overcome. In that way, Hegel insists with Goethe that each viewpoint represents a stage in the development of spirit. Thus, in reading Hegel's extensive lectures on history and on the history of aesthetics, religion, and philosophy, we do not merely trace a sequence of changing events, cultures, or ideas across time. Rather, we come to learn of the human mind in its very becoming.[3]

Beyond this more general influence, Kaufmann claims multiple times to have uncovered a more explicit connection between Goethe and the young Hegel.[4] He identifies Hegel's early work *The Spirit of Christianity and Its Fate* as a turning point in the philosopher's development, in particular through the explicit critique of Kantian *Moralität* by means of the *Sittlichkeit* articulated by Jesus. Kaufmann here points to the influence of Goethe's play *Iphigenia in Tauris*. He argues, "Hegel, who had previously put Kant's *Moralität* into the mouth of Jesus, now makes Jesus the prophet of the *Sittlichkeit* represented by Goethe's Iphigenia."[5] On Kaufmann's reading, Hegel has adopted Goethe's understanding of the human being as a harmonious ethical whole, in contrast to Kant's sundering of reason and the inclinations. Furthermore, Hegel's Jesus articulates a nontranscendent concept of faith that is basically "the love and trust between two free spirits."[6] Goethe's Iphigenia, for her part, shows such humanistic faith toward her brother Orestes, who is thereby freed from the torments of his conscience and his fate, and toward King Thoas. By that latter faith, Iphigenia atones the fate of her ancestral house.

Yet the theme of fate alerts us to ways that, in fact, Goethe's Iphigenia differs notably from Hegel's depiction of Jesus in *The Spirit of Christianity*. Both texts describe a distinctive figure—the beautiful soul—who struggles against his or her fate. In eighteenth- and early nineteenth-century moral thought, the beautiful soul was an important figure that emerged in response to the need to establish a new system of ethics based not on Christianity but on human reason. Yet many thinkers realized that reason alone might not suffice to ensure moral action, so they also invoked the notion of beauty. The virtuous soul became beautiful, exhibiting such features as balance, proportion, and harmony. On this view, beauty, based as it was on universal principles but appealing also to the emotions, could unite human reason and sensuality into a harmonious whole.[7] By the time of Goethe and Hegel, however, the figure of the beautiful soul was strained and beginning to succumb to its eventual fate. This fate is exemplified in the contrast between Goethe's Iphigenia and Hegel's Jesus. Whereas Iphigenia is able, through her love and humanity, to achieve a reconciliation with her fate and with those around her, the story Hegel tells of Jesus is a tragic one. The Galilean's beauty of soul clashes with the subservient nature of his surrounding Jewish culture and ultimately leads him and the Christian Church after him to fall victim to their fate.

In this chapter, my primary objective is to show the limits of the identification Kaufmann makes between Goethe's Iphigenia and Hegel's Jesus. Then I would like to gesture briefly toward the ways Goethe's play reappears in Hegel's mature thought, especially in relation to Hegel's reinterpretation of Jesus and Christianity. In that regard, we will see how Hegel thinks the Christian religion surpasses the aesthetic in the cultivation of *Sittlichkeit* and a humanity at home with itself, society, and the world.

Goethe's *Iphigenia in Tauris*

Kaufmann credits Goethe's *Iphigenia in Tauris*, written and reworked several times between 1779 and 1787,[8] with helping the young Hegel move beyond the *Moralität* of Kant toward his mature concept of *Sittlichkeit*. "Like nobody before him," Kaufmann claims,

> Goethe succeeded at one blow in bringing the Greeks to life in eighteenth- and nineteenth century Germany. Winckelmann and Lessing had talked about the Greeks and taught their countrymen, including Goethe, to think about them in a different way, but Goethe made a new generation, including Hegel and Hölderlin, see and hear them. Suddenly, Sophocles' Antigone ceased to be merely the heroine of a tragedy written in the fifth century B.C.; her spirit was present even now and represented a live option and an alternative to Kant's *Moralität*.[9]

The Greek playwright Euripides had written a play of the same name in 412 BCE, and the differences between his work and that of Goethe are instructive. In Euripides's play, Iphigenia, Orestes, and Pylades deceive King Thoas and spirit away the statue of the goddess Artemis—a requirement set forth by Apollo so that Orestes might atone for killing his mother Clytemnestra. When Thoas seeks revenge, Athena appears and instructs him to yield to the divine will. In Goethe's play, by contrast, Iphigenia reconciles with Thoas through honesty and love. These prove, moreover, to be the sufficient *human* means of solving the dilemmas that arise in the story. Let us examine these features of Goethe's work in greater detail.

At the beginning of the play, Iphigenia bemoans her empty, lonely existence. Her father, the Greek king Agamemnon, had been underway to Troy with his armies when the winds became unfavorable, and their ships stalled at Aulis. The goddess Diana declared that if Agamemnon sacrificed Iphigenia she would be placated and allow the winds to carry the Greek ships onward to Troy. Before the sacrifice could be completed, however, Diana rescued Iphigenia and bore her off to serve as her priestess in the barbarian land of Tauris. Iphigenia thus tells Arkas, messenger of the Taurian king Thoas, that an alien curse has befallen her, and she has been separated from her family and nation. Now, she claims, she is nothing but a shadow of her former self.[10]

Since, moreover, it was the goddess herself who allegedly took Iphigenia from her family and enlisted her as a priestess in Tauris, Iphigenia's relationship to the deity appears ambivalent. Iphigenia acknowledges that Diana saved her from death on the altar, but the consequence of that salvation is now an existence of servitude in a land far from her home at Mycenae. In her opening monologue, Iphigenia laments that even after a long tenure of service her spirit feels strange and unaccustomed to the goddess' sacred forest.[11] She is ashamed to admit that she serves the deity reluctantly, although she still places her hopes in Diana for a second rescue—a return to her home in Greece.[12] Throughout the monologue, Iphigenia maintains an attitude of reverence; she will not contend with the gods. Nonetheless, she makes clear that in contrast to a man, who is able to help himself in a strange place, "The lot of women is a piteous thing. . . . But how wretched / If hostile fate drives her to alien lands!"[13] Already in the first scene, it is unclear whether one can attribute fate to divine or human agency. Iphigenia first claims that she is held in Scythia by "a high will," to which she submits herself.[14] But later, immediately after decrying the difficulty of a hostile fate for a woman, she says, "Thus Thoas holds me here, a noble man, / In solemn, sacred bonds of slavery."[15]

When Iphigenia subsequently recounts to Thoas her blighted pedigree, fate more clearly emerges as the consequence of human actions. The fate that plagues Iphigenia's household stems from the action of its progenitor, Tantalus. The gods had invited him to dine with them, and he stole some of their ambrosia and shared it—and some divine secrets—with mortals. Iphigenia mitigates the grievousness of the crime to an extent by arguing that it is natural for humans to become dizzy and act out of character when communing with the gods.[16] Nevertheless, a curse was placed upon Tantalus's house, and thereafter his descendants perpetuated their own fates by repeated acts of deceit and murder.

Although this narrative of accursed internecine bloodshed plays out prior to the events that motivate the dramatic conflict in *Iphigenia*, it still bears upon the immediate dilemma facing Iphigenia. Thoas, the Taurian king, wishes to marry her in order to secure his dynasty and avert revolution by his discontented subjects.[17] But Iphigenia longs to return home and consequently declines.[18] Spurned, Thoas threatens to reinstate a custom that had been suspended ever since Iphigenia appeared on Scythia's shores: the practice of sacrificing all stranded foreigners to Diana.[19] Iphigenia is to offer up to the goddess two recent captives who turn out to be Iphigenia's brother Orestes and his companion Pylades. She is now torn. On the one hand, she feels that she owes kindness and gratitude to Thoas,[20] who spared her life and even halted the practice of human sacrifice on her account.[21] On the other hand, if she refuses Thoas, as she is inclined to do, she will have to kill her brother and his friend, thereby extending fate's claim over her household.[22]

In her anguished deliberations, Iphigenia struggles to find a point of orientation. Arkas, Thoas, and Pylades each advocate a course of action that would accentuate division and hinder reconciliation: the former two say she should marry the king,[23] whereas the latter encourages deception and theft.[24] Thoas and Pylades, though endorsing incompatible paths forward, both insist that Iphigenia listen to reason.[25] But the fact that their adherence to reason would only aggravate division—by either separating Iphigenia from her people or by stoking the animosity between Thoas and the Greeks—suggests that Goethe indeed sees the predominance of reason over the inclinations as an injurious form of heteronomy.[26]

The contrast between reason and the inclinations further relates to Goethe's concept of the divine as found in the drama. Iphigenia and the other characters strive to ascertain the divine will: does Diana will that Iphigenia return to Mycenae?[27] Does she want human sacrifices?[28] Pylades insists that he and Orestes were instructed by Apollo to recover the statue of Diana from the temple in Tauris. When Orestes questions whether his friend is not confusing his own wishes with the divine will, whether he is not merely following his own inclinations, Pylades contends that human intelligence provides sufficient hermeneutic means: "What good is human shrewdness if it does / Not harken heedfully to that high will?"[29] The problem is that he thinks that by stealing the image of Diana they will serve both the gods and the world,[30] when in fact they would only widen the gap of misunderstanding between the Scythians and the Greeks.

While Thoas suggests reason, and Pylades human craftiness, Iphigenia listens steadfastly to her *heart*. Thoas at least implicitly identifies this tendency with submission to her inclinations, but the significance of the heart in the drama suggests something more. In response to Thoas's insistence on reason,

Iphigenia claims that the heart is the true oracle of the divine will: "Through our hearts only do [the gods] speak to us."[31] She is at once listening to the command of the divine—not to marry Thoas, not to sacrifice Orestes and Pylades, not to deceive the king who has been her kind benefactor—and to the particular pulsation of her feelings. In her heart they are one and the same.[32]

Goethe thus imbues his drama with a sense of divine benevolence and the unity of the gods with human beings. The drama, for one, clearly rejects a slavish obedience to positive laws and traditions falsely elevated to the absolute will of the gods. Thoas argues that Diana is angry because he has withheld the human sacrifices from her since Iphigenia's arrival. He therefore wishes to reintroduce the tradition—an ancient law, as he calls it.[33] Iphigenia counters that so-called traditions often merely serve as expressions of personal passion.[34] She insists that one erroneously interprets the divine will if he conceives of the gods as bloodthirsty tyrants, when it is really only humans who desire to kill one another. Did not Diana prove this, Iphigenia asks, when she saved me from the priest's hand at Aulis?[35] The shedding of blood would only bring down fate's horrid curse upon the head of the one wielding the knife.[36]

In the midst of her dilemma, when the continuation of her family's fate seems inevitable, Iphigenia naturally struggles to accept the notion of divine benevolence. She recalls a song that her nanny used to sing when she was young, a song of the Fates, which depicts the gods as capricious overlords who bless and curse human beings according to their whim.[37] However, Iphigenia is not adhering to a negative concept of the divine. It is important to note that the song is sung not by Iphigenia herself but by someone else. The song serves as a reflective exercise whereby she can gain a greater awareness of her own moral agency in contrast to the traditional understanding of the gods.[38] Her real desire is for the gods to confirm her notion of benevolent divinity: "Save me and save your image (*Bild*) in my soul!"[39] The request is later granted, but with a crucial twist: Orestes and Pylades had thought they needed to save the statue of the goddess and return it to Greek shores, when it turns out that Apollo had not meant his sister Diana but Orestes's sister Iphigenia. The image of the divine that proves central to Goethe's play lies in the beautiful human soul.[40]

Iphigenia thus decries Thoas's inhumane manner of ruling, which resembles that of a distant, tyrannical god who issues positive commands to kill but allows someone else to bloody his or her hands and incur (half of the) fate by executing the order. In this case, there is a distinction between the command or law as a concept and its execution in reality.[41] But Iphigenia's comparison implies that, while commanding something inhumane, Thoas wishes *in vain* to hover (*schweben*), untainted, above the fray of human life and that true divinity is marked not by its distance from humankind but by its free and loving unity with it.[42]

Iphigenia accordingly strives to affirm a positive image of the divine, indeed, to affirm gods who do not favor one people over another but who rather love all humankind: "For the immortals bear love unto / The good and far-flung races of men."[43] Although the language of the drama sometimes reflects a distinction between the divine and human spheres, in dramatic "reality" there is a unity. This is most evident in the heart's mediation of the divine will. Iphigenia listens to her heart when she refuses to marry Thoas.[44] She appeals to the heart when she tries to liberate Orestes from his guilt-ridden insanity.[45] Orestes listens to his heart when he is finally healed and recognizes his sister.[46] Thoas, I would argue, does likewise when he offers Iphigenia and her compatriots a farewell blessing.[47] All these actions effect reconciliation, the true end that the gods desire. Moreover, with the exception of Diana's rescue of Iphigenia from the altar at Aulis, which does not take place in the drama itself, all the action is carried out by human beings. Fate is the product of human actions. And just as human deeds give rise to fate, so too do they lead to its reconciliation. In this way, the words of Arkas ring true: "[The gods] tend toward human means to rescue humans."[48]

Over the course of the drama, Iphigenia comes to learn the truth of Arkas's statement not in the sense that humans solve their problems by mastering the world around them but rather by sensing their unity with the divine. Her recognition of this unity and her ability to reconcile her family's fate manifest her beauty of soul. Goethe makes direct reference in the text to Iphigenia as a beautiful soul. When she resists marrying Thoas, who has shown her great kindness, Arkas asks, "Can a beautiful soul (*eine schöne Seele*) feel such repugnance for / A kindness that a noble man extends?"[49] In response, Iphigenia states that such a beautiful soul feels reluctance when the noble person attempts to possess not her gratitude but her person.[50] A beautiful soul cannot see herself under the domination of an alien power.

Yet Iphigenia is able to achieve autonomy while still reconciling herself with the surrounding world. This reconciliation obtains when love proves victorious over the demands of so-called necessity and of rights and duties. When Iphigenia hesitates to deceive the king so that Orestes, Pylades, and she can escape, Pylades argues that the urgency of the situation legitimates their subterfuge. Need, he maintains, demands their covert escape and the theft of Diana's statue. Therefore, both gods and humans will overlook the deceit such a course of action requires.⁵¹ Pylades then adds that one cannot avoid sullying his or her soul when one enters into relations with others in the world. Iphigenia should consequently not be so scrupulous:

> So wondrously is mankind constituted (*gebildet*),
> So various are his knots and interweavings,
> That no one can stay pure and unconfused
> Within himself or with his fellow men.⁵²

Pylades is right to see human beings as wondrously intertwined. It is thus true that Iphigenia cannot avoid acting in the world. She senses as much. Torn between saving her brother and being honest with Thoas, who has shown her such kindness, she soliloquizes,

> Oh my soul, be still!
> Do you begin to waver now and doubt?
> The firm ground of your solitude you must
> Abandon now!⁵³

The question is this: is it possible, contrary to what Pylades maintains, to act in the world and remain pure?

To be sure, Iphigenia must *withdraw* from the rational sphere of rights and duties in order to maintain her pure heart. Pylades advises her to claim her sacerdotal right to secrecy in order to facilitate their escape.⁵⁴ As Orestes's sister, moreover, she could very well make the case for defending his life.⁵⁵ Finally, Thoas has pledged to her free passage home if she is able to show that she has a reasonable chance of returning, which she now does.⁵⁶ But when Thoas confronts her about the delayed sacrifice, which she is intentionally stalling to win time, Iphigenia simply cannot bring herself to deceive the king any longer. She reveals the identities of the captives and their plans to escape with Diana's contraband image in tow.⁵⁷ In so doing, she is in effect relinquishing her rights as priestess, sister, and pledge recipient. Sensing that the king will not waver in his decision to stage the sacrifice, she throws herself at his mercy and pleads to be killed first.⁵⁸ Iphigenia cannot bear the thought of having to slay her brother and, as a result, perpetuating the fate of Tantalus's house.⁵⁹

It seems possible, then, for Iphigenia to avoid contamination and the ensuing fate by sacrificing herself. However, she has in the meantime begun to discover the conciliatory power of love. She has already reached out in love to her brother, guilt-ridden for having killed their mother and unable to recognize Iphigenia his sister in his insanity:

> O let love's pure breath, gently wafted, cool
> The burning deep within your breast. Orestes,
> My dear one, can you not hear what I say?[60]

Indeed, when Orestes begins to listen, to listen to his *heart*, he recognizes his sister and the bond of love they share, and the curse is lifted:

> O let me too, clasped in my sister's arms
> ... enjoy and keep
> With total gratitude what you grant me!
> The curse is lifting; my heart tells me so.[61]

Furthermore, Iphigenia does not restrict her love to itself or to her kinsmen. When Thoas and Orestes stand ready to clash swords to determine their fate, Iphigenia intervenes and overturns fate altogether with love and peace. As a beautiful soul, she is able to unite the realms of rights and duties and of the inclinations. To her brother and the king, she boldly speaks as priestess, sister, and adopted daughter of Thoas. All the while, she speaks directly from her heart as she persuades them to sheathe their swords:

> Do not profane
> The goddess' dwelling place with rage and murder!
> Command your people to lay down their weapons,
> And hear your priestess, hear your sister.[62]

With these words she facilitates reconciliation with fate and loving peace between the Scythians and Greeks. Violence would breed only more division, and the curse of fate would persist. This would occur if Iphigenia were to sacrifice her brother or if Orestes were to fight Thoas. As Iphigenia prays to the goddess Diana,

> O withhold then my hands from blood!
> Blessing and peace it never brings;
> the shape of one murdered by chance
> Will with terror stalk the sombre
> Unwilled murderer's evil hours.[63]

By the same token, Iphigenia's heart recoils at the prospect of gaining her freedom by deception. She realizes that she is leaving behind fellow human beings on Tauris,[64] and she is tormented by the thought of harming Thoas, who has been so good to her. Lies, like violence, would only strengthen fate's grasp on her and her household. Once told, lies return to harm the one who spreads them:

> O woe to lies! They do not liberate
> The heart as other words true-spoken do.
> They do not comfort us, they strike alarm
> In one who secretly invents them, and,
> Like arrows sped and by some god averted
> And made to miss their mark, they backward fly
> To strike the archer.[65]

For a pure soul the truth suffices.[66]

Violence, deceit, and theft would preclude reconciliation. Therefore, when Thoas threatens to reinstate the practice of human sacrifice, because he fears that the goddess is angry that they have failed to obey the ancient law, Iphigenia counters by invoking an even older law. This law is neither the positive command of a deity nor the Kantian universal command of reason. Rather, it is a law enacted by impersonal love: the law of hospitality.[67] In hospitality (*Gastrecht*), the categories of right and duty are taken up and transcended. Here there is no longer a division between races and nations; Iphigenia trusts that all people, barbarian and Greek alike, can listen to their hearts and recognize the bonds of humanity, love, and life,[68] such that no one is ever a stranger on another's shores. Accordingly, after Thoas has decided to keep his promise and permit Iphigenia to sail home with her brother and his companions, Iphigenia pledges that Taurians will always be welcome guests in her land. She will offer them hospitality and request news of the king from them.[69]

At first, however, Thoas only reluctantly and bitterly allows Iphigenia to leave. She protests immediately:

> Not thus, my king! Without your blessing,
> With your ill-will, I shall not part from you.
> O do not banish us. A friendly guest-right [*Gastrecht*]
> Must be the rule between us: that way we
> Are not cut off forever.[70]

Just as she opens her arms in hospitality to Thoas and his people, she cannot leave him behind without his blessing and a reciprocal offer of welcome. Otherwise there is neither love nor reconciliation—just a grudging nod to her *right* to leave. In that case, Iphigenia and Thoas, the Greeks and the Taurians, would remain forever divided. Ultimately, though, love prevails. Thoas listens to his heart and offers Iphigenia and the Greeks his blessing, a farewell that shows—and here I deliberately anticipate the next section on Hegel—that *love* has become *life*: "Lebt wohl!"[71]

Hegel's *The Spirit of Christianity and Its Fate*

Hegel's early writings on religion reflect his effort to uncover the spirit of his society and to ascertain why that spirit had resulted in the societal divisions he saw around him. Hegel believed that the relationship to nature that a certain people's spirit has decisively conditions their understanding of the world and the particular religious, historical, and philosophical categories through which that worldview is expressed. In Greek religion and society, Hegel finds an example of beauteous harmony, of a people at home with each other and the world.[72] However, when he strives to understand the divisions in the German society around him, he turns to his culture's Judeo-Christian roots for insight into its governing spirit and the relation this spirit has to nature and the world. This effort to understand his culture reveals a transformative motive, insofar as Hegel sensed that by grasping the proper relationship of spirit to nature and the world, one could attain true unity and freedom and lead a life in harmony with one's own essential character and the surrounding world.[73] One can properly understand Hegel's early works, then, only within the context of his search for unity and freedom.

In *The Spirit of Christianity* (1798–1800),[74] Hegel thus criticizes what he sees as the spirit of the Jews, who have, according to his reading of Jewish history, perpetuated disunity through alienation from nature and other peoples. Both in the reaction to the destructive flood[75] and in Abraham's departure from his native people to live on his own, Hegel detects an attitude that views nature as a hostile enemy to be conquered rather than as an environment and force with which a people must reconcile themselves. Abraham and his progeny, the Jews, are therefore not at home in the world. In an effort to maintain their autonomy, their freedom from the conditions of life in this world, they seek the unity of their people in an extraworldly God, a universal ideal, who controls for them the hostile elements and guarantees their continued, isolated existence in exchange for their obedience.[76]

The spirit of Abraham, which his descendants inherit, is one of seeming autonomy vis-à-vis the world. However, that autonomy is sustained by a deeper-seated, more deleterious subservience to the Jewish God and his commands. This tenacious separation of the Jews from other peoples and from nature, along with the thoroughgoing dependence on their unifying principle, gives rise in Hegel's view to the Jews' distinctive fate: a perpetually wretched existence in isolation and slavish servitude to the positive laws of their religion. In describing the fateful Jewish existence, Hegel avails himself of aesthetic categories: "In other peoples the state of independence is a state of good fortune, of humanity at a more beautiful level. With the Jews, the state of independence was to be a state of total passivity, of total ugliness."[77]

This caricature of Judaism could be found elsewhere in Enlightenment thought. Immanuel Kant had argued that the true core of religion is ethical.[78] In his *Religion within the Boundaries of Mere Reason*, he thus concludes that Judaism is not, properly considered, a religion at all: it is simply a political union whose laws are consistent with a state's concern with external action, rather than moral intention, and the state's use of coercive force to ensure compliance.[79] By contrast, Kant strove in his ethics to uphold the autonomy of the human person by emphasizing that reason, not a divine being, legislates the categorical imperative whereby one should act according to his or her maxim only if that maxim can serve as a universal law. This rational law, moreover, trumps any sensual inclinations in determining the principle of ethical action.[80] Yet even Kant's attempt to secure the human being's autonomy in an enlightened ethical religion, as opposed to all positive religions, falls victim to criticism in Hegel's search for a higher form of unifying freedom.

The Kantian has, on Hegel's reading, merely assimilated an external overlord to reason, such that opposition between reason and the inclinations persists within the person and hegemonically precludes all other relations not determined by a sense of duty.[81] Hegel argues, furthermore, that a merely formal law of reason claiming universality in scope lacks the means whereby it can actualize itself in particular action. Such a law cannot compel someone in a particular situation to act without involving itself in a contradiction of universal and particular.[82] Through the teaching of Jesus, then, Hegel introduces the concept of love, which is life manifest in a specific mode, as a means of uniting the universal form of law and the particular inclinations of each person. In love there is no sense of duty to the law of reason which would demand suppression of the inclinations. Rather, the inclinations are in complete accord with the "commands" of reason; properly speaking, there are no longer any commands, "since duties require an opposition and an action that we like to do requires none."[83] When Jesus speaks of the fulfillment (πλήρωμα) of the law in his Sermon on the Mount (Mt 5.2–16),

Hegel interprets this to mean the addition of inclination to the concept of law.[84] Through the synthesis of universal law and particular inclination in love, Jesus "exhibits that which fulfils the law but annuls it as law and so is something higher than obedience to law and makes law superfluous." As a result, subject and object and particular reality and universal concept shed all opposition and "restore man's humanity in its entirety."[85]

Jesus, according to Hegel, directs the brunt of his teaching against these forms of heteronomous opposition. With regard to Judaism, he opposes heteronomy in general as well as the infinite God who rules over the Jewish people. The divine, for Hegel, is accordingly not a universal ideal opposed to the world, as the Jews would have it. Nor is it something utterly finite and objective that would preclude one's ability to sense him or herself as a part of the whole of life. To Hegel's mind, the latter is the mistake the early Christians make. In their love for one another, they withdrew from the world, since they regarded all forms of life as consciousness of particular objects and as a result desired to avoid these restricted forms. Such withdrawal from the world, however, prevented them from actualizing their love in *life*, that is, in a sensing of one's existence as a part and manifestation of the whole. Their Christian love therefore remained an ideal, the consciousness of which they could not now achieve apart from a positive command to love each other. The positivity of this command to love in turn drove them to specify dogmatic faith in particular doctrines, especially concerning the human person of Jesus, as the concrete indicator of the common love shared by the members of the group.[86]

Here we gain insight into the young Hegel's concepts of God and religion. Above we saw how he attempts to achieve unity in the realm of morality through love. Just as Kantian *Moralität* affirms the human being's autonomy in the realm of consciousness—that is, it replaces the concept of a divine lawgiver with a sense of duty to the categorical imperative which reason legislates for itself—so love overcomes the gulf between reason and the inclinations in the realm of *Moralität*. Love itself, however, fails to attain completeness for the human being in his or her sociality. While happy love enables people to live unreflectively in their joyful, albeit undeveloped union, unhappy love compels them to reflect upon the cause of their unhappiness, upon the finitude of the feeling of love. This reflection reintroduces opposition, insofar as one becomes conscious of the fact that the intuition of love, the representation of love that one has before his or her mind's eye, necessarily has a delimited object—that group of relations to which the love extends

—and thus cannot encompass the infinite object of the divine. Hence Hegel observes that one must rise from love to the level of religion: "What is religious, then, is the πλήρωμα of love; it is reflection and love united, bound together in thought."[87]

For Hegel, then, religion is neither simply an expression of rational operation nor just of feeling or sensation. Rather, it unites the two aspects of the human person and eliminates the opposition between them. Hegel describes this unification in terms of a process or development, and, in this description, he employs aesthetic terms. Love, he argues, is not equivalent to religion but must rather develop into it. As in the case of the early Christians, love is at first an ideal that must become objective in the imagination. Hence Hegel stresses the religious need for images that give shape to love. But these representations are not mere symbols of a common feeling, since symbolization requires mediation *in thought* by a third element that connects the symbol and its referent. They are instead manifestations of *living* bonds that surmount the opposition between the ideal and the objective and allow those who participate in them to sense their living, spiritual union together.[88] Thus while multiple, disparate religious images, in their objective form, introduce divisions by their restrictedness in the imagination, this division is a requisite part of love's development into religion and life, which ultimately erases any opposition.[89] The religious group thereby comes to the self-consciousness, in the union of reflection and love, of their unity in spirit and life. They become aware of their harmony in "their developed many-sidedness."[90]

Here the strong social emphasis in Hegel's understanding of religion and the divine becomes apparent. But we should remind ourselves that at this point in his development Hegel evaluates Christianity according to the standard of the harmonious religious and political experience of the Greek polis. In particular, he wants to show that because of its excessive subjectivity—its resistance to objective expression through the imagination—Christianity never rises from love to religion. According to Hegel, the entirety of the Christian religion, as taught by Jesus, is contained in the idea of the Kingdom of God. By the terms "love" and "life," Hegel underscores the unity of the divine and the human spirit and, moreover, the unity of all human beings in that spirit:

> In the Kingdom of God what is common to all is life in God. This is not the common character which a concept expresses, but is love, a living bond which unites the believers; it is this feeling of unity of life, a feeling in which all oppositions, as pure enmities, and also rights, as unifications of still subsisting

oppositions, are annulled.... This friendship of soul ... is the divine spirit, is God who rules the communion.[91]

The faith that Jesus preaches has as its proper object (*Gegenstand*) this unifying divine spirit that the human being already contains in some way within him or herself and not any finite object (*Objekt*) distinct from the believing subject.[92] Hence Jesus tried, by Hegel's reading, to downplay his own personal identity so that his disciples would not place their faith in a finite object—the man Jesus. By the same token, Jesus opposed any notion of a personal God distinct from the persons who believe in him.[93] In an impersonal divine spirit uniting all human beings through the bond of love, where there is no subjection to an objective principle, Hegel discovers true freedom and beauty: "In the Kingdom of God there can be no relation save that which proceeds from the most disinterested love and so from the highest freedom, save that which acquires from beauty alone its mode of appearance and its link with the world."[94]

As we have already seen, though, Jesus's teaching of beauty and freedom met with misunderstanding in the minds of his immediate followers. Their spirit, their withdrawal from the world and objectification of faith into doctrines for belief, have all determined their fate: namely, their inability throughout history to unite spiritual and worldly affairs.[95] But even before the early Christians bungled Jesus's message, the battle between beauty and fate raged in Jesus's own life. To understand Jesus as a fated beautiful soul, then, we need to explore Hegel's concept of fate in greater detail.

In *The Spirit of Christianity*, the contours of fate emerge quite lucidly when Hegel contrasts fate with penal law. Penal law, as a concept, stands diametrically opposed to life. The law is a formal, universal condemnation of all acts that violate it and thereby annul its content, namely, the affirmation of a right that has been denied another in the crime under consideration. The law knows no mercy or reconciliation because its universality of form always opposes the particularity of the transgressor and his or her trespass. Were the law to offer mercy in this instance or that, then it would no longer have the form of a *universal* law. The law's enforcement depends, however, upon a judge, who as a living being possesses the ability to carry out the universally deserved punishment or not. Consequently, a tension persists between the universal concept of justice embodied in the form of the law and the execution of justice in particular cases. Punishment meted out by a judge and endured by the trespasser cannot erase the reality of the past crime because the universality of law remains, even after punishment, always opposed to the particularity of life. Punishment leads to reunification only in a concept, in terms of pure justice, but not in the realm of relations whereby the unity of life manifests itself, in virtue. Thus, if the universal law persists, so does the condemnation of the particular crime. The law relentlessly hounds the conscience of the transgressor, who is constantly reminded of his or her misdeed, a crime that is henceforth ignominiously and irreparably cemented in the past.[96]

But whereas the law, a mere concept, requires something real to enact the punishment it demands, fate in Hegel's view entails both the command and its execution at once, since in fate there is no division between the universal and the particular. This is the case because fate arises from a sundering of life. All life is unified. Consequently, any harm done to another life harms one's own life as well. A violation of life causes life itself to turn back upon the trespasser as his or her own enemy; the transgression gives rise to its own punishment. Yet the very fact that life punishes those who rupture its unity offers the possibility of reconciliation. Punishment by law always betrays a condition of heteronomy, as the law subjects the particularity of life to its domination. It is always some agent of a dominant power who exacts justice by executing the punishment demanded by law, but this punishment amounts merely to one particular violation of rights in response to another. As a result, the living person always views the law as a persisting alien force to which he or she is subject. But when one endures fate, when life itself has been rent in two, then the crime is not merely the annihilation of the content of a law, of a particular right, to which the law's universal form remains opposed. In the throes of fate, one senses not the domination of law but that the wound inflicted upon life forms a part of him or herself. And when one feels that he or she has severed the unity of life, when one yearns to recover the life he or she has lost, one already begins to share again in the unity of life. The division that is felt is, in a sense, necessary for the reconciliation with fate by love. With reconciliation, then, with the recognition that the life violated in another is also violated in oneself, justice is served and one's conscience assuaged. Unlike punishment by law, which forever spotlights the reality of the unchangeable crime, reconciled fate allows the transgression against life to fade into the shadows of memory.[97]

Fate further differs from penal law in that it also afflicts the innocent. One need not be guilty of a crime to sense divisions in the unity of life. Here Hegel traverses the rugged terrain of the tragic, where the guilt of innocence arouses fate, where a beautiful soul cannot avoid harming life in order to maintain his or her autonomy and purity.[98] Yet if Hegel considers fate to arise from one's own actions, what about so much of life, in which a great deal is done or happens *to* someone? Is this also a source of fate? No, Hegel answers, another's action simply serves as the occasion for fate. What is decisive is how one chooses to react to that which befalls him or her.[99]

Hegel delineates three possible reactions to an assault. One could choose to fight back and defend his or her right against the aggressor. Or one could passively yield. In the latter case, one is still insisting upon his or her right. Such a person merely lacks the power to defend it and suffers grief over this impotence. Both reactions subject one to fate: in both there is a conflict between the claim to a right in thought and the reality of that right in life. On the one hand, courageous self-defense perpetuates fate by submitting the conflict of rights, an opposition of universal concepts, to resolution either by physical might or by a judge's arbitration. Heteronomy obtains in the case of self-defense because each combatant must yield to determination by sheer strength, which has nothing to do with right, or to an outside arbiter. Opposition likewise persists because neither force nor a third party can reconcile opposing claims to right or life turned against life. In grieving passivity, on the other hand, one bitterly succumbs to fate and the domination of the other while nonetheless clinging, in one's mind, to one's own right.[100]

Only the third alternative, that of the beautiful soul, enables one to maintain his or her autonomy and transcend the power of fate. The beautiful soul removes him or herself from the sphere of rights altogether; he or she relinquishes his or her right voluntarily and accepts the fate as just. In this way, courage and passivity are united. Life remains because the beautiful soul withdraws from heteronomous relations in order to preserve his or her purity, but the opposition with another living being no longer exists. Moreover, unlike the one who bitterly yields to an aggressor, the beautiful soul accepts his or her fate and can endure it, since the sufferings are now the result of his or her own choice and not of some other being that would exert dominance over him or her.[101]

Hegel seems, then, to be examining what we might call an aesthetics of suicide, which has autonomy and purity of soul as its highest values: "To save himself, the man kills himself; to avoid seeing his own being in another's power, he no longer calls it his own, and so he annihilates himself in wishing to maintain himself, since anything in another's power would no longer be the man himself."[102] Wishing not to injure life through heteronomous social relations, the beautiful soul chooses instead to withdraw from life. By giving up a part or whole of life, however, the beautiful soul must endure the fate of his or her own destruction. Yet this destruction is no longer fate to the beautiful soul because it is voluntarily chosen. The beautiful soul has transcended fate.[103]

It is clear that Hegel regards Jesus as precisely this beautiful soul who removes himself from impure Jewish society. Yet in Hegel's treatment of Jesus as a beautiful soul, several tensions emerge which indicate that, in *The Spirit of Christianity*, Hegel reaches an impasse, if not with the figure of Jesus as the founder of the Christian religion, then at least with the concept of the beautiful soul. Hegel describes how the negative attribute of the beautiful soul's withdrawal is a tremendous freedom, since by relinquishing all ties he or she gains complete autonomy. The pure heart that has fled life in order not to harm anyone is thus fully open to reconciliation with kindred spirits. With respect to Jesus, this is evident in the exhortation to forgive sins. By the standards of justice, when one endures a violation of his or her person, he or she obtains rights over the one who has committed the affront. In forgiving the other's sin, however, one renounces his or her claim to that right. A stringent claim to rights, in Hegel's view, betrays a mistake akin to the one Kant makes: namely, dutifully clinging to universal standards, to concepts, which one has set up in his or her mind and by which he or she is now judging others. Consequently, this subjection of the particular individual to universal standards of right arouses fate. This fate, as a reaction of the whole, of life, turns against the one who judges the other, who sees in the transgressor only a sin made universal by law, rather than a whole person who is more than the sum of his or her errors. Forgiveness, contrariwise, reconciles one with fate and leads to consciousness of the unity of life and spirit with the other person.[104]

The difficulty in Hegel's text lies in the fact that, although Jesus possesses a heart completely open to reconciliation, he is unable to actualize that reconciliation in life because he has withdrawn from his surrounding society. This problem in turn leads to the question of undeveloped beauty in Hegel's reading of Jesus's life and the history of the early church. In Jesus's life, fate comes into direct conflict with beauty:

> The fate of Jesus was that he had to suffer from the fate of his people; either he had to make that fate his own, to bear its necessity and share its joy, to unite his spirit with his people's, but to sacrifice his own beauty, his connection with the divine, or else he had to repel his nation's fate from himself, but submit to a life undeveloped and without pleasure in itself. In neither event would

his nature be fulfilled; in the former case he would sense only fragments of it, and even these would be sullied; in the latter, he would bring it fully into his consciousness, thought would know its shape only as a splendid shadow whose essence is the highest truth; the sensing of that essence he would have to forgo and the truth would not come alive in act and in reality. Jesus chose the latter fate, the severance of his nature from the world.[105]

This passage is quite telling. It reveals the tragedy of Jesus's situation and how, no matter what course of action he chooses, he must innocently suffer. This occurs because Jesus separates his nature from the world. This might sound similar to the Jews' own withdrawal from nature, but there are two major differences. Jesus chooses his fate in order to maintain his complete autonomy. He does not want to blemish the sense of the divine within himself. The Jews, by contrast, opt for a limited freedom supported by an ideal God who stands outside the human being and the world. Furthermore, Jesus does not flee the natural world but rather the unnatural world where the heteronomous ideal is unable to unite with the individual, where the ideal only commands and masters life.[106]

Even though Jesus is able to transcend his fate and endure it, his own life remains undeveloped and his nature unfulfilled. In his mind he can grasp (*erkennen*) the connection with the divine; he can, apparently, preserve his beauty, the idea of the Kingdom of God, as an *ideal*,[107] but his beauty and his freedom—which we saw above are integrally connected for Hegel—are deficient insofar as he and the members of the early church eschew social engagement and are passive vis-à-vis the state:

> Hence with this [passive] relation to the state one great element in a living union is cut away; for the members of the Kingdom of God one important bond of association is snapped; they have lost one part of freedom, that negative characteristic which an association of beauty possesses; they have lost a number of active relationships and living ties.[108]

In thus circumscribing love, in order to avoid all determinate modes of life,[109] Jesus prevents love from developing into life, into the full living self-consciousness of the unity of the divine shared by all in the community. In a foggy way, Jesus can recognize the truth and freedom of the ideal Kingdom of God. However, with regard to truth, Hegel writes, "Truth is something free which we neither master nor are mastered by.... Truth is beauty intellectually represented; the negative character of truth is freedom."[110] We have seen that the intellectual representation of beauty in religion is social by its very nature. Jesus's beauty thus remains confined to consciousness and really only to consciousness of a shadowlike form of beauty. Because Jesus has separated himself from the society around him, he cannot unite his ideal with the senses through religious imagination, at least not in the way that Hegel believed occurred in ancient Greece;[111] Jesus has no feeling (*Gefühle*) of the essence of the Kingdom of God as a living, active reality,[112] and hence truth and freedom do not in fact obtain.[113]

If we revisit the quotation with which I began this essay, it seems to Hegel almost inevitable that the pure soul would be sullied in his or her relations with others.[114] If that soul is not sullied and it withdraws, then it invites its own destruction—a destruction that is itself a consequence of the very fate that the beautiful soul seeks to transcend. Thus while Hegel calls the struggle of the beautiful soul against a tragic fate a "sublime" sight,[115] he simultaneously shows that such a soul's beauty falls short of the beauty manifest in a society at home in the world and one with the divine, a society where love has developed into life. With the figure of Jesus, Hegel appears to have reached an impasse.

Looking Ahead

So is Kaufmann right? Is the Jesus of Hegel's *Spirit of Christianity* the prophet of Goethe's more holistic vision of humanity and Iphigenia's *Sittlichkeit*? To be sure, Goethe's vision of the unity of divine and human and his narrative depiction of how Iphigenia transcends the divisions of duty and right do anticipate important features of Hegel's account in the *Spirit of Christianity*. In other respects, though—both negative and positive—Goethe's Iphigenia already gestures toward developments that will carry Hegel beyond the Jesus of the *Spirit of Christianity*.

First, if Goethe's own chronology is any guide, by the time he wrote the chapter "Confessions of a Beautiful Soul" in his novel *Wilhelm Meister's Apprenticeship* (1795–96), he seems to have realized that the figure of the beautiful soul was intrinsically destined to retreat from social contact and vanish in an inward, isolating void. As Robert Norton has shown, Goethe's depiction of the dissolution of the beautiful soul in *Wilhelm Meister* comes at the end of a century of eager but generally futile attempts to describe just what moral beauty is and how beauty might lead individuals to pursue the good, instead of degenerating into a solipsistic effort at self-fashioning.[116] In his *Phenomenology of Spirit* (1807), Hegel, too, will famously draw this century-long fascination with the figure of the beautiful soul to a close by recounting the enigmatic figure's withering away in a consumptive condition.[117]

At the same time, Goethe's Iphigenia suggests positively where Hegel will end up, especially by means of his later reinterpretation of Christianity. If tragedy comes to represent, beautifully, the internal contradictions that will ultimately cause the breakdown of the polis as a harmonious whole—with the awareness of many *poleis* all grounded upon the free subject[118]—then the successful enlightened critique of the Taurian custom of blood sacrifice that Iphigenia offers as part of a dialogue with King Thoas represents the use of public reason as the means of achieving reconciliation through mutual recognition. So it is that Katerina Deligiorgi has traced important parallels between Goethe's play and Hegel's account of confession and forgiveness in the *Phenomenology*—the very section in which the isolation of the beautiful soul is overcome.[119] So, too, does Stephen Houlgate describe Hegel's account of dramatic reconciliation—and in his *Aesthetics*, Hegel considers Goethe's *Iphigenia* a preeminent exemplar of modern drama[120]—as a "quasi-religious" anticipation of Hegel's mature account of forgiveness and reconciliation in Christianity and, importantly, in ethical life.[121]

Thus, if Hegel's critique of Christianity in the *Spirit of Christianity and Its Fate* is that it is too subjective and that a community based on love will logically transform into a positive religion because it cannot give expression to (and cannot know of) its unity with the divine as real in the world, then Hegel's discovery of the dialectic of reason enables him to show how the Greek religion of art is remembered but sublated in Christianity, where particularity becomes the expression of absolute being and where self-conscious individuality is known as substance. The self-directed practices of Hegel's idiosyncratic post-Enlightenment articulation of Lutheranism, in particular the Eucharist, in which the believer is conformed to the sacrifice and resurrection of Christ[122]—hence, in cultural-pedagogical practices that do justice to the individual while cultivating a disposition toward the universal—can then form the essential basis of the modern, rationally determined state.

Notes

1. This chapter had its origin in a seminar taught by Vittorio Hösle at the University of Notre Dame in fall 2006. I would like to thank Prof. Hösle, Cyril O'Regan, Peter Wake, and Franz-Josef Deiters for their helpful comments and feedback on earlier drafts of this chapter.

2. Friedrich Hegel, "Der Geist des Christentums und sein Schicksal," in *Hegels*

theologische Jugendschriften, ed. Herman Hegel, Geist (1907; repr., Frankfurt: Minerva, 1966), 315. English translation: Hegel, *On Christianity: Early Theological Writings*, trans. T. M. Knox (1948; repr., New York: Harper Torchbooks, 1961), 269.

3. Walter Kaufmann, *Discovering the Mind*, vol. 1, *Goethe, Kant, and Hegel* (New York: McGraw-Hill, 1980), 260–69.

4. Walter Kaufmann, "The Young Hegel and Religion," in *From Shakespeare to Existentialism: Studies in Poetry, Religion, and Philosophy* (Boston: Beacon, 1959), 142–46; Kaufmann, *Mind*, 1:207–9; Kaufmann, *Hegel: A Reinterpretation* (Garden City, NY: Anchor, 1965), 38.

5. Kaufmann, "Young Hegel," 144.

6. Kaufmann, "Young Hegel," 145.

7. Robert E. Norton, *The Beautiful Soul: Aesthetic Morality in the Eighteenth Century* (Ithaca, NY: Cornell University Press, 1995).

8. Joachim Angst and Fritz Hackert, postscript to *Iphigenie auf Tauris: Ein Schauspiel*, by Johann Wolfgang Goethe, notes by Joachim Angst and Fritz Hackert (Stuttgart: Reclam, 1993), 75–76; Charles E. Passage, introduction to *Iphigenia in Tauris: A Play in Five Acts*, by Johann Wolfgang von Goethe, trans. Charles E. Passage (1963; repr., Long Grove, IL: Waveland, 1991), 6–9.

9. Kaufmann, *Hegel*, 16. Kaufmann proceeds to defend his identification of Goethe's Iphigenia and Sophocles's Antigone as similar representatives of Greek *Sittlichkeit*. There is, however, a profound difference between these characters: whereas Antigone's stubborn one-sidedness leads to her destruction, Iphigenia relinquishes any one-sidedness and reconciles with Thoas.

10. Johann Wolfgang Goethe, *Iphigenie auf Tauris: Ein Schauspiel*, notes by Joachim Angst and Fritz Hackert (Stuttgart: Reclam, 1993), 1.2.83-86, 1.2.88-89. References to the German text consist of act, scene, and line.

11. Goethe, *Iphigenie*, 1.1.1–10.

12. Goethe, *Iphigenie*, 1.1.35–38, 1.1.51–53.

13. Goethe, *Iphigenie*, 1.1.23–24, 1.1.31–32; English translation: Johann Wolfgang von Goethe, *Iphigenia in Tauris: A Play in Five Acts*, trans. Charles E. Passage (1963; repr., Long Grove, IL: Waveland, 1991), 21–22.

14. Goethe, *Iphigenie*, 1.1.8; Goethe, *Iphigenia*, 21.

15. Goethe, *Iphigenie*, 1.1.33–34; Goethe, *Iphigenia*, 22.

16. Goethe, *Iphigenie*, 1.2.157–63, 1.3.315–26.

17. Goethe, *Iphigenie*, 1.3.226–50, 1.3.435–36.

18. Goethe, *Iphigenie*, 1.3.437–47.

19. Goethe, *Iphigenie*, 1.3.527–37.

20. Goethe, *Iphigenie*, 4.4.1669–71.

21. Goethe, *Iphigenie*, 1.2.121–27.

22. Goethe, *Iphigenie*, 4.5.1689–717. See also 1.4.549–53.

23. Goethe, *Iphigenie*, 1.2.150–53, 1.2.156–71.

24. Goethe, *Iphigenie*, 4.4.1666–88.

25. The question of reason's role in achieving reconciliation has its place within the broader issue of gender in the drama, a question beyond the scope of this essay. Thoas scolds Iphigenia for acting as a woman (i.e., for allegedly acting according to her inclinations rather than according to his concept of reason):

> Do as your heart bids you do,
> And pay no heed to the voice of good counsel
> And reason. Be a woman through and through,
> Yield to the impulse that without restraint
> Now takes and pulls you one way or the other.
> (Goethe, *Iphigenie*, 1.3.463–67; Goethe, *Iphigenia*, 34)

26. Kaufmann thus appears correct on this point.
27. Goethe, *Iphigenie*, 1.3.444–47.
28. Goethe, *Iphigenie*, 1.3.522–30.
29. Goethe, *Iphigenie*, 2.1.742–43; Goethe, *Iphigenia*, 42.
30. Goethe, *Iphigenie*, 2.1.747–48.
31. Goethe, *Iphigenie*, 1.3.494; Goethe, *Iphigenia*, 35.
32. One observes how Iphigenia's heart encompasses reason and feeling when she admits to Pylades that she has possibly imperiled their deceptive plan by allowing Arkas to report to Thoas the need to postpone the sacrifice while she purportedly purifies the goddess' statue in the ocean:

> Blame me
> Alone, the fault is mine, I realize [*ich fühl es wohl*].
> And yet I could in no way else confront
> That man who reasonably and seriously [*mit Vernunft und Ernst*]
> Asked what my heart [*mein Herz*] acknowledged was his right.
> (Goethe, *Iphigenie*, 4.4.1587–90; Goethe, *Iphigenia*, 67)

33. Goethe, *Iphigenie*, 5.3.1831.
34. Goethe, *Iphigenie*, 5.3.1833–34.
35. Goethe, *Iphigenie*, 1.3.523–26.
36. Goethe, *Iphigenie*, 1.4.549–53.
37. Goethe, *Iphigenie*, 4.5.1726–66.
38. See Franz-Josef Deiters, "Goethe's 'Iphigenie auf Tauris' als Drama der Grenzüberschreitung oder: Die Aneignung der Mythos," *Jahrbuch des Freien Deutschen Hochstifts* (1999): 35–41.
39. Goethe, *Iphigenie*, 4.5.1716–17; Goethe, *Iphigenia*, 71.
40. Kaufmann observes, "Goethe's change of Euripides' plot does not revolve around a superficial ambiguity: what is truly divine and has the power to purify a man is not a statue or anything else supernatural but a harmonious ethical personality whose pride does not preclude humility and whose outstanding courage and honesty are employed in the service of love." *Hegel*, 17.

41. This opposition, as we will see, anticipates Hegel's exposition of penal law, a form of punishment under which reconciliation is impossible.

42. Iphigenia tells Thoas:

> A King
> Who asks inhuman actions will find henchmen
> Enough who for reward and favor will
> With greed accept half of the action's curse;
> But his own presence still remains unblemished.
> He sits within his stormcloud plotting death
> And lets his messengers descend with flaming
> Destruction on the luckless mortal's head,
> While he serenely moves off in the storm,
> An unscathed god across the heights of the sky.
> (Goethe, *Iphigenie*, 5.3.1812–20; Goethe, *Iphigenia*, 74)

43. Goethe, *Iphigenie*, 1.4.554–55; Goethe, *Iphigenia*, 36.
44. Goethe, *Iphigenie*, 1.3.452–53, 1.3.493–94.
45. Goethe, *Iphigenie*, 3.1.1172, 3.1.1190–95.
46. Goethe, *Iphigenie*, 3.3.1355–58.
47. Goethe, *Iphigenie*, 5.6.2174.
48. Goethe, *Iphigenie*, 4.2.1463; Goethe, *Iphigenia*, 63.
49. Goethe, *Iphigenie*, 4.2.1493–94; Goethe, *Iphigenia*, 64 (translation modified).
50. Goethe, *Iphigenie*, 4.2.1495–96.
51. Goethe, *Iphigenie*, 4.4.1645–47.
52. Goethe, *Iphigenie*, 4.4.1656–59; Goethe, *Iphigenia*, 69.
53. Goethe, *Iphigenie*, 4.3.1526–29; Goethe, *Iphigenia*, 65.
54. Goethe, *Iphigenie*, 4.4.1596–603.
55. So implies Pylades. Goethe, *Iphigenie*, 4.4.1640–45.
56. Goethe, *Iphigenie*, 1.3.292–94.
57. Goethe, *Iphigenie*, 5.3.1919–36.
58. Goethe, *Iphigenie*, 5.3.1942–44.
59. Goethe, *Iphigenie*, 5.3.1949–52. Against commentators who do not see any real conversion on Thoas's part and hence no real danger in the story, Stephen Houlgate insists that Iphigenia's situation bears genuine tragic potential. Thoas grows angry at her rejection of his marriage proposal and is intent on having the sacrifice carried out. In speaking honestly with him, Iphigenia renders herself susceptible to tragic fate. See Stephen Houlgate, "Hegel's Theory of Tragedy," in *Hegel and the Arts*, ed. Stephen Houlgate (Evanston, IL: Northwestern University Press, 2007), 165–66.
60. Goethe, *Iphigenie*, 3.1.1157–59; Goethe, *Iphigenia*, 54.
61. Goethe, *Iphigenie*, 3.3.1355–58; Goethe, *Iphigenia*, 60.
62. Goethe, *Iphigenie*, 5.5.2000–2002; Goethe, *Iphigenia*, 80. A few lines later Iphigenia says that Thoas has become to her a second father.

63. Goethe, *Iphigenie*, 1.4.549–53; Goethe, *Iphigenia*, 36.
64. Goethe, *Iphigenie*, 4.3.1522–25.
65. Goethe, *Iphigenie*, 4.1.1405-11; Goethe, *Iphigenia*, 62.
66. Goethe, *Iphigenie*, 5.3.1873–74.
67. Goethe, *Iphigenie*, 5.3.1834–36.
68. Goethe, *Iphigenie*, 5.3.1939–42.
69. Goethe, *Iphigenie*, 5.6.2153–65.
70. Goethe, *Iphigenie*, 5.6.2152–55; Goethe, *Iphigenia*, 84.
71. Goethe, *Iphigenie*, 5.6.2174.
72. For example, the Greek pair Deucalion and Pyrrha. Hegel, *Geist*, 245; Hegel, *Early Theological Writings*, 184–85.
73. Roger Harrison, "Jesus, Abraham, Freedom and Fate in Hegel's Early 'Theological' Writings," *Clio* 9, no. 1 (1979): 53-54. Laurence Dickey has situated the early Hegel's desire to transform his society into the context of Württemberg Pietist efforts at social and political reform. Laurence Dickey, *Hegel: Religion, Economics, and the Politics of Spirit, 1770–1807* (Cambridge: Cambridge University Press, 1987). Pietism, as Norton has shown, played no small role in the history of the concept of the beautiful soul. See Norton, *Beautiful Soul*, 55–99. Peter Wake takes a different approach to Hegel's early works by arguing that Greek tragedy provided a template for Hegel's early effort to discover a new mythology for religion in modernity in a way that would unite rationality and sensuality. Tragedy served as a lens through which Hegel uncovered the roots of positivity and heteronomy in the Christianity of his own day. See Peter Wake, *Tragedy in Hegel's Early Theological Writings* (Bloomington: Indiana University Press, 2014).
74. On the text's composition and dating, see Wake, *Tragedy*, 221–22n1.
75. Hegel, *Geist*, 243–44; Hegel, *Early Theological Writings*, 182.
76. Hegel, *Geist*, 245-48; Hegel, *Early Theological Writings*, 185–88.
77. Hegel, *Geist*, 258; Hegel, *Early Theological Writings*, 202. Hegel is here addressing the Jews' historical loss of power to foreign nations. Because their independent existence was one held in opposition to nature and in control over it (by *their* infinite ideal, *their* God), it was inevitably precarious. Hegel believed the Jews were so concerned with the provision of basic needs that they had no opportunity to develop resources for coming to friendly terms with the world: resources that other peoples who embodied more beautiful, humane existences could employ when coping with adversity. With their loss of temporal power and subjugation to other nations, the Jews thus plunged into an even more miserable and passive state that only further prevented them from achieving the freedom of beauty that results from the proper relationship to nature and the world.
78. See, for example, Immanuel Kant, *Die Religion innerhalb der Grenzen der bloßen Vernunft* in *Kant's gesammelte Schriften*, ed. Königlich Preußische Akademie der Wissenschaften, vol. 6 (Berlin: Georg Reimer, 1914), 167–68. See the distinction, then, that Kant draws between a true moral religion and the

counterfeit service of God, that is, the observance of statutory laws as the condition for pleasing God. See Kant, *Religion*, 6:178–79.

79. Kant, *Religion*, 6:125–26.

80. Immanuel Kant, *Grundlegung zur Metaphysik der Sitten*, in *Kant's gesammelte Schriften*, ed. Königlich Preußische Akademie der Wissenschaften, vol. 4 (Berlin: Georg Reimer, 1911), 433–34.

81. Hegel, *Geist*, 265–66; Hegel, *Early Theological Writings*, 211–12.

82. Hegel, *Geist*, 264; Hegel, *Early Theological Writings*, 209.

83. Hegel, *Geist*, 267; Hegel, *Early Theological Writings*, 213.

84. Hegel, *Geist*, 268; Hegel, *Early Theological Writings*, 214.

85. Hegel, *Geist*, 266; Hegel, *Early Theological Writings*, 212.

86. Hegel, *Geist*, 335-36; Hegel, *Early Theological Writings*, 292-95.

87. Hegel, *Geist*, 302; Hegel, *Early Theological Writings*, 253.

88. Hegel, *Geist*, 297; Hegel, *Early Theological Writings*, 248. Hegel argues, for instance, in respect to the Eucharist: "To eat and drink with someone is an act of union and is itself a felt union, not a conventional symbol." Hegel, *Geist*, 297; Hegel, *Early Theological Writings*, 248.

89. See Hegel, *Geist*, 322; Hegel, *Early Theological Writings*, 278–79.

90. Hegel, *Geist*, 321; Hegel, *Early Theological Writings*, 277.

91. Hegel, *Geist*, 321–22; Hegel, *Early Theological Writings*, 278.

92. Hegel, *Geist*, 312–13; Hegel, *Early Theological Writings*, 266.

93. Hegel, *Geist*, 316; Hegel, *Early Theological Writings*, 271.

94. Hegel, *Geist*, 328; Hegel, *Early Theological Writings*, 285. Elsewhere Hegel asks, "Is there an idea more beautiful than that of a nation of men related to one another by love? Is there one more uplifting that that of belonging to a whole which as a whole, as one, is the spirit of God whose sons the individual members are?" Hegel, *Geist*, 322; Hegel, *Early Theological Writings*, 278.

95. Hegel, *Geist*, 342; Hegel, *Early Theological Writings*, 301.

96. Hegel, *Geist*, 277-80; Hegel, *Early Theological Writings*, 224–29.

97. Hegel, *Geist*, 279-83, 288; Hegel, *Early Theological Writings*, 227–33, 237–38.

98. Hegel, *Geist*, 283; Hegel, *Early Theological Writings*, 232–33.

99. Hegel, *Geist*, 284; Hegel, *Early Theological Writings*, 233–34.

100. Hegel, *Geist*, 284-85; Hegel, *Early Theological Writings*, 233–35.

101. Hegel, *Geist*, 285; Hegel, *Early Theological Writings*, 234–35.

102. Hegel, *Geist*, 285–86; Hegel, *Early Theological Writings*, 235.

103. Hegel, *Geist*, 286; Hegel, *Early Theological Writings*, 236.

104. Hegel, *Geist*, 286–88; Hegel, *Early Theological Writings*, 235–38.

105. Hegel, *Geist*, 328–29; Hegel, *Early Theological Writings*, 285–86.

106. See Hegel, *Geist*, 317; Hegel, *Early Theological Writings*, 271–72.

107. See Hegel, *Geist*, 329; Hegel, *Early Theological Writings*, 286–87.

108. Hegel, *Geist*, 327; Hegel, *Early Theological Writings*, 284. Brackets included by Knox, the translator.

109. Hegel, *Geist*, 324; Hegel, *Early Theological Writings*, 281.

110. Hegel, *Geist*, 254; Hegel, *Early Theological Writings*, 196.

111. Consider Hegel's comments on the Eucharist in comparison to a statue of a Greek god. The Eucharist, on Hegel's early analysis, elicits only a transient *feeling* of unity and reconciliation among the communicants, that is, only until the wafer has dissolved on one's tongue. There is no enduring object or shape for the imagination, which could call forth the experience of love. On the one hand, thought knows that there is bread; on the other, one feels the unity of love. However, the image of bread does not give rise to the feeling of one's unity with the whole: "To faith it is the spirit which is present [in the Eucharistic celebration]; to seeing and tasting, the bread and wine. There is no unification of the two. The intellect contradicts feeling, and vice versa. There is nothing for imagination (in which intellect and feeling are both present and yet canceled) to do; here it cannot provide any image in which seeing and feeling would be unified. In an Apollo or a Venus we must forget the marble, the breakable stone, and see in its shape the immortal only. In looking at the shape, we are permeated with the sense of love and eternal youth." Hegel, *Geist*, 300; Hegel, *Early Theological Writings*, 252. As Peter Wake observes, there is no way for Christianity to give enduring, adequate cultural expression to the subjective unity of love that forms the basis of its union. Any outward cultural practice or institution will inevitably assume the form of positivity. See Wake, *Tragedy*, 172.

112. Hegel, *Geist*, 329; Hegel, *Early Theological Writings*, 286.

113. I must thus disagree with Harrison's conclusion regarding Jesus as one who takes control of his fate, thereby opening up a space for human freedom and self-creation, that is, for history. While this interpretation is to an extent true, it appears that Hegel ultimately sees the freedom to which Jesus attains as deficient. Jesus finds freedom only in a void, as Hegel says. I do not know if the void is in Hegel's view the proper venue for self-creative history. See Harrison, "Jesus, Abraham, Freedom and Fate," 66.

114. Elsewhere Hegel contends, "The struggle of the pure against the impure is a sublime sight, but it soon changes into a horrible one when holiness itself is impaired by unholiness, and when an amalgamation of the two, with the pretension of being pure, rages against fate, because in these circumstances holiness itself is caught in the fate and subject to it." Hegel, *Geist*, 329; Hegel, *Early Theological Writings*, 286.

115. Hegel, *Geist*, 324, 329; Hegel, *Early Theological Writings*, 281, 286.

116. Norton argues, "Perhaps . . . Goethe discerned in the idea of moral beauty —then at the crest of its popularity—an inherent tendency toward the vacant aestheticization of the self that *Bildung* can produce when it is not grounded in genuinely ethical being, which is never selfishly sought as a means of private enjoyment, or even abstract satisfaction, but is always a matter of social and communal responsibility carried out in some sort of action." Norton, *Beautiful*

Soul, 262. The chapter, "Confessions of a Beautiful Soul," is, according to Norton, "a veiled cautionary tale about precisely that process of deluded diminishment performed in the name of inner expansion." Norton, *Beautiful Soul*, 252. In that regard, Norton diagnoses a similar contradictory dynamic to that which Peter Wake has argued dooms Jesus and the Christian Church in Hegel's *Spirit of Christianity*—namely, that any community based on *love* will falter under the competing urges to expand and also to intensify, often by vilifying those outside the group as enemies. Wake, *Tragedy*, 183–89. Andrew Fiala has similarly shown that Hegel's critique of Schiller's notion of an "aesthetic state" rests on that state's ideal or utopian character—its distance from the real—and that such distance can result in a dangerous fanaticism. Andrew Fiala, "Aesthetic Education and the Aesthetic State: Hegel's Response to Schiller," in *Hegel and Aesthetics*, ed. William Maker (Albany: State University of New York Press, 2000), 171–85.

117. G. W. F. Hegel, *The Phenomenology of Spirit*, trans. A.V. Miller (Oxford: Oxford University Press, 1977), 399–400, 406–7.

118. On this dynamic in Hegel's thought, see Paul Cobben, "Religion in the Form of Art," in *Hegel's Philosophy of the Historical Religions*, ed. Bart Labuschagne and Timo Slootweg (Leiden, The Netherlands: Brill, 2012), 99–124.

119. Katerina Deligiorgi, "Dissatisfied Enlightenment: Certain Difficulties concerning the Public Use of One's Reason," *Bulletin of the Hegel Society of Great Britain* 35 (1997): 46–50. Deligiorgi's use of the term "reason" here ought not to obscure the role of the heart in both Goethe's play and in Hegel's account of confession and forgiveness. In the latter, it is worth asking what exactly it is that leads the hard heart to break.

120. Hegel, *Werke in zwanzig Bänden*, ed. Eva Moldenhauer and Karl Markus Michel (Frankfurt: Suhrkamp, 1970), 15:533. For Hegel's discussion of the play, especially as it differs from that of Euripides, see also Hegel, *Werke*, 13:297–300.

121. Houlgate argues, "A play such as *Iphigenie auf Tauris* thus offers a *quasi-religious* alternative, within dramatic art, to the tragedy that is engendered by *aesthetic*, heroic individuality. This quasi-religious alternative—of yielding, forgiveness and reconciliation—in turns holds the key to genuine *ethical* life, which is to be found in communities based not on heroism but on mutual recognition. In drama, in other words, art points to a truth that lies beyond its own aesthetic ideal—an ideal that tragedy reveals to be magnificent but self-destructive." See Houlgate, "Hegel's Theory of Tragedy," 168.

122. See Douglas Finn, "Spiritual Consumption: Eating and the Christian Eucharist in Hegel," *Owl of Minerva* 47, no. 1 (2015–2016): 109–67; Lawrence S. Stepelevich, "Hegel and the Lutheran Eucharist," *Heythrop Journal* 27, no. 3 (1986): 262–74.

Chapter Two

Two Early Interpretations of Hegel's Theory of Greek Tragedy
Hinrichs and Goethe

Eric v. d. Luft

HERMANN FRIEDRICH WILHELM HINRICHS (1794–1861) was Hegel's student at Heidelberg from 1816 to 1818, professor of philosophy at Halle from 1824 until his death, and the first scholar to write a book-length treatise on any aspect of Hegel's thought: *Die Religion im inneren Verhältnisse zur Wissenschaft* [Religion in its internal relationship to systematic knowledge] (1822). He is best known in the latter capacity, not so much for his own efforts but because Hegel wrote the famous preface to the book.[1] As such, Hinrichs is preeminent among the so-called Old or Right Hegelians (i.e., the first generation of orthodox supporters of Hegel's doctrines), such a paragon that when Marx and Engels attacked their fellow Young or Left Hegelians, Bruno Bauer ("Saint Bruno") and Max Stirner ("Saint Max"), in *Die Heilige Familie* [The holy family] (1845), they sarcastically called upon Hinrichs no fewer than six times to help them—*Hinrichs hilf!*[2]

Goethe had known of Hinrichs since at least 1822, when the twenty-eight-year-old upstart boldly sent the seventy-three-year-old titan a copy of his philosophy of religion. Goethe replied on June 10, 1822, that he had read Hegel's preface eagerly and at once—and that he would read the rest of the book when he got around to it (*HHS*, 19).

Hinrichs's second book was on Goethe's *Faust*.³ He consulted Goethe in 1824 while writing it and received some friendly feedback (*HHS*, 23–24).

In 1827 Hinrichs published a thoroughly Hegelian book about Sophocles.⁴ It was the topic of Goethe's conversations with Eckermann on March 21 and 28, 1827.⁵ Goethe lamented that such a brilliant thinker as Hinrichs had become so deeply enamored of Hegel and so thoroughly steeped in Hegelianism that he had, in effect, ceased to think for himself (*HHS*, 3–4).⁶ But besides Hegel, Hinrichs had two other main influences in his theory of tragedy: Aristotle, whose theory of tragedy he judged too "subjective" (*W*, xxxvi–xxxviii, xlii; *E*, 18, 20); and Plato (*W*, xlii; *E*, 20). Even though, as expected, Hinrichs's theory of ancient tragedy did not depart much from Hegel's, he also extrapolated some tangents of his own, fleshing out Hegel's analysis and filling in gaps. Thus Goethe's dismissal of him as a mere epigone is somewhat harsh.

For Goethe, Sophocles is not the pinnacle of ancient Greek tragedy that he is for Hinrichs and Hegel (*GG*, 136–137; *CG*, 231–232) but shares that honor with Aeschylus and even Euripides, both of whom Hinrichs sharply criticizes, mostly along established lines (*W*, xvi–xvii, xx–xxviii, xxxvii–xl, xlvii; *E*, 10, 12–15, 18–19, 22). Hinrichs complains that Euripides spoiled his plays with prologues, which "usually let us know in advance the whole course of the tragedy, while genuine art consists in that we first come to know the tragedy through the necessary development and unfolding of the tragedy itself" (*W*, xxxix; *E*, 19). But Hinrichs is wrong on this point: a Euripidean prologue is not akin to a spoiler for the next *Star Wars* movie. Rather, as Goethe correctly points out, a Greek dramatist would take "some ancient ready-made popular tradition in which a good idea existed" (*GG*, 126; *CG*, 226) and adapt it for the theater. So, the audience would already know the plot. Yet the play itself was not mere mannerism but a cogent and fascinating expression of ideas, especially in the hands of a master like Sophocles. Moreover, Hinrichs argues against Aeschylus that the Theban plays of Sophocles are superior because they emerge from dialectical necessity and the genuinely tragic idea rather than from "natural contingency" (*W*, 44–45, 51; *E*, 43, 46).

For Hinrichs, tragedy comes from fated roles into which powerless humans are inexorably cast (Heidegger would say *geworfen*; see *Sein und Zeit*, § 29); but for Goethe, it comes from idiosyncratic human foibles, flaws, and mistakes (*GG*, 124–125; *CG*, 225). For Hinrichs, tragic persons are "individuations" (*W*, 15–16; *E*, 29); for Goethe, they are individuals. That is, for Hinrichs, tragedy is impersonal, driven by fate, and comes from the incompatibility of roles, regardless of personal idiosyncrasies (W, 46–49, 54; E, 44–45, 47); but for Goethe, it is personal, driven by choices, and comes from the clash of personalities, mostly regardless of their respective birthrights, fortunes, or sociopolitical positions. For Hinrichs, the tragedy in *Antigone* is between state and family as embodied respectively in Creon and Antigone (W, 49–50; E, 45); but for Goethe, it is between Creon and Antigone themselves as individuals. Goethe believes that the most important aspect of the tragedian's task and art is to make the characters come alive as unique individuals (i.e., as subjective flesh and blood), whose very subjectivity, apart from their roles, is the source of their tragic conflict. They represent nothing except themselves. But Hinrichs will have none of that. For him, the characters in a play represent, exemplify, or embody ideas (W, iii–v; E, [5]), and the tragic persons among these characters particularize, actualize, or "individualize" substantial tragic powers (e.g., family and state) or ethical ideas (e.g., family piety and political virtue) and thus become "mental images" (*Vorstellungen*) of these powers or ideas. Personalities are contingent, but tragic roles are necessary as determined within their own dialectic and thus cannot be filled by just anybody: only by those who, because of their pretragic sociopolitical status, adequately represent these roles. "Antigone and Creon, entirely in keeping with the demand of the tragedy, ... bearing witness to the family and to the state as the tragic powers, conduct family piety and state virtue as their pathos against each other" (W, 72–73; E, 56). Other characters, such as Haemon, are just role fillers, necessitated by the trajectory of the plot (W, 52–54, 80, 99–102; E, 47, 59, 69–70). Yet perhaps we could concede a point to Goethe and say that Hinrichs confuses bona fide necessity with mere dramatic logic.

Hinrichs claims that free individuals who follow their own wills or desires, acting autonomously without external constraint or heteronomous influences, can never be tragic. Only those who are caught in conflicting roles over which they have no control and from which they cannot escape are tragic persons. Hinrichs identifies three such roles: member of a family, citizen of a state, and member of a "people" (i.e., a particular ethnic, cultural, or religious group) (W, 7–12; E, 25–27). Accordingly, there are three potentially tragic powers—the family, the state, and the ethnic/cultural/religious group—which could wrest control of lives from individuals. Only the first two of these powers, family and state, are active in the Theban trilogy of Sophocles. All the characters are Greek polytheists; hence, there is no possible tragic conflict involving the third sphere.

Perhaps anticipating Goethe's assertion that Hinrichs reduces Greek drama to expressions of ideas (*GG*, 126; *CG*, 226), Hinrichs writes that the hero's "activity is ... not determined from outside, but rather from his own interiority ... even if a god encourages him toward action and activity.... Since the self-determining spirit underlies all true art ... the ... art of the Greek people ... exists only as an expression of the spiritual" (*W*, xiv; *E*, 9). That is, for Hinrichs, each character in a Greek drama indeed represents an idea and creates for the audience a dynamic mental image of that idea, but the plot activity of that character is not determined by the idea but instead self-determined by the character, either wittingly or unwittingly, and eventually, as the tragedy unfolds, with full self-knowledge. Even though the characters are fated, they know their actions as their own. Through a tragic character's growing self-knowledge, the audience gains knowledge of the idea that character represents. "But whatever in particular concerns Greek art insofar as it becomes an object of knowledge by means of the idea, this knowledge itself still could not emerge from Greek life, because art still constituted the midpoint between the direct beholding and the mental imagery of this life" (*W*, xxxv; *E*, 17).

These dramatically represented ideas are neither abstract nor esoteric. Rather, they belong to real life and present actuality, with which the audience can readily identify (*W*, 18; *E*, 30). Hinrichs claims that "actuality, as disintegrated necessity ... actual freedom ... the orderly ethical ... is ... the essence of ancient tragedy" (*W*, xlvi; *E*, 21). "Thus, what the people is according to its customary morals, what occurred through its power and action, what religious mental images pervade it, all this was what this great creator of tragedy [i.e., Sophocles] had first to formulate dramatically, then to train into the self-conscious pathos of a tragic plot" (*W*, xv–xvi; *E*, 10). Nevertheless, "as long as Greek life was still motivated by customary morals and religion, and as long as this life constituted what motivated art, tragedy also had to rise in its training toward ever greater perfection and purity entirely according to the orderly ethical idea ... it gained for its content precisely this dawning consciousness of the orderly ethical powers of the family and the state as all actuality" (*W*, xviii; *E*, 10–11).

The family is the ground of the state. Thus, even though Creon was within his rights as prince, his decree forbidding the burial of his nephew and his death sentence against his niece, his son's fiancée, both in fact sabotage the state insofar as they attack the family. Thus his power crumbles, and his state virtue comes to nothing. As Teiresias reveals, Creon, in destroying both Antigone's family and his own, likewise endangers the state, which, if it is to be strong, must consist of the unity of strong families (W, 95–98; E, 67–68). Yet only through the suicides of his son and wife does he learn that "his right was the greatest wrong" (W, 103; E, 71) and thus achieves full self-knowledge. He's too late in understanding that the formula for reconciliation must be rational (i.e., "the substantial certainty that true reason consists in not committing outrages against the gods, which entails that family and state, not as opposed, but rather as their own living unity, constitute a properly divine actuality") (W, 105; E, 71).

Hinrichs catalogs and considers all the various interfamilial relationships— mother / child, husband / wife, father / mother, brother / sister, sister / sister, brother / brother, member of immediate family / member of extended family, blood relative / relative by marriage, etc.—in terms of their respective divine sanctions (W, 1–16; E, 22–29). On this basis, due to the naturally asexual closeness and attendant ethical purity of the blood sibling relationship, he follows Hegel in declaring that Antigone obeyed the will of God in giving appropriate funeral rites to her brother despite the decree of the state.

The crux of Hegel's interpretation of *Antigone* is that Creon and Antigone are each correct within their respective spheres: he within the worldly sphere and she within the divine sphere. Since both do their duty according to the separate dictates of these two spheres, both are blameless. The tragedy is that the two spheres are at least penultimately incompatible, barring further dialectic beyond Hegel's time—and ours.

Both Creon and especially Antigone resemble Kantian rational and ethical beings insofar as each does their duty without regard for consequences. Yet he has a rougher task to make decisions than she does. Man is a member of both the state and the family and thus may have conflicting duties. Woman, on the other hand, although subject to the laws and customs of the state, is not in fact a member or citizen of the state but only a member of the family, to which alone she has a duty. Thus Creon is conflicted between his roles as father and ruler, but Antigone is not conflicted at all. Her way is clear, though terrifying; while his way is muddled by dichotomously opposed influences. Only Teiresias clarifies matters for him.

Both Hegel and Hinrichs endorse standard "separate sphere" gender ideology. For Hinrichs, the most basic and natural tragic opposition is between woman and man. And because woman represents or personifies the family while man represents or personifies the state, this tragic opposition is intensified, exacerbated, and indeed almost reified (W, 11–13, 79–80, 85–86; E, 27–28, 59, 62). Specifically, the sister (in this case, but sometimes the mother) "individuates" the family while the prince "individuates" the state. Despite motherly love being the source of all real love on earth, the mother is not the most highly tragic person in the family because her love is tainted by sexual attraction and sexual indulgence. Thus, it is "woman as sister ... [who] senses the purest orderly ethical family love ... [and] woman as the loving sister in whom ... is individualized the tragic power of the family" (W, 15–16; E, 29).

Simon Goldhill complains that Hegel concentrates too much on Antigone's sister/brother relationships and not enough on her sister/sister relationship. This is a valid criticism, but it is not true of Hinrichs, who considers Ismene's role in depth as a foil and counterpoint for Antigone.[7] Nevertheless, Goethe criticizes Hinrichs on this very point (GG, 125–126; CG, 225–226). Hinrichs claims that a sister's love for her brother is the purest sort of love (W, 14; E, 28), but Goethe counters that "the love of sister for sister was still more pure and unsexual" (GG, 125; CG, 225–226). But, at the same time, Hinrichs distills the tragic family down to the devoted sister as the epitome of tragedy (W, 51–52; E, 46–47), regardless of her feelings for either her sister or her brother, since she is essentially without power or authority in either the state or the family but can preserve her integrity only by doing her duty according to the divine sanction of the family. The central role of the devoted sister, Antigone, necessitates the auxiliary role of the not-quite-so-devoted sister, Ismene, whose purpose, both dramatic and dialectical, is to underscore, by contrast, the absolute purity, resoluteness, and piety of Antigone (W, 54–55; E, 47–48). Ismene is conflicted; Antigone is not; and Ismene's confusion, fluctuation, and general uncertainty, born of fear, throw Antigone's fearless resolve and unwavering commitment into sharp relief (W, 65–66, 80–83; E, 53, 59–61).

Motherly love is primordial, the strongest love, the basis of all other love (W, 2–4; E, 23–24). In fact, motherly love is the family's "principle of ethical order" (E, 24),[8] and hence, by extension, the principle of the ethical order of the whole fabric of society. The untranslatable term, *Sittlichkeit*, which is perhaps best rendered as "ethical order," denotes a key concept for Hegel: the ideal of right and justice and the aim of law, custom, and morality. *Sittlichkeit* entails not only an orderly ethical family but also an orderly ethical state.

Conflicts within the ethical order, or between two ethical orders, create tragedy, a dialectical impasse.

Marriages gradually build families into a nation by developing a huge network of interrelated families, but since these families at the same time become increasingly distant, the state and its laws become necessary to hold the nation together and to preserve *Sittlichkeit*, since love is no longer sufficient to do so at such distances (W, 3–5; E, 24). "Thus arises ... legislation as human law, alongside love as divine law ... [and] since mutual recognition is possible only in the legal life of the state ... love and law are equally valid and equally essential for the people ... [so that] customary morals ... consist in the actualized unity of family love and state virtue" (W, 5–7; E, 24–25). This necessity of the state as the legal source and defender of *Sittlichkeit* is the ground of Creon's justification of the righteousness of his decree forbidding the burial of Polynices (W, 49–50, 57–58, 64, 76–79; E, 45, 49, 52, 58–59), yet in this case it inexorably causes the irreconcilable bifurcation of sociopolitical coherence, which destroys *Sittlichkeit* as the state disrespects the family. Eteocles and Polynices erroneously believe that the family is subordinate to the state; thus, their "brotherly love no longer suffices to unify them" (W, 42; E, 42), and their abandonment of it is the root of their downfall. The state is not illegitimate even if it opposes the family; it is merely wrong in such cases. Its error does not affect its legitimacy (i.e., its right to exist) but still vitiates its ability to exist effectively, justly, and popularly.

Despite its divine warrant, the power of the family is not absolute. It cannot, for example, start blood feuds against other families because that would violate the legitimate laws of the state against murder, assault, etc. Nor can the family behave as if it were the state. The general inadvisability of government of the family, by the family, and for the family is the lesson of the Icelandic sagas. Blood feuds, which were rampant in Iceland during the "heroic"[9] period from the time of the settlement in 874 for the next four or five centuries, when government consisted of councils of clan chieftains, have been nearly unknown there since the Icelandic government assumed a more modern structure, partially under the influence of Denmark, in the late medieval era. Indeed, the evolution of the relationship among Icelandic families, clans, heroes, and governments readily admits of Hegelian dialectical analysis and shows positive historical progress, but that is a topic for another paper.[10]

Offenses against family piety pervaded and doomed the clan of Antigone long before Creon's own offense against it. Laius had raped a young boy, the child of his host, and Laius and Jocasta together had tried to kill their own newborn son. Since both of these offenses were committed wittingly, Laius was by no means innocent when Oedipus killed him. Partially as divine punishment for these witting offenses, there ensued the unwitting offenses of Oedipus killing his father and begetting four children with his mother. The corruption, grotesqueness, and doom of this clan is signified by Oedipus being, by blood, half-brother to his own children (W, 21–23; E, 32–33). Hence, Antigone stands by Oedipus not only because she is his daughter (W, 34–37; E, 38–39) but also because she is his sister. Thus, she owes him not only daughterly obedience but also sisterly devotion. The clan's family relationships are skewed, members do not understand their proper roles in the family, and this confusion undermines family piety. Eteocles and Polynices may owe filial love and obedience to their father Oedipus but no more to their brother Oedipus than to each other. The motherly love of Jocasta, which should have been the foundation of a solid family, is undermined not only by her attempted infanticide but also by her unwitting misidentification of motherly and spousal love (W, 32; E, 37). Her family is doomed because the normal, bilateral, well-defined relationships of its members are in fact abnormal, multilateral, and jumbled (W, 24–25; E, 33–34).

Fatal and wide-ranging repercussion for sin against the family is not an uncommon motif in the literary and dramatic arts. An excellent example of such a sinner, analogous to Creon, is Wotan in Wagner's *Der Ring des Nibelungen*. Wotan rules the universe by decree and carves the ensuing laws as runes on the shaft of his spear. But he himself is bound by these laws just like everyone else. If he should ever break any of his own laws, he would become powerless, the social fabric would unravel, and the political structure would collapse. Thus he is unfree, as he laments throughout Act 2, Scene 2, of *Die Walküre* (e.g., "der durch Verträge ich Herr, den Verträgen bin ich nun Knecht" [As I rule by treaties, so I am now the slave of treaties]). When his greed for the ring prompts him to promote the incestuous adultery of Siegmund and Sieglinde and thereby defile the marriage of Sieglinde and Hunding, he indeed loses his power and authority. Thus Siegfried is able to shatter Wotan's spear with the reforged sword, Notung, which that spear had once shattered in the hand of Siegmund, and the plot thereafter moves inexorably toward universal destruction in *Götterdämmerung*.[11]

Whereas Sophocles apparently sees the two tragic powers, family and state, as essentially irreconcilable unless the state capitulates to the divine warrant of the family and thus, in effect, ceases to be the state; Hinrichs sees these two powers as dialectical opposites, neither necessarily nor permanently opposed, but capable of reconciliation. Although he does not directly engage statements from the Theban triology such as "All the generations of these humans amount to nothing" (*King Oedipus*, ll. 1186–1187), Hinrichs opposes a reasoned optimism to the implied pessimism of Sophocles. To do this, Hinrichs takes a strictly Hegelian line of thought.

Both Hinrichs and Hegel intend to show that although Creon and Antigone are each correct within their respective contexts, these contexts, not the two subjective personalities who resolutely fit these contexts, are irreconcilable, at least at this stage of their dialectic. Nevertheless, Hinrichs (and to some extent even Hegel) implies that the rectitude of Antigone, following divine law, is superior to the rectitude of Creon, following human law. That is, if Creon is correct within the context of the state, and if Antigone is correct within the context of the family, then Antigone has moral ascendancy over Creon, insofar as the family is more sacred to the gods and more basic to human solidarity than the state is. Even Creon himself admits that Zeus, the king of the gods, is the god of family love (*Antigone*, ll. 658–659). There is no corresponding god of the state, despite Hinrichs's assertion (*W*, 26–27, 40–41; *E*, 34, 41) that Zeus presides over both family and state.

For Goethe, Creon is an absolute villain, with both abstract right and public opinion firmly against him (*GG*, 127–128; *CG*, 227). Nevertheless, Goethe recognizes that the audience has some sympathy for Creon, not through any virtue of Creon himself but only because Sophocles is such a master of the dramatic art. This Sophoclean suggestion that Creon could be at least partially in the right may have contributed to Hegel's original argument (*PhS*, ¶¶ 436–437, 466–475, 486, 736)[12] that Creon, qua prince with a consummate duty to uphold human law, state virtue, and legal correctness, and from his sincere point of view consistent with his authoritative masculine role, is entirely in the right, especially over against the nurturing feminine role with its purported divine law. Apparently, Goethe regards this sympathy for Creon as what led Hegel and Hinrichs to what he considers a serious misinterpretation. Goethe may have wished that both Hegel and Hinrichs had paid more attention to Teiresias as the voice of not only divine revelation but also potential reconciliation between divine mandates and state duties. Moreover, at least as he portrayed his own characters, Goethe seems to have had more sympathy for the feminine than did Hegel[13] (e.g., more for Gretchen than for Faust, more for Charlotte than for Werther, etc.).

Indeed, Hegel's—and subsequently Hinrichs's—vindication of Creon as the upholder of legitimate political power is hard to swallow. Patricia Mills writes: "Hegel's interpretation of Creon as the just representative of the law of the *polis* is [a] radical departure from Sophocles' tragedy.... The conflict between the just moral law and the unjust political law which is central to Sophocles' *Antigone* is muted in Hegel's interpretation.... Sophocles shows Creon to be a misogynist and a tyrant who requires unquestioned obedience."[14] Nevertheless, Mills seems to agree with Hegel and Hinrichs against Goethe that dramatic characters represent ideas rather than personalities.

Creon and Antigone do not recognize each other's right. Since each is secure in certainty and believes the other's action to be arbitrary and therefore wrong, each knows the other only one-sidedly as a stubborn obstacle to peace and harmony. This one-sided knowledge is tragic because it precludes their mutual recognition (W, pp. 59-60; E, p. 50). We could say, with Goethe, that the tragedy stems from Creon's tyrannical obstinance, or, with Hegel and Hinrichs, that it stems from his embodiment of one side (and Antigone's embodiment of the other side) of a natural dialectical aporia between two equally legitimate sociopolitical entities (i.e., state and family). Haemon, fulfilling his auxiliary role as a loyal but powerless member of both state and family, tries to present the case for reconciling the two powers, but Creon refuses to hear it (W, 85–88; E, 62–63). Creon's demeanor in this scene supports Goethe's low opinion of him. However, Creon's eventual self-knowledge consists in recognizing the reciprocal rights and mutual validity of family and state (W, 8–9; E, 26), as well as the possibility of their reconciliation, but this knowledge—via Teiresias and the chorus—arrives too late for him; by then the tragedy has already occurred.

Hinrichs depicts Oedipus, the solver of the sphinx's riddle, as having thereby figured out what humanity is and what human life is all about. This knowledge does not immediately help Oedipus, however, because he is caught in the inexorable consequences of his parents' attempted infanticide. Thus a significant irony is that Oedipus understands human nature better than anyone else in the trilogy but does not learn the full truth about his own particular nature until long after this self-knowledge could have done him or his clan any good (W, 23–24; E, 33). Subsequently, through his failure to recognize Antigone's righteousness, Creon misses his opportunity to actualize the reconciliation of family and state that Oedipus made possible through his self-knowledge and atonement (W, 41, 63; E, 41, 52).

As Antigone surrenders with equanimity to Creon sentencing her to death, she ceases to be tragic, since she now recognizes the state and thus no longer represents the family over against the state. Similarly, as Creon destroys the family and thereby undermines the very state he had sought to protect, he ceases to be tragic, since he no longer has a particular foil to oppose but only universal opinion against him. (W, 93–95; E, 66). When they cease to be tragic persons, they cease to be anything meaningful: Antigone dies; Creon becomes "nothing" (W, 104–109; E, 71–73).

The general motion of the tragic trilogy is toward the self-knowledge of its main characters, who thus determine and reveal the respective destinies of the tragic powers that they each represent: Antigone the family, Creon the state, and Oedipus both. Resignation to his acquired self-knowledge sets Oedipus free because his self-knowledge is the general knowledge of what a proper human is. Resignation to her acquired self-knowledge leads Antigone to loss of self, because even though she has honorably and completely fulfilled her pious duty to the family, she has also acknowledged the legitimacy of the tragic power of which she is not a member, the state, over the tragic power of which she *is* a member: the family. Resignation to his self-knowledge brings Creon to self-conscious nothingness. As he has single-handedly and one-sidedly destroyed both of the tragic powers of which he was a member, his destiny is to be "nothing," the tragic terminus (W, 104–109; E, 71–73). But in the end, comprehensive self-knowledge accrues only to the people, represented by the chorus and the audience, since they persist after the major players and their respective tragic powers have all come to ruin. Moreover, this self-knowledge is no longer distributed one-sidedly among the major players but *aufgehoben* in the chorus, unified for the audience, and therefore edifying for the people (W,110–114; E, 73–75). The self-knowledge of the people, thus acquired, constitutes a crucial part of the blueprint for the eventual reconciliation of family and state (i.e., the "reconciling certainty" that actualizes "mutual reconciliation") (W, 116–117; E, 76–77).

Although Hegel writes that the purpose of philosophy is not to edify (*PhS*, ¶ 9), Hinrichs appears not to take such a hard line but instead highlights the moral purpose of not only his philosophy of ancient tragedy but also the Theban plays themselves. This moral purpose is to show the reader that any human law or institution, including even the legitimate state, however sociopolitically necessary it might be, is doomed to eventual demise if it should ever come into irreconcilable conflict with the family—a natural human unity that will persist no matter what. Hence, if the state wishes to survive, then it must seek, create, and preserve reconciliation with the family. But the family, on the other hand, has neither reason nor inclination to seek reconciliation with a hostile state but only with a state that is willing unilaterally to make major (if not total) concessions to the family.

Goethe does not object to a dramatist having a moral or edifying purpose, but he says, "When the point is to bring his subject clearly and effectively before his audience, his moral purpose proves of little use.... If there be a moral in the subject, it will appear, and the poet has nothing to consider but the effective and artistic treatment of his subject" (*GG*, 130; *CG*, 228). For Goethe, stagecraft and presentations of plot, characters, and action are more important than "ideas" and their representations or mentally imagined forms.

Hinrichs seems almost like a moralist when he argues that Creon's demise is meant to teach the people what not to tolerate when trying to live in harmony with both family and state. Given that the ultimate concern and goal of the people is the full reconciliation of family and state (i.e., their own secure and sustainable peace and prosperity), then

> the actuality of divine and human law [is paramount] ... [and] to live and to act bearing witness to it is the most which life in general is able to achieve ... [and] this alone is the only true and final goal of life itself ... [which means] that nothing matters except this goal and whatever is not in accord with it.... [In other words] the actuality of the life of the people is the sole content of the self-knowledge of the chorus ... the bifurcation of the tragic powers preserves, cancels, and raises itself to a higher level through their demise ... [and] the tragic plot is merely the movement toward this actuality ... [so that] the tragic powers ... lose their meaning, and nothing matters except the actuality of the life of the people itself. (*W*, 115–118; *E*, 76–77)

The overarching movement of the whole trilogy and its moralistic or edifying interpretation is toward practical self-knowledge, that is, self-knowledge for the people, identical with the actualization of their goal of universal reconciliation in the sociopolitical realm, or that the people can internalize and use to achieve *Sittlichkeit*. That is, for the people, "The becoming of actuality is completely indistinguishable from the becoming of the knowledge of actuality" (*W*, 119–120; *E*, 78).

Conclusion

The true interpretation of the *Antigone* probably lies between that of Hegel and Hinrichs on one side and that of Goethe on the other. For surely, as Goethe says, Sophocles was motivated primarily by concerns of stagecraft and dramatic impact; but at the same time he was quite cognizant of the dichotomous, natural, and apparently irreconcilable conflict between family and state, and as such, his Theban plays admit of Hegelian analysis.

Notes

1. Eric von der Luft, ed. and trans., *Hegel, Hinrichs, and Schleiermacher on Feeling and Reason in Religion: The Texts of Their 1821–22 Debate* (Lewiston, NY: Edwin Mellen, 1987). Also includes a new critical edition of the German text of Hegel's "Hinrichs Foreword." Cited as *HHS*.

2. Friedrich Engels and Karl Marx, *Die heilige Familie, oder Kritik der kritischen Kritik: Gegen Bruno Bauer & Consorten* (Frankfurt: Literarische Anstalt, 1845), 217–219, 222–223.

3. Hermann Friedrich Wilhelm Hinrichs, *Aesthetische Vorlesungen über Goethe's Faust als Beitrag zur Anerkennung wissenschaftlicher Kunstbeurtheilung* (Halle, Germany: Wittwe Bathe, 1825).

4. Hermann Friedrich Wilhelm Hinrichs, *Das Wesen der antiken Tragödie in ästhetischen Vorlesungen durchgeführt an den beiden Oedipus des Sophokles im Allgemeinen und an der Antigone insbesondere* (Halle, Germany: Friedrich Ruff, 1827). Cited as *W*; Hermann Friedrich Wilhelm Hinrichs, *The Essence of Ancient Tragedy: Presented in Lectures on Aesthetics Concerning the Two Oedipus Plays of Sophocles in General and the "Antigone" in Particular*, trans. Eric v.d. Luft (Syracuse, NY: Gegensatz, 2017). Cited as *E*.

5. Johann Peter Eckermann, *Gespräche mit Goethe in den letzten Jahren seines Lebens, dritter Theil* (Magdeburg: Heinrichshofen, 1848), 121–137; cited as *GG*. Johann Wolfgang von Goethe, *Conversations of Goethe with Eckermann and Soret*, trans. John Oxenford (London: George Bell, 1882), 223–232. Cited as *CG*.

6. Goethe (*GG*, 123–124; *CG*, 224–225) specifically cites the end of Hinrichs's penultimate paragraph (*W*, 118–119; *E*, 77–78) as an example of obscure Hegelian jargon and unintelligibility.

7. Simon Goldhill, *Sophocles and the Language of Tragedy* (Oxford: Oxford University Press, 2012), 21–22, 24, 54, 236, 240–241, 244–248 [on Ismene]; 8, 138–140, 148, 164, 168, 173–175, 177–179, 182–183, 185–186, 188–189, 199, 231, 234, 239, 246–248, 254, 260–261, 263 [on Hegel]; 111, 116, 163, 204, 235, 239, 241–242, 244, 246–248 [on the sister/sister relationship].

8. "die Mutterliebe als Princip der Sittlichkeit zu Grunde liegt" (see *W*, 4).

9. See Alasdair MacIntyre, "The Virtues in Heroic Societies," in *After Virtue: A Study in Moral Theory*, 2nd ed. (Notre Dame: University of Notre Dame Press, 1984).

10. Eric v. d. Luft, "Dialectics and Destiny: A Look at Predetermination in *Njál's Saga*," in *Ruminations: Selected Philosophical, Historical, and Ideological Papers, Volume 1* (North Syracuse, New York: Gegensatz, 2010), section X.1.

11. Eric v. d. Luft, "'Who's That in Your Saddle?'—A Hegelian Interpretation of Wagner's *Ring*," in *Ruminations: Selected Philosophical, Historical, and Ideological Papers*, vol. 1 (Syracuse, NY: Gegensatz, 2010), section I.2.

12. G. W. F. Hegel, *Phenomenology of Spirit*, trans. A.V. Miller (Oxford: Clarendon, 1977). Cited as *PhS* with Miller's numbering of paragraphs.

13. Heidi M. Ravven, "Has Hegel Anything to Say to Feminists?" *The Owl of Minerva* 19, no. 2 (Spring 1988): 149–168. See page 160: "A phenomenology of *woman's* consciousness would, for Hegel, stop with Antigone, i.e., with woman as the quintessential spirit of the ever selfsame family."

14. Patricia Jagentowicz Mills, "Hegel's *Antigone*," *The Owl of Minerva* 17, no. 2 (Spring 1986):131–152; here 144.

Chapter Three

Hegel and the Origins of Critical Theory

Aeschylus and Tragedy in Hegel's *Natural Law* Essay

Wes Furlotte

An Introduction to The Problematic Ambiguity of Hegel's *Natural Law* Essay

Hegel's *Natural Law*[1] essay (1802–3) is best understood as an important yet often forgotten text in the history of critical social theory. It aims not only to evaluate the underlying causes of structural problems permeating the socio-politico-economic registers of modern Enlightenment Europe as it found itself in the immediate aftermath of the industrial, French, and Kantian revolutions but also to reconfigure the conceptual schemes and methodology used to think through these problems with complex precision. First published in the *Kritisches Journal* in Jena, the essay announces Hegel's definitive break with the abstract individualism undergirding the critical philosophies of Kant and Fichte, on the one hand, and the metaphysical framework of Schelling's Identity Philosophy, on the other. Here we discover exploratory blueprints of Hegel's emergent dialectical method: the essay places the totality of a community in its historical unfolding at the forefront of the analysis, insisting that dialectical processes of internal differentiation and unity constitute the reality of social life. Hegel maintains that such a method is the only way to properly engage the real processes constituting a community's moral-ethical-economical-cultural life. The *Natural Law* essay, therefore, reads like an embryonic manifesto of methodological principle and thematic motifs that will be systematically developed in the *Phenomenology of Spirit* (1807).

Analyzing the destabilizing effects of property exchange within the modern European nation-state, Hegel enigmatically remarks that these processes constitute "the performance, on the ethical plane, *of the tragedy which the absolute eternally enacts with itself*" [*Es ist dies nichts anderes als die Aufführung der Tragödie im Sittlichen, welche das Absolute ewig mit sich selbst spielt*].[2] Elaborating, Hegel's strikingly original interpretation proposes to illuminate the key elements and players involved in the processes of this "tragedy of the absolute" by way of Aeschylus's *The Eumenides*. In what follows, I contend that Hegel's utterly distinct use of *The Eumenides* is highly ambivalent and ultimately problematic to the precise degree that it advances a metaphysical-aesthetic justification of the institution of private property in the modern European nation-state, thereby framing it as a "metaphysical necessity" that is crucial to the "tragic life of the absolute" as well as to social life. Such a move, however, risks denying the possibility of meaningful critique and social change on this front. That pronouncement, therefore, marks the point at which the text becomes antithetical to the demands of critical social theory, as developed in the works of Adorno, Benjamin, Marcuse, and others where metaphysical claims of this sort are consistently rejected for philosophical inquiry into the possibility of real social change where domination and barbarism are challenged, dethroned, and, ultimately, bypassed with the objective of realizing a higher order of social freedom.

I offer here a preliminary sketch of the ambiguity at the center of Hegel's analysis. On the one hand, immediately preceding the introduction of *The Eumenides*, Hegel's investigation prioritizes the method of historical development. Proceeding historically, Hegel generates an intense sense of the problem the unchecked expansion of property relations, their corresponding legal sphere, poses to the effective purchase of morality, and the living unity binding a society in the modern European world. On the other hand, the analysis' introduction of "the absolute" and tragedy, *The Eumenides*, and aesthetic categories as "instruments of reconciliation," by which the problem of property is sublated, undermine its methodological commitment to developing these contradictory tensions and the possibility of their resolution, historically. Indeed, appealing to aesthetic concepts with the objective of "resolving" the property question entails an untenable aestheticizing of the political wherein problematic forms of social marginalization gain traction, are reinforced, and ultimately framed as "metaphysically necessary." In this precise sense, Hegel's analysis relies on an aesthetic metaphysics for the "resolution" of this problem. The essay's methodological breakthrough insists on the priority of historically developing a sense of the dialectical processes concerning the social totality but capitulates in the final analysis proposing resolution in terms of knowledge, aesthetic criteria, and the atemporal perspective of "the absolute." Hegel's appeal to the absolute, tragedy, and *The Eumenides* consequently offers us a precise sense of what is most valuable *and* problematic in the *Natural Law* essay, revealing the utmost limits of what this exploratory essay offered in advancing what we have come to know as critical social analysis.

Exploring this tension in detail, I will first reconstruct Hegel's critique of Fichte's system of natural law. Hegel argues that Fichte's system is "self-cancelling" [*sich selbst aufhebt*][3] and so the demand for an alternative perspective from which to frame the question of the social realization of freedom. In a second moment, I will trace the constitutive features of Hegel's category of "absolute ethical totality" [*absolute sittliche Totalität; absoluten Sittlichkeit*].[4] I emphasize how it connects to the lexicon of organic process, insists on internal differentiation (class divisions) and relational movement (dialectal process) as critical to the dynamic life of the whole community that unfolds historically. In a final moment, I develop the contradictory tensions that Hegel attributes to the modern European nation-state, particularly the conundrum of the "second class" and its exclusive concern with property relations. I then reconstruct Hegel's account of the "tragedy on the ethical plane," which he connects with the necessary processes of "the absolute" itself and detail how *The Eumenides* exemplifies what he categorizes as the "tragedy of the ethical": it demonstrates the key players in that process and their respective fates. I contend that the dramatic shift in the analysis' focus from the historical to the atemporal and aesthetic counteracts the real advance it simultaneously marks in methodology in terms of developing distinct social tensions historically. Before concluding, I explore the real risks that this appeal to the aesthetic entails. In aestheticizing the political one potentially justifies the social destabilization and marginalization of individuals and groups on the weak side of the power imbalances that the property relation entails. Again, these symptomatic phenomena ultimately reveal the real problem resident in Hegel's appeal to the aesthetic in this context. Despite this setback, I conclude by outlining important lasting advantages for critical social theory that follow from Hegel's underappreciated *Natural Law* essay.

Immanent Critique: Fichte and the System of Coercion

Hegel's essay constitutes a systematic challenge to Fichte's *Foundations of Natural Law* (1796). It develops penetrating criticisms concerning abstraction, first formulated in the *Differenzschrift* (1801) but now redeployed to address the subjects of natural law and morality. Hegel's wager is that a reconstruction of Fichte's analysis will reveal its intrinsic limitations, which introduces the demand for an alternative perspective from which to consider the problematical relationship between law and morality and their respective sciences, thereby clearing the way for his own position.

Fichte, says Hegel, begins from *within* the individualistic standpoint of personhood where one has "a body which is subject to the laws of physical nature."[5] Human action is unthinkable except in terms of material bodies in space x, time y, etc. This *material* aspect of personhood is separate from the domain of morality—namely, concerns of intentionality and goodwill—and so they are distinct fields of inquiry, the one having nothing to do with the other. Society, on the Fichtean model, concerns the legal sphere, and its purpose is to provide the space for each and every free individual to exercise his or her freedom as expressed physically. This objective is achieved *negatively*, in the libertarian sense, each individual's sphere of freedom is restricted such that each and every person is accorded their respective space of self-determination. Fichte writes: "Each is to limit his freedom through the concept of the possibility of the other's freedom, under the condition that the latter likewise limit his freedom through the freedom of the former."[6]

Members of civil society must reciprocally recognize one another as autonomous agents and so devise a mechanism for mutual security. Security cannot hold only for one but must be applicable to *all*. However, there is no way to be certain that each will respect others' claims to freedom. This comprehensive uncertainty introduces the demand for a third party, overseeing the intersubjective register so as to enforce the respective boundaries allotted to all individuals involved, and one avoids transgression to avoid pains of punishment meted out by the Hobbesian authority. There are no guarantees: one can always resist such forces and establish themselves as beyond concerns of security and material comfort. But an omnipresent surveillance and enforcement apparatus would ensure a high rate of punishment for infractions and so deter the populace more generally.

Hegel argues that Fichte's conception of the state emphasizes the physical dimension of persons, their rights to property, etc., and so their *physical security*. This makes sense given Fichte's claim that it is only in the physical sphere that human agency finds reality. Such a framework results, however, in what Hegel characterizes as a "universal system of compulsion" [*diesem allgemeinen Systeme des Zwangs*].[7] The state manifests itself as a *force* that imposes respect for the legal prescripts that the society has agreed on concerning the exercise of individual freedom. The emphasis Fichte places on the restriction of self-interested activity entails a *multiplicity* of restrictive legal prescripts. Yet, Hegel maintains that such a system of compulsion is "self-cancelling," [*sich selbst aufhebt*].[8] Hegel argues that the threat of compulsion cannot, in the final analysis, force an individual into submissive identification with the dictates of the legal regime. One retains the possibility of absolute resistance. Hegel writes: "By his ability to die the subject proves himself free and entirely above all coercion. Death is the absolute subjugator."[9] For Hegel, this example demonstrates a lacuna within the Fictean explanatory matrix, accounting for legal freedom strictly in restrictive terms of individuals' physical security and protection in terms of external force. For Fichte, there is a multiplicity of restrictive legal prescripts that enforce such security. However, Hegel argues that the case of absolute resistance demonstrates a level of freedom that is entirely unaccounted for and yet demands explanation if the Fichtean analysis of the social realization of freedom is to be "absolute."[10]

Hegel's critique operates on two interconnected planes. One the one hand, Fichte's framework does not offer a sense of the dynamical unity that must, for Hegel, connect members of a given society over and above "legal prescripts": it perpetually dirempts the universal sphere of legality from the flux of an individual's self-interested activities, problematically accounting for their unity in terms of fear and intimidation. Hegel characterizes such divisions as "abstractions without substance," "creatures of imagination, without reality." [*daß sie wesenlose Abstraktionen, Gedankendinge oder Wesen der Einbildung, ohne Realität sind*].[11] On the other hand, Fichte's model treats legal violations as arithmetic transactions where one might exchange a "unit" of security violation for one of retribution. However, for Hegel, this model cannot account for the most important kind of freedom—that which outstrips concerns of physical security and that, nevertheless, appears crucial to the foundation and maintenance of a real society and to the sciences of social organization. Hegel's critique unfolds immanently because tracking the conceptual commitments of the Fichtean standpoint leads to the unresolvable problems of dynamical unity and the mode of freedom at the core of "absolute resistance." This impasse therefore demonstrates the system's "self-cancelation," the nullity of its claims to comprehensiveness concerning social freedom.[12]

Absolute Ethical Totality: Internal Class Divisions, Dialectical Process, and Historical Development

As a result of the intractable problems emanating from Fichte's framework Hegel proposes to reorient the analysis in terms of the categories of "absolute ethical life" and "absolute ethical totality" [*absolute sittliche Totalität*; *absoluten Sittlichkeit*].[13] "Absolute ethical totality" signifies, unlike Fichte's starting point of the *Ich*—positing the individual contra society—a unified *people* (*Volk*) (i.e., a nation in relation to others). Hegel's wager with the category of "absolute ethical totality" is that it can account for the living unity of a social community (people) in a way that is impossible from within the coordinates of the abstract individualism of the (Kantian-) Fichtean standpoints and so functions as a significant advance beyond the latter's shortcomings concerning a complete account of the social realization of freedom

This is not to suggest that Hegel sees *no* domain of validity for the Fictean perspective. On the contrary, it constitutes a "system of reality"[14] with the caveat that it applies exclusively to the domain of possession, property, "physical necessity," and "enjoyment" and so to only one *dimension* of human activity such that legal prescripts *alone* are unable to account for the dynamical unity that Hegel sees as crucial to the formation of a people. Such a system cannot therefore claim to offer an exhaustive account of what social freedom ultimately signifies. Hegel writes: "Our treatment of the system of reality has shown that absolute ethical life must take a negative attitude to that system."[15] Concentrating on the unifying bond of a people, Hegel writes that "the individual proves his unity with the people unmistakably through the danger of death alone."[16] Foreshadowing the master-slave dialectic of the *Phenomenology*, it is in the risk of death that the real unity of a people is discovered. Just as for Fichte self-consciousness only has meaning in reference to other self-conscious subjects so too a nation can only exist in a multiplicity of nations with the consequence that they may coexist or risk conflict. War raises the prospect that an *entire* way of life might be negated (not just individuals within it). Contra Kant and Schelling, Hegel soberly maintains that "perpetual peace" is chimerical, whereas the possibility of "annihilation" is real. Yet, in a conclusion entirely in accord with Rousseau,[17] Hegel maintains that such a threat is, in a sense, crucial to statehood. It prevents a people's institutions from calcification, contributing to their "ethical health," which is an unthinkable move within the stasis of perpetual peace.[18] For Hegel, consequently, the absolute ethical totality of a people constitutes their *living* identity, permeating the whole. Undermining abstraction, it is a process with which the people livingly identify such that a significant portion could not maintain their identity apart from it.

This process of (trans-)formative identification between the "absolute ethical totality" and the individual who is "permeated" by that totality is critical to unpacking the full signification of Hegel's position. Hegel maintains that such a vital unity needs to be thought of not only in terms of relation, as in Fichte's system, but also in terms of shape [*Gestalt*][19] while retaining the quality of relation. But what does this mean? Hegel writes that shape is "a relation of organic to inorganic nature."[20] Consequently, Hegel proposes to frame the dynamical identity between the "absolute ethical totality" and the individual in terms of organics such that internal moments of difference (individuals as organs) are preserved and annulled within the unified totality of the whole (totality as body politic). This reorientation of the conceptual schematic on the question of social freedom is highly significant. It expresses Hegel's attempt to reconstruct it in conceptual terms of holistic process, which he associates with the dialecticity of reason with a view to overcoming what he believes are the rigid distinctions of the understanding propelling Fichte's analysis, preventing it from adequately accessing the life of the "absolute ethical totality." In this sense, Hegel rejects the Kantian/Ficthean methodological principle that situates the individual over and against universal laws and maxims. Such an approach elides the *living* communities that ultimately generate and shape individual agents and thus his demand for an alternative viewpoint. Consequently, his line of advance completely reorients the discussion. For Fichte, morality had been entirely bracketed from science of the legal, the former being a matter of conscience and the latter being a question of the state enforcing respect for the law and individuals' freedom. By contrast, Hegel argues that it is the totality of the community and the laws that make possible the emergence of morality and ethical conduct.

The unified body politic of a nation, for Hegel, consists in a tripartite class structure. Hegel takes this model from Plato and Aristotle, although he will significantly rewrite it in light of developments stemming from new modes of production and modern conceptions of property, on the one hand, and their respective levels of freedom, on the other, which he gauges by the criterion of death. Hegel's analysis therefore displays a historical sensitivity to fundamental differences distinguishing modern Europe from antiquity: processes of production, conceptions of property, and modalities of freedom. For each class there is an internal dynamical process involving an organic and inorganic moment therefore reflecting and expressing processual structures permeating the entirety of the "absolute ethical totality."

The first class is "the living movement and the Divine self-enjoyment of this whole in its organs and members."[21] Composed of "single individuals," they are nevertheless unified in a "universal" project. They engage the "inorganic" register of different nations and work together to preserve the nation as an "absolute ethical totality." Hegel says that they must be willing to engage "nullifying death" for "the preservation of the entirety of the ethical organization."[22] Simultaneously, they are committed to the public interest, "the totality" (which Plato connects with philosophy), and the development of the country's political institutions and thus their status as free. My point, here, however, is not to romanticize such "universality." Rather, it is to indicate that such universality must be real for the functioning of the ethical totality itself. Indeed, as we will see, it is this very immanent universality that the second class calls into question.

The second class consists of individuals who Hegel explicitly characterizes as "not free" [*Stand der nicht Freien*]. [23] Their work relates to the domain of transactions: the "inorganic" objects of possession and property and concerns of physical need. The second class is proficient in law and has a sound understanding of the nature of transactions; however, because they do not risk their lives in relation to the preservation of the ethical totality, and such a risk is the criterion of freedom, they are unfree. The third class consists of those individuals who are not versed in the laws of property and are determined by the "crudity of its uneducative work"—those who deal with the "earth as an element."[24] Nevertheless, in entering the standing army "in their elemental being" they are connected to the freedom of the first class; they risk "violent death" insofar as they are subjected to the violence of war in the preservation of the "totality." The social classes' systolic and diastolic movements constitute the dynamical unity grounding the category of "absolute ethical totality." While their unique movements and processes constitute the moments of internal differentiation (organs) within the body politic, they are constantly deployed and aligned within the immanent unity of the "ethical totality."

Contradictions of Modernity: (Absolute) Tragedy and Its Perpetual Reenactment, *The Eumenides*

In a highly condensed section of Hegel's analysis he pays particular attention to the evolutionary transformations this tripartite class structure has undergone in distinct historical epochs, specifically Greece, the Roman world, and emergent modern Europe. This reveals the priority Hegel assigns historical development and comparison in his analysis of the social. While extremely challenging due its level of abstraction, Hegel's account of the historical emergence and evolution of the second class is important and must be tracked. Doing so will bring us into the very center of his conclusions concerning the "tragedy of the ethical plane" and the ambiguous implications of his interpretation of Aeschylus's *The Eumenides*.

Hegel's analysis emphasizes the historical emergence of "the specializing species amongst modern nations" and "the class of earners" [*die erwerbende Klasse*][25] (i.e. the second class). Hegel starts in Greece and contends that the class risking nothing courts the contempt of leadership and in so doing risks "punishment by exile," going as far as to connect the absence of virtue in particular individuals or groups with servitude. Insofar as the threat of death constitutes the criterion by which identity with the "ethical totality" is achieved, those who do not undergo such a risk serve to destabilize the community's immanent unity. Hegel's analysis of the signification of slavery in the ancient world is a sobering refusal to edify. Slavery was crucial to the structure of the Greek "ethical totality" to the precise degree that the freedom of the nobility was intrinsically connected to a class of serfs, with, as Hegel puts it, "the loss of absolute ethical life and the degradation of the class of the nobility, the two formerly separate classes became equals; and, with the loss of freedom, slavery ceased of necessity."[26] This claim is important in several ways, not least of which is that it connects the decline of Greek culture with the dissolution of the class distinctions constituting their unifying life blood.

The emergence of "the Roman Empire" consequently poses anew the question concerning the unity of the "absolute ethical totality." Hegel claims that in contradistinction to the dynamism of Greece the unifying bond crucial to the identity of the Roman world is one of *externality*. He writes: "When the principle of formal unity and equality had to be *imposed*, it generally cancelled the inner true difference of the classes."[27] This external imposition of "formal equality" functions paradoxically in that it signals the dissolution of servitude even though it simultaneously presupposes the *imposition* of unity. Hegel revealingly writes: "These classes are [i.e. nobility and servitude], under the form of universality, in the relation of domination and dependence only as whole class to whole class, *so that even in this relation the two in their bearing on one another remain universal*; while in the relation of slavery the form of particularity determines the relation."[28] This indicates that the real structure of slavery, as in Greece, is grounded in particular differences, that is, the features that are *particular* to the noble class in contrast to *those* constituting the class of servitude. In other words, domination cannot function without these real qualitative differences. However, for Hegel, the Roman Empire, as shaped in part by the ascension of Christianity (an element that remains decidedly muted in his analysis), marks an increased emphasis on formal unity and, concomitantly, the imposition of universal form. It is, ultimately, the application of universal form that "generally cancelled the inner true difference of the classes."[29] Once the principle of universality "mastered the whole," "the first class is in truth entirely cancelled, and *the second alone becomes the people*."[30]

Consequently, the Roman Empire's imposition of formal unity and equality on its citizenry marks the appearance of "universal private life" [*allgemeinen Privatleben*].[31] Hegel writes: "This universal private life . . . immediately establishes the formal legal relationship which fixes, *and posits absolutely, individual separate existence*."[32] Correspondingly, it signifies the proliferation of the "system of property and law," addressing the legal basis of property and contract, which includes "the whole endless expansion of legislation."[33] It would be an error, however, to read Hegel as arguing for a Romantic return to "Greek substance," facilely moralizing against the Roman era. Hegel sees this development as highly significant and necessary, marking an irretrievable fissure between it and the Grecian world. Hegel writes: "This system has to develop . . . it is necessary that this system be consciously adopted, recognized in its rightfulness, excluded from the class of the nobility and given a class of its own realm, where it can make itself secure and develop its whole activity."[34] The integrity of Hegel's analysis is that it soberly outlines the real significance of the advent of "universal private life" and the intensification of its concomitant property and property laws while simultaneously accentuating the problems for social life that necessarily arise out of such developments. Hegel is explicit in this latter regard: there are intrinsic limitations in terms of what "universal private life" can provide the "ethical totality" in terms of identity and unity, and so a state risks radical volatility insofar as it is permitted unlimited reign and not confined within set boundaries of the larger architectonics of the community. Recall that a system of formal unity "consists not in anything absolute and eternal, but wholly in the finite" and so its inability to function as *the* source of unity within the polis. It offers little in this regard and also denotes why, amidst a cacophony of individuals of the second class making claims to possession, Hegel connects the Roman era in its decline with servitude. Quoting Gibbon's *History of the Roman Empire*, Hegel dryly remarks that the uniformity of "private life . . . introduced a slow and secret poison into the vitals of the empire," and, continuing, states that "they received laws and governors from the will of their sovereign. . . . The posterity of their boldest leaders was contented with the rank of citizens and subjects . . . and the deserted provinces, deprived of political strength or union, insensibly sunk into the languid indifference of private life."[35]

Therefore, a unique dimension of the Roman Empire's ascension simultaneously announces its demise. Nevertheless, Hegel writes that "the most complete structure of a system of law based on this relationship has formed and evolved out of such corruption and universal degradation."[36] I believe that Hegel connects the modern European state with this "most complete structure of a system." The fitful development of the second class in Rome finds its *complete* articulation in the modern European state's property dynamics. If this supposition is correct, it would indicate that the *complete* permeation of the second class by the relation of possession results in a situation where each individual is capable of possession (at least formally): each is related to all others in the social whole "as being a burgher in the sense of *bourgeois*" (i.e., one who owns property and its enjoyment).[37] Hegel writes: "Members of this class are private individuals, the burgher finds compensation in the fruits of the system; i.e., peace and gain and perfect security in their enjoyment individually and as a whole. The individual's security as a whole is involved because he is exempt form courage and spared the necessity (laid on the first class) of exposing himself to the danger of violent death."[38] This acerbic assessment likely serves a twofold function: it denotes Hegel's criticism of certain forms of material affluence and indifference that he found in the

"Germany" of his time while also signifying the more universal phenomenon of the intensifying power of, and legal space accorded to, the bourgeoisie's property concerns throughout modern European nation-states.

In this sense, Hegel's nuanced analysis has isolated a potentially lethal scission within the "totality" of the modern state, one which might serve to undermine the polis as in the example of the Roman Empire. In key ways the analysis here then anticipates key insights of young Marx and the destabilizing implications of private property. Hegel then writes:

> As a result of the supersession [aufgehobene] of this confusion of principles, and their established and conscious separation, each of them is done justice, and that alone which ought to be is brought into existence (i.e. the reality of ethical life as absolute indifference, and at the same time the reality of that indifference as real relation in persistent opposition) so that the second is overcome by the first and this compulsion itself is made identical and reconciled.[39]

The question becomes the following: how *exactly* is this supersession/sublation achieved? The opening qualification "As a result" indicates that the very supersession that demands demonstration *has already been achieved*. Having systematically developed an acute sense of the threat that the unrestrained expansion of the second class poses to the "ethical totality," Hegel asserts its "supersession" by the sphere of the first class. But how exactly this is to be effected is passed over in silence. Simultaneously, the analysis's methodological principle of the historical development of the class dynamics constituting the modern European nation-state appears to be jettisoned and an atemporal perspective adopted in its stead. Hegel writes: "This reconciliation lies precisely in the knowledge of necessity [Versöhnung eben in der Erkenntnis der Notwendigkeit], and in the right that ethical life concedes to its inorganic nature, and to the subterranean powers by making over and sacrificing to them one part of itself."[40] Therefore, reconciliation of a distinct historical tension becomes a question of epistemology. In the spirit of Spinoza, rational understanding of things as they *are* introduces real freedom. In truly comprehending the register of the second class, the inorganic domain of things and their exchange, as a necessary dimension of the social, the threat is supposedly dissolved.

Hegel then reveals that this tension is "nothing else but the performance, on the ethical plane, of the tragedy which the Absolute eternally enacts with itself" [Aufführung der Tragödie im Sittlichen, Aufführung der Tragödie im Sittlichen, welche das Absolute ewig mit sich selbst spielt] and states that it does so by "eternally giving birth to itself into objectivity, submitting in this objective form to suffering and death, and rising from its ashes into glory."[41] Consequently, the distinctly modern European configuration of class relations is now framed atemporally in terms of the process in which "the absolute enacts with itself." On this account, the perpetual reenactment of these contradictory tendencies somehow constitutes their overcoming but also, by the same token, their reestablishment. Hegel indeed goes so far as to state that this "perpetual process" is *tragedy*, herein introducing his truly striking interpretation of ancient tragedy as a sort of heuristic framework by which we might better understand the structure of this social phenomenon. He writes: "*Tragedy* consists in this, that ethical nature segregates its inorganic nature (in order not to become embroiled in it), as a fate [*als ein Schicksal*], and places it outside itself, and by acknowledging this fate in the struggle against it, ethical nature is reconciled with the Divine being as the unity of both."[42] The category of fate [*Schiksal*] implicates Hegel's Berne-Frankfurt research concerning the history of Christianity, although here it is redeployed in the exploration of an undoubtedly related, yet distinct, socio-economic problem. Simultaneously, this shift in perspective sterilizes the analysis of historical detail, introducing formal distinctions concerning the "tragedy of the ethical," which ultimately constitutes its identity with the movements of "the absolute." The particulars of class dynamics disintegrate within the crucible of the atemporal: a formal residue remains and obliterates the specifics of early nineteenth-century class dynamics. Tragic art renders these tensions immediately intelligible (*Phantasie*): it has purchase at both the cognitive and sensual levels and, in so doing, forcefully replicates the dynamical movements of the ethical and "the absolute." *Aesthetic sensibility*, therefore, is crucial to rational comprehension.

Comedy [*die Komödie*],[43] by contrast, "will generally come down on the side of absence of fate."[44] In this sense, it lacks a moment of real difference and so its inferiority. Modern comedy: "falls within non-life and therefore presents only shadows of self-determination and absoluteness."[45] Modern comedy lacks the perspective of "the absolute," real difference, and fateful struggle, thus explaining its distance from the dynamics of "the real" and its subordination to tragedy. Elaborating on this defect, Hegel scathingly writes that in modern comedy "the ethical urge . . . must . . . transmute the existent into the formal and negative absoluteness of law. And thereby it must give its anxious mind the impression that its possessions are secure, must lift all its belongings to safety and certainty by contracts and all imaginable varieties of clause and subclause in the formulary."[46] There is a distinct sense in which this verdict functions as an assessment of Fichte's system of natural law. Fichte's framework constitutes the completion of a "system of compulsion," which ultimately focuses exclusively on physical security, property relations, and the legal prescripts pertaining to both. In this precise sense, Fichte's framework, for Hegel, constitutes the philosophical manifesto of that modern comedy.

Continuing, Hegel's provocative interpretation maintains that Aeschylus's *The Eumenides* offers a forceful picture of this "tragedy on the ethical plane." It consists "of that litigation between the Eumenides (as the powers of the law in the sphere of difference) and Apollo (the god of indifferenced light) over Orestes, conducted before the organized ethical order, the people of Athens."[47] Elaborating on how this conflict depicts the movement of the absolute itself *and* the tragedy of modern European sociopolitical life, Hegel states that in the human mode, "Athens, as the Areopagus, puts equal votes in the urn for each litigant and recognizes their coexistence; *though it does not thereby…settle the relation between the powers or their bearing on one another.*"[48] Consequently, the contradictory tendencies that the analysis carefully developed concerning the second class's destabilizing emphasis on property dynamics only finds reconciliation with the ethical totality in the "Divine mode." It is Athena who "separates the powers" of the two registers, each having legitimate claims against the criminal Orestes and in so doing brings about a "reconciliation in such a way that the Eumenides would be revered by this people as Divine powers, and would now have their place in the city, so that their savage nature would enjoy … the sight of Athene enthroned on high on the Acropolis, and thereby be pacified."[49] The originality of the interpretation, however, does not come without questions. Despite claiming "reconciliation," it is not clear how Hegel's appeal to *The Eumenides* in any way resolves the distinct class tensions with which his analysis begins. It is not evident how *recognizing* the necessity of the second class, its concern with property and property law, is supposed to bypass the social instabilities that they themselves are essential in generating. Indeed, Hegel's prior analysis demonstrated the real threat they pose to the unity of the ethical totality. Again, the analysis has already demonstrated what the unchecked expansion of the second class means for the "ethical totality": the burgher finds "peace and gain and perfect security" insofar as one remains ensconced within the ebb and flow of material satisfactions, their corresponding legal sphere.In other words, it is not clear that rational comprehension *alone* of these aspects of social life constitutes meaningful social transformation on this front.[50] I contend that the very shift to the metaphysical standpoint of the absolute and appeal to aesthetic categories, which were meant to demonstrate the overcoming of such questions, instead serves to intensify them and expose the vulnerability of the very justification in question. While objective knowledge of real structural processes will always be paramount in critical-diagnostic social analysis, the absolute, tragedy, and the example of *The Eumenides*, while brilliantly deployed, do not adequately justify or resolve the distinctly modern European sociopolitical problems that the analysis had initially isolated. One could legitimately argue that "fateful" concession to the "subterranean powers" [*unterirdischen Mächten*] only exacerbates the problem: hush money to a corrupt force does not constitute real change. Appeal to "the absolute" in this regard becomes highly suspect.

Consequently, I contend that while Hegel's singular interpretation of Aeschylus provides a unique entry point into thinking about this problem, I also believe that the use of *The Eumenides* and tragedy to explain private property's distinct sociohistorical developments means that the analysis ultimately advances an aesthetic justification (*tragedy* of the ethical) of the phenomenon in question. This move is at bottom, I believe, untenable. Not only does it risk eliminating historical concreteness from the analysis, its mytho-poetical justificatory ground risks serious ideological misuse. This misuse is laid bare in critical social theory. By way of mytho-poetical appeals, private property is justified and schematized as timeless, inevitable, and a "metaphysical power" to be endured by way of fateful concession. Therefore, one might legitimately argue that this aspect of the analysis "aestheticizes the political." That is to say, it seeks an atemporal-aesthetic justification for a historical social problem that remains open to the real possibility of *change*. Yet, doing so effectively serves to obscure private property's contradictory, destabilizing effect on the modern European nation-state, leaving it untouched and categorizing it as a fateful necessity of the "tragic life of the absolute." Critical social theorists have argued that dangerous social conditions emerge when political and economic institutions seek to suppress the question of property dynamics and the possibility of social change: in strategies of avoidance, the populace must instead be mobilized and deployed in the interests of conflict. Walter Benjamin writes: "*All efforts to aestheticize politics culminate in one point. That point is war.*"[51] While Hegel's philosophy is not equivalent to politics, I believe Benjamin's warning still has purchase concerning the *Natural Law* essay's analysis of modern European society's class dynamics. In other words, applying the essence of Benjamin's evaluation to Hegel's analysis would generate counsel worth careful consideration. Such an application would maintain that it is crucial to remain highly critical of Hegel's analysis at the very point at which it introduces aesthetic categories to account for a socioeconomic contradiction that it cannot further concretely conceptualize. This aestheticization of the problem initially isolated ultimately serves to conceal and obfuscate the real social tensions it cannot further track conceptually. The analysis' appeal to aesthetic categories introduces a host of readily questionable metaphysical, ethical, sociopolitical presuppositions that atemporalize—and so preserve and perhaps even intensify—the very social phenomenon in question. This aestheticization of the analysis obliterates—even hijacks—its historical and critical dimension and, in so doing, risks demarcating the entire schema as reactionary. The move, at least in principle, leaves the property dynamic unscathed and in this sense leaves the analysis open to enlistment in the interests of force: controlling powers active in the modern European nation-state. Concomitantly, the anesthetizing of modern class tensions risks reinforcing the marginalized status of individuals and groups on the weak side of the power imbalance that the property relation entails. It hazards marking property, and thus inequality, as a metaphysical inevitability. Critical social theory, to the extent that it challenges inequality—especially when marked as metaphysically necessary and inevitable—must reject this move *in toto*.

In an attempt to counter this criticism, one might argue that Hegel's *Elements of the Philosophy of Right* (1821)[52] abandons the organic, aesthetic metaphysics deployed in the early work and so functions as a break with the *Natural Law* essay's rendering of the ethical totality—the property relations of the second class. However, *Elements of the Philosophy of Right* does *not* consist in the overcoming of these problems but instead functions as their (re-)formulation within Hegel's mature thought, its conceptual milieu. In this sense, it constitutes a more sophisticated conceptual rendering of the problem, not its overcoming. More precisely, *Elements of the Philosophy of Right* still entails Hegel's account of the "rabble class," which highlights nothing other than the *recurrence*, not the sublation, of key problems first explored in the *Natural Law* essay some twenty years earlier. We acquire a particularly vivid sense of the type of marginalization Hegel's late analysis entails when we examine his characterization of economic overproduction, the resultant market saturation, and mass layoffs. Hegel writes: "When the standard of living of a large mass of people falls below a certain subsistence level . . . and when there is a consequent loss of the sense of right and wrong, of honesty and self-respect which makes a man insist on maintaining himself by his own work and effort, the result is the creation of a rabble."[53] The problem only compounds when we consider the untenable "solutions" that Hegel proposes to overproduction, the rabble, and civil society's intrinsic volatility. Hegel writes: "This inner dialectic of civil society thus drives it . . . to push beyond its own limits and seek markets . . . in other lands which are either deficient in the goods it has overproduced, or else generally backward in industry, &c."[54] Similarly, he writes: "Civil society is . . . driven to found colonies . . . it is due in particular to the appearance of a number of people who cannot secure the satisfaction of their needs by their own labour once production rises above the requirements of consumers."[55] Finally, this: "the colonizing activity . . . to which the mature civil society is driven and by which it supplies to a part of its population a return to life on the family basis in a new land and so also supplies itself with a new demand and field for its industry."[56] While Hegel's later text offers a sophisticated sense of the internal working of civil society in the modern European nation-state, it yet again stumbles on a key economic problem irretrievably connected to the question of private property: overproduction and the social consequences of large-scale unemployment. Consequently, even in acknowledging *Elements of the Philosophy of Right*'s advance in methodology and conceptual precision in its rendering of the key institutions of social life, including a definitive break with the Schellingian metaphysical/aesthetical overtones of the *Natural Law* essay, we are still required to critically engage with the highly problematic consequences that permeate its account of economic overproduction and the genesis of a "rabble" class (i.e., social marginalization, colonial-imperialistic market expansion.[57] To the precise degree to which such problems remain at the very center of Hegel's late philosophical rendering of the economic-sociopolitical sphere, we are justified in concluding that the late work, while denoting a significant advance in methodology and terminology, in no way functions as an overcoming of the problem of the second class first explored in the *Natural Law* essay. In a special sense, the recurrence of this problem-set in Hegel's later work actually points to the unique significance of the earlier essay. It is one of Hegel's earliest investigations into a pressing social problem that would not only permeate the remainder of Hegel's social philosophy but would steadily perplex theorists and activists alike throughout the nineteenth, twentieth, and, indeed, twenty-first centuries. That he was able to access this problem, despite the difficulties of the

Schellingian-inflected terminology in which it was initially articulated, its brilliant appeal to metaphysical-aesthetic categories by way of Aeschylus to explain the social problem in question speaks nevertheless to the acuity of his analysis of the social. This is a hidden yet important insight at the core of Hegel's *Natural Law* essay.

Conclusion: Ethical Totality, the Priority of Historical (Dialectical) Development, and Promises for Critical Social Theory

Schiller's *Aesthetic Letters* (1794) is rightfully credited with diagnosing fundamental structural problems permeating the individual and the sociopolitical register of modern Enlightenment Europe as configured in the general upheaval of the period. For Hegel, Schiller was crucial in advancing the principles of "unity and reconciliation as the truth"[58] but did so in terms of aesthetics and how they might meaningfully facilitate sociopolitical reform. It is important to place Hegel's 1802–3 *Natural Law* essay firmly within the same coordinates of early critical social theory while simultaneously marking it as a significant advance beyond the intrinsic limitations of Schiller's analysis. As we have seen, however, Hegel's advance does not come devoid of its own intrinsic problems.

Hegel's essay expresses a distinct break with the critical frameworks of Kant and Fichte, a development that was impossible given the material/form drive distinction propelling Schiller's analysis, which limited it in terms of its access to the social *whole*. Hegel's emphasis on "totality" in its historical development expresses a significant advance in terms of the conceptualization and understanding of the forces constituting social life. Correspondingly, his early organic model of the polis allows the analysis to prioritize contradictory dialectical processes as constitutive of the dynamics of social life, demarcating property relations/legislation as crucial. The real advantage here is that Hegel transcribes all this *conceptually* by way of constant appeal to historical processes and developments. This method of advance was fast becoming the only way to comprehensively engage the real processes constituting a community's moral-ethical-economical-cultural lives. The analysis, nevertheless, enters the domain of the untenable, especially from the privileged vantage point of the contemporary reader who takes seriously the insights of Marx and first-generation critical theorists like Adorno, Benjamin, and Marcuse, at the precise moment that it requires aesthetic categories to explain and justify socioeconomic developments that originate historically, economically, and sociopolitically.

Nevertheless, historically considered, the concept of "absolute ethical totality" [*absolute sittliche Totalität*] and its method of analysis in terms of sociohistorical development introduce the possibility of thinking with precision about the interconnections between individual liberty, social freedom, and the institutions necessary to both in strikingly new ways. Hence, these breakthroughs are significant for critical social theory. By the same token, the ethical totality's formative power in relation to communities and individuals raises a host of pressing problems, not the least of which, as we have seen, concerns making consistent the realms of particularized self-interest and universal life. I might further suggest that Hegel's *Natural Law* essay is an often-forgotten text that anticipates Adorno's famous indictment of advanced industrial society where "the whole is the false."[59] From the standpoint of conceptualization, in other words, it is in the aftermath of a text like Hegel's that it becomes possible to theorize how the totality of a community might prove a corrupting force that actively torpedoes the freedoms of individuals and groups within its jurisdiction.

The essay's value for critical social theory is also evident in the value it assigns the principles of *sublation* [*Aufhebung*] and *reconciliation* [*Versöhnung*]. While the aesthetic metaphysics of "the absolute" appeal to tragedy, *The Eumenides* proves insufficient in fully illuminating and overcoming the social malaise of "the tragedy of ethical"; the very analysis itself reveals the importance of such a methodology, the principle of sublation. It thereby maintains, at least in terms of its initial methodological principle, the possibility of overcoming instabilities at the core of modern European social life. It marks a break with the romantic, despite its indebtedness to Goethe, Schiller, Weimer classicism and elements of *Frühromantik*. It is of lasting historical significance and a valuable source of insight and inspiration for the ongoing project of real social critique—its corresponding praxis.

Notes

1. G. W. F. Hegel, *Natural Law*, trans. T. M. Knox (Philadelphia: University of Pennsylvania Press, 1975); hereafter *NL* followed by page number. Where helpful, original German terms are from *Werke [in 20 Bänden auf der Grundlage der Werke von 1832–45]*, ed. E. Moldenhauer and K. M. Michel (Frankfurt am Main:

Suhrkamp, 1970); hereafter W followed by volume number and page number. Original German terms indicated with square brackets.

2. NL, 104; W2, 495. Emphasis added.
3. NL, 88; W2, 475.
4. NL, 92; W2, 480–81.
5. H. B. Acton, "Introduction," NL, 28.
6. J. G. Fichte, *Foundations of Natural Right*, ed. Frederick Neuhouser (Cambridge: Cambridge University Press, 2000), 49. (
7. NL, 85; W2, 472.
8. NL, 88; W2, 475.
9. NL, 91; W2, 479.
10. NL, 90-91.
11. NL, 88; W2, 476.
12. NL, 88.
13. NL, 92; W2, 480–81.
14. NL, 98.
15. NL, 98.
16. NL, 93.
17. Jean-Jacques Rousseau, "The State of War," in *Basic Political Writings*, ed. Donald Cress, 2nd ed. (Indianapolis: Hackett, 2011), 255–265. Consider the incessant activity that Rousseau assigns to the state: "The essence of society consists in the activity of its members and ... a state without movement would be nothing but a dead body." (See Rousseau, "The State of War," 261) The necessary consequence of this incessant movement is conflict. In this sense, war is crucial to statehood. Rousseau writes: "I therefore call war between one power and another the effect of a mutual, steady, and manifest inclination to destroy the enemy state, or at least to weaken it, by all means possible." See Rousseau, 264.
18. NL, 93.
19. NL, 98; W2, 487.
20. NL, 98.
21. NL, 99.
22. NL, 99–100.
23. NL, 100; W2, 489.
24. NL, 100.
25. NL, 100; W2, 490.
26. NL, 101.
27. NL, 101. Emphasis added.
28. NL, 101. Emphasis added.
29. NL, 101.
30. NL, 101. Emphasis added.
31. NL, 102; W2, 492.

32. *NL*, 102. Emphasis added.
33. *NL*, 102.
34. *NL*, 103.
35. *NL*, 102.
36. *NL*, 102.
37. *NL*, 103.
38. *NL*, 103.
39. *NL*, 101. Emphasis added.
40. *NL*, 104. Emphasis added; W2, 494.
41. *NL*, 104; W2, 495.
42. *NL*, 105; W2, 496.
43. *NL*, 105; W2, 496.
44. *NL*, 105.
45. *NL*, 105.
46. *NL*, 107.
47. *NL*, 105.
48. *NL*, 105. Emphasis added.
49. *NL*, 105.

50. It is worth noting that in Aeschylus's text, the furies *willfully* hand over authority to Athena. Consider lines 440–450. Aeschylus writes: "Athena: And you are set on the name of justice rather than the act. / Leader: How? Teach us. You have a genius for refinements. / Athena: Injustice, I mean, should never triumph thanks to oaths. / Leader: Then examine him yourself, judge him fairly. / Athena: *You would turn over responsibility to me, to reach the final verdict?* / Leader: *Certainly. We respect you. You show us respect*" (emphasis added). See Aeschylus's *The Oresteia: Agamemnon, The Libation Bearers, The Eumenides* ed. and trans. W. B. Stanford, trans. Robert Fagles (New York: Penguin Classics, 1984).

51. Walter Benjamin, "The Work of Art in the Age of its Technological Reproducibility: Second Version," in *The Work of Art in the Age of its Technological Reproducibility and Other Writings on Media*, ed. Michael W. Jennings, Brigid Doherty, and Thomas Y. Levin, trans. Edmund Jephcott, et al. (London: Belknap, 2008), 19–55, 41.

52. *Hegel's Philosophy of Right*, trans. T. M. Knox (Oxford: Clarendon, 1958); hereafter given as *PR* (followed by "para." to denote paragraph number) and *Zusatz* references where relevant.

53. *PR*, para. 244.
54. *PR* para. 246.
55. *PR* para. 248, *Zusatz*.
56. *PR* para. 248.

57. For critical responses see, for instance, Aimé Césaire, *Discourse on Colonialism*, trans. Joan Pinkham (New York: Monthly Review, 2000); Glen Sean

Coulthard, *Red Skin, White Masks: Rejecting the Colonial Politics of Recognition* (Minneapolis: University of Minnesota Press, 2014); and Frantz Fanon, *Black Skin, White Masks*, trans. Charles Lam Markmann (New York: Grove, 1967).

58. G. W. F. Hegel, *Hegel's Aesthetics: Lectures on Fine Art Volume I*, trans. T. M. Knox (Oxford: Clarendon, 1975), 61.

59. Theodor Adorno, *Minima Moralia: Reflections on a Damaged Life*, trans. E. F. N. Jephcott (New York: Verso, 2005), 50.

Chapter Four

The Tragedy of Sex (for Hegel)

Antón Barba-Kay

It seems it must be impossible for organic creatures to come into being from the matter of our world through reproduction in any other way than through the two sexes established for this purpose.—In what darkness does human reason lose itself when it tries to fathom the origin, or even merely undertakes to make a guess at it!—KANT, *Anthropology*

SEX MAKES HISTORY at the beginning of chapter 6 of the *Phenomenology*. I mean that a specific version of sexual difference and its familial expressions is at stake in the question of what spirit as such is in Hegel's account; it is placed at the threshold of the idealized reenactment of historical forms that make up that chapter. This marks a departure from the graduated quasi-Aristotelian order that Hegel had followed in the earlier Jena *Systems*, where the introduction of ethical life had been preceded by preliminary distinctions at the levels of sex, family, and village. In one sense, the departure is no great mystery: it expresses Hegel's new conviction that the notion of ethical substance, the people, must itself be understood within a cumulative, adaptive teleology of increasingly free forms of life. Whereas the 1805–1806 *Philosophy of Spirit* moves directly from a categorical discussion of class and government to the themes of art, religion, and science, the *Phenomenology* transforms those categories into objects of developmental scrutiny in their own right. But this statement of the issue thereby raises the new question of where such a developmental narrative should rightly be said to begin, and why—in view of the historical alternatives present in chapter 7 of the *Phenomenology* itself—it should begin with a form of life that does not simply have tragedy in general as its paradigmatic figure but a tragedy that turns specifically on a sexual conflict.

I realize I am treading on the beaten path here, since Hegel's treatment of *Antigone* has long elicited comment from a number of angles—whether and why Hegel sees fit to render history dramatic here, what his view of women is, how his reading of literature relates to his analysis of agency, and whether his reading is faithful to Sophocles, to name a few.[1] Still, I believe more attention needs to be paid to the implications of the fact that Hegel is intent on presenting the tragedy of the "Ethical Order" as the sexual difference at odds with itself. The assignation of roles here looks at first like the sexism of casual personification—as if, on cosmetic grounds alone, it should make sense that Antigone belongs to the home and Creon to the assembly. The application of sexual difference risks looking as if it has resolved one symmetry too many. But Hegel clearly has more in mind than that, putting "man and woman" into the section heading of the *Phenomenology* and insisting on their differences at length. Given Hegel's consistent and unqualified admiration for *Antigone* throughout his career—he refers to it as "the most magnificent and satisfying work [of tragedy]" in the *Lectures on Fine Art*[2]—given his repeated claim that the paradigmatic conflict of tragedy is in fact that between the state and the family,[3] and given his insistence on the desideratum that tragic characters be entirely and essentially identified with their role,[4] I think we need a better view of the relation between tragedy and sexual difference as such in the *Phenomenology*.

I want to suggest, in sum, that the connection between the sexual and the tragic is an essential and cardinal one for Hegel, since his analysis of it should be read with an eye to addressing and resolving a larger question about the metaphysical significance of sexual difference that was very much alive for Schelling and his fellow idealists. It is because an immediately natural difference may be fully identified with aspects of social agency—when the distinction between men and women becomes congruent with an ethical collision, that is—that the tragic achieves its exemplary setting and consummate expression. And it is for this reason, I suggest, that tragedy makes a beginning to the *Phenomenlogy*'s history: it is when and because sex becomes suffused with ethical significance that our natural, prehistorical situation first gains a foothold in a spiritual narrative of form. The paradigmatic tragedy is sexual tragedy because it is through that passage that human nature assumes a history. None of this obviates the fact that Hegel has a number of cases at his fingertips, ancient and modern, for which sexual difference is not primarily in play. *Oedipus* and *Hamlet* are also tragic to him for reasons not concerned with sex.[5] Yet just as he continued to insist in the *Philosophy of Right* that sexual difference "acquires *intellectual* and *ethical* significance by virtue of its rationality,"[6] it remains to be seen how and why that difference must be tragically required by the opening statement of spirit's riddle.

Let me back up to make a better leap, since the extraordinary significance that sex took on for German idealism requires some preliminary recital. The physiological meaning of sexual difference was shifting in the eighteenth century. The older view, indebted to Aristotle's biology and Galen's medical writings, had conceived of women as relatively defective or imperfect men. Sex was, physiologically speaking, not regarded as a fundamental difference in kind (as it seems to be in other passages in Aristotle) but one of degrees along the same track of development, finally determined by quantities of vital heat and other contingent factors subsequent to conception. It was thus not until early modernity that medical vocabulary began to distinguish male from female reproductive organs unequivocally, rather than accounting for them as male or female versions of the same.[7]

The momentous political causes of this modern distinction between the sexes and its biological and social implications need not detain me, except to note that, whereas the significance of this difference is still relatively muted in Rousseau's writings, it begins to show up as philosophically primary for Hamann's and Herder's Counter-Enlightenment thought. The former is already skeptical of knowledge claims from the Cartesian nowhere ("Do not forget, for the sake of the *cogito*, the noble *sum*"). Hamann follows in Montaigne's steps by insisting on the biographical context of knowledge and on its incarnate characteristics, among which he emphatically includes the passions and sexual difference: "My coarse imagination has never been able to picture a creative spirit without *genitalia*."[8] Herder, likewise, accords essential aesthetic significance to the sexes: in his 1778 *Sculpture*, he says that the two sexes stand at opposed, complementary extremes of a perfection ("stability" and "grace") that they continually approximate without being able to achieve.[9]

It is easy to see how sexual difference, understood as definitive and complementary, then became interesting to a generation of thinkers concerned with the problem of reconciling freedom and nature that they inherited from

Kant. Sexual difference already has a peculiar place within what might be called the very first post-Kantian work in this regard, namely, the *Critique of Judgment* itself: Kant names it as the only admissible instance of an "external purpose." That is, unlike the problematic and qualified sense of final cause that he sanctions throughout the "Critique of Teleological Judgment," he marks off sexual difference as unusual in that it exhibits a purpose that we can objectively ascribe to an organism in connection to something outside itself.[10] Goethe's *Morphology* of 1790 presents sexual difference as a moment of nature's "complementary work," as epitomizing the systole and diastole of her total activity.[11] ("Whenever we perceive this capacity [of life] as divided, we designate it by the names of the two sexes."[12]) The difference between man and woman then serves Schelling and Hölderlin as a concrete, unique manifestation of the *Urtheil* or *Entzweiung*—the original scission into an order of natural differences, the archetype of which it was their program to reconstruct. It is in this context that the opposition therefore acquires wide-reaching metaphysical status. And it is, along these same lines, no accident that both these authors promote both sexual difference and tragedy to first philosophical significance.[13]

Their different articulations notwithstanding, the following passage from Schiller's *Letters on the Aesthetic Education of Man* may serve as a general statement of the family resemblances of these post-Kantian positions on sexual difference:

> even as beauty resolves the conflict between opposing natures in this simplest and clearest paradigm, the eternal antagonism (*Gegensatz*) of the sexes, so too does it resolve it—or at least aims at resolving it—in the complex whole of society, endeavoring to reconcile the gentle with the violent in the moral world after the pattern of the free union it there contrives between the strength of man and the gentleness of woman.[14]

I remark on two points. First, the passage understands the difference between the sexes as an irreducible, polar difference not simply associated with aesthetic qualities—as Schiller, following Herder's lead, had presented them in *Grace and Dignity*[15]—but invested with fully metaphysical (quasi-Empedoclean) resonance. Second, it presents this difference as pursuing resolution through love, while also affirming the failure of that resolution: the outcome of love between the sexes is never some third, mediating sex. Sexual difference bespeaks the fundamental duality of the phenomenal world. Or as Schelling puts his version of the thought in his *First Outline* (1799): "The law which is observed in the [formation of the sexes] must be extended over nature as a whole."¹⁶

Now, within the terms of this discussion, Hegel came early to love but late to sex. Throughout the Frankfurt, Bern, and earliest Jena writings, love shows up as a theological and metaphysical principle of mediation, rather than in any connection to natural or anthropological considerations. It is only within Hegel's first attempts to give compendious expression to his thought in the *System of Ethical Life* and in the first and third Jena *Systems* that he explicitly discusses sexual difference, love, and family as moments of spirit's progress, within the transition from psychology to social theory. These mentions are notable precisely to the extent that, unlike his fellow idealists, they refrain from attributing any cosmic stakes to the difference between men and women. The emphasis is rather on overcoming the biological difference within a relationship of mutual acknowledgment—that is, on the absolution of sexual desire into the "indifference" (in the Schellingian sense) of marriage and family life.¹⁷

There are nonetheless two apposite passages from these early works that I'd like to consider before turning back to the *Phenomenology*: one on sex from the third Jena *System* and one on tragedy from the *Natural Law* essay. The third Jena *System*—the unpublished work immediately preceding the *Phenomenology*—contains a remarkable description of the sexes as expressing contrasting aspects of the will. It follows on the discussion of labor. Hegel claims that the will acquires cunning when it withdraws from brute labor; it comprehends and turns "blind power" against itself. This is the distinction that (somewhat abruptly) motivates his description of sexual difference in the following terms:

> Through cunning, the will becomes feminine....The will has become doubled, split in two.... One sort of character [the male] involves this tension, the power in the confrontation of beings. This power, however, is blind, has no consciousness of the nature of this being. It is fully open, straightforward, driving and being driven. The other sort of character [the female] is evil, [enclosed] in itself, subterranean, knowing what is there in the light of day, and watching something accomplish its own destruction by its own efforts, or else turning actively against the thing, thereby introducing a negative element into its being, indeed into its self-preservation.... The will has divided itself into these two extremes, in one of which it is whole and universal, while in the other it is particular.¹⁸

The description is indebted to Kant's *Anthropology*, to which (I suppose) Hegel alludes throughout these pages.[19] Both authors characterize the sexes in roughly conventional ways (passive wile versus open strength), and both present the relationship between them as a struggle for control.[20] But for Hegel in this text, this is the beginning of the struggle for recognition, the first motion of intersubjectivity. Unlike the more familiar version of this set piece in the *Phenomenology*, the third Jena *System* suggests that the nascent social order sets forth a tension present within the human psyche: a tension that both stands in need of realization and demands practical resolution. It is through their eventual grounding in the family that each is able to self-negate its erotic love and to know itself in its other; the need of each gives way to a third. The sexes die to live in their child.

There are obvious differences between this account and the *Phenomenology*'s. The latter has separated the issue of recognition from that of sexual difference, and "love" has gone missing almost entirely from it.[21] Yet there are helpful resemblances here. For both the third Jena *System* and the *Phenomenology*, the brute fact of sexual difference is an intrasubjective distinction writ large and made flesh—the sexes express aspects that are at once internal to the will and challenges to it from without; each sex summons the other to overcome itself. The female will is a "subterranean" principle—the unconscious shadow—that Hegel associates with Antigone's law in the *Phenomenology* and by means of which the blithe forthrightness of the male view must be undone. (The female thus occupies a place analogous to that of the bondsman in the struggle for recognition.) In the third Jena *System* Hegel also goes on to identify the female will with the "particular" and the male will with the "whole and universal,"[22] as in the *Phenomenology*. Finally, in the third Jena *System*, Hegel observes that in this relationship of love "the totality of ethical life [*Sittlichkeit*]" is already present (though "only a suggestion of it [*nur die Ahndung derselben*]").[23] One might say that this love is pregnant with the ethical—it is the juncture at which the natural assumes the spiritual, and vice versa.

There is an additional (and well-known) text from this period that should be placed alongside the *Phenomenology*. In the 1802–3 *Natural Law* essay, Hegel is describing as essential the social conflict between a courageous, public-minded class, eager to risk life on behalf of the state and a bourgeois, apolitical class that looks to protect its private life and commercial pursuits. The mediation of these two political principles then takes the form of tragedy:

> This reconciliation consists precisely in the recognition of necessity, and in the right which ethical life accords to its own inorganic nature—and to the chthonic powers—by giving up and sacrificing part of itself to them. For the potency of the sacrifice consists in facing up to and objectifying this involvement with the inorganic, and it is by facing up to it that it is dissolved…This is nothing other than the enactment, in the ethical realm, of the tragedy which the absolute eternally plays out within itself—by eternally giving birth to itself into objectivity, thereby surrendering itself in this shape to suffering and death, and rising up to glory from its ashes. The divine in its [visible] shape and objectivity immediately possesses a dual nature, and its life is the absolute oneness of its two natures.[24]

The martial unselfconsciousness of the one faction must thus "sacrifice" itself, must face its own dissolution in the unexpressed truth of its opposite, which it is not in a position to avow. It is in and through this destruction of both parties that the "recognition of necessity" takes place. Hegel follows the passage with a comparison involving Aeschylus's *Oresteia*, in which the Eumenides ("the powers of the right which resides in difference") are in tragic opposition to Apollo ("the god of undifferentiated light").[25]

If the identification of the bourgeoisie with the Eumenides looks clumsy, that clumsiness only serves to clarify Hegel's concern here. As in the Jena *System*, he is describing the basic conditions of ethical life as constituted by competing claims to the significance of ultimate ends: the public ("leading a universal life wholly dedicated to the public interest"[26]) and the private ("which has its being in the differentiation of need and work and in the right and justice of possession and property"[27])—that is, the position that each lives for the good of all against the position that all live for the good of each. The two come into specific conflict on account of the significance they attach to violent death in battle—with one side seeing it as honorable and the other regarding as the worst evil. But it is this second, private-minded position that has the divine on its side (the "inorganic," in the sense of suprabiological), since it attaches a noninstrumental value to the dead warrior. It typifies a view of personality that exceeds its political roles—this bourgeois is "chthonic" precisely in that it sees self-consciousness as independent, as free unto itself, in a way that both cannot and must be acknowledged by the most basic kind of political community. Tragedy "objectifies" a showdown that is foundational, since it is by means of it that the claims of public and private are rendered intelligible to each other.

It is true that sexual difference turns up only tacitly here, in the conflict between Apollo and the Eumenides; and the Schellingian color of the passage suggests the phoenix-like recurrence of the conflict as much as its reconciliation. Yet the similarities to the passage in the Jena *System*—the opposition between what is forthright and what is subterranean, between universal light and the particularity of differences—suggest that, taken together, the themes in both passages have then been synthesized in the *Phenomenology*'s discussion of *Antigone*. Both passages are presented in their respective texts as the opening movement of the ethical. But in the *Phenomenology*, the sexual difference of the third Jena *System* has been severed from love, while the tragic from the *Natural Law* essay has been severed from class warfare. The synthesis of sex and tragedy is therefore a deliberate one: sexual difference now occupies a distinctive place between the psyche and the city, fleshing out the reality of two aspects of practical agency, on the one hand, and the foundational conflict of all political life, on the other. Both passages have been recombined, that is, into the opening shape of spirit in chapter 6 of the *Phenomenology*. It is when natural difference specifically coincides with tragic conflict that opposing heroes cannot but be right to be wrong as they come to grief.

If sex and tragedy are found connected in this train of thought, however, it remains to be said why it is that both are rightly situated at the opening of chapter 6 of the *Phenomenology* and how that opening is justified as such. Let me offer a sketch of the transition to chapter 6, accordingly. What has been unraveled at the end of chapter 5 is a quasi-Kantian model of practical reason, within which right action may be specified by a priori testing. The consciousness deliberating in accordance with such a model first sets out to identify principles of right that are intrinsically true of all times and places and, failing that, to identify a criterion of universalizability that will serve to determine grounds of absolute right in any given case. Hegel's dialectical strategy is then to reveal how such positions are at bottom tautologous, since they cannot in and of themselves specify any particular content; that is, they are dependent on some qualitatively different, underlying register of communally and historically minded commitments, which Hegel will call "Spirit." It is to the logic of this register that Hegel then turns his attention in chapter 6.

The outcome of chapter 5 therefore motivates the outset of chapter 6 in at least two ways. On the one hand, it is important that the new shape be in position to make genuinely universal claims: such claims must not bottom out in "because I say so" or "because that's the way it's always been," but must be able to invoke the absolute form "because this is right."[28] As Hegel puts it, "Reason is Spirit when its certainty of being all reality has been raised to truth, and it is conscious of itself as its own world." It is this very awareness of universality as such that defines ethical life in this context and that makes possible an altogether new sense of agency.[29] Without this stipulation—which is as much the achievement of a normative order as of the collective consciousness of belonging to such an order—we would not yet have a qualitatively better version of practical reason than had been present in chapter 5. And such a possibility, so far from being a primitive given of all forms of human association, already constitutes a spiritual milestone—one that Hegel attaches here to a form of life evocative of classical Greece but that in later formulations he came to identify with the difference between history and prehistory more generally. This helps to account for why chapter 7 of the *Phenomenology* begins its historical narrative of religious forms from a seemingly prior historical moment, since such forms are compatible with preethical worlds.

On the other hand, the ethical must also resolve the limitations of the two concomitant features of modern deontology that had been singled out for criticism in chapter 5: its individualism and its procedural, view-from-nowhere formalism. On this score, Hegel emphasizes the sheer givenness of the body of the ethical *nomoi*, their "unshakeable, intrinsic being," their immediate being, and their opacity to apodictic reason.[30] Hegel uses two lines from *Antigone* to gloss them: "They are not of yesterday or of today, but everlasting/Though where they came from, none of us can tell." The basis of right must supply precisely the contingent, conditioned, and particular content that derivation cannot. Spirit is the actuality of a "substance" that is prior to its analyses.[31] In contrast to the "belief" or "ought" of Reason, "ethical self-consciousness is immediately one with essential being through the universality of itself."[32] The ethical's achievement is to surrender a certain sense of self-certainty, so as to be collectively sure of what is a priori unknowable.

The ethical is therefore organized around the contrast between a rational universality—what one might call the ability to distinguish between *physis* and *nomos*—and a given role that constitutes the circumstantial tissue of the ethical agent's life. Each of the tragic antagonists later in the chapter must meet both of these conditions; and it is the conjunction of these that makes sense of sexual difference. In other words, sex is no longer the occasion of ethical consequence that it had been in the earlier Jena *System*, since Hegel goes out of his way to deny that nature plays a causal role here. It is not because there are men and women that there is an ethical world but because there is an ethical world that sexual difference first takes on meaning: man and woman are (as such) discoveries, not givens. At the same time, two aspects of ethical action are transparently expressed by and exhibited in the difference between the sexes, and this contrast is insisted on as central to the wholeness of ethical life. The structure of the ethical thus rests both on contradiction and affirmation of the role of sex.

I want to elaborate this affirmation and contradiction in turn, in order to show how I take the binding of sex with law to amount to a tragic failure of recognition.

The opening distinction of chapter 6 is between public and private, between "the essential antithesis of individuality and universality."[33] Each of these spheres is then said to have its "law"—its organizing theory of what is unconditionally valuable: one human, the other divine. The former is the distinctive disposition of the *nomoi* that make up the life of a people—its "movement of self-conscious action,"[34] the ways in which it is conscious of governing itself, and of determining its own ends in the agora, the assembly, and the battlefield, which serves to press it into conscious formulation of itself in opposition to other communities. In contrast to this domain in which the community is "conscious of what it actually does, the other side has the form of immediate substance or substance that simply is."[35] Here it is the family that embodies the "natural ethical community," the "unconscious still inner Concept," and the household gods that stand opposed to the "universal Spirit."[36]

It is this symmetrical disposition of laws that lends the ethical world the beauty, harmony, and equilibrium that Hegel ascribes to it. The poetry of this world is that inner commitments are transparently expressed by the different social spheres into which they are articulated; the agents belonging to such spheres are "stainless celestial figures that preserve in all their differences the undefiled innocence and harmony of their essential nature."[37] The ethical world is an "immaculate world . . . unsullied by any internal dissension" in which "each [power] preserves and brings forth the other."[38] This transparency of inner to outer is the deeper reason why the ethical world shows up as the beginning chapter 6: the agents of such a world are able to do what they mean and mean what they do in a sense that, if necessarily lost for good, remains an image of the Christian polis toward which Hegel's spiritual history eventually points. The development of legal personhood, religious belief, Enlightenment, and conscience are all integral conditions of this higher vision, but their development is also attended by social alienation and fragmentation, since they sharpen the differences between avowals and deed, self and society, state and church, and so on. Within the beautiful, dream-like fiction of the ethical world, on the other hand, agents can be just what they seem. And, what's crucial, Hegel explicitly identifies this feature of the ethical world with its sexual differentiation: "The difference of the sexes and their ethical content. . .is just the constant becoming of that [spiritual] substance."[39] "Nature, not the accident of circumstances or choice, assigns one sex to one law, the other to the other law; or, conversely, the two ethical powers themselves give themselves an individual existence and actualize themselves in the two sexes."[40] Ethical life permeates the differences between its spheres so completely as to identify with the immediate, natural being of every agent. It is as though the law may be read off from the flesh.

But Hegel is also bent on denying the fact that sex, as a biological characteristic, has any causal or explanatory force at all in these passages. For one, "nature" is exclusively spoken of on the side of the divine law—"nature" is what the publicly manifest world is rooted in but cannot encompass.[41] Furthermore, of the three pairs of family relationships that make up the divine law—husband and wife, parents and children, and brothers and sisters—Hegel claims that the first two of these are not properly ethical; they are only an "image" of spirit, insofar as their motives are mixed with natural emotion. This culminates in the extraordinary claim that it is only the relationship between brother and sister that is fully ethical. It is only their relationship that is based "not on feeling, but on the universal" and it is only between them that there is a pure moment of recognition.[42] This is concentric with the earlier (rigorist) remark that "the ethical connection between members of the family is not that of feeling or the relationship of love."[43] Even as Hegel puts sexual difference at the very core of ethical life, he also takes pains to sunder it from the act of sex itself. He insists on sex even as he unsexes it. Why so?

It is true that the suppression of procreation is in line with Hegel's antiempirical commitments—he is partly intent on emphasizing that ethical life is not a consequence of biological imperatives; unlike a beehive, it is not a social arrangement convened for the satisfaction of bodily needs. This is consistent with the fact that, unlike Schelling, Hegel does not discuss sexual difference at any length in his *Philosophy of Nature*—he sets no spiritual stock on the physiological fact of sexual difference as such.[44] But this suggests that something else is up, since Hegel might have easily distinguished sex from gender altogether here, and a brother-brother relation might have done just as well to exemplify the inextricability of the two laws. Sex is neither a cause nor an effect here, it seems, but something like a living spiritual function: it is a natural difference that has been specifically selected for and raised to a higher power as the expressive medium of ethical life. Much like the difference between lord and bondsman in chapter 4, that is, the difference between male and female is inseparably of intersubjective and of intrasubjective moment.[45] And this feature makes it, finally, into a question of recognition.

It is the death of the brothers on the battlefield that precipitates the implicit or "unconscious" conflict between human and divine law because the corpses belong to both "laws" (as a dead sister would not).[46] The human law can only acknowledge the ends of life as they serve the common order. The divine law, for its part, refuses to view the dead warrior as cannon fodder—as merely subordinate to the political. It sees him as this particular self-consciousness, autonomous unto himself. It is the chthonic that has the power to take things personally, as the corporate human law cannot: "The individual himself is the power of the nether world, and it is *his* Erinys, *his* 'fury', which wreaks vengeance."[47] The divine law thus serves as the location of the long-term impulse toward the modern view of persons as "particular individualities" or unique ends-in-themselves.[48]

More than this conflict of ends, however, it is because and insofar as the ethical self-consciousness finally fails to understand the meaning of her own deed (of burial) that she is tragic; it is by attempting to assert the validity of the divine law within the political reality of the human law that she must "acknowledge its [her] opposite as its [her] own actuality" and so the actuality of her own wrongdoing.[49] More than the straightforward collision between polis and family per se—that is, more than the failure of each law to recognize its other as its other—this is the heart of the tragedy: the ethical agent's appalling discovery that she must and cannot disavow her opposite, that she has failed to see herself in her own doing, and that she cannot tell what she had meant to mean. At the end of the series of symmetrical elements—two laws, two brothers, two sexes—the ethical agent discovers that she cannot recognize her own self as herself. One might say that, in burying her brother, she is in a sense burying herself, and that in burying herself she is thereby transgressing against herself.[50]

Even at this deeper level, Antigone's act of burying her brother is said to itself contain and be vitiated by the failure of each sex to recognize the other: "The ethical action contains the moment of crime, because it does not do away with the *natural* allocation of the two laws to the two sexes."[51] In other words, Antigone stands to Creon in the relation that she stands toward her own misdeed. Both are confused and at odds *within* each other as aspects of each other's action in a way that they can neither acknowledge nor rid themselves of—the human law is still "in" her act. She has done what she despises. It is insofar as these standing aspects of the city must fail to recognize each other that they must in this way continue to fail to recognize themselves. And so it is when sexual difference is galvanized into the recognition of its intrasubjective bearing, in this sense—when I am bound to but cannot see the other as myself—that the tragic collision ensues.[52] Sexual difference at once establishes and reflects this failure to express the self as the other and the inner as the outer.

Sex is not meaningfully dealt with again in the *Phenomenology*. If Hegel had in the earlier *Systems* described love and children as the mediation of sexual difference,[53] the sexual conflict in the *Phenomenology* is resolved into the notion of the person as such, personhood as an "empty unity":[54] the discovery of the concept of right requires an "abstract universality" that is notionally indifferent to sexual difference. Roman rights are neuter. This point concludes Hegel's tacit argument against Schelling by demonstrating that sex is not a permanent, ever-renewed spiritual antithesis but a riddle answering to determinate world-historical meaning.

By way of conclusion, however, let me try to connect the discussion of *Antigone* in chapter 6 with what is at stake in Greek tragedy in chapter 7 and perhaps generally. I do so by way of a different text. In the *Philosophy of Right*, after claiming that sex is a rational difference all the way down because it is intrinsic to ethical substantiality,[55] Hegel adds:

> In one of the most sublime presentations of piety—the *Antigone* of Sophocles—this quality is therefore declared to be primarily the law of woman, and it is presented as the law of emotive and subjective substantiality, of inwardness which has not yet been fully actualized, as the law of the ancient gods and of the chthonic realm as an eternal law of which no one knows whence it came, and in opposition to the public law, the law of the state—an opposition of the highest order in ethics and therefore in tragedy, and one which is individualized in femininity and masculinity in the same play.[56]

Both the conflict of *Antigone* and of *Oedipus* (which Hegel stresses in chapter 7 of the *Phenomenology* as the emblematic tragedy) may be said to hinge on this same lack of subjective "inwardness" that is said to be lacking from the Greek polis. Oedipus, like Antigone, cannot repudiate the meaning of the act that he has committed and so demonstrates the collision between the "known and the unknown" aspects of action that govern the tragedy of chapter 6.[57] Agency collapses in on itself here; and Hegel seems to gather both Antigone and Oedipus under the general formulation that "actuality . . . holds concealed within it the other aspect which is alien to this knowledge."[58] For Oedipus, however, the hidden "inwardness" of his act corresponds to no particular person or kind of person—his fate is faceless and nameless—whereas one might venture that Antigone actually instantiates that same opacity that prevents Oedipus from seeing the meaning of what he has done: she shows what the polis cannot avow by day, a notion of subjective inwardness, even as she also then experiences estrangement from herself.[59] Unlike Oedipus's case, the estrangement between Antigone and the city personifies or "individualizes" spirit's first awareness of itself as alien to and divided against itself.

I point to this connection between the two tragedies to explain why Hegel regarded *Antigone* as a more "concrete" tragedy than *Oedipus*[60] and to emphasize that the former's relative superiority for him is related to the sexual conflict. *Antigone* is a tragedy because "nature as such enters into the ethical act, the reality of which simply reveals the contradiction and the germ of destruction inherent in the beautiful harmony and tranquil equilibrium of the ethical Spirit itself."[61] It is because sexual difference is capable of being invested with this opposition—because what is alien in another can coincide with the limits of my self-knowledge—that it demands the ruin of the characters in order to resolve it into higher terms. The two sexes in this way reflect and constitute these deeper differences about what a human being is and what it means to be free in deed.[62]

It is true Hegel does not take pains to distinguish between sex and gender—he is no Plato—and that the essentialism of these ascriptions is likely to strike us as quaint.[63] Elsewhere in the *Philosophy of Spirit*, for instance, sexual difference is again presented as externally analogous to the alternation between day and night, sleep and waking, and the outer and inner organs,[64] and this begins to sound again like the facile rhapsody of association he criticizes in Schelling. But the point in chapter 6 of the *Phenomenology* is more specific than that: that sexual difference may under some circumstances be capable of expressing rival aspects of practical agency and that tragedy results, as I've argued, when sex is asked to bear a significance that it cannot sustain. In a different *Phenomenology*, Merleau-Ponty writes that the sexual, far from being reducible to the genital, is an agent's general power of "taking root in different settings, of establishing himself through different experiences, of gaining structures of conduct. It is what causes man to have a history."[65] Just so, in Hegel's *Phenomenology*, it is when sex becomes a matter of action that tragedy affords spirit a real beginning to its life in time.

Notes

1. See Allen Speight, *Hegel, Literature, and the Problem of Agency* (Cambridge: Cambridge University Press, 2001); Judith Butler, *Antigone's Claim* (New York: Columbia University Press, 2002); and Kimberly Hutchings and Tuija Pulkkinen, eds., *Hegel's Philosophy and Feminist Thought: Beyond Antigone?* (London: Palgrave Macmillan, 2010).

2. *Hegel's Aesthetics: Lectures on Fine Art*, trans. T. M. Knox (Oxford: Oxford University Press, 1975), 1218 (henceforth *LFA*). Hegel was not the only author to give *Antigone* this laurel: for the play's place in Hölderlin's thought and throughout the nineteenth century, see George Steiner's excellent *Antigones* (New Haven, CT: Yale University Press, 1996).

3. *LFA*, 1213.

4. *LFA*, 1194.

5. Though Hegel weighs their tragic bona fides against *Antigone* and finds them wanting: see *LFA*, 1213, 1225.

6. *Elements of the Philosophy of Right*, trans. H. B. Nisbet (Cambridge: Cambridge University Press, 1991), section 165 (henceforth *PR*).

7. Thomas Laqueur, *Making Sex: Body and Gender from the Greeks to Freud* (Cambridge, MA: Harvard University Press, 1992), 149–92.

8. Walther Ziesemer and Arthur Henkel, eds., *Briefwechsel* (Wiesbaden: Insel, 1955–79), 2:415. See for discussion Daniel Dahlstrom's *Philosophical Legacies: Essays on the Thought of Kant, Hegel, and Their Contemporaries* (Washington, DC: Catholic University of America Press, 2008), 67–92.

9. Johann Gottfried Herder, *Sculpture: Some Observations on Shape and Form from Pygmalion's Creative Dream*, ed. and trans. Jason Gaiger (Chicago: University of Chicago Press, 2002), 85.

10. Immanuel Kant, *Critique of the Power of Judgment*, trans. Paul Guyer and Eric Matthews (Cambridge: Cambridge University Press, 2000), section 82.

11. *Goethe's Botanical Writings*, trans. Bertha Mueller (Woodbridge, CT: Ox Bow, 1989), 48, 61.

12. Goethe, *Sämtliche Werke, Briefe, Tagebücher und Gespräche* (Frankfurt am Main: Suhrkamp, 1991), 13: 179.

13. See Martin Thibodeau's *Hegel and Greek Tragedy*, trans. Hans-Jakob Wilhelm (Lanham, MD: Lexington, 2013), 10 (for the connection between tragedy and Kant's antinomies); and, more broadly, Joshua Billings's *Genealogy of the Tragic: Greek Tragedy and German Philosophy* (Princeton, NJ: Princeton University Press, 2014).

14. Schiller, *On the Aesthetic Education of Man*, trans. Elizabeth Wilkinson and L. A. Willoughby (Oxford: Clarendon, 1982), 213. See Catriona MacLeod's very interesting observations on how this sexual polarization results, in turn, in Schiller's quest for an "androgynous" view of the aesthetic ideal (*Embodying

Ambiguity: Androgyny and Aesthetics from Winckelmann to Keller (Detroit: Wayne State University Press, 1998), 52–66.

15. See especially *Grace and Dignity*, trans. Jane V. Curran (Rochester, NY: Camden House, 2005), 153–54.

16. *First Outline of a System of the Philosophy of Nature*, trans. Keith R. Peterson (Albany: State University of New York Press, 2004); 38. There are, admittedly, other passages in which Schelling vacillates on whether duality or unity is more basic to nature (see 158 and 184–85). On this point see David Farrell Krell's "Three Ends of the Absolute," *Research in Phenomenology* 32 (2002): 60–85 (esp. 64–67).

17. Hegel, *System of Ethical Life and First Philosophy of Spirit*, ed. and trans. H. S. Harris and T. M. Knox (Albany: State University of New York Press, 1979) (henceforth *SEL*), 127–8. The discussion of marriage follows immediately on the relation of master and bondsman, but Hegel emphasizes the specifically ethical, contractual dimension of marriage. It cannot be a natural relation, since "to treat oneself as an absolute *thing* [as a mere bearer of certain sex organs], as absolutely bound up with a specific characteristic, is supremely irrational and utterly disgraceful." See Hegel, *System of Ethical Life*, 128.

18. *Hegel and the Human Spirit: A Translation of the Jena Lectures on the Philosophy of Spirit (1805–6)*, trans. Leo Rauch (Detroit: Wayne State University Press, 1983), 104–105 (henceforth *JPS*).

19. See Kant's *Anthropology from a Pragmatic Point of View*, trans. Robert B. Louden (Cambridge: Cambridge University Press, 2007); 374, 399–407. Compare esp. 402–403 ("woman wants to dominate, man to be dominated (especially before marriage).—This was the reason for the gallantry of ancient knighthood.") with Hegel's mention of "high chivalric love." See *JPS*, 107.

20. This passage in Hegel's 1805–6 *Philosophy of Spirit* thus occupies a place analogous to the struggle for recognition in the 1807 *Phenomenology*: it is the first expression of intersubjectivity.

21. For a fuller picture of love in Hegel's early thought, see Antón Barba-Kay, "Why Recognition Is a Struggle" *Journal of the History of Philosophy* 54 (2016): 307–32. The connection between the pairings of male/female and master/bondsman is more than superficial, I think, inasmuch as both pairs look like they express an intrapsychic distinction in intersubjective, natural terms (to the extent that the bondsman can be read as a natural category, a "natural slave," a reading that cannot but lead to a particular kind of failure). No other conflicting pair combines natural and normative roles in quite the same way for Hegel.

22. *JPS*,105.

23. *JPS*, 107.

24. Hegel, *Political Writings*, trans. H. B. Nisbet (Cambridge: Cambridge University Press, 1999), 151 (henceforth *PW*). Pöggeler worries, rightly perhaps, that this formulation, in its promise of Christian, phoenixlike reconciliation, is not as classically tragic as it ought to be in *Hegels Idee einer Phänomenologie des*

Geistes (Freiburg and München: Alber Verlag, 1973); 106–7. For the Christian influence on Hegel's view of tragedy, especially at the beginning of his career, see Peter Wake's *Tragedy in Hegel's Early Theological Writings* (Bloomington: Indiana University Press, 2014).

25. *PW*, 152.
26. *PW*, 147.
27. *PW*, 147.
28. See *The Phenomenology of Spirit*, trans. A. V. Miller (Oxford: Oxford University Press, 1977) [henceforth *PS*]; §437. See also Alznauer's discussion of the point in *Hegel's Theory of Responsibility* (Cambridge: Cambridge University Press, 2015); 83–97.
29. See Pierre Manent's fine description of the connection between tragedy and agency in *Les métamorphoses de la cité* (Paris: Flammarion, 2010); 10 ("*la cité rend capable d'agir*").
30. *PS*, §436.
31. *PS*, §440.
32. *PS*, §436.
33. *PS*, §446.
34. *PS*, §449.
35. *PS*, §450.
36. *PS*, §450.
37. *PS*, §437.
38. *PS*, §463.
39. *PS*, §460.
40. *PS*, §465.
41. *PS*, §474.
42. *PS*, §457. For a suggestion that this point might not be just wishful anachronism on Hegel's part, see the passage in Aeschylus's *Libation Bearers* (ll. 167–78)—later mocked by Aristophanes—in which Electra recognizes a lock of her brother Orestes's hair, as if to betoken the singular kind of kinship that exists between them. (I'm grateful to Andrew Davis for making this connection for me.)
43. *PS*, §451.
44. So that when Michelet compiled the "additions" to the *Encyclopedia* from various extant sources, he had to help himself to the 1805–1806 Jena notes on sexual difference, *faute de mieux*. See Alison Stone, "Sexual Polarity in Schelling and Hegel," in *Reproduction, Race, and Gender in Philosophy and the Early Life Sciences*, ed. Susanne Lettow (Albany: State University of New York Press, 2014); 259–81 (esp. 266); and Alison Stone, "Matter and Form: Hegel, Organicism, and the Difference between Men and Women," in *Hegel's Philosophy and Feminist Thought: Beyond Antigone?* (London: Palgrave Macmillan, 2010), 211–32 (esp. 216).

45. Aristotle examines four relationships of household friendship: father/sons, husband/wife, brother/brother, and master/slave (*Ethics* 1160b22–1161b10). It is interesting to note that whereas the first three are present in Hegel's account, brother/sister has replaced master/slave. I owe this observation to Eliza Little.

46. See *PS*, §452 and §455.

47. *PS*, §462.

48. See *PS*, §464.

49. *PS*, §470.

50. Lydia Winn helped me formulate this paradox.

51. *PS*, §468.

52. For the point that the conflict between human and divine law mirrors divisions that are found throughout all octaves of this spiritual shape, see Dahlstrom, *Philosophical Legacies*, 146.

53. *SEL*, 128.

54. *PS*, §480.

55. *PR*, §165.

56. *PR*, §166.

57. *PS*, §467.

58. *PS*, §469.

59. To put the matter more boldly still: Antigone is tragic for reasons parallel to Socrates. She enacts in mythic fact a version of what was at stake in his trial: she is the principle of autonomy that the polis cannot acknowledge. For Socrates as a cardinal pivot toward the modern state in this regard, see Richard Velkley's helpful "On Possessed Individualism: Hegel, Socrates' Daimon, and the Modern State," *Review of Metaphysics* 59 (2006): 577–99. (There is a passing connection to Antigone on 583.)

60. *LFA*, 1213.

61. *PS*, §476.

62. My reading follows Christoph Menke's in this regard, though he does not insist on the meaning of sexual difference as such: see his *Tragödie im Sittlichen: Gerechtigkeit und Freiheit nach Hegel* (Frankfurt Am Main: Suhrkamp, 1996); 156–76.

63. Though for a good account of why the sex/gender distinction is inadequate to characterize Hegel's position, see Laura Werner, " 'That Which Is Different from Difference Is Identity'—Hegel on Gender," *Nordic Journal of Feminist and Gender Research* 14 (2006): 183–94.

64. Hegel, *Hegel's Philosophy of Mind*, trans. W. Wallace, A. V. Miller, and M. J. Inwood (Oxford: Clarendon, 2007), §398z.

65. Hegel, *Phenomenology of Perception*, trans. Colin Smith (London: Routledge & Kegan Paul, 1962), 158.

Chapter Five

Substantial Ends and Choices without a Will

Greek Tragedy as Archetype of Tragic Drama

Allegra de Laurentiis

Tragedy is not an imitation of men but of actions.... Without action there could not be a tragedy, but there could be without character.—ARISTOTLE, *Poetics* 6 1450a

Introduction

The focus of this essay is not a generic concept of "the Tragic" to which, as pointed out by Robert Williams in 2012,[1] Hegel dedicates no particular doctrine. The focus is on Hegel's theory of the tragic form of drama as artwork, that is, as a work of fiction: *das Trauerspiel*. This essay aims to make plausible the reasons Hegel thinks that the Greek tragedies of the classical age, due to their peculiar *ethical* content, embody the essential type of all tragic drama and that this ethical core consists of the unique *historical import* of the deeds narrated.

It is well known that Hegel explicates the artwork in general as aesthetic, that is, sensible and physical embodiment of the human spirit's drive to fulfill the Socratic command *gnōthy seauton*. The artwork is, briefly put, an expression of spirit's self-knowing in sensible form. This general definition applies of course as well to the poetic artwork, its genres and styles. The first part of this essay is devoted to briefly recalling this systematic context. My synopsis is based on Hegel's explicit treatment in the *Lectures on Aesthetics* edited by Hotho.[2] This chapter then examines three radical forms of estrangement that together constitute, according to Hegel, the essential feature of tragic Greek δρᾶμα, understood as a "deed done" to accomplish an end that transforms individual action (*Handlung*) into historical deed (*Tat*). Here I also reference texts from Karl Hegel's edition of the *Lectures on the Philosophy of History*[3] and from the 1820 *Outlines of the Philosophy of Right*.[4] Finally, I discuss the main reason why Hegel thinks of Greek tragedies as embodying the essence of all tragedy: namely, the fact that they represent a unique (in the sense of unrepeatable) event in the history of humankind, a transformation affecting the essence (what L. Feuerbach would call the "*Gattungswesen*") of the human species.

My use of the word "history" here is broad, as it crucially includes early archaic, (pre-Homeric) epochs (which would normally be referred to as prehistorical) and archaic, (i.e., Homeric and Hesiodic epochs). As for the word "ethical," I follow Hegel's usage, which encompasses the political, juridical, religious, and moral realities that complement our natural existence without replacing it. This usage is the German philosopher's modification of the Rousseauian *seconde nature*, to which Hegel refers as *die Sittlichkeit*, *das Sittliche*, and even, depending on context, as "the worldly divine": "The ethical life [*Die Sittlichkeit*] ... is ... substantial right, second nature, as it has been rightfully called, because the first nature of humanity is its immediate, animal being" (*PhGesch W* 12, 57); and "The ethical [*das Sittliche*], if considered in its pristine immediacy ... is the divine in its *worldly* reality ... the driving content of genuinely human action" (*Aesth* III, *W* 15, 522).

The following discussion offers some answers to legitimate skepticism regarding Hegel's assignation of an archetypal function to ancient tragedy: Why does it tell of radical forms of conflict, allegedly unmatched in later tales of human disasters and calamities? What is it about the ancient heroes that condemns one side in the tragic conflict to obliteration? What are the motive forces of heroic action in Greek tragedy, and how do they differ from the motive forces of modern tragic figures?

The Systematic Context:
Structural and Temporal Features of the Artwork

Hegel's explication of tragedy presupposes a matrix in which logical relations and historical stages of spirit intersect. This is the same framework he uses to account for all products of human artistic activities—spatial, tactile, visual, aural, or language-bound arts. In this matrix, the principal logical feature that distinguishes each art form from the others consists of the peculiar relation of spirit to itself (the particular way in which it knows itself); the historical stages of spirit's overall development mark epochal transformations in its self-knowing. This self-relation is, as already announced in the preface of the 1807 *Phenomenology of Spirit*,[5] a relation of spirit as subject to itself as substance, one that Hegel defines as "absolute" relation: "That the substance is essentially subject, this is expressed in the conception that utters the absolute as *spirit*" (PhenG W 3, 28). One expression of this absolute relation is the production of the artwork. As for the temporal transformations that affect this absolute constellation and its aesthetic expressions, they define epochal stages in the development of the arts (as well as different stages in the two further modes in which absolute knowing expresses itself: religion and philosophy).

In this overall framework, Hegel chooses to refer to the first phase of spirit's sensible self-relation as the symbolic (or archaic) stage or form of the artwork (*symbolische Kunstform*); the second major phase is that of the classical (for short: ancient) artwork (*klassische Kunstform*); the third, that of the romantic (medieval and modern) artwork (*romantische Kunstform*). In each of these epochs, one *kind* of artistic output (*Kunstart*) is the culturally dominant one. While all epochs and civilizations produce architectural, sculptural, pictorial, musical, and poetic artworks, each of these predominates in specific times, geographical settings, and the cultural spaces they define.

The following discussion centers first on the structural features ("qualities") and temporal developments ("changes") of the artwork in general, and then on the variety of dramatic genre we call "tragedy," in particular. The focus is on the contrast between archaic and classical ways of self-knowing in the arts because Greek tragedies are set in archaic times but written, read, and performed in the classical age. As argued below, this historical displacement is, for Hegel, pivotal for understanding the elemental character of ancient tragedy vis-à-vis later forms of the same poetic type.

STRUCTURAL FEATURES OF DRAMA AND OF TRAGIC DRAMA

Like poetry's epic and lyric genres (*Gattungen*), the dramatic genre exists in different types (*Arten*), mainly tragedy, comedy, and the stage play (*Schauspiel*)[6]—all of which, if we follow Hegel's manner of exposition, derive from connotations intrinsic to the general concept of the genre "drama" (see *Aesth* III, W 15, 520). The difference between dramatic types is determined by the particular relation of the individual agent to the object of her striving: "The principle of the various types can only be derived from the relationship in which *individuals* stand to their *goal* and its content" (*Aesth* III W 15, 520). The defining features of tragic drama in particular are the ethical nature of the agent's end and the iron necessity of the chain of events triggered by her striving for this end.

In the following, I briefly discuss first the distinguishing criterion of dramatic types and, second, the main structural features of tragedy.

(i) The principal elements of all drama (or, if we like Hegel's expository strategy, the principal connotations of the concept of "the deed done") are a human individual and the end of her action. While the agent represents the subjective side, the end pursued represents the objective side of the drama. Neither side can be missing if the events unleashed by the action are to be worthy of dramatization. Hegel refers to these two sides as drama's "substantiality" and "subjectivity." "Substantiality" refers to the significance (or irrelevance, as the case may be) of the ends pursued, hence also to the gravity (or pettiness) of the conflict. The substantive element, in Hegel's words, forms "the content of the individual character and purpose" (*Aesth* III W 15, 520). "Subjectivity" instead denotes the kind and degree of independence autonomy (or lack thereof) by which the agent chooses and pursues the end: the subjective element of the deed done consists of the individual's "self-determination and freedom [*Selbstbestimmung und Freiheit*]" (*Aesth* III W 15, 520). For example, while unwarranted or foolish certainty of self in the pursuit of petty goals is the mark of successful comic characters, the mark of the most magnificent protagonists of tragedy is their compulsive, maniacal determination in pursuing substantial ends.

Although the distinctions among the three basic dramatic kinds types are not clear-cut, as exemplified by Plautus's tragicomedy[7] or various types of modern literature, Hegel believes that a specific imbalance between subject and substance provides a reasonable criterion for the distinction between tragedy and comedy. Either the substantial element dominates the subjective element, or vice versa. Briefly put, if the moment of substantiality determines the outcome of the "deed done," the drama qualifies as tragedy; if subjectivity triumphs, it qualifies as comedy. If neither element is decisive, we have the stage play. Types of the latter carry the day in the modern theatrical output because, as befits modern perceptions—or perhaps illusions—of individual sovereignty over fate and circumstances, in the stage play even severe adversity may ultimately fail to destroy the modern protagonist; or the frivolousness of modern characters' purposes may fail to elicit genuinely cathartic laughter.

(ii) In the particular case of tragic drama, further crucial features obtain. One is that the objectives of the agents can never be personal goals. They are always political purposes, and this means that they are ethical ends. A harrowing story of failed pursuits of love or wealth or social status may yield a novel, a stage play, even a modern *Trauerspiel*. It will not bring forth the quintessential tragedy.

The other features of tragedy are ones that Hegel adopts (as much else) from Aristotle's *Poetics*. First, any story leading to a genuinely tragic end must be "organic" as opposed to being disjointed or episodic. This does not amount to a mere requirement of aesthetic harmony. Rather, it means that the tragic plot is to be based not just on the chronological succession but also on the logical sequence of the events narrated. Given a set of anthropological, psychological, or historical presuppositions, the tragic end *must* follow. The dramaturge does not force the outcome: he just brings its necessity to light. Aristotle spells this out as follows:

> Many and in fact an infinite number of things happen to any individual, some of which do not form a unity; similarly, many are the actions of one, from which a unity is not produced ... [Instead,] the parts of the [tragic] plot are so organized that if any one of them is displaced or taken away, the whole will be shaken and put out of joint. (*Poetics* 8 1451a)

The tragic plot, in other words, is like "a living creature [*zoōn*]" (*Poetics* 7 1450b) because what confers to each animal its proper measure is the suitability of the animal's parts to their functions, and of the functions to the end of the whole organism. This is in turn the necessary condition of the animal's intelligibility and beauty: whether in living nature or in the poetic artwork, "beauty depends on magnitude and order" (1450b).[8] Despite Hegel's lengthy and explicit argument (in *Aesth* I W 13, chapters 2 and 3) that natural and art-beauty differ in fundamental respects,[9] still he subscribes to the Aristotelian analogy, according to which "just as ... animals, if they are to be beautiful, must have a magnitude ... easily taken in by the eye, so plots, for the same reason, must have a length ... easily held in the memory" (1451a). The objective beauty of the living animal is a function of the concordance (we would perhaps say "adaptation") of organs and capacities to its overall purpose. Its, while its subjective beauty derives from our ocular discernment of it as one perfectly functioning or adapted whole. Likewise, the terrible beauty of tragic drama derives objectively from the end pursued and subjectively from our capacity to retain the fateful progression of the deed in one coherent memory. This "memorable" character of tragedy is the condition of its intelligibility, and intelligibility depends on one further Aristotelian requirement: namely, that reversals, changes of fortune, and *dénouements* "follow from preceding events according to likelihood or necessity" (1451a).

When it comes to authentically tragic deeds, Hegel is less open to the "likelihood" of their sequence than Aristotle seems to be. For Hegel, the end advances inexorably, which is why fate (*Schicksal*), or the ancient "apportioners"—the three spinning, measuring, and cutting *moirai*—make up the subtext of every ancient tragedy. In a concise passage in the *Science of Logic's*[10] section on "Measure," Hegel gives a bare-bones account of the inescapable logic that connects in the Greek mind right measure, necessity, arrogant overreach, and just rebalancing (*moira, ananke, hybris,* and *nemesis*):

> The still indeterminate Greek consciousness [i.e., Pre-Socratic thought—AdL] that *everything has a measure* ... is the beginning of a much higher concept. ... The more developed, more reflected measure is necessity; the fate, the *nemesis* is limited in general to determining the measure, in order that what *mismeasures* itself [*was sich* vermesse], what makes itself too great, too high be brought down to the other extreme of being reduced to nullity [*Nichtigkeit*]. (WdL I W 5, 390)

It would be difficult to sketch the logic of Sophocles's Theban Trilogy or of Aeschylus's *Oresteia* in a more succinct and yet accurate way. Their protagonists are individuals who unfailingly and *voluntarily* mismeasure themselves and their ethical context. It is the iron inevitability of the conflict between, on the one hand, the intrinsic measure of characters and existing *Sittlichkeit*, and on the other, characters' *choice to overstep* this measure, that lends organic unity to the plot; and it is this tension-ridden unity in turn that renders even the most outlandish, insane, and self-destructive deeds of heroes intelligible, bearable, and in the end convincing to the audience.

TEMPORAL FEATURES OF DRAMA AND OF TRAGIC DRAMA

If all artworks are sensual embodiments of spirit's self-knowing, and if spirit knows itself in different ways at different times, then the core features of tragic artworks cannot be only functions of the *logical relation* of subject and substance in the action, nor only of action's *organic* nature. Historical time must be a further determinant of tragedy. Like all other kinds of art forms and kinds (*Kunstformen* and *Kunstarten*), tragedy changes in correspondence with spirit's transformations. It is the *historical stage* of the relationship of spirit as subject to itself as substance that explains the difference between epochal variants of the same dramatic type. For this reason, a tragic event in an archaic Mediterranean community differs essentially from one unfolding in the Italian or English Renaissance; and Oedipus's relation to the ethical substance that surrounds him differs radically from Hamlet's relation to the ethical substance that he is desperately seeking in himself.

Since, as noted, ancient Greek tragedies are classical artworks with archaic content, the following discussion pertains exclusively to Hegel's explication of kinds of art that are dominant in the archaic and classical ages (i.e., the symbolic and the classical forms).

"Symbolism" is, historically, the primary form of artistic production because it expresses a logically immediate configuration of our self-knowing. We mark our presence and seek to carve out a home in the natural and hostile world from which we have emerged. Dwellings and emblems are primal (or primitive) signs by which we both distinguish ourselves from nature and seek shelter in it. Life is represented through lifeless shapes. The power of the species is expressed through the magnification of reproductive organs, and the emerging self appears sensually in what is conspicuously devoid of selfhood. The human figure comes into view in reptilian and other monstrous forms—hence the often enigmatic and sometimes even repugnant character of prehistorical and archaic artworks. Our species' drive to know itself first becomes objectified in the erect stone, the dolmen, the cairn, the totem or the lingam, and in the half-animal-half-human figures of Sobeks, Sphinxes, Ganeshas, Kalis, Centaurs, or Harpies. The urge to make the world our home materializes in cave dwellings and cave paintings, in mud villages and cities carved in mountain cliffs, and eventually in monumental gateways, labyrinths, stone enclosures, pyramids, and temples. Of all artistic output, architecture—the art of fashioning a human space and inscribing a human presence in the world—is the symbolic art par excellence.

In time, the dominance of architecture is displaced by less immediate configurations of self-knowing in which spirit is represented as both human and divine. In Greece,[11] this transformation results in the stunning classical sculptures of charioteers, winged *nikes*, resting athletes, thundering gods and martial or mourning goddesses, all of which testify to spirit's recognition of itself as towering above the animal kingdom. In contrast to symbolism's "distorted" representations of spirit, Hegel comments, the shaping of physical materials is now entrusted with displaying

> its ... spiritual meaning. A shape of this kind is ... the *human* shape because the exteriority of the human being alone can reveal what is spiritual [*das Geistige*] in a sensuous way. ... Face, eye, posture, gesture ... in this very physicality [*Körperlichkeit*] the human exterior is the kind of body [*Leiblichkeit*] that mirrors spirit in itself. (*Aesth* II W 14, 21)

In the classical age, then, self-knowing is sought prevalently in the ideal shape of the exquisitely human body. No other form is deemed more fitting to express the potentialities and actualizations of spirit. Sculptural representations of the human body are the classical art-kind par excellence.

Yet even this representation of spirit in flawless human physicality suffers from an intrinsic limitation. Despite the persistence of interpretations of Hegel as a devotee of nineteenth-century Graecomania, he is actually quite explicit about the fact that classical beauty is no adequate expression of spirit. In Walter Jaeschke's fitting remark, for Hegel, "Spirit is not a beautiful thing and the attempt to represent it as such belongs to a historical stage on which spirit still knows itself in unity with nature."[12]

After the collapse of classical civilization, sculpture's dominance recedes in favor of mediums no longer centered on three-dimensional (ultimately tactile) embodiments of self-knowing. These are the so-called Romantic arts: painting, music, and poetry. Of course, since for Hegel the past is always conserved in new historical developments, the ancient sculptural medium does survive (as does architecture) in the church-enclosed statuaries of the Christian demigod, one no longer shown, however, at the peak of bodily power but in the anguished postures of a human being entirely bereft of Olympian bliss. Already Hellenistic sculpture presages medieval Jesus imagery: to choose but one example, Jesus's iconic chest wound can be traced back to that of the Dying Gaul of the pre-Christian era, just as the riddle of the paradoxical triumph of a crucified semigod can be traced back to that same sympathetic portrayal of a "loser" from Hellenistic times—a sympathy that would have escaped classical viewers' taste and understanding entirely.

Over the centuries, however, the overwhelming physicality of the dominant artistic kinds gives way to increasingly "intellectualistic" expressions of self-knowledge. Two-dimensional as well as nonspatial self-representations of spirit in painting, music, and literature become the preferred productions of medieval and modern art making.

With regard to our subject matter, Hegel claims that fifth-century BC tragedies represent the encounter between symbolic and classical art forms. More precisely, they are staged representations of the conflict-ridden historical shift from the archaic world to the contemporaneous life of the audiences. Moreover, these tragic stories are built around the essential assumption that archaic spirit's self-knowing does not just happen to succumb to classical self-knowing, but *must* do so with iron necessity. The dramaturge confronts the classical audience with the enigmatic and unsettling constellation of two mindsets, the archaic and the contemporary, that are intimately connected and yet at the same time remote and alien to one another.

Dramatic Estrangement, Strange Justice, and Ancestral Strangers

The notion of self-estrangement, therefore, plays an important role in Hegel's conceptualization of Greek tragedy as an expression of absolute knowing in the arts. He describes the dramatic estrangement effect[13] as operating at distinct levels: (i) it refers to the impact exercised by the drama on the audience; (ii) it also pertains to a core content feature of the subject matter itself; and finally (iii) it informs the plot's explicit recollection of the foreign, unfamiliar origins of classical civilization.

(i) The estrangement-effect results from the epochal dislocation between the time of the story (Minoan, Mycenaean, or other) and the audience's present time. Composed without exception in the fifth century BC, Sophoclean, Aeschylean, and Euripidean tragedies stage events unfolding in ethical settings that no longer exist and depict individuals whose moral outlook is no longer or only subconsciously shared by the audience.[14] No tragic plot unfolds in the Colonus of Sophocles's time, in Aeschylus's Eleusis, or in Euripides's Salamis. The virtues displayed on stage are incompatible with the official doctrines of philosophers and educators (as Plato's comments on drama make abundantly clear). Bonds of blood and tribal kinship no longer define the political experience and juridical self-understanding of the citizen-spectator. When Hegel stresses the "sculptural" quality of tragic protagonists (see e.g., *Aesth* III W 15, 522), he is drawing attention to the fact that tragedy's epochal dislocation parallels that of classical sculptural works: the bronze and marble figures in the *agorà* or on the Parthenon's pediments represent mythological individuals, not historical leaders and commanders. The Greek artwork's "plasticity," as Hegel calls it, is not limited to the shaping of marble or bronze but extends to the poetic shaping of humans engaged in extraordinary (indeed super-human) deeds.[15] The supremely self-confident and inattentive, truly hieratic expression of statuary's demigods is the tangible counterpart of heroes' character in tragedy.

(ii) "Estrangement" also refers to a feature of the story being told: it is a story *of* estrangement. The more outlandish the story is, the more powerful its repulsive force; and the more strangely familiar the characters and their motives are, the stronger is the attraction. Hegel thinks that this double arousal of "fear and empathy" (which already Aristotle attributes to "the very structure of the events": see *Poetics* 14 1453b1–2) is most radical in stories unfolding at the threshold of history proper, that is, (i.e., in humanity's transition from the prepolitical to the political life). The historical basis of this fictional transition is described in the *Philosophy of Right* in the following terms:

> To emerge from [mere bonds of] marriage and husbandry into the rule of law and objective institutions . . . is the absolute right of the Idea, whether . . . this actualization appears as divine legislation and beneficence, or as [sheer] might and wrong;—this right is the *right of heroes* to bring about states. (*RPh* W 7 § 350)[16]

The prepolitical quality of historical right in a right-less world applies equally to the fiction's heroic deeds, as these are imitations of prehistorical deeds that were guided by far-reaching ethical ends. The life of stage protagonists shares fundamental traits with the life of the real founders of political states:

> If we look at the destiny of these world-historical individuals, whose task it was to be executors of world spirit, we can see that it has not been a happy one. They never came to reposeful enjoyment, their entire life was toil and effort, their whole nature was only their passion. (*Ph.Gesch.* W 12, 46)

Even more importantly, the personality of real and fictional heroes is equally irrelevant vis-à-vis their deeds: "Once their end is achieved, they fall away, empty shells falling off the core" (*Ph.Gesch.* 47). But the genuinely tragic quality of fictional heroes additionally consists of the fact that they are portrayed as always failing to achieve their ends. As shown below, their predicament lies in the peculiar nature of their will, that is, in their subjective disposition to choose ends that they neither freely posit nor will ever live to see.

The incestuous and cannibalistic background of the House of Atraeus,[17] the ensuing harrowing stories of parricide and matricide, child sacrifice, live burial, retaliation in kind, voluntary martyrdom, and mad wrath unfold in a world of patriarchal rule, not in the world of the Law. In the former, antagonists may claim equal justification (*Berechtigung*) for their incompatible ethical aims because in this world, "right" (*Recht*) is not yet actualized in laws and institutions. Fifth-century spectators are confronted with two kinds of aberrant agents: those whose only claim to right is might and those on the wrong side of history. This is also why, incidentally, Hegel reminds us that "in the state there can no longer be heroes: these occur only in the uncultured condition [*im ungebildeten Zustande*]" (*RPh* W 7 §93A).

(iii) Finally, estrangement in ancient tragedy also consists of the fact that all the featured heroic dynasties of the protagonists originate from non-Greek populations and cultures:

> We have just talked about foreigness as one element of the Greek spirit, and it is a known fact that the beginnings of [their] culture [*Bildung*] are connected with the arrival of foreigners in Greece. The Greeks preserved this origin of ethical life with grateful remembrance in what we may call mythological consciousness.... Thus we also witness here a colonization by cultivated peoples who were already ahead of the Greeks in civilization [*Bildung*]. (*PhGesch* W 12, 280–281)[18]

Tragic drama is a constant reminder to Greek audiences that agriculture, the forging of iron, the uses of fire, the taming of horses, the art of weaving, the alphabet, and even the olive tree were introduced to the Hellenes by Schythians, Caucasians and Phoenicians. In *Oedipus Rex*, for example, Sophocles just mentions as a well-known fact that the founder of Thebes is Cadmus of Phoenicia; in the *Histories*, Herodotus mentions casually that the Egyptian Kekrops is the founder of Athens.

In sum, the plots of classical tragedies pull their audiences' imagination into archaic forms of the ethical life that are foreign to them in more than one sense. The royal houses of foreign stock, whose demise is being staged, produce larger-than-life agents, enforcers of cruel acts of "justice," strange women with the moral fiber of men, and humans communing with gods. Hegel points out that in the dramatic structure this is reflected in the role of the chorus representing the voice of the Greek people. The chorus never participates in the action but comments on it as if it only comprised of outsiders: only the heroes "perform the deeds and carry the blame" (*Ph. Gesch. W* 12, 285). Once the deed is done, royal individuals and their aristocratic kin become superfluous to the point of annulling the necessity of popular revolt against them: "The royal houses destroy themselves in themselves or decay without hatred, without struggle by the people.... What a contrast with the stories of other times!" (*Ph. Gesch* 285).

On Choosing without a Free Will

In the previous sections I have highlighted, first, the centrality of the conflict between archaic and classical forms of self-knowing for an understanding of Greek tragic drama; second, the impersonality of the protagonists' ends, whose actions are guided by antagonistic visions of justice; third, the inevitable demise of one side in the conflict despite the ethical equivalence of their rival conceptions of justice in absence of actual institutionalized "right."

The question I wish to address now is why Hegel considers Greek tragedy to represent the quintessence of all tragic drama. In general terms, the reason seems to be that Greek tragedies reenact the drawn-out, violent, and irrevocable abandonment of the state of nature, broadly conceived as a lawless state of humanity, and that this upheaval, far from concerning only external modes of survival and ways of life, is also reflected in a radical change of the essence (*Wesen*) of the species (*Gattung*).

Hegel thinks of Hobbes's *exeundum e statu naturae* as a seismic event: not just a cataclysmic change in human interactions but, not unlike in Rousseau's vision of the same epochal transition, *a transformation of human nature*. In the species *Mensch*, nature becomes irreversibly enmeshed with history.[19] This alteration is the deeper subject matter of Greek tragedy. The upheaval affects the species at two levels: on the one hand, it marks a transition from dependency on first nature—including humanity's own animality—to dependency on second nature; connected with this, it is also a transition from the mere exercise of the natural will to the emergence of the capacity for free will. By portraying various forms of this sweeping transformation, classical tragedies revive it on stage and even confront the spectators with the prospect of the ever-present hazard of a relapse into prepolitical forms of life, of the will, and of self-knowledge.

If Hegel is right in thinking of Hobbes's *exeundum* as a radical change in the nature of the human will, and since the denizens of the polis only stand at the beginning of a millenarian development of that capacity, then the classical audiences must feel a formidable affinity (alongside fear and revulsion) with tragedy's heroes. The dramaturges, in other words, confront their fellow citizens with a terrifying past as well as with the singularly ephemeral, precarious status of their civilization.

By presenting the outcomes of human actions not as mere misfortunes but also as voluntary choices, classical tragedy exhibits the human will as an enigma. In light of the already quoted description from the Greater Logic pertaining to Greek conceptions of the intrinsic measure of things and of our capacity for trespassing our own intrinsic measure (*WdL* I W 5, 390), we see how for Hegel tragic actors neither stumble nor are thrust upon the threshold dividing right measure from *hybris*. Their peculiar heroic capacity lies in their *choosing* to trespass. At the same time, and paradoxically, these individual choices are prompted—from without as it were—by a preternatural alteration of the natural will: tragic agents make choices they have *not consciously* willed. Their individual passion is filled with imperatives over which they have no command—a cryptic condition that fictional heroes share with the prehistorical founders of the political life:

> These are the great human beings in history, whose particular purposes contain what is substantial, which is the will of world spirit. They are ... *heroes* insofar as they have drawn their purposes and calling...from a source, whose content is hidden, ... from the still subterranean inner spirit that knocks on the external world as on a hull and bursts it open because it is a different core than the core of that hull—[people] who appear to draw [only] from within themselves. (*PhGesch* W 12, 46)

Like the state founder who seems motivated by personal goals while being actually driven by world spirit, so the fictional hero, seemingly guided by personal passions, is instead following the overpowering, inexplicable ends of a heavenly agent.

Meticulous studies of Greek works by classicists and scholars of ancient philosophy[20] fully corroborate Hegel's reading of ancient conceptions of the will (though without once citing Hegel). For example, in a seminal series of lectures entitled *A Free Will* (2011) M. Frede highlights the absence of any reference to a concept of free will or of individual autonomy in the extant Greek literature;[21] and in an essay on "Stoic Autonomy" (2003) Cooper identifies the first century AD historian Dio Chrysostom as the first textual source containing a reference to individual autonomy as source of the "free will."[22] To use Hegel's formulations: there is no reference in ancient Greek texts to "the will . . . free not only *in* itself but *for* itself also" (*RPh* § 21); nor to the urge "of free spirit . . . to make its freedom objective for itself . . . in order to be for itself, as Idea, what the will is in-itself: "*the free will which wills the free will*" (§ 27). There is no Greek expression uniting the concept of "(to) will" with that of "freedom" to form a notion of "free will," though there are of course copious separate employments of each notion. An act of willing is expressed either by *boulēsis*, referred mostly to a community's "counsel" and, occasionally, to counsel with oneself or deliberation; or by *proairesis*, an individual's actual choice and, occasionally, a disposition to choose among existing alternatives. As for freedom, *eleutheria* denotes a people's political independence and by extension a characteristic of the male citizens of such a community (*eleutheroi*). Contrary to modern expectations (and as testified, for example, in Euripides's *Iphigenia in Aulis*, to be quoted shortly), being a free people or even a free individual is for Greek authors not a consequence of one's position of dominance as much as a presupposition of one's legitimate rulership. Conversely, servile status—*douleia*—is not so much a consequence of having been subjected as it is a presupposition of justified subjection by another.[23] Hegel, well aware of all this, interprets these ancient conceptions of subjection, freedom, and voluntariness as evidence of a still naturalistic and hence inadequate self-comprehension of humanity:

> According to its *immediate* existence, the human being [*der Mensch*] is to itself a natural being, an externality to its concept; only through the *development of its own body and spirit*, *essentially* through *its self-conscious grasp of itself as free*, does it take possession of itself. . .
>
> The standpoint of the free will, with which begin Right and the science of Right, has already left behind the untrue standpoint . . . on which the human being is a natural being. (*RPh W* 7 § 57 and R)

Developing "body and spirit" includes growing away from the mere naturalness of the will. In ancient texts, the intimate connection of freedom with nature and status—maleness, citizenship, even Greekdom—makes it impossible to conceive of self-legislating individuals who freely posit their ends and wind up obeying themselves. Cooper can document only three passages spanning about six centuries, in which "autonomy" is predicated of individuals as opposed to ethnic or political communities. Two of these passages have unequivocally negative connotations: both refer to the lawless or unsupervised behavior of young males.[24] The third is found in Sophocles's *Antigone*, where the chorus qualifies her the heroine's live descent into Hades as occurring *autonomōs* (i.e., "in a self-legislating manner"). The key to this unique passage is, however, not to convey that Antigone follows *her own* law but that she prefers or chooses—in an act of *proairesis*—one existing law over another existing law. Not unlike the Christ's 'Thy will be done,' what Antigone chooses is heavenly over earthly will. Her defiant explanation to Creon famously appeals to the fact that divine justice "did not enact these human laws. / Nor did I deem that you, a mortal, / Could by a breath annul and override / The immutable unwritten laws of heaven. / These were not born today nor yesterday; / They do not die, and no one knows whence they come" (*Antigone* 450–457). Antigone's choice is a tragic one between already existing ends (what the Roman legislators would eventually identify as *jus naturale* and *jus civile*). Hers is not a triumphant positing of her own end.

An often-voiced objection to this conception of the ancient mind must be met. To say with Hegel and with contemporary classical scholars that neither tragic heroes nor Sophocles's or Aeschylus's contemporaries grasp persons as free, willing agents does not imply that they grasp them as natural automata. Just like ourselves and just like their audiences, Greek dramaturges and philosophers fully recognize individuals' capacity to act without external coercion and thus to be responsible—or rather, in ancient parlance, to be either blameworthy or praiseworthy—for their actions. Yet ancient authors always present moral agency as impelled by divine counsels and apparitions (Homer), by a *daimon* (Socrates), by one part of the soul (Plato), or by virtuous training (Aristotle). Under no circumstances are individuals free to act against these outer or inner motives. There is no free choice, for example, between acting on reason or acting on the appetites because there is no third or higher criterion from which to make the choice. Frede makes a convincing case that for Plato, for example, acting on reason simply means following reason's desire, just as acting on the appetites simply means following appetitive desire. But Aristotle's *aristoi* are an even more glaring example of this ancient conundrum: the virtuously trained are no doubt better people than the uneducated vulgar, but they are no *freer* in that, while the vulgar cannot choose noble actions, the *aristoi* cannot choose ignoble ones. To use a Hegelian formula: the agency of the ancient individual is an expression of the in-itself free will, never of the will that is for-itself-also.

It is therefore Hegel's contention that there is a significant difference between archaic and postarchaic understandings of volition. The difference can be easily gleaned from works of classical literature in which the archaic representations of all-moving gods as motive forces of human action have morphed into allegories that now stand for inward forces or "divinities in the human breast" (*Aesth* I W 13, 295). The classical work of literature, and foremost the classical drama, is therefore the *locus* of "a peculiar difficulty":

> The gods and universal powers in general are the moving and driving force, but in the real world genuine individual action is not apportioned to them; rather, the action is attributed to a human being.... On one side stand those universal powers, ... on the other, human individuals who own the deliberation and the final resolution to act, as well as the actual execution. In truth, the eternal ruling powers are immanent in the self of the human being, constituting the substance of its character; ... but the divine powers are themselves individuals and hence ... related to the subject in an external manner. In this relationship between gods and humans there lies immediately a contradiction ... [insofar as] this imperils both the free independence of the gods and the freedom of the individual agents. (*Aesth* I W 13, 292–3)

In a manner that must have been quite shocking though not entirely undecipherable to classical audiences, archaic heroes perform as "mere instruments of alien caprice [*Willkür*]" and the gods themselves as "dead machines" (*Aesth* I, 294). Oedipus blames himself for actions committed in utter ignorance—a circumstance that in classical Athens would have led to his juridical (and possibly moral) acquittal. Even more incoherently, he is both perpetrator and victim of entirely unfree actions: namely, his own. His daughter Antigone on her part embraces eternal laws of whose authorship she is entirely ignorant. And even Euripides's Iphigenia, perhaps a more nuanced character, in the end still chooses to be the willing captive of an alien will.

Iphigenia's initial grasp of the life worth living is anything but heroic, signaling rather an atheist stance, brash to the point of shamelessness: "Nothing is sweeter to mankind than to see the light of day, / What lies below is nothing: He is mad [*mainetai*] who prays / for death. To live ill is better than to die well" (*Iphigenia in Aulis* 1250–52). Yet a short time later, in "a flash coming upon me" (1374), Iphigenia embraces that very madness. Her personal interest is suddenly obliterated by an all-consuming interest in justice writ large. Her self-sacrifice, she now claims, will bring "Safety for Hellas' daughters from barbarians in the days to come, / That the ravisher no more may snatch them from a happy home, / When the penalty is paid for Paris' outrage, Hellen's shame" (1378–82). Were she to hold on to her life against the will of Artemis, the goddess who has been requiring her body in exchange for the razing of Troy, then "what would the justice in this be [*ti to dikaion toũto*]?" (1392).

The full import of Iphigenia's self-obliterating ethical choice becomes explicit in her closing words: "And it is only equitable [*eikos*], mother, that Hellenes should rule barbarians, and not barbarians / Hellenes; because they are of servile status [*doũlon*], but we are free [*eleutheroi*]" (1400–1). The freedom at issue here is the freedom of a people in its political life. This is Iphigenia's "substantial end." Ancient heroes and heroines do not attempt their own nor the kingdom's salvation through Hamletic anguish, self-doubt, or self-discovery. Their factual or moral ignorance is revealed to them abruptly. After the revelation, they choose the ends of their actions through no will of their own but in spells of divine madness. Through these tragedies, Hegel claims, the tragedians erected the poetic version of the "Temple to Mnemosyne" built by the historians of origins—Herodotus and Thucydides—who first provided the Greeks, and us, with a radical new way of being and of knowing ourselves: historical consciousness.

> [Original historiography] transposes what has been a mere occurrence . . . *into the realm of mental representation*. . . . What in reality is a past gone by, scattered in fortuitous subjective memories . . . becomes assembled as one whole . . . in the *Temple of Mnemosyne*, thereby securing for it immortal duration . . . a . . . better soil than that of the ephemeral . . . just like the ancients describe *the Elysium*, where *heroes* carry on forever the deeds they did *only once* in their lives. (*PhGesch W* 12, 544)

Notes

1. See Robert R. Williams, *Tragedy, Recognition and the Death of God: Studies in Hegel and Nietzsche* (Oxford: Oxford University Press, 2012), 1: "In contrast to Nietzsche's *Birth of Tragedy*, Hegel offers no comprehensive general theory of tragedy; instead he discusses particular Greek tragedies, notably his personal favorites which include Aeschylus' *Oresteia*, Sophocles' *Antigone*, *Oedipus Rex* and *Oedipus at Colonus*."

2. G. W. F. Hegel, *Vorlesungen über die Ästhetik: Werke in zwanzig Bänden*, vols. 13–15 (Frankfurt am Main: Suhrkamp, 1970). Cited as *Aesthetics* I–III W 13–15.

This edition, based on the transcriptions by Hotho, is the second edition (1842) of the four cycles of lectures in "Aesthetics or Philosophy of Art" held by Hegel in Berlin 1820–1829.

3. G. W. F. Hegel, *Vorlesungen über die Philosophie der Geschichte: Werke in zwanzig Bänden*, vol. 12 (Frankfurt am Main: Suhrkamp, 1973). Cited as *PhGesch W* 12. Hegel lectured five times on the topic (1822–1831). The textual basis for this edition is Karl Hegel's 1840 edition, reprinted in *G.W.F. Hegel Sämtliche Werke*, vol. 11: *Vorlesungen über die Philosophie der Geschichte*. Edited by Hermann Glockner (Stuttgart: Frommann Holzboog, 1971).

4. G. W. F. Hegel, *Grundlinien der Philosophie des Rechts oder Naturrecht und Staatswissenschaft im Grundrisse: Werke in zwanzig Bänden*, vol. 7 (Frankfurt am Main: Suhrkamp, 1970). Cited as *RPh W* 7.

5. G. W. F. Hegel, *System der Wissenschaft. Erster Theil, die Phänomenologie des Geistes. Werke in zwanzig Bänden*, vol. 3 (Frankfurt am Main: Suhrkamp, 1972). Cited as *PhenG W* 3.

6. Hegel refers to the stage play also as "drama in the narrower sense" or "intermediate genre" (*Aesthetics* III *W* 15, 521).

7. Hegel quotes Plautus's saying (in *Amphitryon*) that a god could commute tragedy into comedy (*Aesthetics* III *W* 15, 531), but already Aristotle mentions their potential for transmogrification. The reasons given by Plautus for coining the word "tragicomedy" relate to conceptions of social hierarchy: tragic plays feature gods and human elites, comedies feature the lower ranks. Since Plautus's *Amphitryon* features all classes, it is a combination of both.

8. In drama, the criterion of order includes cases of a character's inconsistency: in this case, says Aristotle, it will be "portrayed as consistently inconsistent" (*Poetics* 15 1454a). This would seem to apply to comedy more than to tragedy, but Aristotle considers characters to be secondary features in tragedy, as testified by the quote that opens this essay chapter. Euripides's Iphigenia does show radical "inconsistency" when changing her mind about the life well lived. But hers is a one-time irreversible reversal, not a "consistent inconsistency."

9. *Aesthetics*, Part I, chap. 2: "The Beauty of Nature"; chap. 3: "The Beauty of Art, or the Ideal."

10. G. W. F. Hegel, *Wissenschaft der Logik I. Werke in zwanzig Bänden*, vol. 5 (Frankfurt am Main: Suhrkamp, 1972). Cited as *WdL I W* 5.

11. Hegel exemplifies classical art with its flourishing in Attic civilization, but it is not impossible to identify the same transitions from "symbolic" to "classical" to "Romantic" epochs in the arts of other world civilizations. See Lindsay DeWitt, "The Universal Human Spirit in Japanese and Greek Art" (unpublished manuscript), 2018.

12. Walter Jaeschke, *Hegel-Handbuch. Leben—Werk—Wirkung* (Stuttgart/Weimar: Metzler, 2003).

13. Brecht dubbed this the "*V-Effekt*" (from *Verfremdungseffekt*) and made it

into a staple of theatrical production in general. See Bertolt Brecht, *Gesammelte Werke in 20 Bänden* (Frankfurt am Main: Suhrkamp, 1967), 15:301.

14. Nor is this ethical perspective shared, as Dover points out, by the dramaturge. See J. K. Dover, *Greek Popular Morality in the Time of Plato and Aristotle* (Indianapolis: Hackett, 1974), 15–16.

15. Further references to the "sculptural" quality of Greek spirit in general ("the plastic artist" and the "reshaping shaper [*umbildende Bildner*]"), including the "*beautiful individuality*" of fictional heroes, can be found in *PhGesch W* 12, 294–5.

16. On the "right of heroes" as founders of states, see also *RPh* § 93 Remark.

17. This is the royal stock of Agamemnon. Atraeus, Agamemnon's father, is offered human flesh by his brother Thyestes at a banquet—the flesh of Atraeus's own sons no less. In doing so, Thyestes is repeating the actions of his own grandfather, Tantalus, who was the first to attempt testing divine omniscience by offering to the gods his own son as a feast.

18. The next sentence in this passage is of interest as a corrective to simplified readings of Hegel's philosophy of history and its notion of "colonization": "But one cannot compare this colonization [of the early Greeks] with that by the English in North America, as these have not mingled with the natives but rather displaced them, while the colonists of Greece mixed together imported and autochthonous elements" (*PhGesch W* 12, 281).

19. The natural-historical essence of the human species would become pivotal in Marx's enhancement of the concept of *Gattungswesen* he adopted from Ludwig Feuerbach, whose conception of the human being, ostensibly related to Hegel's, was largely ahistorical.

20. I consider here only the following: Michael Frede, *A Free Will: Origins of the Notion in Ancient Thought. Sather Classical Lectures 1997–98*, ed. A. A. Long (Berkeley: University of California Press, 2011); K. J. Dover, *Greek Popular Morality in the Time of Plato and Aristotle* (Oxford: Basil Blackwell, 1974); John M. Cooper, "Stoic Autonomy," *Social Philosophy and Policy* 20, no. 2 (2003): 1–29 (2003); and W. D. Ross, *Aristotle* (London: Methuen, 1923), especially 201–2.

21. Frede, *A Free Will*. Chapter 2 is entitled "Aristotle on Choice Without a Will," which inspired the title of this essay.

22. See Cooper, "Stoic Autonomy," especially 3–7.

23. On the meaning of *douleia* in the ancient Greek and Roman worlds see Walter Beringer, "'Servile Status' in the Sources for Early Greek History," *Historia: Zeitschrift für alte Geschichte* 31 (1982): 13–32. As is so often the case, J.-J. Rousseau is best at capturing the historical inversion of perspective from antiquity to modernity: "Aristotle was right but he took the effect for the cause. Every man born in slavery is born for slavery, nothing is more certain ... Hence if there are slaves by nature, it is because there have been slaves against nature." See *Social Contract* bk 1, chap. 2. of *J.J. Rousseau. Du Contrat Social*, ed. M. Halbwachs (Paris: Aubier Editions Montaigne, 1943).

24. The passages are from Xenophon's *Constitution of the Lacedaemonians*, 3.1, http://www.perseus.tufts.edu/hopper/text?doc=Perseus%3Atext%3A1999.01.0210%3Atext%3DConst.+Lac.%3Achapter%3D1; and Isocrates's *Panathenaic Oration*, 215, http://www.perseus.tufts.edu/hopper/text?doc=Perseus%3Atext%3A1999.01.0144%3Aspeech%3D12%3Asection%3D17.

Chapter Six

Freedom and Fixity in Shakespeare's Tragic Heroes

Rachel Falkenstern

Introduction

According to the popular account of Hegel's theory of tragedy, ancient tragic heroes are one-sided and unwavering in pursuit of their aims, while modern heroes, in contrast, are not so solid and may even waver.[1] However, Hegel actually holds that early modern tragic heroes are one-sidedly fixed to their goals, in much the same way that ancient heroes are—indeed, this is a necessary attribute for all tragic heroes for Hegel.[2] Yet, he also holds that individuals in modernity have achieved a deeper, freer, and more reflective subjectivity than individuals in antiquity. Thus, early modern tragic heroes, which for Hegel are primarily Shakespeare's, pose a double problem for Hegel's theory of tragedy and for the historical aspect of his wider philosophy: on the one hand, modern subjective freedom seems to preclude the one-sided fixity necessary for tragic heroes, and, on the other, such fixity seems to jeopardize their very status as modern.

    This chapter argues that early modern tragic heroes are indeed one-sidedly fixed to their goals, which allows for their aesthetic greatness, and also possess a depth and freedom that their ancient counterparts did not, due to their particular historical standpoint. Hegel's theory of subjectivity and freedom as historically coined shows Macbeth, Hamlet, and Shakespearean tragic heroes in general to be presenting the unique brand of *early* modern subjectivity, which is partially but not yet fully self-determining or reflective. Further, Shakespearean tragic heroes display their subjective freedom and depth through such aesthetic elements as simile and the supernatural while remaining fixed to their aims.

The first section "Fixity and One-Sidedness" argues how, for Hegel, Shakespeare's tragic heroes are one-sidedly fixed to their goals, in keeping both with the historical progress of subjective freedom and with Hegel's theory of tragedy. The next section then lays out how these heroes are problematic in that they seem to lack self-determination in their subservience to witches and ghosts; as it turns out, the hero displays self-determination and reflection through their very dealings with these supernatural characters. The third section argues that the subjective depth of early modern tragic heroes is further displayed through their use of simile and in their tragic reconciliation or demise. Ultimately, through the lens of Hegel's philosophy, Shakespeare's tragic heroes show us what we have gained in early modernity, what is lacking at this stage of spirit's progress, and the contradictions that result.

Fixity and One-Sidedness

In Hegel's general view of the historical progress of subjective freedom, spirit's freedom increases and gains greater subjective depth at different moments in history. In various places throughout his corpus he points out important shifts and differences between human subjectivity and freedom in different historical moments and cultures—most notable for our purposes is the contrast between antiquity and European modernity. Ancient Greeks had not yet broken from a natural, unreflective standpoint; they transformed or interpreted the given but did not take the materials of self-production and expression from within themselves and therefore were not fully self-determining (*LPH* 238–39).[3] Spirit becomes unsatisfied with the immediate and the natural, and searches within itself for freedom, which is eventually realized (*LPH* 250).[4] This very progress of spirit is presented to itself in absolute spirit (i.e., in art, religion, and philosophy), so that art's content concomitantly becomes increasingly self-reflective and free.[5] Thus, with the advent of Christianity, art displays a greater degree of subjective depth and freedom than the classical art of ancient Greece (*LFA* 79).[6]

However, it is not until the Protestant Reformation that individuals begin to truly know themselves as subjects possessing self-determination (*LPH*

438). With this subjective turn in early modernity, seen not only in religion but also in all aspects of spirit—such as Descartes' philosophy and Romantic art—drama now presents subjective freedom and is focused on the character's "inner subjective life" (*LFA* 193).[7] Modern dramatic heroes embody, enact, and are aware of subjective freedom. Shakespeare's Hamlet and Juliet, for example, present their inner life through poetic expression, reflecting not only on the objective situation but also on their own inner, subjective condition, in a way that ancient heroes such as Antigone and Oedipus do not.[8]

Yet, at the same time, and perhaps surprisingly, in Hegel's view early modern heroes are firmly fixed to their aims, much like their ancient counterparts are, as epitomized by Hegel's famous description of Sophocles' Antigone. Indeed, Shakespeare's heroes are so fixed to their goals that he describes them as "simply the one power dominating their own specific character" (*LFA* 1194). But such a description is clearly problematic in light of his view of modern subjective freedom and its prominence in modern art. Further, it may also seem problematic in light of two tendencies in Hegel scholarship: the prevailing tendency is to read Hegel's theory as placing ancient and modern tragedy in direct contrast to, or necessarily very different from, each other.[9] This would make such a similarity between ancient and modern tragedy—the one-sided fixity of all tragic heroes—questionable. The other tendency takes Hegel's view to be that the deeper subjectivity and greater freedom of modern characters allow them to waver, thus preventing them from being completely fixated on anything.[10] This would make it impossible for them to be one-sided and, therefore, also impossible for them to be proper or great tragic heroes according to Hegel's theory of tragedy. Nonetheless, it is Hegel's view that Shakespeare's heroes are firmly and one-sidedly fixed to their aims. This one-sidedness manifests itself in early modern tragic heroes as two types.

The first type of early modern hero is a "*subjective* totality, but one which persists undeveloped in its inwardness and undisclosed depth of heart," exemplified by Hamlet and Juliet (*LFA* 577). In other words, these are "substantial hearts which incorporate a totality but in their simple compactness generate every deep feeling only in themselves without developing it outwardly and unbosoming themselves of it" (*LFA* 580). Miranda in Shakespeare's *The Tempest* is also of this type, somehow unable to externalize the depths of her inner life (*LFA* 585).

Such figures never fully realize their aims because they have no support from others; they are prevented from acting by accidental circumstances or by their own inwardly turned nature. Yet, despite the deeper subjectivity exhibited in these characters, Hegel sees them also as being completely fixated on their aims. Hegel posits that even characters that may seem hesitant or weak, such as Hamlet and Juliet, are formally fixed, just "based in inwardness" (*LFA* 580). They never realize their aims, but they never let go of them: this unwavering solidity is part of their aesthetic greatness, much like ancient heroes.

One might argue, however, that Hamlet is the epitome of a vacillating hero and famously so.[11] But according to Hegel, Hamlet "was not doubtful about *what* he was to do, but only *how*," and Hegel suggests in this part of the lectures that Hamlet is an ideally unified character (*LFA* 244).[12] That is, in contrast to popular readings, Hegel actually sees Hamlet as one-sidedly fixed on his aim of revenge, not split or wavering. What he lacks is not fixity but the resources to go about fulfilling his goal, as he never finds definitive proof or the perfect opportunity to exact his revenge. This is seen when Claudius is praying and confessing his sins (at the end of Act III), and Hamlet is deterred from killing him by the possibility that Claudius could go to heaven—something Hamlet Sr. was deprived of. Likewise, Hamlet is not satisfied with Claudius's reaction to *The Mousetrap*. Even though Claudius's stern silence could be read as guilt, the murderer in the play is the play-king's nephew, not his brother, and Claudius's reaction could thus also be seen as being insulted by or afraid of the thought of his *own* nephew murdering him. Because he must be sure his revenge is justified before he acts, Hamlet is left without sufficient proof and remains unable to reach his goal to the bitter end. Indeed, I posit that this is exactly what makes Hamlet a great tragic hero according to Hegel: amidst so much madness and turmoil, he remains inwardly fixed to his cause, but because he never figures out how to act, he remains stuck to the fence, as it were.

Lear and Macbeth are the second type of early modern tragic hero and just as fixated on their subjective aims as the first type; however, they are able to outwardly direct their energy into fulfilling their goals. Hegel describes this trademark quality as the "self-sustaining firmness of character which limits itself to specific ends and puts the whole power of its one-sided individuality into the *realization* of these ends" (*LFA* 577). This type of hero may easily be seen as one-sided, as she is so focused on realizing her goals that she succeeds.

For example, Macbeth's formalism entails his complete concentration on his aim, "which he made emerge completely in its firm severity, which he expressed and carried through" (*LFA* 580). Hegel describes Macbeth's one-sided pursuit of power as "what he has, does, and accomplishes, he draws immediately, without any further reflection, from his own specific nature which is just what it happens to be" (*LFA* 577). Macbeth takes his personal aim immediately from himself and keeps it directly in front of him. Even when facing his demise, Macbeth remains "inflexible" and unreflective: Hegel asserts that "what he meets, whether from the rule of fate, from necessity, or from chance, likewise just *is*, without his reflecting on whither or why" (*LFA* 580).

However, this fixity is complicated by the fact that these goals are an intrinsic part of the character, so that the hero is accomplishing her own self-actualization at the same time. This "is not merely a development out of the individual's *action*, but is at the same time an inner growth, a development of his *character* itself" (*LFA* 579).[13] This is tricky because any change in character is actually a development of "something that was implicit … from the start. For example, in *King Lear*, Lear's original folly is intensified into madness in his old age, just as Gloucester's mental blindness is changed into actual physical blindness" (*LFA* 1229).[14] What was within Lear and Gloucester is now outwardly developed, not simply displayed but "intensified" and made actual, fully brought to light.[15] Gloucester physically actualizes his blindness *through* his metaphorical blindness, and Lear's folly develops *into* madness. The expression of what was implicit, or the accomplishment of aims, makes the character more of what he already was.[16] Their pathos may be intensified, but this second type of tragic hero ultimately remains what they always were at core.

While this description may seem overly literal, it has a deeper, crucial meaning for Hegel. Although in modernity we have gained a deeper subjectivity than we had in antiquity, in early modernity we do not have the true freedom that we come to have later. The progress of subjective freedom does not stop at Descartes, Luther, or Shakespeare.[17] Although "Protestantism had introduced the *principle* of Subjectivity," humanity does not fully realize subjective freedom until it can hold itself under the scrutiny of its own reason, as introduced by the philosophical and cultural movements of the Enlightenment (*LPH* 438). That is, the *last* stage of this progress only *begins* near the end of the eighteenth century, when modernity truly starts for Hegel (*LPH* 412). By this point in history, individuals have gained an even greater depth of subjectivity and freedom than they possessed in the early modern period (*LHP* 131). In Hegel's view, individuals in late modernity know (indeed, they must know) they possess greater freedom and a deeper subjectivity than individuals did before (*LFA* 187).

This highlights a subtle but important distinction Hegel makes within romantic art. While all romantic art displays a greater degree of subjective depth and freedom than classical art, artworks of Hegel's own post-Enlightenment era present an even greater degree of subjective freedom and a deeper spirituality than works of early modernity. Thus, I posit that for Hegel the firm characterization of early modern tragic heroes is directly related to the historical progress of subjectivity and freedom and, further, that the wavering that plagues some dramatic heroes is only possible in *late* modern drama. The kind of radical subjectivity that leads to split or wavering characters is seen in post-Enlightenment drama—for example, in the context of Hegel's critique of early German Romanticism and forms of irony, or in Schiller's tragedies—but it is not available to Shakespeare's heroes, who remain firm to the bitter end.[18]

Self-Reflection and Self-Determination

However, if early modern tragic heroes are indeed one-sidedly fixed to their aims, we are left with a problem: this one-sidedness leaves us with seemingly little room for the deeper, reflective subjectivity that Hegel argues we moderns have gained. That is, Hegel's reading of Macbeth's one-sidedness and Hamlet's fixity seems to contradict his own theory of the historical progress of modern subjectivity as involving a greater depth of personality and freedom. Hegel partially answers this problem of early modern heroes, I posit, by turning to a dramatic device employed in modern tragedy: supernatural characters.

In *Macbeth*, Hegel sees the witches as revealing what was already implicit within Macbeth (in keeping with the self-actualizing type of modern hero he is), rather than seeing them as giving him new knowledge or being an external influence. The witches are "only the poetic reflection of his own fixed will," showing to him and to us what is lying within him but otherwise unarticulated (*LFA* 585). They are disclosing to him the realm from which he is cut off due to his tragic fixity, revealing the truth of his subjectivity to himself and to the audience. In this way, the witches are a part of his self-actualization, as described earlier. Just as what was within Lear and Gloucester developed outwardly, the witches are a way for Macbeth's inner realm to be more fully brought to light.

However, one may argue that viewing the witches in this light is problematic: they could be seen as a completely outside or alien force, thus suggesting that Macbeth was lured to evil deeds by an external influence. This would suggest that he is weak or less firm, making him less aesthetically great and less heroic. And if the witches are on the side of evil, and he listens to them, is he even more evil—and perhaps even less heroic? Further, their influence might also mean he was acting less freely than if he were fully driven by his own passions and ideas, putting him back in the problematic situation of not being a free modern subject. If he is lured to his deeds by external circumstances, would that not limit his self-determination and self-actualization, making him un-modern?

Since the first productions of *Macbeth*, the problem of the witches' power over Macbeth has been answered in a variety of ways, as witchcraft was both popular and controversial during Shakespeare's lifetime. King James was a self-proclaimed witchcraft expert and was well known for his persecution not only of (supposed) witches but also of those who did not believe that witches existed.[19] However, with the Enlightenment, the outlook on witchcraft changed considerably (although violent witch hunts and persecution continued in Europe and the United States well into the eighteenth century). This shift in attitude about actual witches (as opposed to characters in drama) is reflected in the stagings and interpretations of Shakespeare's plays during Hegel's era—and Hegel was well aware both of the history of witch hunts and of the reception of Shakespeare during his own lifetime.[20]

Shakespeare was a central figure in Germany during Hegel's time, so how people, in an era when they supposedly no longer believed in witches, dealt with Shakespeare's witches was a live issue. For example, in Schiller and Goethe's *Macbeth* (with Schiller as translator and Goethe staging their 1800 production in Weimar), the witches are less ambiguous. Their witches are clearly evil, although in a symbolic fashion: they are less visually grotesque and more humanlike than earlier versions, and they clearly state their evil intentions.[21] As a result, the Weimar witches bring Macbeth to ruin, rather than Macbeth doing this to himself. Their Lady Macbeth also has more power over her husband than in Shakespeare's original, so that this production paints a less evil Macbeth (perhaps as a result of Schiller and Goethe's moral aims for art in this period).[22] These choices present both a less free and a less heroic Macbeth.

Hegel's reading, by contrast, paints the witches as more ambiguous and also as having less power over Macbeth. He gives Macbeth more freedom and responsibility for his actions (including for his own demise) than Schiller and Goethe do, leaving both his evil and heroic natures more intact. In this way, Hegel can use the witches as an answer to the problems of how Macbeth could be a reflective subject and how he could exercise his freedom as a modern agent. The witches are thus both necessarily ambiguous and fitting in this early modern tragedy.

Further, from his standpoint in late modernity, Hegel argues that he can explain Shakespeare's use of such otherworldly figures as witches and ghosts in a way that Shakespeare himself, entrenched in the early modern mindset, could not. In Hegel's view, we are influenced by the legends and stories of Christianity and *invent* witches and ghosts (LFA 230; LPH 425). Because they are products of our imagination, we should not obey them; in truth, we have the freedom to act on our own (LFA 230–31). Macbeth, who seems at first to be an unreflective subject under the spell of external supernatural forces, turns out to be a modern agent freely pursuing his goal.

However, the witches in Macbeth could pose another problem for Hegel's aesthetics: because, for Hegel, "in art nothing is dark ... everything is clear and transparent," the "truly ideal character has for its content and 'pathos' nothing supernatural and ghost-ridden but only true interests in which he is at one with himself" (LFA, 243). The witches' influence would take away from Hegel's aesthetic requirement that dramatic characters be unified and whole within themselves, making Macbeth less aesthetically ideal. Modern characters, for the most part, should not be attuned to visions or other supernatural phenomena, as this would take away from their tragic fixity.[23] Nonetheless, I posit that supernatural forces are appropriate in modern art for Hegel if they do not overpower the individual's freedom—and that this is the case in *Macbeth*.

Macbeth believes—wrongly according to Hegel—that the idea to be king was prophesied and given to him by the witches, not that his ambition was a preexisting condition, as it were. As Hegel describes it, the witches "appear as external powers determining Macbeth's fate in advance. Yet what they declare is his most secret and private wish which comes home to him and is revealed to him in this only apparently external way" (LFA, 231). Here we see Hegel's confirmation that what seems to come from without truly comes from within. Just as Hegel sees the witches' words as ultimately stemming from or corresponding to Macbeth's already existing desires, so too can we see his actions stemming from those desires as his own and that he is freely acting of his own will. Hegel does not view the witches as having any real power over

Macbeth; the witches are a manifestation of his will, making Macbeth the doer of his own deeds. In his explanation of the witches, Hegel implies that they serve as an aesthetic device to display Macbeth's self-reflection and to exercise subjective freedom, however limited, on the way to the realization of his one-sided aim.[24]

Similar to witches, ghosts in early modern tragedy are, I argue, a spiritual and yet objective revelation of the subjective—a manifestation of what was implicit within the subject, who makes it explicit to herself in this supernatural way. In "The Spirit of Christianity and Its Fate," Hegel discusses the meaning and significance of Banquo's ghost. For Hegel, it is Banquo's ghost, and not Macbeth's conscience, that shows Macbeth he was wrong. Although the ghost may actually be a product of his conscience, Macbeth sees the ghost as completely other, not as self-created or self-related. For us, Macbeth is projecting the truth, but as an early modern tragic hero he is too one-sided to see that the truth comes from within himself. In my view, a similar argument could be made of Hamlet's ghost—that Hamlet is unable to *completely* externalize his thoughts naturally. That is, deep in Hamlet's mind he knows what evil Claudius has done, but Shakespeare relies on another means for Hamlet to know the truth, revealed to Hamlet and to us as an audience as coming from the ghost (*LFA*, 583). The ghost could be seen as the truth attempting (but not fully able) to reveal itself, mirroring Hamlet's own limitations.

Along these lines, what we know to be Macbeth's own doing seems to him to be fate; although it is truly of his own making, it seems to him that he is inescapably trapped in a bloody circle of uncontrollable events. Hegel views this trap as indeed of Macbeth's own doing, yet, in "The Spirit of Christianity and Its Fate," Hegel also describes it as a fate. This is because, in this early essay, Hegel's view of fate is that it is a reaction to our action, not a completely external force: we bring about our own fate. He describes Macbeth's demise as a reaction to his own evil deeds, that is, as ultimately stemming from him.[25] Hegel writes that "punishment as fate is the equal reaction of the trespasser's own deed, of a power which he himself has armed, of an enemy made an enemy by himself" (*ETW*, 229–30).[26]

In light of Hegel's reading of *Macbeth*, another important role of ghosts and witches in early modern tragedy, I posit, is to highlight the very ambiguity of early modern subjective freedom.[27] As we have seen, early modern tragic heroes are somewhat un-modern in their lack of subjective freedom, just as they are also not able to be fully self-reflective without these "supernatural" figures. In truth, humans possess self-determination, yet these heroes are only abstractly free because they do not know their implicit freedom.[28] As in the earlier description of their merely formal subjectivity, modern heroes who are cut off from others are also merely formally and not concretely free.[29] For Hegel, freedom is not solipsistic or pure autonomy but involves, as famously put, "being at home with oneself in one's other" (*EL*, §24A2). We are truly free when we know that our freedom depends on others in various social contexts. Macbeth, however, does not know this until perhaps the end—although one might argue that Hamlet often seems to be closer to this truth.

Using Hegel to explain the supernatural figures in *Macbeth* shows them to be both illustrative and a result of what I see as Hegel's view of the tensions in early modern Europe—tensions, for example, between myth and Christianity and between feudalism and later social systems that allow for true freedom. These otherworldly figures and their intimate relationship to tragic heroes reflect the deeper subjectivity of modernity in contrast to that of antiquity but in a way unique to *early* modernity in contrast to late modernity. In this light, we see that for Hegel, agency in early modernity is a gray area of limited freedom yet radical self-determination. It is with the otherworldly figures of witches and ghosts that we can see how early modern heroes, despite their one-sidedness, display the freedom that spirit has achieved so far.

Self-Expression and Self-Destruction

However, while we can see some aspects of freedom in Macbeth's and Hamlet's dealings with supernatural characters, some aspects of self-reflection are still left unexplored, and the element of subjective depth is also left unaccounted for. Hegel contends that "if these one-sided characters . . . are to interest us not only superficially but profoundly, we must . . . see in them that this restrictedness of their personality is . . . an entanglement of their peculiar restricted character with a deeper inner life" (*LFA*, 585).[30] Throughout his discussions of heroes like Hamlet, one can also catch the tone of admiration when he describes them as deep but firm and untouched hearts.[31] In this final section, I argue that the poetic self-expression and eventual self-destruction of Shakespeare's tragic heroes are two additional displays of early modern subjectivity.

Through the hero's use of simile, we see both their heroic strength and the greatest "depth and wealth of spirit" (*LFA*, 585). The poetic self-expression of Shakespeare's characters is engendered by and reveals their subjective creative world, presenting their inner truths to themselves and to the audience in a way more concrete and more truly human than characters of lesser (in Hegel's opinion) modern playwrights or than any ancient characters. According to Hegel, Shakespeare equips his characters with a "wealth of poetry" and "actually gives them spirit and imagination" (*LFA*, 1227–28). It is through the artist's imagination that the characters themselves have imagination and thus exhibit freedom. Yet for Hegel art is not merely the artist's self-expression; it is the larger truth of spirit at that moment of its historical progress. Spirit in early modernity is subjectively free but still pushing forward, searching for reconciliation or reunification with the substantial that it had been unreflectively aligned with in ancient Greek life. Macbeth exists in an ambiguous state of remaining tethered—not weighed down in shackles but hovering above himself in "beautiful and tranquil peace" (*LFA*, 417).

By objectifying their ideas and spirit in simile, these characters can *know* their freedom—and such knowledge is a necessary part of true freedom for Hegel. Macbeth "tries by comparisons to free himself from his immediate unity and makes the liberation actual and obvious by showing that he is still capable of making similes" (*LFA*, 419).[32] In his poetic self-expression, with the similes he creates, Macbeth can see and hear his own desires externalized, similar to how he sees himself in the ghosts and witches—a form of self-objectification. The hero sees her own freedom *in* her creative act, once it is actualized, so that these heroes develop themselves through creative and aesthetic means. When Hegel says that Shakespeare's characters are "free artists of their own selves," I take him to be referring to the type of tragic hero that Macbeth is—self-same, yet self-actualizing and self-creative (*LFA*, 1228). What was implicit in them, they freely and creatively express and make explicit, which is a positive display of freedom that the audience witnesses. We see them as the free poets and artists they truly are, who "manifest to us the nobility of their disposition and the might of their mind" (*LFA*, 418).

Although the formal characteristics of heroes like Macbeth (described earlier) also end up leading to their demise, I posit that their self-destruction displays an aspect of their freedom and that it is also related to their use of simile. Because these heroes are so firm, they eventually break; fulfilling their personal aims at all costs eventually costs them their lives.[33] Macbeth puts such a concentrated effort into obtaining his goal that in accomplishing it, he simultaneously brings about his own downfall. He is so fixated on his aim that he *becomes* his aim at all costs; his one-sided fixation on his freely chosen subjective aim blinds and prevents him from changing his course of action. The determinate aim that Macbeth keeps in front of him is one that he draws from within himself and one that he also realizes objectively; thus his goals, actions, and very character are all self-determined and, finally, bring about a self-imposed ruin (*LFA*, 1199, 1230).

In this way, the subjective freedom of these early modern heroes is displayed in their self-destruction. It is not always the case that the tragic hero dies, but they often do—and if not, the one-sidedness of all tragic heroes ends up fundamentally destroying their lives. Further, while is it rarely the case that the hero commits suicide, in Hegel's theory the modern hero's death is *always* a self-destruction in some way. To maintain their heroic stature and legacy, Hegel's theory requires that heroes be responsible for their own death rather than being victims. Even what seems an accidental switching of swords is not the ultimate cause of Hamlet's death; in Hegel's view it lay in Hamlet's mind from the start (*LFA*, 1231).

In Macbeth's case, death is one form of self-development for this character type. He cannot reconcile his purely subjective aims with the objective world he has set himself against—the same world in which he must realize those aims. Due to his fixity, the only way to move beyond this contradiction is to die; the development of his purely subjective aim combined with his formal freedom necessarily results in self-destruction. What makes him who he is also destroys him. Hegel describes this tragic reconciliation as being possible most often through the death of the hero, and in this sense, death can be described as an affirmative move.[34]

In a discussion of the "greatness of spirit" in Shakespeare's characters, Hegel quotes Macbeth's sound and fury speech, "when his hour has struck" (*LFA*, 420; *Macbeth* V.v, 25–30). Here, the connection between his poetic self-expression and his self-destruction most fully comes to light. When expressing themselves in simile, Shakespeare's characters compare themselves to something other than what they are, exhibiting their ability to imagine themselves differently and the possibility to change.[35] Macbeth's use of simile shows his awareness that death is a way of being something other. In this way, simile also points to freedom, albeit as death.

IN CONCLUSION, then, Hegel views Shakespearean heroes as self-contradictions because early modernity itself engenders ambiguous and contradictory positions (*LFA*, 240). I posit that this is for Hegel the essence of early modern tragic heroes: a combination of, on the one hand, a particular brand of early modern subjective freedom—self-determination not tied to anything external—and, on the other, a tragically fixated character. In his contradictory blend of fixity and freedom, Macbeth is ambiguous, located somewhere between ancient plasticity and truly free late modern subjectivity. It is only the tragic action itself—Macbeth's own activity—that opens the possibility for Macbeth's reflective thought. Shakespeare can only give us a tragic character that *must* act according to her passion, a passion that she just *is* but at the same time reaches beyond. Thus, in Hegel's reading, what Shakespeare's tragedy leaves us with is the tragic vision of a radically free subject pursuing her personal aims at all costs, yet hinting at the possibility of change as her freedom and creativity point toward the future.[36]

Notes

1. See, for example, Julian Young, *The Philosophy of Tragedy: From Plato to Žižek* (New York: Cambridge University Press, 2013), 110–138; Mark W. Roche, "Introduction to Hegel's Theory of Tragedy," *PhaenEx* 1 (Fall-Winter 2006); Mark W. Roche, "The Greatness and Limits of Hegel's Theory of Tragedy," in *A Companion to Tragedy*, ed. Rebecca Bushnell (Oxford: Blackwell, 2005), 51–67 (the two articles by Roche are very similar); A. C. Bradley, "Hegel's Theory of Tragedy," in *Oxford Lectures on Poetry* (New Delhi: Atlantic, 1999). One notable exception to this trend is Stephen Houlgate: see Houlgate, "Hegel's Theory of Tragedy," in *Hegel and the Arts*, ed. Stephen Houlgate (Evanston, IL: Northwestern University Press, 2007), 146–78; and Houlgate, "Hegel and Nietzsche on Tragedy," in *Hegel, Nietzsche and the Criticism of Metaphysics* (Cambridge: Cambridge University Press, 1986). Another exception is Leonard Moss, "The Unrecognized Influence of Hegel's Theory of Tragedy," *The Journal of Aesthetics and Art Criticism* 28 (1969): 91–97 (unfortunately, this article itself seems to have gone unrecognized in the literature on Hegel's theory of tragedy).

2. I will be using the following abbreviations for Hegel's works cited (all quotes retain original emphasis and capitalization unless otherwise noted). *EL*: G. W. F. Hegel, *The Encyclopedia Logic: Part I of the Encyclopedia of Philosophical Sciences with the Zusätze*, trans. T. F. Geraets, W. A. Suchting, and H. S. Harris (Indianapolis: Hackett, 1991). *EM*: G. W. F. Hegel, *Hegel's Philosophy of Mind: Part Three of the "Encyclopaedia of the Philosophical Sciences" (1830)*, trans. William Wallace and Arnold V. Miller (Oxford: Clarendon, 1971). *ETW*: G. W. F. Hegel, "The Spirit of Christianity and its Fate," in *Early Theological Writings, with an Introduction & Fragments*, trans. T. M. Knox and Richard Kroner (Philadelphia: University of Pennsylvania Press, 1971). *LFA*: G. W. F. Hegel, *Hegel's Aesthetics: Lectures on Fine Art*, trans. T. M. Knox, 2 vols. (Oxford: Oxford University Press, 1975). *LHP*: G. W. F. Hegel, *Lectures on the History of Philosophy, The Lectures of 1825-1826: Medieval and Modern Philosophy*, ed. Robert F. Brown, trans. R. F. Brown, J. M. Stewart, with the assistance of H. S. Harris, vol. 3 (Berkeley:

University of California Press, 1990). *LPH*: G. W. F. Hegel, *The Philosophy of History*, trans. J. Sibree (New York: Dover, 1956). *PR*: G. W. F. Hegel, *Hegel's Philosophy of Right*, trans. T. M. Knox (London: Oxford University Press, 1967).

3. That is, while ancient individuals could willfully or freely act, they still took direction from what was given to them by things such as their social roles, disposition, or oracular divination—even the gods are at the mercy of the fates (*LPH*, 249–50). They are immediately connected to their roles and lack the ability to see themselves as separate from them (*LFA*, 436–37). See William Allan, "Tragedy and the Early Greek Philosophical Tradition," in *A Companion to Greek Tragedy*, ed. Justina Gregory (Malden, MA: Blackwell, 2005), 71–82.

4. For accounts of ancient individuality and the emergence of modern subjectivity see: Allegra de Laurentiis, *Subjects in the Ancient and Modern World: On Hegel's Theory of Subjectivity* (New York: Palgrave Macmillan, 2005); David James, *Hegel's Philosophy of Right: Subjectivity and Ethical Life* (London: Continuum, 2007); Terry Pinkard, *Hegel's Phenomenology: The Sociality of Reason* (Cambridge: Cambridge University Press, 2005); David Carlson, *Hegel's Theory of the Subject* (New York: Palgrave Macmillan, 2005); and Robert B. Pippin, *Hegel's Idealism: The Satisfactions of Self-Consciousness* (Cambridge: Cambridge University Press, 1989).

5. Robert Pippin explores this idea of art's content becoming historically increasingly self-reflective and self-conscious as it relates to abstract painting, arguing that Hegel's theory shows it to be a logical culmination of the self-consciousness of painting and of modern subjectivity, in his "What Was Abstract Art? (From the Point of View of Hegel)," *Critical Inquiry* 29 (2001): 1–24. Pippin also explores this idea in relation to literature in "The Absence of Aesthetics in Hegel's Aesthetics," in *The Cambridge Companion to Hegel and Nineteenth-Century Philosophy*, ed. Frederick C. Beiser (Cambridge: Cambridge University Press, 2008), 394–418. Pippin looks more broadly at modern painting in Robert B. Pippin, *After the Beautiful: Hegel and the Philosophy of Pictorial Modernism* (Chicago: University of Chicago Press, 2014).

6. When God appears before us as human and in his death, resurrection, and ascension, the true essence of both God and humanity is revealed. God's human manifestation shows humans to be spiritual and infinite, not merely natural but also divine. His resurrection and ascension show him to be limitless, beyond the ancient Greek gods whose highest phases are merely material manifestations in products of the imagination, and not as truly human or pure spirit (*LFA*, 521; *LPH*, 249–50, 456; *LHP*, 17–18; *EM*, §564; *EL*, §147A).

7. For a relevant discussion of connections between Hegel's readings of Descartes and of *Hamlet*, see Kristin Gjesdal, "Reading Shakespeare, Reading Modernity," *Angelaki* 9 (2004): 17–31, esp. 18–21.

8. Paul Kottman makes a case for how Shakespeare's *Romeo and Juliet* presents a struggle for individual freedom and self-realization for each Romeo and

Juliet, via Hegel's *Phenomenology of Spirit*; see Paul A. Kottman, "Defying the Stars: Tragic Love as the Struggle for Freedom in Romeo and Juliet," *Shakespeare Quarterly* 63 (2012): 1–38. For my take on Sophocles's Oedipus, see "Hegel on Sophocles' *Oedipus the King* and the Moral Accountability of Ancient Tragic Heroes," *Hegel Bulletin* (Cambridge: Cambridge University Press, 2018).

9. See note 1.

10. In addition to those mentioned in note 1, see Gjesdal, "Reading Shakespeare, Reading Modernity"; and Lydia Moland, "An Unrelieved Heart: Hegel, Tragedy, and Schiller's *Wallenstein*," *New German Critique* 38 (2011): 1–23.

11. For example, A. W. Schlegel blames Hamlet's inaction on too much reflection, and in Goethe's *Wilhelm Meisters Lehrjahre* he is a Werther-like noble but weak soul, an image Freud helped perpetuate. See A. W. Schlegel, *A Course of Lectures on Dramatic Art and Literature*, trans. John Black and A. J. W. Morrison (London: George Bell and Sons, 1846); J. W. von Goethe, *Wilhelm Meisters Lehrjahre* in *Goethe: The Collected Works*, ed. Eric Blackall, vol. 9 (Princeton, NJ: Princeton University Press, 1995); and Sigmund Freud, *The Interpretation of Dreams*, trans. James Strachey (New York: Avon, 1965), 298. Also see Moland, "An Unrelieved Heart," 9; and Gjesdal, "Reading Shakespeare, Reading Modernity."

12. Here, Hegel immediately continues: "The Ideal consists in this, that the Idea is *actual*, and to this actuality man belongs as subject and therefore as a firm unity in himself" (*LFA*, 244).

13. What the tragic hero "has, does, and accomplishes, he draws immediately ... from his own specific nature," and, Hegel says, "Shakespeare's characters especially are of this kind" (*LFA*, 577).

14. This may have interesting implications for Hegel's reading of Sophocles' *Oedipus the King*: if there is no character development in ancient heroes, and Oedipus remains the same from start to end, then perhaps his act of literal self-blinding is an intensification of his inner blindness, and he never was the seer he claimed to be (and was famed for being); certainly this makes sense when he was so blind and deaf to the truth all along, taking quite some time to truly know himself.

15. This character development follows the pattern of conceptual development from implicit to explicit, which could be seen as the basis of all of Hegel's philosophy. For Hegel, the concept is the principle of reality, which unfolds in every aspect of life—in pure thought, in nature, and in all aspects of human activity—as it develops itself from its implicit to explicit truth.

16. Hegel states that "the achievement of the action is *eo ipso* a further development of the individual in his subjective inner life and not merely the march of events" (*LFA*, 579).

17. Thus, for example, it took post-Cartesian philosophy to eventually complete what Descartes started, such as mediating the alienating subject-object divide he opened (*LPH* ,440). See also *LHP*, 131–151, 272.

18. See, for example: *PR*, §140R; *LFA*, 243; and his criticism of Tieck and the Schlegel brothers, not just for their use of irony but also for their own personal self-centeredness at *LFA*, 1175.

19. Before *Macbeth* was written, King James had published his own well-known account of witchcraft, *Daemonologie* (indeed, it was published before his version of the Bible appeared), so Shakespeare was most likely aware of it, although whether he read it or not is unknown to me.

20. For Hegel on witches, see *LPH*, 426–27.

21. Simon Williams, *Shakespeare on the German Stage, 1586–1914*, vol. 1 (Cambridge: Cambridge University Press, 2004), 95. See pp. 94–100 for the discussion of Schiller and Goethe's *Macbeth*.

22. Williams, *Shakespeare on the German Stage*, 96.

23. However, in Schiller's *Wilhelm Tell*, Hegel allows for Attinghausen's prophecy because he is on the brink of death and thus, I presume, closer to the spiritual world (*LFA*, 243).

24. Jennifer Ann Bates has also argued that in Hegel's reading, the witches are not responsible for Macbeth's actions; she also points to the ambiguities and problematic nature of Macbeth's self-determination and self-reflection. However, in contrast to my argument and against what I argue is Hegel's view, she posits that Macbeth is not free and is not operating as a modern agent but as a premodern one. See Jennifer Ann Bates, *Hegel and Shakespeare on Moral Imagination* (Albany: State University of New York Press, 2011), see esp. 201–221.

25. This point is also made in a different context by Robert Williams in *Tragedy, Recognition, and the Death of God: Studies in Hegel and Nietzsche* (Oxford: Oxford University Press, 2012), 122, where he also refers to the same passage of Hegel's *ETW*.

26. Hegel also says that in killing Banquo, Macbeth really injures himself because "the destruction of life is not . . . the nullification of life, but its diremption, . . . transforming life into an enemy" (*ETW*, 229). This is what Hegel means by the "equality between the injured, apparently alien life and the trespasser's own" (*ETW*, 229–30).

27. In this light, one could speculate about why Gertrude cannot (or refuses to) see the ghost in *Hamlet* III, iv: Perhaps she refuses to see the truth, or perhaps, as an early modern figure, she is unable to—whether she refuses to admit she is also a guilty party in the murder is a question left open, just as Shakespeare leaves it ambiguous at the end of Act I whether Marcellus and Horatio hear the ghost telling them to swear. These are all instances in tragedy of the ambiguity of early modernity.

28. The "responsibility for oneself alone and the greater subjective independence thus gained is . . . only the abstract independence of the person" (*LFA*, 189).

29. "True independence consists solely in the unity and interpenetration of individuality and universality" (*LFA*, 180).

30. Shakespeare's characters are "men of free imaginative power and gifted spirit, since their reflection rises above and lifts them above what they are in their situation and specific ends" (*LFA*, 585).

31. A hero such as Hamlet is one who "grasps with deep feeling the substance of existing circumstances" but is "not complicated by the whole concatenation of particular interests, concerns, and finite ends," nor "distracted by ordinary emotions or by the seriousness and sympathies ordinarily involved" (*LFA*, 581).

32. The context of the following passage indicates that Hegel is referring to Shakespeare's dramatic works, and I quote it at length because it is extremely helpful in understanding how simile operates as an artistic means of presenting early modern subjectivity: "[S]imiles have the aim of showing that the individual has not merely immersed himself directly in his specific situation, feeling, or passion, but that as a high and noble being he is superior to them and can cut himself free from them. Passion restricts and chains the soul within.... But greatness of mind, force of spirit, lifts itself above such restrictedness and, in beautiful and tranquil peace, hovers above the specific 'pathos' by which it is moved. This liberation of soul is what similes express.... It is only a profound composedness and strength of soul which is able to objectify even its grief and its sorrows, to compare itself with something else, and therefore to contemplate itself *theoretically* in strange things confronting it; ... it is the *dramatis personae* who appear as themselves the poets and artists, since they make their inner life an object to themselves, an object which they remain powerful enough to shape and form and thus to manifest to us the nobility of their disposition and the might of their mind" (*LFA*, 417–18).

33. "[T]he more idiosyncratic the character is which fixedly considers itself alone and which therefore is easily on the verge of evil, the more has the individual not only to maintain himself in concrete reality against the hindrances standing in his way and blocking the realization of himself, but the more he is also driven to his downfall through this very realization. In other words, because he succeeds, he is met by the fate proceeding from his own determinate character, i.e. by a self-prepared destruction" (*LFA*, 579).

34. As Hegel puts it: "[D]eath is only a perishing of the *natural* soul and *finite* subjectivity, a perishing (related negatively only to the inherently negative) which cancels nullity and thereby is the means of liberating the spirit from its finitude and disunion as well as spiritually reconciling the individual person with the Absolute" (*LFA*, 523).

35. Shakespeare "lifts especially his criminal characters above their evil passion by endowing them with a greatness of spirit alike in crime and in misfortune.... [H]e gives them this force of imagination which enables them to see themselves not just as themselves but as another shape strange to them" (*LFA*, 420).

36. My gratitude to Kristin Gjesdal for her generous feedback on multiple early versions of this essay. Many thanks to Wes Furlotte, Fiacha Heneghan, Eric v.d. Luft, Lydia Moland, Jason Yonover, and others for their insightful comments at the 2018 Hegel Society of America Biennial Conference. Thank you to Lydia Moland also for the invitation to present a version of this chapter at Colby College in the fall of 2018, where I enjoyed everyone's comments, especially those of the colloquium senior commentators. Thanks to Susan Feagin, Espen Hammer, and Paul Kottman for comments on earlier stages of this chapter.

II
Comedy

Chapter Seven

Taking the Ladder Down

Hegel on Comedy and Religious Experience

Peter Wake

The comic comes into being just when society and the individual, freed from the worry of self-preservation, begin to regard themselves as works of art.—BERGSON[1]

THE RELATION BETWEEN COMEDY AND PHILOSOPHY is undoubtedly an ancient one, but whether it can be reduced to a quarrel is less evident. What I will consider here from this long history is the role that Aristophanic comedy plays in the "Religion" section of Hegel's *Phenomenology of Spirit*.[2] Hegel considers both ancient Greek tragedy and Old Comedy as moments in the development of religious experience, and what is of particular interest is that within this specific context ancient comedy is, for Hegel, the logical fulfillment of tragedy.[3] Comedy is also the final form of what Hegel calls "art religion," and its limitations as a form of religious consciousness necessitate the further development toward "revealed religion," of which Christianity is the exemplar. My focus on this section of the *Phenomenology* is motivated by two related questions: Why, for Hegel, must the path from ancient Greek tragic religious consciousness to "revealed religion" pass through comedy? What does Hegel's account of comedy as a moment in the dialectic of religious experience reveal about the broader philosophical significance of comedy, as well as the relation between comedy and philosophy itself? I will enlist the work of Bergson to help clarify the contributions and implications of Hegel's thinking on comedy. Alongside these philosophical studies,

I would also like to consider—albeit to a far lesser degree—the comedian's reaction to philosophy. Hegel introduces Aristophanic comedy in the "Religion" section of the *Phenomenology* in conjunction with Socrates, and, as is well known, the comedian and the philosopher reflect on each other.[4] Aristophanes writes Socrates into his comedy, and Plato returns the favor in the *Symposium*, each incorporating the other according to the logic and conventions of his own "genre."

Aristophanes and Socrates

I begin with a joke at the expense of philosophers not least because it is self-directed:

> How can you tell a philosopher enjoys talking with you? He looks at your shoes instead of his own.

The target of the joke is not, of course, a philosophical thought but rather the physical gaze of a philosopher—and not just any gaze, but a misdirected one. It is trained downward when it ought to be directed upward, toward the sky, searching for the immortal forms that nourish the soul, the forms that Plato describes in the *Phaedrus* as inhabiting a place beyond Olympus, "outside heaven."[5] This upward gaze has itself been the mainstay of laughter directed at the philosopher since the origin of the Greek philosophical tradition itself. In *Theaetetus*, Socrates draws attention to the absentmindedness of philosophers: "The philosopher does not hold himself aloof from these [worldly] matters [politics, law courts, etc.] in order to get a reputation, but because it is in reality only his body that lives and sleeps in the city. His mind, having come to the conclusion that all these things are of little or no account, spurns them and pursues its winged ways, as Pindar says, throughout the universe" (*Theaetetus* 173e). Socrates then offers an illustration of the danger of this focus on the heavenly at the expense of what is nearest at hand: "They say Thales was studying the stars . . . and gazing aloft, when he fell into a well; and a witty and amusing Thracian servant-girl made fun of him because, she said, he was wild to know about what was up in the sky but failed to see what was in front of him and under his feet" (*Theaetetus* 174a).[6] Socrates makes a point of showing that he knows how and why people react to him in the way that they do. Beyond his notoriously ugly visage, why does the majority find him funny? He puts it bluntly as "partly for the philosopher's superior manner, and partly for his constant ignorance and lack of resource in dealing with the obvious" (*Theaetetus* 175b). Socrates knows that others find him comical and he knows why; in a similar way, he makes it perfectly clear in the *Apology* that he knows why his self-defense will fail to persuade a majority of the jury of his innocence. Socrates knows his philosophical discourse will lead to both laughter and a guilty verdict, and yet he continues.[7]

In the *Apology*, Socrates mentions Aristophanes by name and acknowledges the connection between comedy and his execution explicitly (*Apology* 19c). At the outset of his self-defense, he makes the point that he is not overly concerned about confronting the explicit charges brought against him by Meletus, but he is skeptical about the possibility of circumventing the implicit accusations that have been circulating about him for years, namely that he is guilty of studying things in the sky and below the earth, making the weaker argument appear the strongest and teaching these things to others (*Apology* 19b). In the *Clouds*, Aristophanes has Strepsiades say the following to his son, Pheidippides, as he points out Socrates's school:

STREPSIADES: That, my boy, is the house of clever souls, the "Thinkery" [*phrontistērion*].

> The men who live there are able to talk us into believing
> that the universe is a casserole dish that covers us all
> and that we are the hot coals, nestling inside.
> What's more, for a small fee, these gentlemen will teach you
> how to successfully argue any case, right or wrong. [...]

PHEIDIPPIDES: Ughh! I know who you mean, that godforsaken bunch of pasty looking

> frauds, going around barefoot!
> You're talking about Socrates and Chaerephon![8]

Aristophanes portrays Socrates as guilty of both these implicit charges and the explicit charges raised some twenty-two years after the play was first performed:[9] Pheidippides eventually enrolls in Socrates's Thinkery and learns how to argue against the existence of Zeus and justify beating his own father. Hegel's view of this portrayal was that Aristophanes subjected Socrates to legitimate criticisms;[10] he defends the playwright by arguing that his exaggerations in the *Clouds* harbor a clear-eyed understanding of the dangers inherent in Socrates's enterprise of (i) uprooting the established Greek absolute and (ii) grounding truth "on the judgement of inward consciousness."[11] In light of this, we might be tempted to portray the relation between comedy and philosophy as simply antagonistic. Aristophanes lampoons Socrates, leaving the fateful image of a natural philosopher and sophist in the minds of his audience. Plato, for his part, includes Aristophanes in the *Symposium*, giving him a truly extraordinary speech, and yet one could certainly see this gift in light of Nietzsche's claim that "mercy remains the privilege of the most powerful."[12] Despite the excellence of Aristophanes's contribution, it is surpassed by Socrates's own account of eros. As a creator of mimetic works, the comedian is put in his place by philosophy, as the tragic poets are relegated to their proper place outside the city walls at the conclusion of the *Republic*.[13]

This antagonistic reading of the relation between comedy and philosophy is bolstered by the undeniable affiliation between laughter and enmity. A Greek proverb passed on by Sophocles reads, "To laugh at the enemy is the sweetest of laughter."[14] Comedy is a weapon to wield against one's enemies and harsh medicine to administer against the shortcomings of one's friends. Laughter paves the way for the execution of Socrates; it is implied in the mock praise of Jesus as "King of the Jews" (Matt. 27:27–31), as well as in the scorn he is subjected to by the crowd witnessing his crucifixion (Matt. 27:44).[15] In contemporary jargon, a stand-up comedian who has her audience in stitches would say of her performance, "I killed." Monty Python captures this affiliation well in a skit built on the premise of a joke so good that anyone who hears it dies of laughter.

While this piercing edge of laughter is undeniable, to find in it cruelty alone would be to overlook the levity, even joy, that is a part of the phenomenology of comedy. Hegel, for his part, makes a clear distinction between comedy and laughter.[16] Comedy may make us burst out laughing, but everything that makes us laugh does not warrant the designation "comedy." The comic implies "an infinite light-heartedness and confidence felt by someone raised altogether above his own inner contradiction and not bitter or miserable in it at all: this is the bliss and ease of a man who, being sure of himself, can bear the frustration of his aims and achievements" (A 2:1200). Comedy proper appears to somehow sidestep the destructive nature of the laughter provoked by satire, follies, ridicule, senselessness, derision, and scorn.[17] And while the agonistic interpretation of the relation between the philosopher and comedian is certainly understandable, it is not the only one. According to Plutarch, Socrates responded to his portrayal in the *Clouds* by claiming, "I feel that I am being made fun of by friends at a great party."[18] It has also been reported that after the performance of the *Clouds*, when the mask-makers were being applauded, Socrates stood up when his double appeared on stage so everyone could compare the imitation and the original.[19] Regardless of whether these stories are apocryphal, they do indicate a fuller conception of the relation between comedy and philosophy, one that points in the direction of (i) Hegel's own idea of comedy, (ii) his incorporation of the comedic within his system, and (iii) his conception of the comic negation found in Aristophanes's treatment of his subjects, Socrates included.

Hegel and the Temporary "Triumph" of Comedy over Tragedy.

In the *Phenomenology*, Hegel locates a distinctly comic consciousness in the dialectic of religious experience at a point where a strict division between art, religion, and philosophy had yet to be rigorously drawn. As previously mentioned, it arises as the final moment of the "spiritual work of art," the third and final category of Greek "art religion." What we today might call the three *genres* of Greek poetry—epic, tragedy, and comedy—were, in effect, the repository of Greek practical wisdom; they constituted the fundamental ways in which the community reflected upon the union of the human and the divine.[20] In what way is comedy called forth by the limitations inherent in the tragic form of religious consciousness, and, further, how does it mark the completion of "art religion" as a whole?

Before turning to comedy, we must first consider the way tragedy sets the stage for it. And before we get to tragedy, some brief remarks about epic poetry:

(i) *Epic*. For Hegel, Homeric epics as a religious phenomenon drew together the distinct and often warring poleis of the Greek world.[21] Thus, what unites a people as a people in this case is neither blood nor a common language but a narrative of how they came to be a people in the first place. The rhapsode's retelling of *The Illiad* works to construct the Greeks as Greeks and not merely Athenian, Thebans, Spartans, and so on. Recounting their shared history of joining together to fight an external enemy serves to unite the Greeks in the present.

(ii) *Tragedy*. Tragedies make use of the same raw material as epic poetry: they bring on stage figures and events from the Heroic Age and in this way maintain the role of providing a common point of reference. As Hegel writes in an unpublished fragment from his Bern period, "The Athenian citizen whose poverty deprived him of the chance to vote in public assembly, or who even had to sell himself as a slave, still knew as well as Pericles and Alcibiades who Agamemnon and Oedipus were when Sophocles or Euripides brought them on the stage."[22] Instead of the sprawling account of the Trojan War and its aftermath, the more condensed action of the tragedies is the mythopoetic means of presenting and reflecting upon the current contradictions that confront the ethical life of the poet's own polis. Thus, for Hegel, Sophocles's *Antigone* portrays a conflict between the different ethical demands of the family and state, and these demands are fully embodied in the dramatis personae of the play. As intermediaries between fully formed modern literary "characters" and mere abstractions, Antigone and Creon "simply are what they are" (see A 2:1209). They exist without inner conflict and act without hesitation from their animating pathos. As described in the *Aesthetics*, pathos must be distinguished from mere passion, which has the connotations of something "trifling and low," reflecting mere "subjective caprice." Pathos, by contrast, is "an inherently justified power over the heart, an essential content of rationality and freedom of will" (A 1:232–33). As a motive for action, it is "wholly deliberate," but this is not a form of deliberation that results from the protracted reflection associated with "conscience," for this kind of "extreme inwardness" had not yet found a place in the Greek world (A 1:458). Instead the pathos motivating Antigone to act *is itself* the presence of the Divine. Hegel makes the point that "it is both right and wrong to interpret the gods in general as always either purely external to man or purely powers dwelling in him. For they are both" (A 1:228). That is to say, the pathos that drives the action of ancient dramas is evoked by ethical substance—the institutions of the family and state that were conceived of as the divine actualized in the world.[23] These substantial determinants of the will are necessarily limited; Hegel provides some examples: "the fortune and misfortune of love, fame, honour, heroism, friendship, maternal love, love of children, of spouses, etc." (A 1:234). As such, pathos forms "the proper center, the true domain of art." True pathos moves both the tragic hero and the audience, then and now, because "in and for itself it is the mighty power in human existence." It is, as he writes, something that "resounds in every human breast" (A 1:232).

The ancient Greek tragic heroes act out of an unwavering certainty grounded in *pathos* (A 2:1214). Conflict is not internal but external:

insofar as both of the demands embodied by Creon and Antigone have ethical value (and for Hegel they do), their conflict is a clash of rights (Creon cannot but impose a prohibition against burying enemies of the state; Antigone cannot but bury her brother). They are both justified in their actions; and because of the one-sidedness of their animating pathos, they are equally unjustified (see A 2:1214). The necessary reconciliation for the audience between their conflicting positions typically takes place in exile, death, or the renunciation of the character's original one-sided aim (A 2:1217–18; PS 448).[24] Hegel stresses, however, that a successful tragedy reestablishes the unity and harmony of the entire ethical order in the face of the conflict between ethical powers. Tragedy ends, as Hegel writes, by establishing in the audience an "absolutely reconciled and cheerful heart" (A 2:1220).

Grasped *theologically*, this conflict was an expression of the clash between the older, chthonic gods—the Furies—who were associated with the family and the underworld, and the serene Olympian gods, who protected the political order and represented, among other things, an inchoate form of self-conscious reason (see PS 447–48). Considered on their own, these Olympian gods are not the stuff of tragic conflict. For Hegel, the unity of the divine nature is of the essence of the "blessed gods": any apparent opposition stemming from their individuated human form is not serious and can be dissolved with irony directed at the poetic license assumed in their representation (A 2:1074, 1210). In themselves, the Olympian gods manifest "free perfect beauty" (A 1:485), and while our modern sensibilities might lead us to condemn their loftiness and apparent frigidity, Hegel locates in their austere repose a "warmth and life [following from] an indifference to the transient" (A 1:485). When, however, we grasp the tragedies from the perspective of the dialectic of religious experience in the *Phenomenology*, they reflect the emergence of *fate* as a force of necessity into which the traditional Greek gods are subsumed. In the *Aesthetics*, Hegel is quick to point out that he does not think of tragic fate as blind, in the sense of "irrational." Although it falls short of self-conscious Providence, fate *is* rational, for it punishes those who are driven to overstep their proper authority. Indeed, Hegel equates the absolute power of fate with eternal justice (A 2:1230). The crowds leaving the theater in Greece do so with a reconciled and cheerful heart precisely because, as Hegel understands it, justice has been reestablished. And yet, as he writes in the *Phenomenology* apropos the religious experience of tragedy, we see that "Fate completes the depopulation of Heaven" (*PS* 449).[25]

The religious significance of the Greek tragedies in this regard is that they foretell the dissolution of Greek religious beliefs and practices. Hegel points to the inevitable demise of the Olympians in the *Aesthetics* as well. Despite their "lofty freedom and spiritual peace," he notes "the breath and air of affliction that gifted men have felt in ancient pictures of the gods even in their consummate beauty and loveliness" (*A* 1:484–85). "The blessed gods mourn as it were over their blessedness or their bodily form": they mourn the fate that will manifest itself as the contradiction between their spirituality and sensuous existence and their loftiness and particularity (*A* 1:485). This renunciation of the earthly and evanescent coupled with the particularity of their bodily form contains within it the contradiction that classical art will be unable to overcome.

(iii) *Comedy*. Hegel speaks of comedy at times as the *opposite* of tragedy (see, e.g., *A* 2:1220). We might consider in this regard Aristotle's distinction between the heroes of tragedy who are better than us (although not so much better that we fail to identify with them) and comic characters who are baser than us (although not wholly vicious).[26] And yet despite the ways in which the two can be set in opposition, a dialectical approach invites us to witness how both tragedy and comedy reflect upon the same situation. We see this most clearly in gallows humor. When, for example, in the *Phaedo* Socrates states that the aim of philosophy is the practice of death and dying, Simmias cannot help but laugh, even though he was in no mood to do so: "I think the majority, on hearing this, will think that it describes the philosophers very well, and our people in Thebes would thoroughly agree that philosophers are nearly dead and that the majority of men is well aware that they deserve to be" (*Phaedo* 64b).[27] Comedy's proximity to tragedy can intensify its comic effect. Apropos the dialectic of religious consciousness, Aristophanic comedy offers another means of contemplating the flight of the Greek gods. As such, it is something of the flip side of the same phenomenon that tragedy reveals:[28] instead of an expression of divine pathos, comedy embodies the experience of *relief* that comes with the *liberation* from an authority to which one once submitted.[29] Beyond this, comic consciousness comes to see itself as the creative source of these divine figures. The masks that the tragic actors wore to hide their identity, in effect, *slip* to reveal the actors themselves.

What is the status of the Furies, the Olympian gods, and all-powerful fate? The phenomenological significance of Greek comic consciousness is that it declares, *We made it all up!* What is thought to be all powerful is not something over and against us but, as Hegel says, "Fate is now united with self-consciousness. The individual self *is* the negative power through which the gods ... vanish" (*PS* 452). Self-conscious individuality in the form of an artistic creator assumes the role previously reserved for fate. Thus, "art religion" comes, finally, to understand its status as art, and the creative power of the artist is acknowledged to be the source of his or her creations.[30]

This explains the levity that Hegel presents as essential to genuine comedy. He writes of Aristophanes in his *Aesthetics*, "If you have not read him, you can scarcely realize how men can take things so easily" (*A* 2:1221; more literally, "You can scarcely realize how men can feel as good as hogs"[31]). That is to say, comic consciousness, in this discreet moment, is characterized by an entirely bearable lightness of being. In Hegel's words, "It is the return of everything universal into the certainty of itself which, in consequence, is this complete loss of fear and the complete loss of essential being on the part of all that is alien. This self-certainty is a state of spiritual well-being and of repose therein, such as is not to be found anywhere outside this Comedy" (*PS* 453). Comic consciousness is buoyed by the realization that what it took to be a foreign necessity was, in truth, a product of its own will, and this is experienced as a being-at-home in a completely *human* world. We might note at this point that Hegel's portrayal of Aristophanic comedy gives credence to Plutarch's account of Socrates and his supposed reaction to the *Clouds*: "I feel that I am being made fun of by friends at a great party." Plutarch used this anecdote as an example of the unflappable character of the wise man, and the assumption is that Socrates was in fact abused by Aristophanes's portrayal of him. Yet we can also see his observation as a sincere reflection of the mood of great comic drama: a disarming honesty, a "frank joviality" (*A* 2:1235).[32]

HEGEL'S ACCOUNT OF COMEDY in the *Phenomenology* as a moment of the dialectic of religious experience can be corroborated and fleshed out when compared with his presentation of comedy in the *Aesthetics*. Here, too, Hegel makes the point that comedy begins where tragedy ends, with, as we have said, "an absolutely reconciled and cheerful heart" (*A* 2:1220). In the

Aesthetics, Hegel defines the comic figure concisely: it is "a personality or subject who makes his own actions contradictory and so brings them to nothing, *while remaining tranquil* [ruhig] *and self-assured in the process*" (A 2:1220, my italics). The comedic, versus the merely laughable, is the union precisely of self-assurance and a certain lack of substance. This is not to say that Old Comedy has no relation to the substantive. Hegel makes the point that, like the tragedies of Aeschylus and Sophocles, Aristophanes focuses intently on the state of morality, art, religion, and politics: "What principally counts in Greek drama, whether tragedy or comedy, is the universal and essential aim which the characters are realizing" (A 2:1206). (The *Clouds*, for example, confronts the threat of sophistry to true philosophy.[33]) Old Comedy addresses the objective and substantive sphere, but unlike tragic heroes, Aristophanes's characters are simply not invested in these higher pursuits. Comedy is populated by those like Strepsiades "with lower views, tied the real world and the present" (A 2:1220–1). Indeed, the comic conceit of the *Clouds* is not based fundamentally on, to use Gilbert Murray's phrase, "any suggested roguery of Socrates," but on the clash of "humors" that arises when Strepsiades, with his lower, quotidian interests, finds himself in a school of "ascetic contemplative students with minds set on mathematics and *ta meteōra* and things not of this world."[34] Any higher, substantive aims are undermined by "subjective caprice, vulgar folly, and absurdity" (A 2:1221); the aims they *are* invested in are not serious (Strepsiades turns to philosophy to avoid his creditors), and yet they pursue them with a self-assurance born of naivety.

This absence of doubt seems to mirror the unwavering certainty that Hegel locates in the tragic heroes, but unlike Oedipus or Antigone, the comic character lacks genuine pathos (see A 2:1221). And yet despite this lack, comic characters "reveal themselves as having *something higher in them*" (A 2:1221, my italics). What is this "something higher"? Hegel explains that it arises from this lack of substance: comic subjects "are not seriously tied to the finite world with which they engage but are raised above it and remain firm in themselves and secure in the face of failure and loss" (A 2:1221). They *hover*—although never very far off the ground. And this reflects the intimation, prefigured in the consciousness of the skeptic, of their dominion over the world. Hegel describes this as an absolute freedom of spirit "utterly consoled in advance in every human undertaking." The comic character resides in a "world of private serenity" (A 2:1221). This, then, is what Aristophanes puts on display: *the self-confidence of an emerging subjectivity that has yet to give substance to itself.* Hegel confirms the role he assigns to comedy as a moment in the phenomenology of religious experience when he writes the following in his *Aesthetics*:

> In comedy there comes before our contemplation, in the laughter in which the character dissolves everything, including themselves, the victory of their own personality which nevertheless persists self-assured. The general ground of comedy is therefore a world in which man as subject or person has made himself completely master of everything that counts to him otherwise as the essence of what he wills and accomplishes, a world whose aims are therefore self-destructive because they are unsubstantial. (A 2:1199)

For whom is the triumph of the insubstantial subject an object of contemplation? For Aristophanes and his audience? In the *Aesthetics*, Hegel describes Aristophanes's intent in the following way, "Long ago Aristophanes conducted a polemic in his early comedies against the domestic affairs of Athens and the Peloponnesian war" (A 2:1180). Aristophanes is no "malignant scoffer"; he is a true patriot, possessing a most gifted mind (A 2:1222). He does not make fun of what is "truly moral in the life of the Athenian, or of their genuine philosophy, true religion faith, and serious art" but rather "the sophistry, the deplorable and lamentable character of tragedy, flighty gossip, litigiousness, etc., and the aberrations of the democracy out of which the old faith and morals has vanished" (A 2:1202). Hegel summarizes Aristophanes's achievement in this way: Aristophanes presents to us the absolute contradiction between

> The true essence of religion and political and ethical life; and the subjective attitude of citizens and individuals who should give actuality to that essence. But in this very triumph of the subjective attitude, whatever its insight, there is implicit one of the greatest symptoms of Greek corruption, and thus these pictures of a naïve fundamental 'all is well with me' [attitude] are the final great outcome of the poetry of this gifted, civilized and ingenious Greek people. (A 2:1222)

Aristophanic comedy presents the often giddy descent to a thoroughly human, finite world, and he lays before his audience this "absolute contradiction" that characterizes it. In terms of its explicit engagements with substantive matters, comedy here is critique. But it goes no further than this. Although it can present this contradiction as an object of contemplation, its critiques—its jokes—do not have the resources, as comic, to show a way forward. The genius of Aristophanes's work is in the portrayal of this contradiction and the aesthetic experience that it creates: a momentary relief and thoroughly immanent, worldly elevation born, as we have seen, of the mindless self-assurance of its comic characters. Whereas Aristophanes rests with this absolute contradiction, we phenomenologists see, retrospectively, in the self-certainty of the individual consciousness and in the "inherently firm personality which is raised in its freedom above the downfall of the whole finite sphere" (*A* 2:1202) an intimation of the subject as the power of the negative (*PS* 452).

Comedy beyond Ancient Comic Drama

Hegel's approach to comedy in the *Phenomenology* has been to unearth the significance of comic consciousness as it emerges at a specific moment in the reconstruction of the experience of religious consciousness. By way of conclusion, I would like to return to the fact that Socrates and Aristophanes arise together, after tragedy, in this reconstruction. What can we extrapolate from this about the "fate" of comedy, beyond Hegel's more narrow concentration on comic drama? And what does this say about comic consciousness as such, about a genuinely comic disposition toward the world? To begin addressing these questions, I will follow the lead of Bergson in his *Laughter: An Essay on the Meaning of the Comic* (1900) and turn to the three observations that he thinks are fundamental for guiding an investigation into the "comic spirit": [35]

"the absence of feeling ... usually accompanies laughter."
"Our laughter is always the laughter of a group."
"the comic does not exist outside the pale of what is strictly *human*."[36]

Let us consider these in the following order:

1. *The detachment of comedy*. Aristophanes and Socrates come on the scene when fate was completing "the depopulation of Heaven," and they both respond to this with detachment. The mimetic spell is broken. Nowhere is this more evident in Old Comedy than when the chorus addresses the audience directly in the parabases; and Socrates's arguments against mimesis are well known, as is the fact that Plato's presentation of Socrates in the dialogues resides somewhere between art and life.[37] It is precisely this detachment, this emotional disinvestment, this absence of divine pathos, that characterizes comic elevation. Bergson writes, "the comic demands something like a momentary anesthesia of the heart."[38] It demands the

stance of the disinterested observer. Insofar as it is empathy or compassion that is anesthetized, this detachment certainly opens the door to the cruelty that can be expressed through laugher. Yet Hegel's great admiration for Aristophanes's comedy, as we have seen, stems in part from the playwright's ability to convey a sense of levity that undercuts this threat of cruelty. We see, then, a kinship with the stance of the Socratic philosopher: both are invested in the polis while also removed from it. That is to say, comedy shares with philosophy a disinterested, ultimately cognitive relation to itself and the world. Socrates is not overcome by the pathos of tragedy but is known, of course, for detached reflection and ironic distance.[39] And in the same way that this depopulation was, according to Hegel, the condition of the possibility of the frank, self-consciously critical dimension of Aristophanic comedy, it also opens the space for Socrates to replace fate with the practice of philosophy.

2. *The sociality of comedy.* As the moment in "art religion" when art comes to a self-consciousness of itself as art, comedy is for Hegel a vehicle for the collective enterprise of self-reflection and insight that is a unifying trait of the moments of Absolute Spirit. But what can we say about the object of this collective reflection? For Bergson laughter is an inherently social phenomenon: "However spontaneous it seems, laughter always implies a kind of secret freemasonry, or even complicity, with other laughers."[40] His position is that the element in which comedy swims is society; even when we laugh alone, we do so before an imagined audience. He argues further that if society is the element of comedy, its function is a social one. What is this function? He claims that there is always an extra-aesthetic dimension to laughter: beyond laughter for laughter's sake, it always pursues, if unconsciously—and in some instances, immorally—the aim of general improvement. It is pedagogical. As Bergson sees it, life is fluid, mobile, elastic, and filled with tension; when it is rendered inelastic, repetitive, or mechanical it is not as it ought to be. Human beings reduced to a *thing* are, for example, the stuff of comedy, as is the body imposing itself in an elevated context: he writes of a funeral oration where the deceased is described as "virtuous and plump." This distortion of life, this rigidity, is the potential source of the comic and "laughter is its corrective."[41] The laughter that comedy produces is directed toward altering our clumsiness, pomposity, hypocrisies, fixed ideas, and our absentmindedness. Indeed, absentmindedness is, for Bergson, close to the very source of comedy: "How profound is the comic element in the overly-romantic,

Utopian bent of mind!" Captivated by a fixed idea, it runs after its ideal and trips over reality: "child-like dreamers for whom life delights to lie in wait"[42]—Thales falling into a well, Socrates standing immobile for twenty-four hours straight while on a military campaign (*Symposium* 220c–d), and philosophers gazing intently at the shoes of their interlocutors.

3. *The humanity of comedy.* Absentminded "utopians" provoke laughter when their relation to the world around them is seen to be out of joint. This invites a final observation from Bergson, one that points forward to the "fate" of comedy and so the fate of that which unmasks the power of fate: "The comic does not exist outside the pale of what is strictly human."[43] Comedy brings the absentminded back to the surface of the earth—up from the underworld, down from Olympus. Napoleon tells of an interview he had with the Queen of Prussia after the battle of Jena that illustrates the point nicely: Napoleon recounts, "[The Queen] received me in tragic fashion like Chimène: 'Justice! Sire, Justice! Magdeburg!' Thus she continued in a way most embarrassing to me. Finally, to make her change her style, I requested that she take a seat. This is the best method for cutting short a tragic scene, for as soon as you are seated it all becomes comedy." Bergson tells this story because he agrees: "The transition from tragedy to comedy is effected by simply sitting down," thereby coming back down to earth, or at least closer to it.[44] In our ancient Greek example, comedy entails a crowd of Athenians in the theater watching themselves. Aristophanes may bring a God on stage in his mask, as he does with Dionysus in the *Frogs*, but the mask, to quote H. S. Harris, "is transparent; at no time does the character pretend to be anything but an ordinary man, whose like is to be found in every row of the audience."[45]

If, as Bergson claims, laughter is a *corrective*, it corrects here in the context of a phenomenology of religious experience—the belief in an inscrutable, transcendent power of fate—and it corrects or critiques the concomitant denial of human agency that this notion of fate entails. Comedy's element is the social, and this is a strictly human social world. It is the source of the state of spiritual well-being that Hegel attributes to the comic; but it is also the source of its fleeting nature. The well-being or repose that comedy can instill is, qua religious consciousness, temporary. What we see retrospectively is that although comedy liberates consciousness from fate conceived of as an external, alien force, the labor of spirit will be to bring comic consciousness to the full recognition that nothing of substance has been put in its place. That is, spirit must recognize that in sacrificing the infinite on the altar of comedy, it will run up against the proper aim of religious consciousness to unite the finite and infinite. What looms is the full recognition that it is, as Hegel writes near the outset of the "Revealed Religion" section of the *Phenomenology* that

> the consciousness of the loss of all *essential* being in this *certainty of itself*, and of the loss even of this knowledge about itself—the loss of substance as well as of the Self, it is the grief which expresses itself in the hard saying that "God is dead." (*PS* 454–455)

When this occurs, needless to say, the levity of comic consciousness is punctured, and it ceases to be funny. It becomes, instead, unhappy.[46]

If the slip of the actor's mask marks the shift in religious consciousness from tragedy to comedy, then at the end of Greek "art religion," the comic character—Socrates, for example—walks off the stage and joins the crowd, such that the opposition between spectacle and audience collapses. As such, the site of the Greek presentation of the Divine is lost. The labor of spirit will be to reveal the Divine as what walks among us, rather than as what can only appear when placed over and against an audience, on a stage.

Notes

1. Henri Bergson, *Laughter: An Essay on the Meaning of the Comic*, trans. C. Brereton and F. Rothwell (Mineola, NY: Dover, 2005), 10.

2. Aristophanes's plays stand for Hegel at the pinnacle of ancient Greek comedy, and with Cervantes, Ariosto, and especially Shakespeare, the pinnacle of comedy as such. When I refer to ancient comedy I mean the Old Comedy of Aristophanes, unless otherwise stated. See G. W. F. Hegel, *Hegel's Aesthetics: Lectures on Fine Art*, trans. T. M. Knox, 2 vols. (Oxford: Oxford University Press, 1998), 2:1236. And when I refer to Hegel's *Aesthetics*, it is to this volume. Knox has translated the second (1842) edition of H. G. Hotho's three-volume compilation of Hegel's various Berlin lecture series on aesthetics, and the question of where Hegel ends and Hotho begins remains. See Annemarie Gethmann-Siefert, introduction to *Lectures on the Philosophy of Art: The Hotho Transcript of the 1823 Berlin Lectures*, trans. R. F. Brown (Oxford: Clarendon, 2014), 18, n.17. The references I make to the *Aesthetics* are for the most part in the service of showing how the Berlin lecture material on Greek drama corroborates Hegel's account of comedy in the *Phenomenology*. Hegel's *Aesthetics* will be cited in the body of the text as *A*, followed by volume and page number.

3. See G. W. F. Hegel, *Phenomenology of Spirit*, trans. A.V. Miller (Oxford: Oxford University Press, 1977), 450–53. Referred to subsequently in the body of the text as *PS*. Gary Shapiro makes the point that Hegel's reconstruction of Greek art is only apparently chronological; it is rather "a logical sequence of increasingly adequate attempts to realize its purpose"—the purpose of religious consciousness as such. See Gary Shapiro, "Hegel's Dialectic of Artistic Meaning," *Journal of Aesthetics and Art Criticism* 35, no. 1 (1976–1977): 24.

4. In his description of comic consciousness in the *Phenomenology*, Hegel references the concomitant rise of dialectical thinking that is itself a ripe subject of comic drama: "Rational *thinking* frees the divine Being from its contingent shape and, in antithesis to the unthinking wisdom of the Chorus which produces all sorts of ethical maxims and gives currency to a host of laws and specific concepts of duty and of right, lifts these into the simple Ideas of the Beautiful and the Good." See *PS* 451. H. S. Harris argues more pointedly that Socrates is the appropriate hero of comic consciousness at its highest moment. See H. S Harris, *Hegel's Ladder II: The Odyssey of Spirit* (Indianapolis: Hackett, 1997), 638.

5. Plato, *Phaedrus*, in *Plato: Complete Works*, ed. J. M. Cooper (Indianapolis: Hackett, 1997), 247b. All references to Plato are from this volume.

6. This is a revision of an Aesopic fable about an astronomer (*astrologos*) who falls, like Plato's Thales, into a well while gazing at the heavens. See Hans Blumenberg, *The Laughter of the Thracian Woman: A Protohistory of Theory*, trans. S. Hawkins (New York: Bloomsbury, 2015), 5.

7. Michael Naas argues that while Socrates may accept and even invite the ridicule and laughter of those who do not know him, he will not, for example, pander to the jury at his trial for fear of being laughable "in his own eyes or those of anyone who dons the perspective of philosophy." See Michael Naas, "Plato and the Spectacle of Laughter," *Angelaki* 21, no. 3 (2016): 23.

8. Aristophanes, *The Clouds*, trans. P. Meineck (Indianapolis: Hackett, 2000), 9–10.

9. Because of the brutality of the Peloponnesian War and its aftermath—not to mention the cynicism it instilled—Gilbert Murray argues that what was presented in the spirit of "a harmless jest in 423 might easily become deadly denunciation in 399." See *Aristophanes: A Study* (Oxford: Oxford University Press, 1933), 101.

10. "The attacks which Socrates experienced are well known, and were from two sources; Aristophanes attacked him in the *Clouds*, and then he was formally accused before the people." See G. W. F. Hegel, *Lectures on the History of Philosophy*, trans. E. S. Haldane and F. H. Simson, vol. 1 (London: Routledge and Kegan Paul, 1955), 426.

11. Hegel, *Lectures*.

12. Friedrich Nietzsche, *On the Genealogy of Morals and Ecce Homo*, ed. W. Kaufmann (New York: Vintage, 1989), 73.

13. Not only are the tragedians to be exiled from the just republic but the comic poets as well. See the *Republic* 606c.

14. Cited in M. A. Screech, *Laughter at the Foot of the Cross* (London: Allen Lane, 1997), 18, n. 4.

15. Screech argues that these scenes *imply* laughter: Jesus's agony is an object of fun, to be scoffed at (*empaizō*) with the pitiless laughter of children. In the Latin Vulgate, "laughter" is made explicit (*derideo; rideo*—to laugh). See Screech, *Laughter*, 24–27.

16. Comedy, laughter, *and* humor: the latter is, for Hegel, a modern aesthetic invention imported from England in the eighteenth century. See Lydia Moland, "Reconciling Laughter: Hegel on Comedy and Humor," in *All Too Human: Laughter, Humor, and Comedy in the Nineteenth-Century Philosophy*, ed. L. Moland (New York: Springer, 2018), 20.

17. This is Hegel's list, see *A* 2:1200. On the destructive nature of satire, see Stephen C. Law, "Hegel and the Spirit of Comedy: Der Geist der Stets Verneint," in *Hegel and Aesthetics*, ed. William Maker (Albany: State University of New York Press, 2000), 114.

18. Plutarch, *Moralia*, 10c–d. Cited in Ian C. Storey, introduction to *The Clouds* by Aristophanes, trans. P. Meineck (Indianapolis: Hackett, 2000), xl.

19. Moses Hadas, *A History of Greek Literature* (New York: Columbia University Press, 1950), 106.

20. From the *Aesthetics*: art "only fulfils its supreme task when it has placed itself in the same sphere as religion and philosophy, and when it is simply one way of bringing to our minds and expressing the *Divine*, the deepest interests of mankind, and the most comprehensive truths of the spirit. In works of art the nations have deposited their richest inner intuitions and ideas, and art is often the key, and in many nations the sole key, to understanding their philosophy and religion." *A* 2:8.

21. See Harris, *Hegel's Ladder*, 625.

22. G. W. F. Hegel, *The Positivity of the Christian Religion* in *Early Theological Writing*, trans. T. M. Knox (Philadelphia: University of Pennsylvania Press, 1992), 148.

23. See Lydia L. Moland, "'And Why Not?' Hegel, Comedy, and the End of Art," *Verifiche: Rivista Trimestrale di Scienze Umane* 45, nos. 1–2 (2016): 82.

24. While tragic reconciliation typically arises in this way, Hegel does in fact locate a distinct form of *inner* reconciliation in Greek tragedy. This is best represented by Oedipus in *Oedipus Coloneus*: as is the case with all great ancient tragedies, we move from the strife of the ethical powers to the unity of the ethical order as a whole, and yet this is achieved *without* the destruction of Oedipus. Instead, he is able to experience the expunging of the discord that exists within him. This turn toward the subjective satisfaction of Oedipus points us forward to comedy, and to the modern treatment of the subject (see *A* 2:1219).

25. See *PS* 447–49. As Shapiro writes, "Tragedy shows the partiality of the divine powers and their reconciliation through death or absolution, suggesting that only the totality of these powers is real. Conceptually this is the Notion (*Begriff*); artistically, it is Zeus as the sole deity who has shed some of his anthropomorphic traits." See Shapiro, "Hegel's Dialectic of Artistic Meaning," 31.

26. Aristotle, *Poetics*, trans. S. Halliwell, Loeb Classical Library 199 (Cambridge, MA: Harvard University Press, 1995), 1448a17–18, 1149a31.

27. See Naas, "Plato and the Spectacle of Laughter," 16. John Sallis makes the point that "among the dialogues there are few that are richer in comedy than the *Phaedo*." This despite its clear relation to tragedy. See John Sallis, *Transfigurements: On the True Sense of Art* (Chicago: University of Chicago Press, 2008), 146.

28. Flip side or potential outcome: Martin Donougho cites the following line from Hayden White, "Comedy is the form which reflection takes after it has assimilated the truths of Tragedy to itself." See Michael Donougho, "Hegelian Comedy," *Philosophy & Rhetoric* 49, no. 2 (2016): 204.

29. A. C. Bradley writes in "The Rejection of Falstaff" of a "bliss of freedom gained in humor" and a "humorous superiority to everything serious and freedom of soul enjoyed in it." Ann Paolucci finds in his description of Falstaff the distinct echo of Hegel's characterization of the heroes of Aristophanic comedy. See Ann Paolucci, "Hegel's Theory of Comedy," *Comedy: New Perspectives* (New York: New York Literary Forum, 1978), 103.

30. In creating the gods as a means of presenting an "image of pure or perfect self-consciousness," the Greek artist comes to see that "what he was seeking is in fact exemplified in his own activity." See Shapiro, "Hegel's Dialectic of Artistic Meaning," 33.

31. "Ohne ihn gelesen zu haben, läßt sich kaum wissen, wie dem Menschen sauwohl sein kann." See Rodolphe Gasché, "Self-dissolving seriousness: on the comic in the Hegelian conception of tragedy," in *Philosophy and Tragedy*, ed. M. de Beistegui and S. Sparks (London: Routledge, 2000), 41.

32. Harris claims that comedy, stripped of divine pathos, is left with nothing but the *pathos* of being *honest*. See Harris, *Hegel's Ladder II*, 634. What, then, is being frankly addressed in the *Clouds*? Martha Nussbaum, for example, lists three main criticisms inherent in Aristophanes's portrayal of Socrates: "(1) his lack of attention to the necessary role, in moral education, of character . . .; (2) his lack of a positive program to replace what he criticized; (3) his openness to misunderstanding—his failure to make clear to his students the difference (if there is one) between his aloofness and the immoralism of Anti-Right [*Adikos Logos* in the agon]." See Martha Nussbaum, "Aristophanes and Socrates on Learning Practical Wisdom," in *Aristophanes: Essays in Interpretation*, ed. J. Henderson, Yale Classical Studies Series, vol. 26 (Cambridge: Cambridge University Press, 1980), 81.

Despite her claim that the *Clouds* ends in anguish rather than "Hegelian reconciliation and *Grundwohlsein*," Nussbaum is, broadly speaking, in agreement with Hegel when she affirms in Aristophanes the negative effect that Socratic *elenchus* can potentially have on young people like Pheidippides when they are not properly screened and prepared. See Nussbaum, "Aristophanes and Socrates," 79. For Hegel's criticism of the destructive potential of the Socratic dialectic, again see Hegel, *Lectures*, 1:426, as well as the following: "It cannot be said that injustice is done to Socrates by this representation. Indeed we must admire the depth of Aristophanes in having recognized the dialectic side in Socrates as being a negative." Hegel, *Lectures*, 1:430.

33. See Moland, "And Why Not?," 84.

34. Murray, *Aristophanes*, 95.

35. Bergson, *Laughter*, 1. Bergson presents these observations at the very beginning of his study and then works to substantiate them in the analyses that follow.

36. Bergson, 2–3.

37. "Comedy lies midway between art and life." See Bergson, 83. Donougho notes the similarities between Bergson's point about comedy blurring the line between art and life—"the artful breakup of art"—and Hegel's view of comedy as transcending art altogether. See Donougho, "Hegelian Comedy," 207, 211.

38. Bergson, *Laughter*, 3.

39. Socratic irony is a "manner of speech, a pleasant rallying" deployed in the service of "leading men, through thought, to the true good and the universal Idea." Hegel, *Lectures*, 1:402. As such, it is markedly distinct from modern or romantic irony which, adopted as a universal principle, leads to "the destruction of the noble, great, and excellent" (A 1:67). Cited in Law, "Hegel and the Spirit of Comedy," 124.

40. Bergson, *Laughter*, 3.

41. Bergson, 10.

42. Bergson, 7.

43. Bergson, 2. Bergson is initially thinking concretely about the fact that animals, for example, are the stuff of comedy only insofar as they remind us of human attributes or behavior.

44. Bergson, 26; translation altered.

45. Harris, *Hegel's Ladder II*, 633.

46. The legacy of the comic does last for a time. The secularity of the Hellenistic *Weltgeist* and the triumph of the subjective attitude is the inheritance of the comic moment of Greek religious life. For Harris, comic consciousness is still there in Epictetus, but Marcus Aurelius is already well on the way to unhappiness. See Harris, 656.

Chapter Eight

From Comedy to Christianity

The Nihilism of Aristophanic Laughter

Paul T. Wilford

*Gott ist gestorben, Gott ist tot—
dieses ist der fürchterlichste
Gedanke.*[1]

THE QUARREL BETWEEN PHILOSOPHY AND POETRY is an ancient one. When Socrates censured Homer and the dramatists for their unedifying depictions of the gods, the quarrel became a political and theological one. As Socrates contends, the well-being of the sociopolitical order depends on our images of the gods, and the poetic conjurations of the dramatists appear to undermine rather than inculcate civic virtue. But which activity, philosophy or poetry, should decide what counts as politically or theologically salutary? And who can adjudicate their quarrel?

Such questions spring to mind when reading Plato's *Republic,* yet there is a further dimension to the quarrel. In the *Symposium* and *Philebus,* we see Socrates engage with the foremost representative of comedy about "the tragedy and comedy of life."[2] The competitive rivalry intimated in these encounters indicates that Aristophanes threatens or challenges Socratic confidence in philosophy as the best way of life. Comedy's laughter certainly seems more akin to Socratic irony than the *pathei mathos* of Aeschylus, Sophocles, and

Euripides. Accordingly, there is reason to think that for Plato the ancient quarrel is more specifically between philosophy and comedy.

Hegel shares this judgment; but for him the proximity of philosophy and comedy implied by their rivalry suggests a perennial danger—the possibility of descending into an ironic, self-referential, self-satisfied cynicism. Philosophy and comedy both flirt with nihilism, and Hegel is profoundly cognizant of this danger.[3] Hegel knows that both comedy and philosophy must pronounce "Gott ist gestorben"; but whereas that hard saying, "God is dead," remains the logical conclusion of comedic consciousness, philosophy passes through such a moment of crisis, comes out the other side, affirms the world, and finds itself therein.[4] Thus, like Plato, Hegel believes the quarrel concerns not just the political consequences of religious representations but also the very meaning and status of philosophy. Yet, unlike Plato, Hegel's response to the challenge of Aristophanes turns on the reconciliation of religion and philosophy. Christianity proves to be the logical riposte to Aristophanes's ridicule of the gods.

The presentation of Christianity as the determinate negation of Aristophanes occurs in the *Phenomenology of Spirit*, where Hegel's analysis of comedy's insalubrious effects is sharpest. Hegel's treatment of Aristophanes as the exemplary instance of *Das geistige Kunstwerk* differs significantly from that encountered elsewhere in Hegel's corpus. In particular, the presentation of Aristophanes in *Lectures on Aesthetics* and *The History of Philosophy* is far less one-sided than that encountered in the *Phenomenology*, where Hegel stresses Aristophanes's impious mockery and the ethical consequences of his iconoclasm.[5]

Furthermore, by treating Aristophanes in "Religion" Hegel not only underscores the theological import and the sociopolitical ramifications of comedy but prompts us to ask: why is blasphemy the logical perfection of religion in the form of self-consciousness, and why does awareness of such blasphemy usher in the unhappy consciousness? Moreover, the structure of Hegel's text prompts us to ask about the logic connecting Aristophanic comedy and Christianity's Good News, and, given that Hegel's account of Aristophanes climaxes in a treatment of the *Clouds*, we are lead concurrently to ask about the relation of philosophy to these two shapes of consciousness.

To reiterate, in order to grasp Hegel's teaching, we must begin by asking why or how Christianity constitutes a response to Aristophanic comedy, or, more precisely and internally to the text of the *Phenomenology*, why is the central mystery of Christianity—the incarnation—the determinate negation of Aristophanes's self-certainty that was achieved by the "crushing of Gods and men?"[6]

While I will proceed through careful exegesis, my aims are not narrowly textual. Rather this essay is intended as a meditation on a possible posture or comportment that self-consciousness can take toward the world. Like other shapes of consciousness, comedy is not just a description of a peculiar historical moment, and Hegel gives us ample indication that his analysis is not merely a commentary on antiquity's most irreverent wit.[7] Instead, to understand Aristophanes is to understand a dimension of that being for which laughter is, as Aquinas says, an essential accident—attendant upon us as rational animals.[8] But, as we will see, although laughter is far more than the sudden glorying in our own superiority, the self-conscious being nevertheless risks finding everything risible or, what amounts to the same thing, nothing sacred.[9] By arguing that comedy is the consummation of *Kunstreligion*, Hegel prompts us to view comedy as a mode of consciousness making knowledge claims about the absolute. Consequently, comedy is about God, and, as Hans Küng reminds us, "The question of God is always also at the same time a question about man."[10] And, for Hegel, the question about man is the questionableness of self-consciousness.

My inquiry proceeds in five sections: First, I contextualize Hegel's treatment of comedy within the *Phenomenology*; second, I focus on the final moment of *Das geistige Kunstwerk*; third, I examine the inversion of Aristophanic lightheartedness into the suffering of the unhappy consciousness; fourth, I consider Christianity's central mystery as the first act in a divine comedy; and finally, I explore the philosophic import of this dialectical move from comedy to Christianity.

Self-Conscious Spirit, Absolute Art, and Language

Let us begin with a brief recapitulation of the dialectical movement of "Religion" preceding the advent of comedy. In *Natural Religion*, spirit attempts to know itself in an immediate, natural object; failing to know the absolute as substance, spirit then pursues the opposite tack, positing the absolute as self, which it seeks to know in the form of "a sublated natural existence" (i.e., in a work of art). Accordingly in *Religion of Art*, the creative activity of consciousness (*das Hervorbringen des Bewußtseins*) is central and the *geistiger Arbeiter* supplants the *Werkmeister*.[11] In broad terms, spirit pursues self-knowledge in three distinct moments, each exemplified by a unique form of aesthetic-religious production, which reflects a unique understanding of both the divine and the human as well as their relation to one another. Schematically described, each stage becomes increasingly expressive of human subjectivity, as spirit moves from sculpting statues, to ecstatic cultic revelry, to poetic representations: that is, from the abstract, to the living, and finally to the spiritual work of art.

This shape of religious consciousness, Hegel reminds us, is parallel to the ethical or true form of spirit (*Sittlichkeit*), wherein the universal substance of individuals is known as their own essence and work (*ihr eigenes Wesen und Werk*).[12] The spirit of *kunstreligion* is therefore that of a "free people" for whom custom constitutes "the substance of all, whose actuality and existence each and every individual knows as his own will and deed."[13] Reflecting this substance, the "absolute art" of this world expresses free spiritual activity.[14] Such freedom is most manifest in "speech—an existence (*Dasein*) which is immediately self-conscious existence."[15] Thus, language, which Hegel defines as the soul existing as soul (*die als Seele existierende Seele*), plays an increasingly prominent role in the dialectic.[16] The whole movement of the religion of art from the oracle, to the cult, to the divine hymn, and finally to forms of poetry can be read as the search for an adequate form of language that overcomes the dichotomy between interiority and externality.[17] This development, however, is but a reflection of the increasing self-consciousness of the spiritual laborer—the ever increasingly lucid, cognizant self-awareness of the creative activity of the artist. Language is the most pliable of artistic mediums, allowing for the greatest range of representations. In speech, self-conscious creativity is not even bounded by logical consistency.[18] From this perspective, the movement from epic poetry to tragedy to comedy is the development of the ever heightening awareness of the essence of self-consciousness as expressed in poetic power.

Comedic Exultation

Tragedy culminates in "the persons of the divine essence" being swallowed up by necessity. The characters of the drama, unable to find themselves in that substantiality, simply perish (*unterzugehen*).[19] Self-consciousness, however, as the simple certainty of self, is "the spiritual unity into which everything returns."[20] Although consciousness remains present in the play's characters, it appears as *hypocrisy*, since the unity of self, fate, and substance is merely external (*äußerliche*).[21] The previous unity of mask and actor now appears before the spectators as divided into persona and the actual self. Both actor and audience are cognizant of the underlying discrepancy between self-consciousness and substantiality.

Comedy begins by announcing this shared awareness: self-consciousness lays aside "its mask and exhibits itself as knowing itself to be the fate both of the gods of the chorus and of the absolute powers themselves."[22] In breaking the fourth wall, the actor not only acknowledges the theatricality of the theater but also the fact that the dramatic spectacle depends on the activity of both audience and actor. The willing suspension of disbelief, required for tragic drama to provoke a salutary catharsis of passions, is now the object of self-conscious reflection. By calling attention to what tragedy consciously ignored, comedy appears as parasitic on tragedy; laughter is posterior to fear and pity. Moreover, this drawing back of the curtain is not limited to the actor–mask relation. The whole cosmos of beliefs governing the world of tragedy and undergirding the relation between actor, mask, chorus, playwright, and audience is now the object of ridicule.

Accordingly, in comedy, "Actual self-consciousness exhibits itself as the fate of the gods."[23] Self-consciousness stands over and above the gods, whose individuality now exists only in the imagination. "The subject, is thus elevated above that sort of moment as it would be elevated above an individual property, and, wearing this mask, the subject expresses the irony of something that wants to be something on its own."[24] The claimed universality, however, is but a posturing, as the self is "trapped in actuality, and it lets the mask drop precisely because it wants to be something rightful." Playing with the mask as something to put on in order to be a "persona," the self just as readily takes it off and comes "forward in its own nakedness and ordinariness, which it shows not to be distinct form the authentic self, from the actor, nor from the spectator."[25] The comic actor is torn between the power he has over the gods and the attempt to present his authentic self.

But why this desire to step forward in his nakedness? What motivates the subject to reveal that its claim to universality is but a posturing (*Aufspreizen*)? In this desire, we see premonitions of what is so problematic about comedy for both the individual reveling in his ironic posture and for the community for which comedy is a form of worship.[26] Evident already is a desire that cannot be fulfilled, and as "this universal dissolution (*allgemeine Auflösung*) of the shaped essentiality" becomes increasingly serious, comedic destruction becomes likewise more willful and bitter.[27]

This destruction occurs along two axes. First, comedy sunders the relation between the divine and the natural, which Hegel illustrates by recalling the "mystery of bread and wine" and reminding us that in the cult of Bacchus and Ceres, self-consciousness had made nature's essentiality its own, appropriating its independence and transfiguring its significance.[28] In Aristophanes's *Frogs*, however, the Eleusinian mysteries are reduced to absurdity, exposing the spiritual transformation of the naturally given as mere pretense. With this example, Hegel not only points back to the natural–divine relation expressed in ritual sacrifice but also foreshadows the Eucharistic mystery and provides the first indication of precisely what relation between the natural and the divine might address the longings of self-consciousness.

Second, comedy ruptures the relation between the divine and the sociopolitical community. The demos, acknowledging no higher authority, believes itself "to be master and regent." As origin of all

> understanding and insight which are to be respected, [it simultaneously] compels and bewitches itself through the particularity of its actuality, and it exhibits the laughable contrast between its own opinion of itself and its immediate existence, between its necessity and contingency, its universality and its ordinariness.[29]

Although it is the source of all normativity, the demos cannot take itself seriously: the grounds of authentic democracy begin to teeter.[30] Not only does comedy mock the great discrepancy between democratic theory and Athenian practice, but the citizen is cut adrift from the universal, and comedy presents "the scorn which that individuality shows for such order."[31] Ironic contempt is the only posture available for a citizen caught in this self-referential game. Continually distanced from the ground of his own being, he must beware looking down lest he realize he is dancing over an abyss.[32]

And yet that's not all! Comedy attains to even greater heights in its skewering of philosophy's pretensions. Rational thought aims to free the divine essence from all contingent shapes and to elevate the wisdom of the chorus "into the simple ideas of the *beautiful* and the *good*,"[33] but the consciousness of the movement of abstraction that generates these maxims amounts to "the consciousness of the vanishing of the absolute validity" of moral and ethical norms.³⁴ Having dispelled the imaginary and superficial individuality of the gods, all that remains is "the nakedness of their immediate existence"—a nakedness that recalls the comic actor's condition when dispensing with illusions.³⁵ Such immediacy is figured in clouds and evanescent mist, as insubstantial as the representational thoughts themselves, which are vacuous, "suitable to be filled with any kind of content."³⁶ The dialectical procedure becomes the plaything of youthful frivolity (*Leichtsinn*) and the tremendous "force of dialectical knowledge" becomes a weapon for deceiving "anxiety-ridden old age." Unmoored from the ethical world that could give them determinate content, the abstract pure thoughts of the good and beautiful as well as the consciousness that "resolutely clings to them" amount to a "comic spectacle of emptiness;" and rational thought is "on the way to being a game played by the arbitrariness of contingent individuality with opinions."³⁷

Supplanting unconscious fate (*bewußtlose Schicksal*), the individual self is now "the negative force through and in which the gods ... vanish (*verschwinden*)."³⁸ The self, however, resides above this nothingness. Opposing itself to the "mere emptiness of disappearance," the self is the sole actuality; it preserves "itself within this nothingness" and in its self-sufficiency understands itself as the absolute power.³⁹ In contrast to all previous forms of *Kunstreligion*—whether sculpture, athletic excellence, cultic song and dance, the epic song of the troubadour, or the powers and persons of tragic drama—nothing remains foreign to individual consciousness. Thus, "the genuine self of the actor coincides with the persona he plays, just as the spectator is perfectly at home in what is presented to him and sees himself playing a role therein."⁴⁰ Aristophanes steps forth as the chorus in the *Clouds*' *parabasis*, and this self-conscious appeal to the audience is paralleled by Socrates's own identification of and laughter at himself being depicted on stage.⁴¹

Self-consciousness achieves a hitherto inconceivably elevated position as anything whatsoever that claims independent validity is "brought to dissolution." The activity of self-conscious thought confronts any essentiality and after working its analytic magic, moves on, leaving in tatters what once appeared substantial. In this perfect self-certainty, everything alien loses "all its fearfulness and essentiality." There remains no pious awe or humble obedience, no recognition of the divine as a power over and above us mere mortals, and no fear or trembling before a mysterious other.⁴²

Before turning to the inversion of this satisfaction, we should underscore that each step in Hegel's presentation of comedy tracks an ever-increasing awareness of the negativity inherent in self-consciousness. For one familiar with Aristophanes, one striking feature of Hegel's presentation is the almost complete absence of Aristophanes's scatological humor or debauchery. Instead, Hegel's treatment of comedy peaks in an account of the *Clouds*.[43] However, rather than oppose Aristophanes and Socrates, Hegel emphasizes what they have in common. His focus throughout is on the ascendency of self-consciousness in both philosophy and comedy—with comedy perhaps coming out on top, since it mocks philosophy, which foolishly sought for the good and the beautiful in earnest. Philosophy did not know this quest was absurd, and Aristophanes mercilessly exposes its pretensions. Here, we see Hegel's great genius and deep insight. Comedy exemplifies a corrosive power that can be arrayed against the gods, the city, philosophy, and perhaps even itself. The deep source of Aristophanes's humor is the negativity inherent in self-consciousness. The subject's capacity for reflection is also an inverting power: a power of turning everything on its head, a power of making the serious appear absurd. So we might laugh when Pheidippides makes the weaker argument the stronger or when he beats his father, but we might also pause and in the disquiet of our souls ask: In laughing at the spectacle, am I condoning this madness? And if I were to turn this power back on myself, what then?[44]

The Tragedy of Comedy

The raucous laughter that once reverberated around the theater of Dionysus turns to dust and ashes in the mouths of the audience, for the truth of comedy is nihilism, and woeful despair replaces lightness of being. In comedy, spirit completes the incarnation of the divine essence (*Menschwerdung des göttlichen Wesens*), but the cultic unity of interior and exterior has passed "over into the extreme term of the self," and all essentiality is submerged in "the individuality of consciousness." The self stands preeminent and lightheartedly proclaims: *"The self is the absolute essence."*[45] Comedy thus inverts the previous relation of subject to substance, accident to essence. Essence is now a mere predicate, and "spirit has lost its *consciousness*."[46] The self's elevation is the diminution of substance; the undermining of values, gods, heroes, and ideals not only depopulates heaven but also hollows out that communal substance "whose actuality and existence each and every individual knows to be his own will and deed."[47] But what then is the ground of recognition in light of comedy? What becomes of spirit's I–We relation?[48]

Hegel's explicit connection between this development in the religious realm and the previous collapse of the ethical world highlights spirit's dual theological and political suffering.[49] In *Sittlichkeit*, the self was submerged in the spirit of a people and consciousness was immersed in, and so at one with, substance. But when the simple singularity (*die einfache Einzelheit*) distanced itself from this substance and in its levity (*Leichtsinn*) purified "itself into a legal person, into the abstract universality of law," it raised itself out of submersion in thick ethicality into a godforsaken world. A pantheon of merely "abstract universality, of pure thought" reflects the legal-person's "being-in-and-for-itself."[50] Philosophy, comedy, and legality conspire in their assault upon heaven, but the victory is only the spiritless self (*geistlosen Selbst*) whose lightheartedness is a far cry from genuine happiness.[51] Might comedy likewise cause a citizenry to shatter into a multiplicity of atomistic, unyielding selves (*spröden Selbst*)?[52]

The parallels with *Rechtszustand* culminate in the reappearance of three figures—the stoic, the skeptic, and the unhappy consciousness—that together signal a turn inward and a restive longing for an absent absolute.[53] But Hegel is not just repeating the previous movement of *Rechtszustand*; the truth of comedy is disclosed in that iteration of self-consciousness most acutely aware of its lacking, its deficiency, its nonabsoluteness.[54] This shape is the only possible posture in which the true meaning or actual value (*wirklichen Gelten*) of the abstract person can be recognized for what it is, namely, a complete loss (*vollkommenen Verlust*). The unhappy consciousness is the experience of being a self without content.

The unhappy consciousness is the logical counterpoint of the comic consciousness because the return of divine essence back into the comic consciousness is concomitantly "the complete *self-emptying* [or *alienation*] *of substance* (die vollkomme Entäußerung der Substanz)." The unhappy consciousness is the obverse of Aristophanic comedy because both are extreme forms of self-consciousness wherein the alienation of subject from substance reaches a climactic intensity. Although the negativity of the former is directed at itself in its pursuit of a relation to an absolute located in an otherworldly beyond, and the negativity of the latter is directed against all that is not the self, both postures are without limitation or mediation; they are both totalizing, and for this reason they are both ultimately concerned with the absence or presence of God.

Thus, the unhappy consciousness is "the tragic fate of the certainty of the self that aims to be absolute."[55] The irony of the comedic consciousness is that its happiness is achieved in its negation of the very ground it stands on. Its satirical posture cannot be maintained. Comic self-consciousness presumed itself to be the fate of the gods (*das Schicksal der Götter*), but nemesis returns and punishes hubris.[56] Unhappy consciousness recognizes that the loss of all *essentiality* (*Wesenheit*) in this *certainty* of itself is really knowledge of the loss of substance and of self; it voices such grief "in the hard saying: *God has died*."[57]

The world is now in Weber's sense disenchanted (*entzaubert*). The ethical world and the religion of that world are "lost in the comic consciousness" and the unhappy consciousness is but the knowledge of "this *total* loss." Inhabiting a world drained of meaning, consciousness loses all self-worth (*Selbstwert*); its former "trust in the eternal laws of the gods has vanished."[58] If we recall that even to ask about the origins of the law was to walk an "unethical path," we see how far down that road comic consciousness has traveled. It not only asks, but debunks.[59] Comic consciousness surpasses even the activity of philosophy, which sought to demythologize the gods in order to replace them with pure ideals of the good and the beautiful. Socrates, at least, held out the possibility of virtue. Aristophanes seems bent on a complete iconoclastic desecration. Comedy, in its own very different way, appears just as destructive as the negativity of absolute freedom.[60]

All previous forms of religious life are now void: oracles are silent, statues are lifeless stones, hymns are mere words, and games and festivals no longer express the joyful unity of man and the divine. Worst of all, that mode of externalization, language, which was the medium of the soul existing as soul, is no longer a vehicle for the divine.[61] "The works of the muse lack the power of the spirit which brought forth its certainty of itself from the crushing of the gods and men (*der Zermalmung der Götter und Menschen*)."[62] In comedic consciousness even the greatest poetic creations of antiquity are for consciousness what they are for us now (us moderns): "beautiful fruit" already plucked. Consciousness can never return to the world that produced them. The source of the fruit has passed, drowned in waves of laughter.

Hegel even suggests that the great distance that separates us modern, post–French Revolution Europeans from the works of Homer and Aeschylus is already present in comedic consciousness. Our relation to such works is not and cannot be an act of divine worship (*gottesdienstliche*); for us, it can only be an "external activity." We might try to recover these artistic products, but we can gather only "the dead elements of their outward existence" through philological research and historical studies.[63]

Ludwig Siep has argued that Hegel's language here evokes the spiritual malaise of his own epoch.[64] If this is correct, then Hegel is drawing a comparison between the despair of consciousness at this moment and the danger spiritual life faces in his own age of autonomous reason. Hegel's turn to Christianity is framed by a poetic analogy that bears out this supposition.

As a young girl who presents us the plucked fruits as a gift is more than the nature that immediately provided them, . . . so too the spirit of fate that provides us those works of art is more than the ethical life and actuality of that people, for it is the *inwardizing-recollecting (Er-Innerung)* of the spirit in them that was still *alienated*—it is the spirit of the tragic fate that collects all those individual gods and attributes of the substance into the *one* pantheon, into self-conscious spirit conscious of itself as spirit.[65]

While Hegel's subsequent recapitulation of the movement of spirit peaking in the unhappy consciousness prepares the reader for the next dialectical step—the true incarnation of the divine in a single individual self-consciousness—it is simultaneously a programmatic statement of everything that Hegel's philosophy will attempt to take up, do justice to, and make sense of.[66]

Let us now follow Hegel's dialectic one step further and consider how Christianity is the response to the despair engendered by comedy.

Christianity's Divine Comedy

All previous forms of consciousness stand expectant at "the birthplace of self-conscious spirit." They have "as their focal point the all-permeating pain and yearning of the unhappy consciousness."[67] The division of the world into two worlds—one of actuality and one located in an otherworldly beyond—is to be overcome, but such reconciliation of the doubleness that has plagued previous modes of consciousness can only emerge out of the nadir of total loss.[68] The unhappy consciousness appears here as the crucial figure for understanding the development of the *Phenomenology of Spirit*. This figure expresses most poignantly the longing at the heart of the dialectic.[69] Self-consciousness as desire above all (*Begierde überhaupt*) finds its sharpest expression, its most intense instantiation, in this inversion of comedy.[70] Self-consciousness in this guise is far removed from the self-assertiveness that led to the struggle for recognition, and yet if self-consciousness is that which seeks to find itself in the other, it is here in the shape of the unhappy consciousness that it most manifests the intensity of its need for something other.[71] But, as we have learned from comedy, this absolute other must be able to withstand the onslaught of self-consciousness's corrosive negativity. Can self-consciousness achieve its self-certainty without the crushing of gods and men?

Through spirit's twofold development—as the self-emptying substance that becomes self-consciousness and as that self-consciousness that makes itself into the universal self or thinghood—spirit has prepared itself for a final uncovering of a unity of self-consciousness and of substance. In other words, spirit through this movement proves itself to be that truth that is just as much subject as substance.[72] Although spirit will continue to be hobbled by a representational mode of self-understanding, the determinate negation of *Die Kunstreligion* that yields *Die offenbare Religion* nevertheless can achieve "the true absolute *content*."[73] That is, the *Umkehrung des Bewußtseins* expressed in the transfiguration of Aristophanic comedy into the unhappy consciousness begins the final iteration of that process, as described by Ardis Collins, whereby the concept under consideration expands "to include its necessary connection to its opposite," which results in a reconceiving of the hitherto opposed determinations "in terms of a common principle that determines both their necessary difference and their integration in the same differentiated dynamic."[74] This formulation of the determinate negation linking these two moments in the *Phenomenology* underscores that revealed religion must encompass the truth of Aristophanic comedy. Christianity subsumes the potentially destructive negativity of self-consciousness. In revealed religion, God's death is but a moment of God's life.

The incarnation is thus the moment when actual world-spirit (*der wirkliche Weltgeist*) achieves knowledge of itself. Absolute spirit is now present in the *hic et nunc* as a self-conscious being existing for immediate certainty that "*sees, feels,* and *hears* this divinity."[75] This "moment of *immediate* being" constitutes the return "of all essentiality into consciousness." The religious spirit as the inverse of the unhappy consciousness is "the *simple* positive self" that displaces spirit as "*simple* self-conscious negativity." Being simple, the self in the form of complete immediacy is neither conceived, represented, nor produced. Rather "this God is sensuously intuited immediately as a self, as an actual individual person, and only so *is* he self-consciousness."[76] Incarnation is the simple content of absolute religion: essence is now known as spirit, and essence is now "conscious of itself as being spirit." Accordingly, this substance remains within itself in its accidents, and finds itself therein, insofar as it is *subject* or *self*.[77]

Revelation proves to be the means to self-knowledge. If we recall that "self-consciousness attains its satisfaction only in another self-consciousness," the incarnation is the moment when self-consciousness finally encounters its own depth, i.e., an "essence that is essentially *self-consciousness*."[78] In revelation, therefore, there is no discrepancy between being and being known.[79] The self is now certain of itself, not through negation of what is other but through encountering itself *in* the other. "Spirit is known as self-consciousness and is immediately revealed to this self-consciousness, for it is this self-consciousness itself. The divine nature is the same as the human nature, and it is this unity which is beheld."[80] Consciousness knows itself immediately in the object and attains confirmation of its self-certainty.[81]

Retrospectively, we realize that "the hopes and expectation of the preceding world" were essentially oriented "towards this revelation, towards the intuition of what the absolute essence is and towards findings themselves within that revelation."[82] Although Hegel's claim seems paradoxical when comedy is understood as solipsistically contented, when viewed as the peak of self-conscious anguish (a perfection [*Vollendung*] paralleling the perfection of self-consciousness "in the shape of the *unhappy* consciousness"), we see comedy's negation of gods as the expression of a longing for something more—for a divinity that is equal to the power of self-consciousness.[83]

In light of the revelation of this good news—the return of God—self-conscious joy (*Freude*) permeates the world.[84] The possibility of knowing oneself transforms the world from being disenchanted to being a realm of meaning. The finite world is no longer opposed to infinity but redeemed as a moment of creation; and together with this reanimation of the world comes the possibility of communion with others. Whereas comedy was the height of a civic-religious festival, its end was the sundering of the ties that bind us to others. Self-consciousness stood alone—revealed as a poor naked wretch. But the affirmation of our finitude in the revelation of the divine–human unity provides a new ground for communion, for now spirit is recognized not as "the individual on his own but the individual together with the consciousness of the religious community; and what the individual is for this religious community is the complete whole of that consciousness and the community."[85] The incarnation of the divine ultimately makes possible reciprocal recognition—and thereby a genuine communion. It provides the sort of common ground in shared beliefs, ideals, and representations that Aristophanes had so pitilessly mocked. With Christianity, we thus uncover the basis for a stable and enduring "I that is We and We that is I."[86]

Conclusion: Hegel and Strauss on the Meaning of Philosophy

In a series of public lectures entitled *The Problem of Socrates*, Leo Strauss called Hegel "the profoundest student of Aristophanes in modern times" and "the greatest mind who has devoted himself in modern times to Aristophanes."[87] These are striking claims, especially if one bears in mind that Nietzsche, too, was a great student of Aristophanes, and Strauss held Nietzsche in the highest esteem. Given Strauss's principal preoccupations, it seems safe to conclude that Strauss's judgment concerns, on the one hand, the relation of poetry to philosophy, and, on the other, the nature of philosophy itself. Strauss explicitly concurs with Hegel on a number of essential points: (1) Aristophanes's comedy is the culmination of poetry, i.e., it is higher than tragedy. (2) Comedy's blasphemies are essential to its teaching. (3) Comedy's connection to philosophy is not incidental. (4) Comedy constitutes a triumphing "over everything objective and substantial—over the city, the family, morality, and the gods." (5) In comedy, "Man has made himself the complete master of everything which he formerly regarded as the substantial content of his knowledge or action."[88]

Yet Strauss and Hegel ultimately diverge in their judgment of the basis of Aristophanic comedy, and their disagreement turns on the relation of self-consciousness to nature or, what amounts to the same thing, the status of Christianity.[89] Whereas Hegel argues that the basis of the dissolution of *nomoi* is self-consciousness and that self-consciousness thereby learns "the insubstantiality of everything alien to self-consciousness," Strauss insists that "what Hegel calls the triumph of subjectivity is achieved in the Aristophanic comedy only by virtue of the knowledge of nature, i.e., the opposite of self-consciousness."[90] Thus, Strauss insists on the absolute and inviolable opposition of nature and self-consciousness. The two cannot be reconciled, and their incongruity is the basis of Aristophanes's comedy. Furthermore, this antithesis also accounts for Strauss's disagreement with Hegel regarding Christianity and philosophy.

Curiously, while Strauss directs the audience's attention to the *Phenomenology*, he does not mention that Hegel's interpretation of Aristophanes is immediately followed by an account of Christianity, nor does he mention the inversion (*Umkehrung*) of comedic consciousness into the unhappy consciousness.[91] This silence is not a mere oversight but is indicative of a deep disagreement as to whether spirit or nature is the fundamental ground of being—a disagreement that accounts for their divergent views of Christianity.[92] Although Strauss is reticent to speak of Christianity, by referencing Thomas More's *Dialogue of Comfort against Tribulation* he indicates that he believes Christianity resembles tragedy more than comedy, whereas Socratic philosophy is more akin to comedy than tragedy, noting that we never see Socrates weeping, but we have record of his laughing and joking and that "his irony is a byword."[93]

In contrast, Hegel stresses the joy that abides in the world at the revelation of the Good News. A crucial component of this joy is a reconciliation with natural existence, with the limitations of finitude, expressed in Christ's death and resurrection.[94] Through the "*death* of the divine man (*der Tod des göttlichen Menschen*)," death as such loses its natural significance. The natural finitude that is the basis of the absurd incongruity in comedy is transfigured in spiritual self-consciousness "into the *universality* of spirit which lives in its own religious community, dies there daily, and is daily resurrected."[95] If the incarnation signals the unity of man and God, Christ's resurrection reconciles man and nature. Whereas Strauss sees Christianity as teaching that life is a veil of tears, Hegel thinks Christianity's central teaching is an affirmation of this world and communal life in it. Christianity is not tragic. We are not in the end alienated from either God or nature; for there is, in fact, nothing simply other—wholly antithetical—to self-consciousness.

We can approach this fundamental issue from another perspective. Hegel is preeminently concerned throughout his philosophic career with responding to the hard saying, *Gott ist gestorben*. From the early programmatic statement in *Faith and Knowledge* to the lectures on the *Philosophy of Religion*, Hegel is committed to the proposition that philosophy must confront the darkest of possibilities—the meaninglessness of existence. Modern religion as a whole is based on the "feeling that 'God is Himself Dead.' " What existed formerly only in a historical mode, namely, "infinite grief," is now central to man's experience of the world. Accordingly, philosophy must establish "the Idea of absolute freedom and along with it the absolute Passion, the speculative Good Friday in place of the historic Good Friday." In terms of the logic of the *Phenomenology*, this requires responding to the awesome god-destroying power latent in self-consciousness and exemplified by Aristophanes.[96]

Such an interpretation is consonant with Hegel's insistence that the *Phenomenology* is a pathway of despair.[97] From this perspective, comedic consciousness's awareness that it has become the absolute power is the most acute instance of despair, and the unhappy consciousness is the figure most expressive of the negative moment inherent in spirit's dialectical journey.[98]

Perhaps the unhappy consciousness also stands for the philosopher who faces up to the harsh truth of his time—a time described in the *Differenzschrift* as one of deep disharmony—and yet who aims to pass through that harrowing existential state when he says to himself: *Gott ist gestorben*.[99]

Long before Nietzsche's and Heidegger's insistence on the death of God, Hegel had seen with complete clarity the possibility that the modern world could become drained of meaning and that the elevation of autonomous reason risked being the elevation of an ironic posture conducive to sophistic games but ultimately hollow.[100] Hegel was keenly aware that modernity as the apogee of a self-conscious reflexivity risks being disenchanted and therefore tragic.[101]

Yet such apprehensions must be met head on, for as Hegel reminds us, philosophic speculation easily "descends to the level of edification and even triteness when lacking the earnestness, the pain, the patience and the work of the negative."[102] Philosophy must, rather, wrestle with the negative, for "the life of spirit is not a life that shuns death and avoids destruction, keeping clean of it; rather it endures death, and in death, maintains itself. Spirit wins its truth only through finding itself within absolute diremption.... [But] Spirit is this power only by looking the negative in the face and tarrying with it."[103]

Notes

1. *Vorlesungen über die Philosophie der Religion, Werke in zwanzig Bänden*, ed. Eva Moldenhauer and Karl Markus Michel (Frankfurt am Main: Suhrkamp Verlag, 1971), 17:291 (hereafter cited as *Werke*).

2. Plato, *Philebus*, 50B. See Seth Benardete's insightful commentary on this section of the dialogue in *The Tragedy and Comedy of Life* (Chicago: University of Chicago Press, 1993), 198–208.

3. For an account of the metaphysical reasons for both comedy's and philosophy's flirtation with nihilism (or why philosophy is necessarily concerned with nothingness) see Carl Page, "It's Nothing to Laugh About: The Limits of Determinacy and the Altogether Not," in *Being and Dialectic*, ed. William Desmond and Joseph Grange (Albany: State University of New York Press, 2000), 85–100.

4. On the philosophic meaning of the "death of God," Tracy Strong provides a helpful formulation: "The so-called death of God ... refers not (simply) to the decay of Christianity but to a set of problems that develop over time and correspond to the gradual unavailability of authoritative foundations for human

knowledge and actions." See Tracy Strong, *Politics Without Vision: Thinking Without a Banister* (Chicago: University of Chicago Press, 2012), 14. For an introduction to the centrality of this theme in Hegel's corpus see Deland S. Anderson, *Hegel's Speculative Good Friday: The Death of God in Philosophical Perspective* (Atlanta: Scholars, 1996). For a treatment that situates Hegel within the context of his predecessors, see Michael Gillespie, *Nihilism Before Nietzsche* (Chicago: University of Chicago Press, 1995), 115–121. For a broader philosophical context (in particular Nietzsche and the subsequent existentialist tradition) see Julian Young, *The Death of God and the Meaning of Life* (London: Routledge, 2003), 57–79. For a rich and thorough comparison between Hegel and Nietzsche on the theme of the "death of God" see Robert R. Williams, *Tragedy, Recognition, and the Death of God* (Oxford: Oxford University Press, 2012), especially 290–321. While all of these treatments are helpful, they do not explore the connection presented here between comedy and nihilism and its implications for philosophy.

5. The *Phenomenology*'s Aristophanes is a far cry from the conservative patriotic poet, who apparently "did not make fun of what was truly moral in the life of the Athenians, or of their genuine philosophy, true religious faith, and serious art" and who was neither "a cold nor malignant scoffer" but rather "a man of most gifted mind, the best of citizens to whom the welfare of Athens was always a serious matter and who proved to be a true patriot throughout. See G. W. F. Hegel, *Hegel's Aesthetics: Lectures on Fine Art*, trans. T. M. Knox, vol. 2 (Oxford: Oxford University Press, 1975), 1202; *Werke* 15:530; Hegel, *Hegel's Aesthetics*, 1222; *Werke* 15:554). Similarly, consider Hegel's treatment of Aristophanes in relation to Socrates in the *Lectures on the History of Philosophy*, where Aristophanes is described as "no shallow jester who seized every opportunity to make the Athenians laugh, for he was thoroughly and deeply patriotic, a proper Athenian citizen. Genuine comedy does not consist of superficial jests, but presupposes earnestness of the most profound sort." See Hegel, *Lectures on the History of Philosophy 1825–6, Volume II: Greek Philosophy*, ed. Robert F. Brown, trans. Robert F. Brown, J. M. Stewart, and H. S. Harris (Oxford: Oxford University Press, 2006), 143. Accordingly, the following argument is not intended as a reconstruction of Hegel's comprehensive teaching on Aristophanes. For a more general treatment of Hegel and Aristophanes see William Desmond's "Can Philosophy Laugh at Itself? On Hegel and Aristophanes," *The Owl of Minerva* 20, no. 2 (Spring 1989): 131–149. By restricting my focus, I aim to bring out the dangerous aspect of comedy and what philosophy might learn about itself by keeping this in mind.

6. Hegel, *Phenomenology of Spirit*, §753 (hereafter cited as PhG), *Werke* 3:547. All references to Hegel's *Phänomenologie des Geistes* will be given by paragraph number, following the tradition of Miller's 1979 translation, followed by page number(s) in *Werke*. I have consulted the complete translations of A. V. Miller, *Hegel's Phenomenology of Spirit* (Oxford: Oxford University Press, 1977); Terry

Pinkard, *The Phenomenology of Spirit* (Cambridge: Cambridge University Press, 2018); and Michael Inwood, *Hegel: The Phenomenology of Spirit* (Oxford: Oxford University Press, 2018).

7. Accordingly, I will be bracketing several important features of Hegel's broader treatment of comedy. By focusing my attention solely on comedy as it appears in the *Phenomenology*, I end up presenting a more destructive and dangerous Aristophanes than other scholars. For example, Andrew Huddleston treats the sociopolitical virtues of comedy, and while there is a persuasive case to be made for the salutary effects of Aristophanic comedy in light of the presentation in the *Aesthetics*, the *Phenomenology* gives no such indication. See Andrew Huddleston, "Hegel on Comedy: Theodicy, Social Criticism, and the 'Supreme Task' of Art," *British Journal of Aesthetics* 54, no. 2 (April 2014): 227–240. Similarly, by focusing primarily on the *Aesthetics*, Mark W. Roche argues that Hegel cannot account for "dark" comedies and subsequent developments in the genre, whereas I hope to demonstrate that Hegel is fully aware that "even murder" can be an object of comedy and that this is part of what makes it dangerous. See Mark W. Roche, "Hegel's Theory of Comedy in the Context of Hegelian and Modern Reflections on Comedy," *Revue internationale de philosophie* 56, no. 221 (September 2002): 424–425. Finally, although I will be focusing on the *Phenomenology*, it is nevertheless worth bearing in mind that one can plausibly argue that Hegel thinks comedy is the highest form of art—or the *telos* of art; for a defense of this view see Stephen Law, "Hegel and the Spirit of Comedy: *Der Geist der Stets Verneint*," in *Hegel and Aesthetics*, ed. William Maker (Albany: State University of New York Press, 2000), 113–14. As the foremost representative of comedy, this would imply that Aristophanes is the consummate artist.

8. Thomas Aquinas, *Basic Writings of St. Thomas Aquinas*, ed. Anton C. Pegis (New York: Random House, 1945), 33.

9. See Hobbes, *Leviathan*, ed. Edwin Curley (Indianapolis: Hackett, 1994), 32.

10. Hans Küng, *The Incarnation of God*, trans. J. R. Stephenson (New York: Crossroad, 1987), 1.

11. Spirit in the shape of self-consciousness, which "seeks to behold in the object its [own] act or the self," engages in the sort of transformative labor that characterized the bondsman (PhG §683, *Werke* 3:502; see also PhG §§195–6, *Werke* 3:153–5).

12. PhG §700; *Werke* 3:512.

13. PhG §700; *Werke* 3:513.

14. PhG §702; *Werke* 3:514. On the meaning of the appearance of "absolute art" at this stage of the dialectic see Allen Speight, "Religion, Art, and the Emergence of Absolute Spirit in the *Phenomenology*," in *The Oxford Handbook of Hegel* (Oxford: Oxford University Press, 2017), 148–165.

15. PhG §710; *Werke* 3:518.

16. PhG §710; *Werke* 3:518. For the importance of the theme of language in the *Phenomenology* see Howard P. Kainz, "The Phenomenon of Language in Hegel's Phenomenology," in *Hegel's Phenomenology of Spirit: Not Missing the Trees for the Forest* (Lanham, MD: Lexington, 2008), 1–16.

17. PhG, §726; *Werke* 3:528–9.

18. This is not to say that the medium might not impose certain criteria for poetry as Lessing argues in *Laocoön*, only to highlight that the poet is far less restricted than any form of art that fashions natural materiality. Furthermore, much comedy turns on playing with the limits of logic and language; consider, for example, the "nonsense" poems of Lewis Carroll, such as *Jabberwocky*, and the humor of *Alice in Wonderland*.

19. PhG §742; *Werke* 3:541.

20. PhG §742; *Werke* 3:541.

21. Compare Hegel's previous use of "hypocrisy" to describe the discrepancy between inner and outer in his discussion of the beautiful soul; there, too, Hegel uses the language of playing with masks (PhG §§660–666; *Werke* 3:485–490).

22. PhG §743; *Werke* 3:541.

23. PhG §744; *Werke* 3:541.

24. PhG §744; *Werke* 3:542. Other than the discussion of comedy, irony appears only in Hegel's discussion of *Die sittliche Handlung* in his description of the feminine as "die ewige Ironie des Gemeinwesens" (PhG §475; *Werke* 3:352).

25. PhG §744; *Werke* 3:542. See Allen Speight's account of what comedy reveals about the "theatricality involved in self-knowledge and action." See Allen Speight, *Hegel, Literature and the Problem of Agency* (Cambridge: Cambridge University Press, 2001), 70–71). See also Speight's broader discussion of the different forms of theatricality in Hegel's *Phenomenology*, especially his treatment *Rameau's Nephew* in Bildung (Speight, 71–93).

26. While comedy may no longer appear as a collective form of worship, it remains a possible collective orientation to the absolute, especially in our "ironic" and "cynical" age. Consider Friederich Nietzsche, "Uses and Disadvantages of History for Life," in *Untimely Meditations*, ed. Daniel Breazeale, trans. R. J. Hollingdale (Cambridge: Cambridge University Press, 1997), 107.

27. PhG §745; *Werke* 3:542. Compare Hegel's discussion of the essence of self-consciousness as the power for "universal dissolution" (PhG §§194–5; *Werke* 3:152–153). Although potentially destructive, this power is an essential feature of the rational animal.

28. PhG §745, *Werke* 3:542. (See PhG §718, *Werke* 3:523; PhG §724, *Werke* 3:527.)

29. PhG §745, *Werke* 3:542–3.

30. Hegel most likely has Aristophanes's *Knights* in mind here, but regardless of the specific play, the point is that the basis of democratic politics is now

an object of ridicule. The Athenian's identity as a member of the very polis that supports the ritual activity, in which the polis itself is portrayed, is the object of ridicule.

31. PhG §745; Werke 3:543.

32. Genuine community (*Gemeine*) will only reappear with the development of Christianity (see PhG §§763–766; Werke 3:555–557). Hegel's stress on individualism is all the more striking, given that, as Lauer observes, "Religious experience is from the very beginning a corporate experience." See Quentin Lauer, *Essays on Hegelian Dialectic* (New York: Fordham University Press 1977), 235.

33. PhG §745; Werke 3:543.

34. PhG §745; Werke 3:543.

35. PhG §746; Werke 3:543.

36. PhG §746; Werke 3:543. Compare Hegel's critique of Stoicism and his account of virtue in *Virtue and the Way of the World* (PhG §200; Werke 3:158–159; PhG §390; Werke 3:289–290).

37. PhG §746; Werke 3:544.

38. PhG §747; Werke 3:544. For an interpretation of the systematic meaning of *verschwinden* see Andrew Norris, "The Disappearance of the French Revolution in Hegel's *Phenomenology of Spirit*," *The Owl of Minerva* 44, no. 1/2 (2012–2013): 37–66.

39. PhG §747; Werke 3:544. Certain of itself, the absolute power is not "something *represented*, something separated from consciousness in general and thus alien to it (von dem *Bewußtsein* überhaupt *Getrennten* und ihm Fremden)."

40. PhG §747; Werke 3:544.

41. For Aristophanes's appeal to the audience that he should be awarded the prize for best comedy, see the *Clouds*, 518–626. According to tradition, during the performance of the *Clouds*, Socrates rose from the audience, pointed to himself on stage, and joined in on the joke. See Plutarch, *Moralia* 10c–d; W. K. C. Guthrie, *Socrates* (Cambridge: Cambridge University Press), 55. See also Aristophanes's description of Socrates (*Birds* 1280–83).

42. PhG §747; Werke 3:544. Comedy's satisfaction, which Hegel describes as the unrivaled state of consciousness's "well-being and letting-oneself-be-well (*Wohlsein und Sichwohlseinlassen*)," recalls the satisfaction of self-consciousness fleetingly enjoyed by the master before consciousness knew the "fear of the lord." As previously in the dialectic, this self-sufficiency is also only apparent.

43. Compare Hegel's presentation with Lessing's in *Laocoön*; there, too, Socrates is an object of ridicule, but Lessing mentions a scene where a lizard defecates into Socrates's mouth in order to illustrate how "the disgusting" may be bound up with the "laughable." See Gotthold Ephraim Lessing, *Laocoön: An Essay on the Limits of Poetry and Painting*, in *Classical and Romantic German Aesthetics*, ed. J. M. Bernstein, trans. W. A. Steel (Cambridge: Cambridge University Press, 2003), 124–125.

44. Moreover, in Athens something very peculiar occurred (perhaps something without precedent and unrepeatable): the comedic spectacle was part of a public religious activity. The Dionysian festival lay at the heart of the civil-religion of Athenian democracy. Can a civilization survive this self-conscious ironic lampooning of gods and heroes, of citizens, and the state?

45. PhG §748; *Werke* 3:545. Compare Hegel's previous description of this same moment at §701; *Werke* 3:513: "The consummation of ethical life in free self-consciousness and the fate of the ethical world is therefore the individuality that has taken the inward turn, that is, the absolute lightheartedness of ethical spirit, which has dissolved within itself all the fixed distinctions of its durable existence and the social spheres of its own organic structure, and, now possessed of self-certainty, has achieved a boundless joyfulness and the freest enjoyment of itself." See also the description of the pleasure seeker as being characterized by levity or *Leichtsinn* (§370; *Werke* 3:276) and the connection between such lightheartedness and boredom in Hegel's description of our present age (PhG §11; *Werke* 3:18).

46. PhG §748; *Werke* 3:545.

47. PhG §700; *Werke* 3:512: Compare the previous description of spirit, which provides a criterion of judgment for what the relation between self and substance ought to be and how this undergirds communal life: "Spirit is the *substance* and the universal selfsame persisting essence—it is the unshakable and undissolved *ground* and *point of origin* for the activity of each and all—it is their *purpose* and *goal* as the *in-itself* of all self-consciousnesses, an in-itself which has been rendered into thought—This substance is equally the universal *work*, which engenders itself through the *activities* of each and all as their unity and their self-sameness, for this substance is *being-for-itself*, that is, the self, activity." See PhG §439, *Werke* 3:325, and PhG §444; *Werke* 3:327–8.

48. Recall that "the cognizance of reciprocal recognition" first possible in the family between wife and husband is predicated on the divine law (See PhG §455; *Werke* 3:335–6). If these laws have been obviated, can there be mutual recognition?

49. PhG §749; *Werke* 3:545. Although Hegel may have a historical development in mind and may consider Aristophanes's comedies as reflecting that period when a civilization begins to decline, the implications of his discussion of comedy are by no means restricted to an analysis of a peculiar historical moment. As argued below, the essence of the comedic consciousness's posture to the world is a perennial possibility for the self-conscious being.

50. PhG §750; *Werke* 3:546.

51. It certainly does not resemble that contentedness of self-consciousness that marks Hegel's first description of the ethical world found in "Reason" (PhG §§353–7; *Werke* 3:266–269).

52. See PhG §477–8; *Werke* 3:355. On the surface, this account of *Sittlichkeit*'s

demise differs markedly from the previous transition of VI.A.b to VI.A.c (§§476–479, *Werke* 3:354–6), where the emphasis is the submergence of all in fate—an undifferentiated universality. However, the negativity of comedy exhibits the same lack of differentiation. Just as all ethical determinations were swallowed up in fate, so too are all identity-forming norms drowned in laughter.

53. PhG §751; *Werke* 3:547.

54. If we recall that at the start of "Religion," when Hegel provides a retrospective summary of the journey thus far and indicates the presence of religious impulse in consciousness as far back as "Force and Understanding," he asserted that the shape of self-consciousness reached its perfection or fulfillment in the shape of the unhappy consciousness, we begin to grasp the significance of the reappearance of this figure (PhG §673; *Werke* 3:495). While the unhappy consciousness has received less attention in recent scholarship, the figure seems crucial to understanding the movement here. For an account of the importance of understanding the unhappy consciousness as not restricted to a specific historical moment see John W. Burbidge, " 'Unhappy Consciousness' in Hegel: An Analysis of Medieval Catholicism?" in *Hegel on Logic and Religion* (Albany: State University of New York Press, 1992), 105–118. For an argument that the unhappy consciousness is central to the whole dialectic of the *Phenomenology* see Jean Wahl, "Commentary on a Passage from Hegel's *Phenomenology of Spirit*," in *Jean Wahl: Transcendence and the Concrete, Selected Writings*, ed. Alan D. Schrift and Ian Alexander Moore (New York: Fordham University Press, 2017), 54–89.

55. PhG §752; *Werke* 3:547.

56. PhG §744; *Werke* 3:541.

57. PhG §752; *Werke* 3:547; see also §785; *Werke* 3:572.

58. PhG §753; *Werke* 3:547.

59. See PhG §437; *Werke* 3:321–323, especially Hegel's description of the laws: "It is in that way that they count for Sophocles' *Antigone* as the *unwritten* and *unerring* law of the gods: 'Not now and yesterday, but forever/It lives, and nobody knows from whence it appeared.' They *are*." Note the contrast Hegel makes with the immediate positivity of the laws: "However much I inquire about their emergence and confine them to their point of origin, still I have gone far beyond them, since it is *I who am henceforth the universal*, and they are the conditioned and restricted." Compare §712; *Werke* 3:520: "simplicity of truth as essential being . . . knows it *as the sure and unwritten law of the gods, a law that is 'everlasting' and no one knows whence it came*."

60. Compare the outcome of Aristophanes's destruction with that of the Terror: neither shape of consciousness yields positive content outside its self-affirmation through negation. "Universal freedom can thus produce neither a positive work nor a positive deed, and there remains for it merely the negative act. It is merely the fury of disappearing" (PhG §589; *Werke* 3:435–6). For an

analysis of Hegel's depiction of the self-consciousness of the French Revolution as a subjectivity that brooks no objectivity or essential other, see Rebecca Comay, *Mourning Sickness: Hegel and the French Revolution* (Stanford, CA: Stanford University Press, 2010). Note Comay's connection between this episode and the "ruination into which beautiful *Sittlichkeit* was thrown." See Comay, *Mourning Sickness*, 79.

61. The value and import of language will also be recovered in Christianity's emphasis on "das Wort" (PhG §770; *Werke* 3:559).

62. PhG §753; *Werke* 3:547. Compare Hippolite Taine's description of the depiction of the gods in Aristophanes: "Gods so closely resembling man soon become his companions, and later his sport." See Hippolite Taine, *Art in Greece*, trans. John Durand (New York: Holt & Williams, 1887), 43. This is clearly the opposite of Homer's *Iliad*, in which men are the sport of gods. Contrast this with Plato's ostensibly more politically salutary relation of gods and men, spectators, and actors (Laws I, 644–645c). If we conceive ourselves as playing before the gods rather than as the gods' playthings, our activity is ennobled. The inversion of this order, however, entails the elevation of the human to ultimate arbiter of good and evil. The danger of self-consciousness lies in recognizing man as the source of value and therefore the meaninglessness or arbitrariness of any and all values. If merely our products, why these values rather than those?

63. Compare Hegel's surprising interjection, warning his reader against antiquarianism, with Nietzsche's treatment of the same scholarly tendency (Nietzsche, "Uses and Disadvantages," 70–75). See also Hegel's judgment of a similar historico-philological impulse among those who confuse "the *origin*, as the *immediate existence* of the concept's first appearance, with the *simplicity* of the *concept*" (PhG §766; *Werke* 3:557). Such efforts can only yield a "spiritless recollection" (*geistlose Er-innerung*).

64. Ludwig Siep, *Hegel's Phenomenology of Spirit*, trans. Daniel Smyth (Cambridge: Cambridge University Press, 2014), 219.

65. PhG §753; *Werke* 3:548.

66. Siep, *Hegel's Phenomenology of Spirit*, 220. Also see the description of the task of philosophy in the modern age in G. W. F. Hegel, *Faith and Knowledge*, ed. Walter Cerf and H. S. Harris (Albany: State University of New York, 1988), 190–191; *Werke* 2:431–3.

67. PhG §754; *Werke* 3:549. Although Miller's interpolation "round the manger in Bethlehem" is heavy handed, it nevertheless reminds the reader of what Hegel is suggesting with this imagery. The unhappy consciousness that was the inversion of the comedic consciousness awaits the true incarnation of God in a genuinely finite and anthropomorphic form and therefore first as a child. As Hegel remarks in the *Lectures on the Philosophy of World History*, the Greek gods are "not anthropomorphic enough." See Hegel, *Lectures on the Philosophy of World History, Volume I:*

Manuscripts of the Introduction and The Lectures of 1822–3, ed. and trans. Robert F. Brown, Peter C. Hodgson, and William G. Geuss (Oxford: Oxford University Press, 2011), 391. In addition, this image recalls the stations of the cross imagery invoked in the Introduction (PhG §77; Werke 3:72) as well as foreshadowing the final image of the book: "the Golgotha of absolute spirit" (PhG §808; Werke 3:591).

68. PhG §672–79; Werke 3:495–498.

69. If the unhappy consciousness is that shape of consciousness for which "the in-itself is the beyond of itself" (PhG §231; Werke 3:178) it exemplifies the basic structure of consciousness as such as described in the introduction (PhG §80; Werke 3:74–75).

70. For a lucid account of why desire is at the heart of self-consciousness see Robert B. Pippin, *Hegel on Self-Consciousness: Desire and Death in the 'Phenomenology of Spirit'* (Princeton, NJ: Princeton University Press, 2011). However, Pippin is largely silent about the unhappy consciousness and its inflection of desire. The unhappy consciousness's longing to find its satisfaction in another self-consciousness understood as an absolute seems to be an erotic desire for the whole that transcends the sociopolitical order.

71. See Hegel's description of the unhappy consciousness as "yearning for" (*ersehnend*) precisely that content that emerges in this final stage of the dialectic (PhG §767; Werke 3:558).

72. PhG §755; Werke 3:550, "Geist . . . als diese ihre Einheit ins Dasein tritt." See also Hegel's discussion of the "three elments" of actual spirit (§786; Werke 3:573). Compare his programmatic statement on his philosophic aim: "Everything hangs on apprehending and expressing the truth not merely as *substance* but also equally as *subject*. At the same time, it is to be noted that substantiality comprises within itself the universal, that is, it comprises not only the *immediacy of knowledge* but also the immediacy of being, that is, immediacy for knowledge" (PhG §17; Werke 3:22–23). Such immediacy of being and knowing is precisely what is made possible by the incarnation.

73. PhG §786; Werke 3:572. Hegel also states that in religion spirit attains its "true shape" but that shape itself (*Gestalt selbst*) and the representation (*Vorstellung*) of it remain to be overcome (PhG §683; Werke 3:502–3. Compare PhG §678, Werke 3:497–498). See also discussion of *begreifende Wissen*, §798; Werke 3:582 (see also *begreifende Denken*, §59; Werke 3:56–57).

74. PhG §749; Werke 3:545; compare PhG §87; Werke 3:79. See Ardis Collins, *Hegel's Phenomenology: The Dialectical Justification of Philosophy's First Principles* (Montreal: McGill-Queen's University Press, 2013), 383. From one perspective, Aristophanes is so close to the principle of revealed religion that "God as spirit [knows] himself in us (as the eternal or logical side of our knowing ourselves in Him)." See Harris, *Hegel's Ladder*, 546. Yet the proximity is also an infinite distance—one that can, nevertheless, be encompassed by a broader conceptual ground.

75. PhG §758; *Werke* 3:551. This immediacy of the beholding is an indication of what remains to be sublated for religious consciousness (§§762–764; *Werke* 3:554–6; note especially, "die Ungleichheit der Gegenständlichkeit nicht aufgehoben, nicht ins reine Denken zurückgenommen hat").

76. PhG §758; *Werke* 3:551–2.

77. PhG §759; *Werke* 3:552.

78. PhG §175; *Werke* 3:144; PhG §759; *Werke* 3:552.

79. Although the concealment (*Geheimsein*) of essence that has hitherto attended all consciousness's attempts to know ceases when the "absolute essence as spirit is the object of consciousness," nevertheless, one further step remains and Hegel foreshadows the subsequent development of religion into absolute knowing with his remark that spirit's true shape is the concept (*Begriff*), which is also "solely its essence and substance" (PhG §759; *Werke* 3:553). While a great distance remains between revealed religion and absolute knowing, note Hegel's assertion that "speculative knowledge is the knowledge of revealed religion" (PhG §761; *Werke* 3:555).

80. PhG §759; *Werke* 3:553.

81. Since nothing remains hidden to consciousness when the absolute appears in this mode, nothing is alien or other to it (PhG §759; *Werke* 3:553). Recall that nothing was alien to comedy, but the grounds of this condition of nonalienation are now entirely different.

82. PhG §761; *Werke* 3:554.

83. PhG §673; *Werke* 3:495.

84. PhG §761; *Werke* 3:554. This formulation echoes Hegel's previous description: "Since the *other* unchangeable is a *shape of individuality* like itself, consciousness becomes, *thirdly*, spirit. It has the joy (*Freude*) of finding itself therein, and it is aware that its individuality is reconciled with the universal" (PhG §210; *Werke* 3:165). In other words, Hegel distinguishes joy (*Freude*) from happiness (*Glück*) (see also PhG §§353–357). My understanding of the significance of this "joy" is shaped by Chesterton's argument that Christianity makes possible true comedy, whereas all forms of paganism must remain tragic (see, inter alia, *Orthodoxy* in *The Everyman Chesterton*, ed. Ian Ker (New York: Alfred A. Knopf, 2011), 404–405.

85. PhG §763; *Werke* 3:556.

86. PhG §177; *Werke* 3:145. This condensed summary of *Die offenbare Religion* draws on subsequent developments of revealed religion, especially the conceptual meaning of the crucifixion (PhG §§758–764; *Werke* 3:551–556).

87. Leo Strauss, "The Problem of Socrates: Five Lectures" in *The Rebirth of Classical Political Rationalism*, ed. Thomas Pangle (Chicago: University of Chicago Press, 1989), 115; 118 (hereafter cited as *RCPR*).

88. See Leo Strauss, *Socrates and Aristophanes* (Chicago: University of Chicago Press, 1966), 4–6; 36; 43–48; 78–79; 311–12. Also see *RCPR*, 116–118.

89. As Strauss remarks, "Differences of interpretation ultimately proceed less from the consideration or the neglect of this or that particular fact or passage, than from a primary and fundamental disagreement" (*RCPR*, 105).

90. *RCPR*, 116. Compare Strauss's reformulation: Hegel's account "does justice to almost everything in Aristophanes except to one thing of, indeed, decisive importance. The basis of this taking back (or however we call it), of this subjectivism, is in Aristophanes not the self-consciousness of the subject, but knowledge of nature, and the very opposite of self-consciousness" (see *RCPR*, 118). As Strauss states very clearly, "The basis of Aristophanean comedy is knowledge of nature, and that means, for the ancients, philosophy" (*RCPR*, 118).

91. That this silence is deliberate is supported by the fact that some of the passages Strauss quotes from the *Phenomenology* occur in *Die offenbare Religion* section and in the context of explaining how comedic consciousness has become the unhappy consciousness, about which Strauss is also silent.

92. Soon after the public delivery of the Problem of Socrates Lectures in 1958, Strauss published "Relativism," which includes a discussion of the meaning of Christianity for Hegel as the absolute religion, indicating his full awareness of Hegel's teaching regarding the relation of *The Religion of Art* and *Revealed Religion* (see *RCPR*, 24–25).

93. *RCPR*, 106; for the reference to Thomas More see the version of the lectures published in *Interpretation: A Journal of Political Philosophy* 23, no. 2 (Winter 1996): 141. This claim is repeated almost verbatim at the end of Strauss's essay "On the Euthyphron," which addresses the question of divinity and piety. See *RCPR*, 206.

94. PhG §784; *Werke* 3:570.

95. PhG §784; *Werke* 3:570–71. The transformation of the meaning of death recalls that encountered in *Sittlichkeit* (PhG §452; *Werke* 3:332).

96. G. W. F. Hegel, *Faith and Knowledge*, 190–191; *Werke* 2:431–3. This grief is an indication of the opposition of philosophy and religion that characterizes the modern age. Hegel's response to the hard saying will only come by way of resolving the hitherto antagonistic posture of philosophy and religion. Perhaps the moment of theoretical consummation, or the ultimate realization of independent thought freed from authority, which Hegel identifies as the core principle of Protestantism, *must* risk descending into nihilism.

97. PhG §78–79; Consider Hegel's comparison of spirit's journey to the stations of the cross in the introduction (PhG §77; *Werke* 3:72).

98. See Hans Küng, *The Incarnation of God*, 204. See also Donald Verene's insightful speculations regarding the relation between the figure of the unhappy consciousness and philosophy: Verene, *Hegel's Absolute* (Albany: State University of New York Press, 2007), 63–69. Another way of understanding the challenge posed by the unhappy consciousness would be in light of "bad infinity"; philosophy is continually tempted by a false dialectic that obviates resolution and leads one to despair.

99. Hegel's insistence on the importance of this moment and facing up to it squarely is the basis of his criticism of Dante's *Divine Comedy*, which he judged overly confident and self-assured, since it lacked internal opposition. See Hegel, *Natural Law*, trans. T. M. Know (Philadelphia: University of Pennsylvania Press, 1975), 105–6. For the essential need that motivates philosophy see G. W. F. Hegel, *The Difference between Fichte's and Schelling's System of Philosophy*, ed. and trans. H. S. Harris and Walter Cerf (Albany: State University of New York Press, 1977), 89.

100. See Martin Heidegger, "Nietzsche's Word: 'God is Dead,' " in *Off the Beaten Track*, ed. and trans. Julian Young and Kenneth Haynes (Cambridge: Cambridge University Press, 2002), 157–199. For Hegel's critique of clever sophistic games, see his withering criticism of the destructive irony of Schlegel: "But the ironical, as the individuality of genius, lies in the self-destruction of the noble, great, and excellent; and so the objective art-formations too will have to display only the principle of absolute subjectivity, by showing forth that has worth and dignity for mankind as null in its self-destruction." See Hegel, *Hegel's Aesthetics*, 64–69. Hegel notes that this irony is a peculiar product of "Fichtean philosophy" and "borders nearly on the principle of the comic" (*Hegel's Aesthetics*, 66, 67). Hegel's critique of such a position remains apropos as a riposte to postmodernism: for example, Richard Rorty's advocacy of an ironic stance to the world. See Richard Rorty, *Contingency, Irony, Solidarity* (Cambridge: Cambridge University Press, 1989).

101. See Ronald Beiner's description of Max Weber: Weber thought of the world "as tragic, and thought that human beings only rose to being fully human insofar as they comported themselves as self-conscious protagonists in a classical tragedy." See Ronald Beiner, *Political Philosophy: What It Is and Why It Matters* (Cambridge: Cambridge University Press, 2014), xlix. For an argument that Hegel remains the preeminent diagnostician of this possibility see James Doull's response to Emil Fackenheim's charge that today Hegel would no longer be a Hegelian. See James Doull, "The Doull Fackenheim Debate: Would Hegel Today Be a Hegelian?" in *Philosophy and Freedom: The Legacy of James Doull*, ed. David G. Peddle and Neil G. Robertson (Toronto: University of Toronto Press, 2003), 334–342.

102. PhG §19; *Werke* 3:24.

103. PhG §33; *Werke* 3:36–37.

Chapter Nine

Hegel and "the Other Comedy"

Martin Donougho

THIS CHAPTER HAS FIVE PARTS: it's not quite a *comedy* in five acts, true, and there is only a perfunctory gesture at the usual happy ending. First comes a short prologue on Hegel's idea of the self-reflexive artwork, then a second part on German *Lustspiel* and on Hegel's articulation, in his *Natural Law* essay (1802), of his own theory of comedy, classical or modern (the latter he dubs "the *other comedy*"). There follows a third part on what I take to be Hegel's main theory of comedy, as found in the chapter on religion from his *Phenomenology of Spirit* where Aristophanes plays a central role; this approach contrasts with the thorough marginalizing of modern comedy in the Berlin *Aesthetics*. A fourth part examines a brief exception to Hegel's dismissal of comedy, with his 1826 review of a play by Ernst Raupach, *Die Bekehrten* (The converted). Finally, I offer a brief discussion of possible escapes from a dispiriting *endism*—the end of comedy and the end of art.

PROLOGUE: Hotho's edition of Hegel's *Aesthetics* has a wonderful passage at the very point where the exposition shifts from a consideration of the beauty of (or in) nature to the treatment we owe "Art-beauty"—*das Kunstschöne*—a notion that Hegel seems to have borrowed from Aloys Hirt, his colleague at the University of Berlin.¹ Under the rubric of "beautiful individuality," Hegel argues that human form and liveliness (*Lebendigkeit*) are uniquely suited to displaying the "Ideal" (the "Idea" in sensuous shape), in stark contrast to, say, natural symmetry, rocks, amoeba, plants, or nonhuman animals. The eye, especially, is best suited to reveal spirit or mindedness. For the soul not only *sees* but is also *seen* through the eye—*its* eyes. Communicability is inherent to the human figure. In turn, the task of the artwork, Hegel declares,

> is to convert every shape at all points of its visible surface into an eye.... Or, as Plato cries out to the star in his familiar [*bekannten*] distich: "When you look on the stars, my star, oh! would I were the heavens and could see you with a thousand eyes," so, conversely, art makes every one of its productions into a thousand-eyed Argus, whereby the inner soul and spirit is seen at every point. And it is not only the bodily form, the look of the eyes, the countenance and posture, but also actions and events, speech and tone of voice, and the series of their course through all conditions of appearance that art has everywhere to make into an eye, in which the free soul is revealed in its inner infinity.²

The passage derives ultimately from Hotho's own transcript of Hegel's 1823 lectures, reciting Plato's distich (not yet *bekannt*), though without mention of Argus—who knows where *he* comes in?—while "Aster" is tacitly present.³

Other transcripts steer essentially the same course, even if the paradox is expressed less piquantly than in 1823. What matters above all is the self-reflexive step implicit in the Ideal or *das Kunstschöne*, which seems to touch on the "absoluteness" of art, in a Hegelian perspective. Observers regard or interpret the work as it seems to observe or interpret themselves, almost in *mise-en-abyme*; the artwork presents or manifests their own truth, namely, their individuality as expressed in bodily demeanor, posture, gesture, action, speech, etc.⁴ In that respect art—that is, the art*work*—escapes natural determinacy, just as spirit continues to inhabit the natural body and its phenomenal actions and deeds: the work "manifests" human self-expression. And this self-reflexive feature will continue to hold, presumably, in *post*classical (i.e., "romantic"—art), although aesthetic mediation (via character, plot, or gesture) will become somehow attenuated, less cheerful or festive, more nuanced, displaced, even ironic—the self-reflexivity constitutive of art expressly foregrounded. Pippin calls this feature in Hegel's account the "double doubling" (or "dual doubleness") of art, whereby spirit is conscious of its dual nature (as nature and mind), while art communicates to the observer the artist's individual perspective upon human duality (it presents the artist's own "take" on what matters).⁵ Pippin addresses the doubling of subjectivity in Hegel's account of painting. Yet doubling of thematic content is implicit (I'd argue—though much more needs to be said) even in classical sculpture or epic, according to Hegel: there's always the potential for artistic self-awareness, a nod to the audience as to how the represented gesture or action appears to others.

I rehearse the starry passage above as a prelude to my discussion of Hegelian comedy. If comedy is to qualify as art (in Hegel's book)—that is, as absolute spirit—it must present some essential truths about individuals and how they present or express themselves in the world. More subtly, the *experience* of comedy—in the theater or as the text we read—should allow us to understand ourselves, our real-world experiences, in some noncontingent way. We—or ancient Greeks, eighteenth-century Germans, etc.—discover ourselves (they discover themselves) in the work or performance. Such is Hegel's claim. In this chapter I ask what *sort* of self-reflexive truth Hegel thinks comedy might convey and what kind of *truth-telling* the comic-artist might embody or personify—*for us*. And I note that comic knowledge and enjoyment may be focalized at several points: in the *characters* played onstage, in *authorial* subjectivity, or by extension in audience *reception* (whether contemporary or later).

In Hotho's 1823 transcript,

> comedy begins where tragedy leaves off: with an internally and absolutely reconciled and serene heart which gets tangled up, inducing an opposition that attempts to remove the entanglement, yet is so clumsy in the means used that it undermines its purpose through those very means, while yet remaining calm throughout and certain of itself.⁶

This alludes especially to Aristophanes, whose characters—Hegel adds—end up *laughing at themselves*, not just *being laughed at*. Characters experience a change of heart, a discrete *movement* from folly to recognition and cheerful acceptance rather than just static celebration—what Erich Segal in his book *The Death of Comedy* dubbed "a revel without a cause."⁷ And returning to my previous point, *we* laugh *with* the characters, seeing and experiencing *ourselves* on their journey to enlightenment and reconciliation, as far as we're able. My questions are directed at the complex *balance* to be struck between sympathetic *identification*, on the one hand, and madcap *revelry* or derisive (even moralistic) *negation* on the other.

LUSTSPIEL, AND "THE OTHER COMEDY": "*Komödie*, or *Lustspiel* as it is often called in German, has never been a major genre within German literary history, and as a consequence, German comedy has suffered a bad reputation and received relatively little attention." So writes Bettina Brandt, in her succinct description of "German Comedy" (2005).[8] She credits the theorist and critic Johann Christoph Gottsched with popularizing the term *Lustspiel* and also with imposing Enlightenment order upon the form in the interest of challenging the successes of classical French theater.[9] For Gottsched: "Comedy is simply an imitation of an immoral (*lasterhaften*) action which by its ridiculous nature can entertain yet at the same time edify the spectator."[10] Gottfried Lessing's plays in turn allowed audiences to feel sympathetic *identification* with virtuous, bourgeois characters, beyond the previous moralizing *censure* or *ridicule* of deviance. Much impressed by Diderot's *genre sérieux*, Lessing succeeded in bringing a middle-class realism to the German stage: prose replaced verse, acting acquired a more naturalistic tenor, the dramatic action could extend to scenes of domestic life, and a principal aim of drama was assumed to be the cultivation of moral sentiment.

That furnishes a brief historical background to Hegel's earliest treatment of comedy: the 1802 essay on natural law.[11] This highly original work is notable for offering a general picture (*bild*) of political legitimacy as, in a well-known (if highly opaque) formulation,

> nothing other than the performance [*Aufführung*] in the ethical [arena] of the tragedy which the Absolute eternally enacts [*spielt*] with itself . . . by sacrificing itself to forces of objectivity. (104/2, 495)

It represents a sacrifice, that is to say, to the forces of unconscious nature (articulated, we are to understand, by the laws of Scottish political economy). Natural law comprises both classical ethical theory and modern political economy. History is portrayed as assuming aesthetic shape, specifically the cyclical form of tragic sacrifice, epitomized, Hegel suggests, in *The Oresteia* of Aeschylus. But whereas in *tragedy* the state "segregates its inorganic nature as a fate (in order not to become entangled [*sich verwickele*] in it)" (105/495–6), *acknowledging* nature precisely by putting it in its proper place, *comedy* instead *submits* to the messy entanglements of sheer circumstance or contingency. With clear reference to Dante's *Divine Comedy*, Hegel maintains therefore that comedy wholly *lacks* tragic fate, lacks opposition, seriousness and inner truth (105–6/496). He explains: *Either* comedy expresses an "absolute vitality [*Lebendigkeit*]," as in Dante, when it presents "shadows of clashes, or mock battles with a fabricated fate and fictitious beings"—although it's true that Hegel would later change his tune completely, as witnessed in a celebrated passage in the *Aesthetics* on Dante's modern epic.¹² *Or else* it falls within a general "non-vitality"—code for a modern or civil society ruled by economic laws—when it "presents mere shadow images of self-determinacy and absoluteness." The *first* kind—Hegel continues in a page filled with arcane allusions (106/497)—is able to sustain dream traces about autonomous persons, or it can yield up visions of "perfect individuality," though without force or effect. Hegel's words seem to hint at the glories of ancient Greece but also at their mirror image in the work of poets such as Homer, Sophocles, Plato, and not least, Aristophanes—the figure above all associated with Old Comedy.¹³ Hegel gives us comedy both in life *and* in art. But *secondly* there exists what Hegel dubs "the *other comedy*" (107/498), which is to say, modern comedy, "whose entanglements [*Verwicklungen*] are without fate or true struggle," because ethical nature is itself caught in that fate, too—by which I take Hegel to mean that virtue for us moderns simply obeys "the way of the world." Such a world is made up of contingent abstractions, contracts, legal obstructions, and the like. Events climax in conflicts and collisions that the participants themselves may take seriously but which prove risible for us spectators. "And salvation . . . is sought in an affectation of character and [an] absoluteness which is [then] continually deceived and put down."¹⁴ Each character looks anxiously to the security of possessions and legal protections, in a world supposedly bound by reason where all suppose themselves sovereign. An alternative perspective would instead find reason absent from what amounts to an intrinsically *absurd* universe, where people can only beseech the gods for help or protection from sheer baffling contingency. In either case, the finite self "merely enacts the farce [*die Farce*] of its faith and of its undying delusion" (107/499). In the first mode of modern comedy "conflicts and finitude are shadows without substance . . . while in the other the Absolute [itself] is a delusion" (*eine Täuschung*) (108/499). This somewhat foreshadows the dialectic of Enlightenment in the *Phenomenology*, where we find secular business and religious faith at odds, yet operating as mutual supplements. Each exists solely in relation to the other. But, Hegel declares, "the absolute relation . . . is set forth in tragedy [*Trauerspiel*]" (108/499). Modern comedy—reading between the lines—gives us two halves that ethically don't add up: on the one hand, serious business without legitimate foundations; on the other, laughable absurdity and continual disillusionment.¹⁵

COMEDY IN THE PHENOMENOLOGY VERSUS MODERN COMEDY IN THE AESTHETICS: The middle-class "entanglements" characteristic of "the *other comedy*" barely feature in the *Phenomenology* (although you could find traces of bourgeois shenanigans in the chapter on "Reason," say, with "Virtue and the Way of the World," or "The Animal Kingdom of Spirit," understood as modeling civil society). Besides a more articulated concept of tragedy (as not just ethical *content* but also religious *form*—or rather, form*ing*), what we nevertheless find there, in chapter 7 ("Religion"), is Hegel's mature account of comedy. I would maintain that it provides a paradigm for his thinking even in the Berlin period. Comedy comprises the unmasking of ancient character or ethos, when the agent lets persona or mask fall—the mask he or she essentially *is*—whether its removal is performed literally on stage or figuratively in the dramatized action. Chapter 7, on "Art-religion," exhibits the language of tragedy as it gives way to that of comedy—the Old Comedy of Aristophanes. The player doffs the mask she or he wears so as to appear simply as a *self*, a *person* (¶743–44)—just as in turn audience members become selves or persons enjoying their new social status. Hegel speaks (¶742) of *hypocrisy*, in the original sense of playacting, yet also in the sense of the artist/playwright's *self*-deception.[16] It is fair to say that Aristophanes gets his due in these few compressed paragraphs. For example, the "superficial individuality" of divine beings is said in the text to dissolve into "clouds," a vanishing mist (¶746)—a nod at Aristophanes's play. The gods are shown up as wholly lacking a "self": mere figments of representation that display no more than "the *form* of individuality" (¶744/541–2, my emphasis). In a further dig at Socrates, the pure thought of the Beautiful and the Good, following dialectical liberation from mere opinion, is shown empty of content; it becomes comic spectacle (*Schauspiel*), subject to the whim of contingent individuality (i.e., the "singular" philosopher or dialectician). Finally, conversion of all universals into subjective self-certainty, into a "well-being and letting-oneself-be-well" (*ein Wohlsein und Sich-wohlsein lassen*) is, so we read, no longer to be found outside of comedy—which is to say, Aristophanic comedy (¶747). In Hegel's Berlin lectures on *Aesthetics* the same phrase (*wohlsein*) appears, though more pointedly as the vernacular *sauwohl* (happy as a pig in clover), to capture Hegel's particular enthusiasm: "If you haven't read him, you cannot know how hog-happy humans can be."[17] Hegel's resort to Aristophanes as someone driving the last nail in the coffin of Greek community reflects, indeed, a wholesale change in critical opinion, after two millennia dominated by the satiric (or Menandrine) tradition—a deviation that began with Schiller's appreciation for Aristophanes and Old Comedy and continued with the Romantics' extolling his zaniness and then with their own ideas about comedy. Where orthodoxy appealed to attitudes of superiority to the comic figure or "butt," Romantics turned inward to focus on human subjectivity, appealing to an incongruity between reason and passion: an inner theater of the mind that Jan Hokenson suggests—in a superb study, *The Idea of Comedy*—anticipates twentieth-century populist developments.[18]

Aristophanes supplied Hegel with the paradigm of comedy. For he epitomized the subjective self-satisfaction and sense of well-being found in comic action and comic authorship alike. In Hotho's official edition we read that comedy presents subjectivity "in its unfettered self-determination and freedom" (15: 520/1194). It offers, "in the laughter in which the individuals dissolve everything, including themselves," a view (*Anschauung*) "of the victory of their own subjectivity, which remains self-assured nevertheless [*dennoch*]"(15, 527/1199). In other words, comic individuals end up laughing at themselves, and we laugh with them, not (just) at their amusing characters and antics.[19] More fundamentally—as Allen Speight shows in his contribution, "Philosophy, Comedy and History"—Hegel's sees Aristophanes ushering in the end of the entire classical Ideal, the end of art proper; this is a meta-aesthetic role Hegel has him continue to play at the end of the various student transcripts from Berlin. (Amusingly, Hotho misspells the name twice in his 1823 transcript, whether through his own unfamiliarity or because of Hegel's notoriously poor enunciation.[20]) Thus from the last series (1828–9), in the third division devoted to the "individuality" (*Individualität*) of artworks, we read: "Aristophanes is one of the clearest symptoms of the fall of Greek art; in him is expressed the contradiction between gods or state and the citizens' subjectivity" (Heimann).[21] He exemplifies the critical edge comedy may display when it takes on sacred cows with gleeful abandon—though not indiscriminately, Hegel adds. In the *History of Philosophy* Hegel is quick to stress the playwright's loyalty to Athens, arguing that his targets (politicians, philosophers, gods) wholly deserve their staged comeuppance. In the *Aesthetics*, too: "Aristophanes was serious, patriotic, portraying the folly of people and of the gods" (Heimann), we read in the 1828–9 series. In other words, without shifting gears wholly into satire—a transitional form for Hegel, on the borderline of art proper—Aristophanes found a balance between sheer gusto and sharp political or cultural critique.[22] His only rival in the Hegelian canon would be Shakespeare, especially with his Falstaff, who similarly throws off all civilized restraints.

By comparison, what Hegel called "modern" comedy turns out to be marginal in the *Aesthetics*. Hegel argues that its main deviation from "genuine" comedy lies in a tendency to laugh *at* the comic figure rather than *with* him or her. Molière compares unfavorably with Shakespeare in this regard, especially for Shakespeare's more generous understanding of character. There's nothing comical about the narrow-minded *hypocrite, pedant, misanthrope*, or *miser*—the stock characters Molière pokes fun at (perhaps a relic from *commedia dell'arte*). Hegel prefers sentimental (*larmoyante*) comedy, tending toward *sympathetic identification* with characters onstage—in league with, for example, Diderot and Lessing. But it is not clear where to situate that historical development in Hegel's larger scheme of things.

RAUPACH IN BERLIN: Yet there was a peculiar moment when Hegel showed unusual enthusiasm for contemporary comedy, or *Lustspiel*. He is known to have been an enthusiastic opera- and theater-goer; contemporary accounts mention his hurrying off at half-past six of an evening to catch some performance or other. He belonged to an informal club promoting such sociability, its members including Moritz Saphir, founder of the *Berliner Schnellpost für Literatur, Theater und Geselligkeit*. In January 1826 Hegel published in that paper, under the subtitle "Anti-Critical," a five-part rebuttal of an anonymous review (most probably by the paper's owner Saphir) of a play he had just seen, *Die Bekehrten* (The converted), by Ernst Raupach.[23] Hardly a household name today, even in Germany, Raupach was nevertheless highly popular in Berlin and Hamburg, writing well over a hundred plays, including a serial history of the Hohenzollern dynasty, as well as a string of farces and entertainments. (I might add that a piece of his on the Niebelungen myth was translated into English, and there is another translation, of his *Isidor and Olga*, a title Hegel mentions in passing. Not least, an early vampire story, "Wake not the Dead"/"Bride of the Grave" [1823], well-known in English and often attributed to Ludwig Tieck, is in fact by Raupach.[24])

I confess I had never noticed Hegel's attempt at literary criticism (or "anti-criticism") until I found a reference in Jaeschke's *Hegel-Handbuch*. There have been several other mentions, notably a 2010 essay in *Hegel-Studien* by Stephan Kraft, and several pages in Niklas Hebing's comprehensive monograph, *Hegels Ästhetik des Komischen* (2015).[25] I have never seen a reference to it in English, but I think Hegel's lively intervention—he seems really pleased with himself—more than deserves discussion.

Raupach's comedy takes place at an indeterminate time, in a loosely Italian location peopled with a mix of aristocrats and servant types. It tells of a young pair, Clotilde and Torquato, who though close in childhood have since grown apart: she suspects him of some infidelity, and he treats her with an exaggerated show of pride. Torquato's rich uncle, an old count officially betrothed to Clotilde, contrives to reunite the couple (a neat inversion of the conventional device of a *senex* blocking the path of young love). The intrigue involves a trip to Rome in search of papal annulment, followed by an elaborate pretense that the uncle has died and then his reappearance first as a hermit and then later as his own ghost. (Hegel adds that we don't require the backstory to make much *sense*, when what counts is the dramatic *present*—he instances *King Lear* among other works to make his point.) The intrigue is driven by the "knave" Burchiello and Clotilde's maid Fiametta—but they only manage to complicate things: for example, when Burchiello tries to persuade Clotilde to leave Torquato well alone, on the theory that women will *always* do the opposite of what they're told. This is a psychological ploy that totally fails in this instance. Still, in the end Clotilde's jealous suspicions prove unfounded—it was his page, not a lover, that Torquato had contacted—and everything ends happily. We might say, *of course* it ends happily! Even Burchiello and Fiametta wind up together.

Saphir's review was lukewarm. While allowing that the play had some neat touches and effective scenes worthy of their esteemed author, the review argued that there was little in the way of action. Motivation and plot were threadbare and drawn out, the dramatic "discoveries" quite implausible, and the characters from the start "soft and suggestible" (*mürbe und bekehrlich*) (16, 9).[26] (*Mürbe* hints at a flaky lack of character—puppetlike, perhaps, the lovers fall into each other's arms.) All told, the play was full of "non-essentials," depended too much on ingrown resentments, and everywhere "blind chance" ruled. Worse, it involved not so much contingencies as forced outcomes. It was, in short, no *Lustspiel*, merely trivial "farce" (*Possenspiel*), the "knave," for example, being reduced to a mere clown figure (*der Hanswurst*).

Hegel responds on several (though not on all) counts. First, *Lustspiel* by its nature engages with contingency, the "cheerful entanglements of life," although it is often mixed with a serious element as well—lacking which, indeed, it would descend into farce, if not lower (4–5). As weighty authority for injecting nonplayfulness into *Lustspiel* Hegel appeals first of all to Aristophanes and his mixing of the madcap with the serious, even the political; then he appeals to Shakespearean comedy for its use of fools and nonsense even in high tragedy and yet still more for its combining of "deep and noble passions, of worthy characters," even when occasioned by the comic entanglements of subordinates (5). Second, comic events count as no more than the external arena for a display of characters and their passions—the real material of art (6). Fables or "hackneyed" stories typically serve as the mere *frame* on which to hang our literary concerns, the external conditions for mounting the "spectacle." Hegel notes that our critic (addressed directly as "you") seems as concerned with the disturbing violence of events or situations as with sheer contingency, and Hegel admits that the comic pair may verge on vehemence, cruelty, or anger in expression. But verisimilitude is a relative matter (7–8), Hegel argues, citing Raupach's use of a ghost and arguing that comedy has always to strike a balance between real fear and mere farce. As for the intrigue put in play by the old count (though implemented by the servants), Hegel finds that the piquant combination of wild confusion and halfway plausible explanation makes for "a true (*echt*) comic action." It is at least as successful as other common devices—eavesdropping and the like (8). Third, Hegel considers what might be called the psychological angle and how that was effectively conveyed in the play by its talented actors. The characters aren't "squishy," moreover, but instead display reflectiveness, inwardness, even shades of embarrassment as they recall their shared pasts (10).[27] They are shown undergoing a mutual conversion, indeed, as each comes to realize their shared situation (*Grundlage*) and their parity of man and woman. (We might even be reminded of the Cavellian theme of a Hollywood comedy or melodrama of remarriage: not so much first as *second* love, its palpable internalization, and even conversion by conversation.)

Finally, Hegel argues that some of the play's "disharmony" lies in its *irony*, a trope that usually "comprises making everything that passes for beautiful, noble and interesting straightaway self-destruct and turn into its opposite" (11). Irony is understood (by *some* theorists) as the peak of an author's art, Hegel continues. But he draws our attention to how irony works *within* this play, so that while our characters really do undergo conversion, the journey involves a certain amount of tortuous deception at the hands of subordinate characters (Burchiello is a self-conscious ironist, for example) in a kind of double plot. Hegel admires how the action can both sort out and combine straight with crooked and serious with zany on the same stage. Again, Shakespeare is invoked for his mixing of high and low, sincere and ribald (12). Even though Raupach in the past "tinkers about" (*herumversuchen*) with various dramatic forms, from serious drama to farce, here he's praised for finding a happy medium (13).

In his 2010 essay Stephan Kraft raises the interesting question of whether Hegel's brief encounter with Raupach's light comedy might have left its imprint on the lectures of 1826. He cites Kehler's transcript:

> Modern comedy is quite distinct from ancient. *Drama* stands in between, [where] duty or right carries off the victory; vice is punished, and those mixed up in it are at least shamed and turn towards reform; in them [we encounter] a reconciliation of the good with itself.[28]

This "middle" genre recalls Diderot's (or Lessing's) "serious" comedy. At the opposite pole: "What the French call high comedy [*'haute comédie'*] is really little different, but [they] have taken a radical position"—that is, *against* any mixing of censure and sympathy.[29] Hegel cites Molière's Tartuffe and Orgon, or *L'Avare* (the miser). Molière's ridicule (mixed with moralizing animus) is then contrasted with a third form, which Hegel calls here "absolute comedy": "Folly self-consciously negates itself, a high aim is promoted yet is merely entertained [*ein gemeinter*]," while the means employed serve only to undermine the actual carrying out of any such aim. "In modern comedy the means also involve servants and chambermaids, who [may] assist those in charge but through self-interest or misunderstandings imperil or spoil the aim." In a "true" *Lustspiel*, by contrast, the characters are so engrossed with their constitutive aims that they remain quite carefree when things misfire; they display an Olympian cheerfulness, just like that of Aristophanes. His comedies present lofty purposes in disarray—a "deliberate irony," a self-jesting that remains blissful (*selig*) throughout. It is notable that in 1826, unlike other years (1820–21, 1823, 1828–29), the emergence of comic subjectivity (in character or artist) is *not* followed by hints of an end to art and the Ideal. With the second edition of the *Encyclopedia* (1827), however, and again in the final lecture series (Kraft quotes an anonymous transcript, but Heimann corroborates), the "end-of-art" thesis returns with what Kraft calls "its old vehemence." The positive engagement with modern comedy remained "a brief episode," and a "disruption," he concludes.[30] Heimann, I'll add, renders the final verdict even bleaker than in Kraft's telling. We read of "bad" comedies, "bad" sons and servants, "deceiving guardians" moved by "false interests and prejudices" so that "contingent battles contingent." And little more than "the crooked or random," constantly falling short, becomes the object of mirth.

No wonder the following sentence concludes—and it *is* the conclusion—that only philosophy of art remains necessary now that we've left art behind.

What then to make of Kraft's argument, which presses fairly hard on a handful of phrases from Kehler's *Mitschrift*? (Von der Pfordten is no help—just one sketchy paragraph.[31]) If nothing else it underlines the interpretive challenge we face in factoring in Hotho's (often bewilderingly opaque) editorial procedures, plus the uncomfortable circumstance that readers today have as it were to make bricks without straw: most of Hotho's sources are now missing, while only a handful of student transcripts have been published. Kraft remarks that Hotho's edition interpolated a section on "modern drama" (15, 555–69/1222–33) *between* his treatment of Old Comedy (552–5/1220–2) and modern comedy (569–72/1233–6). The effect of Hotho's editing was to align *Lustspiel* with the main line of "New" or "Menandrine" comedy, which runs via Plautus and Terence all the way to Molière: we laugh *at* these ridiculously base creatures appearing onstage. Hotho leaves no room for a more sympathetic approach. In the Kehler extract we've seen that Hegel takes note of the "middle" genre of "drama"—"*Drama* stands in between, [where] duty or right carries off the victory"; Diderot's 'comédie sérieuse' (or *bourgeoise*). But Hotho's edition manages to shoehorn that passage into a brief, one-page discussion of (ßß) "dramas midway *between* tragedy and comedy," having Hegel then dismiss the whole thing rather briskly (15, 568–9/1232–3). Either the genre indulges a German taste for social and family life, often in a medieval setting (e.g., *Götz*[32]), or more often it celebrates "the triumph of *morality* [*Moralischen*]" (568/1232), the pointing of moral lessons. It is a form entirely taken up with money and property, with class differences, petty love affairs, and the like, where virtue simply gets rewarded and vice punished. The particular danger Hegel identifies with such dramas (in Hotho's words) is that the poet will focus either on the inner life of characters rather than the *action* proper, or else on mere theatrical *effect* or *entertainment*. The "middle genre" recedes entirely from view at this point, as we find Hegel racing through his last lecture to reach a final judgment: that modern comedy sounds the death knell of comedy and, indeed, art.

All the same I can't help but feel that—perhaps under pressure to finish up—Hegel misses an opportunity here, if we recall the mordant lines about "the *other comedy*" from 1802 (concerning either a prosaic world full of legal constraints or a disenchanted modern society), or if we imagine what a fuller treatment of "drama" as "*comédie sérieuse*" might yield. A focus on "middle" people and their finite social situations would seem of interest precisely in announcing an emergent nineteenth-century realism, linked perhaps with the Hegelian notion of "the prose of the world," when "*serious*"-minded bourgeois characters are caught at *comic* cross-purposes, or else seek respite from the intrinsically absurd operations of modern circumstance. To invoke Franco Moretti, it is the world of "everyday" waiting and absorption and of time-marking "fillers" lodged between narrative turning points.[33]

One might extend the point to include Moretti's theory of the bildungsroman, specifically *Wilhelm Meister*, a work Hegel appears to slight in his relatively few mentions of it—oddly perhaps, given his usual reverence for Goethe.[34] I realize that it comes under the rubric of the novel, a genre considered elsewhere in the *Aesthetics*. But for one thing, this is a novel much taken up with *theater*—more with tragedy, it's true, though Wilhelm does end up a somewhat comic figure—but also with its social and historical preconditions and with poetry and its modes of performance. As Moretti sees it, the individual feels acutely his or her finitude but feels at the same time a strong sense of possibility: seemingly unconnected events might yet resolve themselves—who knows?—into a larger plan, the very plot of one's life. "It is a new, truly *secular* way of imagining the meaning of life: dispersed among countless minute events, mixed with the indifference or petty egoisms of the world: but always tenaciously there."[35] That's Moretti, admittedly, not Hegel—though it could well have been Hegel, I'd suggest. Moreover, that perspective would open a space for ordinary middle-class individuals to find themselves portrayed—perhaps even caricatured—in a dual aspect: (a) their subjective experience or situation, or (b) within the objective structures of modern life (contracts, civil society, family, etc.). It gestures at the survival of comedy beyond the kind of entertainment (mixing irony, empathy, and revelry) he had once found embodied, for a brief if vibrant moment, in Raupach's piece of theater.

That I confess is reverse my previous conclusion[36] that the comedic genre threatens to pack its bags and leave the realm of art altogether, whether for ordinary reality or for a quasi-philosophical (and highly ironic) perspective on the comedy of world history. Perhaps this gesture of renewal strikes a "reconciliationist" tone—within Allen Speight's survey of outcomes—although the fact that Hegel's late idea of "objective humor" (from January 1829) coincides precisely with the turn *against* reconciliation (which Speight has clearly demonstrated in Hegel's various lecture series) leads us to doubt whether *Versöhnung*, classical or romantic, is its real aim. For as I see it, the middle genre of "drama" doesn't so much put the mind to rest as leave it in productive tension. The tension derives partly from its emergent status as autonomous art, in theory and/or as cultural institution, partly from its transitional status and its precarious balance of subjective and objective moments.

ROADS NOT TAKEN: In this brief concluding section I propose three contexts promising to escape the gloomy "endism" of modern comedy, which just leaves us (and art) in the lurch. I admit these are speculative attempts to make bricks without straw, each building on a moment of transition—Hegel's present—when subjective and objective elements are in play.[37] They all return, notably, to Hegel's citation of Plato's epigram invoking Aster, and to the redoubled gaze of the artwork: subject and object seem to mirror each other.

My first example concerns Hegel's enthusiasm for T. G. Hippel, attested to in both 1826 and 1829 (Heimann gives the date as January 20, 1829). Hippel's *Lebensläufe in aufsteigender Linie* (*Biographies in an Ascending Line*: 1778–81) was a special favorite of Hegel's from youth on, even though this rather ungainly four-volume work was largely forgotten by the 1820s, and it has never been translated into English.[38] Hegel notes that Hippel was a *Bürgermeister* in Königsberg "and is the author of one of few great original works of the German Nation, surpassing Jean Paul."[39] Hotho's official edition fills in the details. It remarks that fixity of character and attitude are often found (as with comic figures) among the lower orders where individuals prosaically *identify* with their fixed and finite roles, never doubting themselves (see 15, 571/1220). In 1826, Hegel says of Hippel: "He has great characterizations of repressed souls who don't know how to express themselves" (literally, create space for themselves); they are persons of typically "frightful" (read "lower class") social origin (Von der Pfordten). "Many sink back into sheer form [*Formalismus*]" (Kehler)—simply following convention. I must admit that *Lebensläufe* seems quite uneventful, even tiresome—far less amusing than Sterne (and many people can't stand *him*, I realize). Nevertheless, quotidian pointlessness *is* the point here. In contrast to Jean Paul, Hippel's narrator tends to vanish. He is a mouthpiece through which to present characters and events, with minimal comment or interpretation, and with *no* attempt to provide causal linkage (a different sense of "revel without a cause"). Plot is of little concern to Hippel; he is content to infuse events and concerns with a sense of gusto, sadness, loss, haplessness, and so on. Again, it's quotidian reality that we encounter. We might be reminded of Dutch genre painting but also of the everyday life found on the modern stage, not to mention the various scenes of "absorption" extolled by Diderot. Hamilton Beck (in his 1987 study) dubbed Hippel less a dramatist—his situations are hardly "dramatic" —than a *protocolist*, by which he presumably means "minute taker" (from the German), but it also signifies "registrar of formalities."[40] Hippel knew all too well how much we are ruled by social artifice, by the formal, constructed, secondhand nature of our lives—women's lives especially. (He wrote pioneering books on marriage and on the status of women and has been hailed as an influence on Hegel's own views in this area.[41]) In sum, awareness of the social categories or roles defining and confining us can result in either political critique or else laughter, perhaps both together. Moreover, Hippel's fiction may itself be described as transitional in nature, when the "romantic" art form/worldview is gradually ebbing, and we encounter various uncanny juxtapositions of objective fact and subjective infusion of feeling. His novel displays mildly comic tableaux rather than proper stories. By suppressing narrative voice, relying instead on readers' amused reactions, it offers scenes blending object and subject, bourgeois reality and reader's share, absorption and theatricality.

Another transitional form to mention is the epigram. Hegel remarks that its formal artifice emerges between classical and romantic worldviews— and again with the dissolution of the romantic artform.[42] Epigram fuses and confuses subjective and objective moments and does so actively, as a performative, its "garlands" of flowers matching distichs or verses exchanged with others. "*Xenien*" Goethe dubbed them, recalling the ancient custom by which for ancient Greeks giving and receiving, just like host and guest, are wholly reversible.[43] It is, moreover, a historicizing practice: painting about painting practices, poems about past poems. But space being short, I'll cite a different example. It isn't even literary, I admit, though it remains distinctly comedic.

In explicating what "the Ideal as such" amounts to, along with sculpture and poetry, Hegel cites Dutch genre studies as well. Genre paintings are not mere "pictures of vulgarity," Hegel maintains, yet neither do they *escape* the vulgar: they are vulgar "inside and out," he says, in both content and formal means (13, 222/168). The last lecture series took sharp aim at von Rumohr's recent materialist assault on the Ideal, and this sharp angle on things was Hegel's neat riposte—the Ideal *lives in* the ordinary, as (we might say) caviar for the general.[44] Genre images perform or enact a popular taking-pleasure-in-life, ordinary objects spiritualized both by their *display* and by our *reception* of that display: they regard us regarding them. But the dialectical interaction is still more complex, briefly, because it seeks to reveal a certain *otium*—play, leisure—*in* the art. Hegel selects unusual works to praise: Murillo's little pictures of beggar boys, which he had recently seen in Munich. In one, the mother picks lice out of the boy's hair; in the other, boys eat grapes and or melon slices. Hegel comments, in Hotho's edition:

> We see that they have no wider interests and aims, yet not at all because of stupidity; rather they squat on the ground content and serene, almost like the gods of Olympus; they do nothing, they say nothing; but they are people all of a piece without surliness or discontent; and since they possess this foundation of all excellence, we get the idea that anything might become of these youths.[45]

It is Hippel inverted: a display of ordinary figures and situations, yet unencumbered and care*free*, not at all awkward, cramped, or repressed—they are like Olympian gods. Jacques Rancière advances a complex interpretation of Hegel's choice of example, in an attempt to do justice to its overdetermined actuality.[46] He finds Hegel taking note of Dutch genre painting as symptomatic of national hardworking virtues. But at the same time, he adds, it has now become *art displayed in museums*—a historical legacy of the French Revolution, the termination of the hierarchies of schools and genres, and the rise of the free market (including the market for Dutch genre scenes). Hegel picks up on the wonderful correspondence—or rather, the ineffable *gap*—between a free *art* (in the singular) and a free *people* (the civic-minded Dutch). Murillo, too, bears a fraught relation to imperial power (Spain/Netherlands), but we catch his beggar boys during a precarious moment of freedom, in a painting we can now see about the very *conditions* of painting. Of course, this moment could not last, Rancière admits. Succeeding generations of artists would come to bear witness to art's essential pastness. Even so, we today can catch a glimpse of what it would be for the correspondence between artwork and social circumstance to be actual, what it might be for us to regard the artwork regarding us regarding the artwork, and so on.

Notes

1. Hegel, "Versuch über das Kunstschöne," *Die Hören* 3, no. 7 (1797): 1–37. In 1828 Hegel allowed Hirt's definition pride of place. See Hegel, *Vorlesungen zur Ästhetik (Adolf Heimann)(1828/1829)*, ed. Alain Patrick Olivier and Annemarie Gethmann-Siefert (Leiden, The Netherlands: Brill/Fink, 2017), Heimann ms. 6–7, 12–13. See also Donougho, "Hegel's 'Characteristic' (*die Charakteristik*) in 1828/29," forthcoming in *Studi di estetica*, 2020.

2. I cite the *Aesthetics* in the Suhrkamp edition, 1970, vols. 13–15) and in

T. M. Knox's translation (Oxford: Oxford University Press, 1975), sometimes amended (here, 13, 203–4/153–4). Robert Pippin has drawn attention to the importance of this passage in Pippin, *After the Beautiful: Hegel and the Philosophy of Pictorial Modernism* (Cambridge: Cambridge University Press, 2014). Plato's distich, as reported by Diogenes Laertius, runs "Star-gazing (*astares*) Aster, would I were the skies/To gaze upon thee with a thousand eyes."

3. Hegel, *Vorlesung über die Philosophie der Kunst (transcript H. G. Hotho, 1823), Gesammelte Werke* 28.1, ed. Niklas Hebing (Hamburg: Meiner, 2015), 286 (Hotho ms. 70): "Plato declares in a distich to his star that he would like to be the heavens, to see with a thousand eyes." Another transcript from Carl Kromayr (Kr. ms. 113), footnoted on the same page, reads "his beloved Asper" (*sic*), the error only reinforcing the probability that Hegel mentioned the name. I refrain from comment on the homoerotic subtext of Plato's (supposed) words. As for the name "Argus," given its total absence from extant transcriptions, Rebecca Comay's comments on the monstrous "ambivalence" of the figure—in Comay, "Defaced Statues: Idealism and Iconoclasm in Hegel's *Aesthetics*," *October* 149 (2014): 123–42—seem beside the point (a wild Argus chase?).

4. This way of putting things is suggested by Allen Speight's remarks, in his conference paper "Philosophy, Comedy and History," concerning the inescapable "theatricality" built into art. Art is presented as being for the beholder, even when it also works to "neutralize" that condition in favor of 'absorption' (in Michael Fried's terms).

5. Robert Pippin, "Hegel on Painting," in *The Art of Hegel's Aesthetics: Hegelian Philosophy and the Perspectives of Art History*, ed. Paul Kottman and Michael Squire (Paderborn: Fink, 2018), 211–237, especially 219 (note).

6. Hegel, *Vorlesungen über die Philosophie der Kunst (Berlin 1823)*, ed. Annemarie Gethmann-Siefert (Hamburg: Meiner, 1998) (Hotho ms. 286, my translation). Compare the wording at 15, 562/1220.

7. Erich Segal, *The Death of Comedy* (Cambridge, MA: Harvard University Press, 2001), 7. Cited in Donougho, "Hegelian Comedy," *Philosophy and Rhetoric*, 49, no. 2 (2016): 196–220, 204.

8. Chapter 23 of Maurice Charney, *Comedy: A Geographical and Historical Guide*, ed. Maurice Charney (New York: Praeger, 2005), 350–62, at 351.

9. *Versuch einer kritischen Dichtkunst* (1730).

10. Quoted by H. B. Nisbet in his comprehensive biography, *Gottfried Ephraim Lessing: His Life, Works, and Thought* (Oxford: Oxford University Press, 2013), 45. Chapter 2 offers a helpful introduction to the eighteenth-century genre that Lessing would transform.

11. "Ueber die wissenschaftlichen Behandlungsarten des Naturrechts," published in *Kritisches Journal* 2. See Hegel, *Natural Law: The Scientific Ways of Treating Natural Law, Its Place in Moral Philosophy, and Its Return to the Positive Sciences of Law*, trans. T. M. Knox, intro. H. B. Acton (Philadelphia: University of

Pennsylvania Press, 1975). I cite page numbers in this edition, and in *Werke*, vol. 2 (Frankfurt: Suhrkamp, 1970).

12. *Aesthetics* 15, 358–9/1103–4; and "Hegel, Philosopher of the Secular [*irdischen*] World: On the Dialectics of Narrative," in *Hegel and the Tradition: Essays in Honour of H.S. Harris*, ed. Baur and Russon (Toronto: University of Toronto Press, 1998), 111–39.

13. The passage would repay detailed study, impossible here. It showcases the development, in Attic society and its art, of subjective individuality and particular selfhood, Socrates epitomizing the latter. It represents both the flowering and the decadence of classical culture. In this context Dante would count as a late articulation of the latter.

14. "*Affectation*" [sic], in Hegel, *Gesammelte Werke 4, Jenaer Kritische Schriften*, ed. Hartmut Buchner and Otto Pöggeler (Hamburg: Meiner, 1968), 461.

15. The text is a lot more complex than my rapid perusal can suggest. Indeed, following the claim about (modern?) tragedy constituting the "absolute relation" comes a dense paragraph on how the particular self (we can't yet call it "individual") "looks on" (*an-schaut*) the ethical life of the political community, intuiting that it is at once alien and its own self. From this perspective, comedy might seem to involve a similarly split vision: we identify with serious issues but also distance ourselves from them through laughter—ultimately they count for nothing. But the question then becomes, why bother with it in the first place if it's all ridiculous? Finding a dynamic balance seems to be the trick. For detailed interpretation and discussion of how it bears on the official (Hotho) edition see Niklas Hebing, *Hegels Ästhetik des Komischen* (Hamburg: Meiner, 2015), 275. See *Hegel-Studien*, 63, 275.

16. Hegel, *Phenomenology of Spirit*, trans. A. V. Miller (Oxford: Oxford University Press, 1977), cited by paragraph (pilcrow ¶) followed by page number of *Werke*, vol. 3. Allen Speight brings out very clearly how unmasking reveals the human face or countenance but also reveals the *self*, in its "singularity" (rather than classically Hellenic "individuality"), or as particular persons "who could actually be in the audience" (as he puts it). He is right (in my view) to draw our attention to Hegel's ambivalent focus on the tragic *character* and on the comic *artist*.

17. See Hotho (1823), 310. Knox: "how men can take things so easily" (15, 553/1221).

18. See Jan Hokenson, *The Idea of Comedy: History, Theory, Critique* (Madison, NJ: Farleigh Dickinson University Press, 2006), 73; cited in "Hegelian Comedy," 201.

19. In a recent issue of the *New York Review of Books* (October 11, 2018)—"LOL."—Gavin Francis situates "laughing with" under Aristotelian "wit" (*eutrapelia*, agility in social interaction). Review of *Studies of Laughter in Interaction*, eds. Philip Glenn and Elizabeth Holt (London: Bloomsbury, 2013).

20. Hegel, *GW* 28.1, 510, note: "Ariphases," "Aristophanes."
21. See Heimann, 207 (ms., 141). On Aristophanes's patriotism, 206, ms., 141.
22. *Aesthetics* 14, 121/512; also see 15, 469, 528/1152, 1200.
23. Ernst Benjamin Salomo Raupach, 1784–1852. See Hegel, "Über die Bekehrten [von Ernst Raupach]," in *Berliner Schriften 1818–1831* (Suhrkamp), 11:72–82. Citations in the text refer to *Gesammelte Werke* 16, 2001, 3–16, which includes about 1,500 words previously unpublished.
24. *Popular Tales and Romances of the Northern Nations*, vol. 1 (London: Simkin & Marshall, 1823), attributed to Tieck—see 233–91. The year 1823 saw its original publication in *Minerva*, Leipzig (for details see http://desturmobed.blogspot.com/2012/05/george-blink.html). *Isidor und Olga* appeared as *The Serf: A Tragedy in Five Acts*, in *Cumberland's British Theatre*, vol. 19 (London: Cumberland, 1828). See also *The Niebelungen Treasure: A Tragedy in Five Acts* (London: Williams & Norgate, 1847), https://catalog.hathitrust.org/Record/10013922.
25. Walter Jaeschke, *Hegel-Handbuch: Leben-Werk-Schule*, 3rd ed. (Stuttgart: Metzler, 2016), 263–4; Stephan Kraft, "Hegel, das Unterhaltungslustspiel und das Ende der Kunst," *Hegel-Studien* 45 (2010): 81–102; Stephan Kraft, *Zum Ende der Komödie: Eine Theoriegeschichte des Happyends* (Göttingen: Wallstein, 2011), chap. 6; and Hebing, *Hegels Ästhetik des Komischen*, 266–75. See also Helmut Schneider, "Komödie des Lebens-Theorie der Komödie," in *Geist und Geschichte: Studien zur Philosophie Hegels*, ed. Helmut Schneider (Berlin: Peter Lang, 1998), 340–46.
26. See Saphir, *Berliner Schnellpost*, January 3, 1826, 11–12, https://sammlungen.ulb.uni-muenster.de/um/periodical/pageview/1994599. Saphir: "die Leutchen sind so mürbe und bekehrlich, daß eine Bibelgesellschaft ihre Freude an ihnen hätte."
27. *GW*, 16, 9–10 is not in previous editions (e.g., Suhrkamp, 11,78).
28. My emphasis. Kehler (1826), 234, ms. 457–8. Cited in Kraft, "Hegel, das Unterhaltungslustspiel," 94. For the contextualizing of this "middle" form, see Hebing, *Hegels Ästhetik des Komischen*, 286.
29. "Was die Franzosen die hohe Komödie nennen, is zum Teil nichts anderes, [sie] haben sich aber sehr dagegen erklärt." See 15, 516/1190, where the Hotho edition refers to "*haute comédie*," that is, in French classical theater. Sometimes that expression denotes the classical comedy of Molière and Corneille, or it can allude to Molière's innovations—in *Misanthrope* especially—comedy of words and manners.
30. Kraft, "Hegel, das Unterhaltungslustspiel," 100 (98 for "old vehemence"); Kraft, *Zum Ende der Komödie*, 307 ("disruption"). For Heimann, 206–7: "Comedy is the ultimate form of art, the dissolution of art, where the import [*Gehalt*] of art is itself negated. . . . Comedy is then the extreme of art, in which the plastic [i.e., perceptual shape] is negated. The nullity of art emerges in the recently employed Irony."

31. Hegel, *Philosophie der Kunst: Vorlesung von 1826*, ed. Annemarie Gethmann-Siefert, et al. (Frankfurt: Suhrkamp, 2005), 252 (just nine lines in all).

32. Goethe's early drama *Götz von Berlichingen* (1773), which Hegel mentions several times in various lecture series as an original work yet not wholly successful in assimilating the externals of history.

33. A renowned theorist of "the prose of the world," Franco Moretti writes about "fillers" in Moretti, "Serious Century," in *The Bourgeois: Between History and Literature* (London: Verso, 2013), chap. 2, 74–5. Here I expand on brief remarks in Donougho, "Hegelian Comedy."

34. Benjamin Rutter, *Hegel on the Modern Arts* (Cambridge: Cambridge University Press, 2010), 258. Rutter plausibly suggests that Hegel was put off by Friedrich Schlegel's extravagant praise of the novel as a genre, and indeed, its promotion to a paradigm of literature and the modern.

35. Moretti, *Bourgeois*, 75.

36. Donougho, "Hegelian Comedy."

37. I should thank Lydia Moland for showing me an early draft of a chapter on Hegel and "Humor," which first provoked my own thoughts about Hippel and epigram. See Moland, *Hegel's Aesthetics: The Art of Idealism* (Oxford: Oxford University Press, 2019), 138–39 (Hippel) and 75–76 (the epigram).

38. See his well-known letter to Schelling (April 16, 1795), recommending Hippel's words "Strive towards the sun, my friends." See Clark Butler, ed., *Hegel: The Letters*, trans. Clark Butler and Christiane Seiler (Bloomington: Indiana University Press, 1984), 36. Hegel calls Hippel "the most excellent humorist" in his 1828 review of Hamann's writings, translated (by Lisa Marie Anderson) as *Hegel on Hamann* (Evanston, IL: Northwestern University Press, 2008), 43; Hotho's edition follows that passage quite closely.

39. Kehler, 148; also see Heimann, 123. Kehler states that Jean Paul "hat das [Werk] vor sich gehabt": (i.e., was inspired or influenced—perhaps merely anticipated—by Hippel). On Hegel and Hippel, see Hebing, *Hegels Ästhetik des Komischen*, 354–55.

40. Hamilton Beck, *The Elusive 'I' in the Novel: Hippel, Sterne, Diderot, Kant* (New York: Peter Lang, 1987), 81. See also the following note 41.

41. David MacGregor, *Hegel, Marx, and the English State* (Boulder, CO: Westview, 1992), 97ff. See also Hippel, *The Status of Women: Collected Writings*, trans. Timothy Sellner (Bloomington: Xlibris, 2009), containing a brief selection from *Lebensläufe* (80–102) sufficiently appealing to make one wish for more. A rare appearance of a first-person "I" exceeding the protocolist role comes when Herr von G. asks "Why didn't *you* say anything?" *I*: "a young man . . . is nothing more than a secretary who writes everything down" (*Status of Women*, 97).

42. *Werke*, 14, 239–40/608–9; on Goethe's *Xenien* and offending "rockets," 13, 524–5/409; on poetic garlands, 14, 173/555.

43. Norman Bryson discusses '*xenia*' as magical phenomena, illusive and reversible, which exist solely in the eye of the beholder. In Bryson, *Looking at the Overlooked* (London: Reaktion, 1990) (see 17ff.). Hegel seemed drawn to this liminal sort of figure, constantly shifting *between* object and subject.

44. Carl Friedrich von Rumohr (1785–1843) was a pioneering art historian and food writer. His *Italienische Forschungen* (Berlin: Nikolai'schen Buchhandlung, 1827) aroused Hegel's particular scorn. Rumohr had attacked the "Ideal," and Winckelmann in particular for applying it (along with "allegory") so as in his view to distance art from nature. For context, see Donougho, "Hegel's 'Characteristic'" (2020).

45. *Werke*, 13, 223–4/170. Heimann (1828) matches some of the wording, at 49, ms. 28 (he dates the lecture November 17).

46. Jacques Rancière, *Aesthesis: Scenes from the Aesthetic Regime of Art* (London: Verso, 2013), chap. 2: "The Little Gods of the Street: Munich-Berlin, 1828," 21–37. It is one of his "Auerbachian" scenes, after Erich Auerbach's *Scenes from the Drama of European Literature* (1984). Compare a Rancière-influenced account of post-Hegelian painting: Alexander Potts, "The Romantic Work of Art," in *Communities of Sense: Rethinking Aesthetics*, ed. Hinderliter et al. (Durham, NC: Duke University Press, 2009), 51–78. Potts frames Turner in comic aspect, as what he nicely terms "anti-autonomous autonomy" (see p. 60). Some of Turner's images have texts appended, as if to frame their autonomy in our eyes.

Chapter Ten

The Comedy of Public Opinion in Hegel

Jeffrey Church

THE "PRINCIPLE OF SUBJECTIVE FREEDOM" recognized in the modern age poses a difficult problem for the modern state (PR 185A).[1] Namely, it must confer "recognition" on the subjective freedom of individuals while ensuring that this subjectivity "pass over" into "the interest of the universal" and "willingly acknowledge this universal interest even as their own substantial spirit" (PR 260). The liberty of individuals and the duty to community must be combined. As has been well explored in the literature, the unity of subjectivity and ethical substance is achieved in large part on Hegel's view through education within the "Estates" and "Corporations." Hegel's theory of the estates remains an unexpected and unappreciated feature of his practical philosophy. In fact, it is the key element of his social philosophy, which grounds his more properly political philosophy. Most fundamentally, it plays this role because the estates provide the forms of visibility required by Hegel's distinctive theory of self-determination, and so the estates constitute conditions for the possibility of human agency as such. With respect to political agency in particular, this ramifies into the view that the estates are *social preconditions* for legal and political practices, forms of *political participation* in their own right, and conditions of possibility of *moderate government* (three functions also attributed to the estates by Montesquieu.²

However, Hegel discusses another political form of the education of subjectivity that remains underexplored in the literature—namely, the education of public opinion through the public forum of the Estates Assembly (PR 315). By introducing public opinion in these sections of the *Philosophy of Right*, Hegel recognizes the limits of the integrative efforts of the mediating institutions of civil society. For Hegel, individuals demand recognition of their subjective freedom not simply as members of particular groups but also as part of the will of the people as a whole, expressed as public opinion. In Hegel's terms, public opinion is the "most external manifestation" of the "subjectivity" of the state, while the "monarch" is the true manifestation (PR 320Z). The task, then, is to recognize public opinion while still educating it to acknowledge the government's rationality (PR 317Z). To achieve this end, Hegel suggests that the Estates Assembly's deliberation proceedings with government be public so that "public opinion" can become "familiar with, and learns to respect, the functions, abilities, virtues, and skills of the official bodies and civil servants," thereby "educating" the people (PR 315).

What does this education consist in, and how does it work? Unfortunately, Hegel offers an all-too-brief discussion. Scholars who have examined this part of *Philosophy of Right* have stressed the "cognitive" nature of this education.³ That is, the public learns by understanding the main issues and arguments at stake in the debate, as well as the government's reasons for its activity. Indeed, Brod places Hegel's argument in dialogue with Habermas, who famously details the emergence of the "public sphere" in which the public will can be formed through reasoned debate.⁴

There is an element of truth in this cognitivist account. After all, the public assembly provides an "opportunity of [acquiring] knowledge" so that "public opinion" can "form more rational judgments" (PR 315). However, the cognitivist reading cannot be the whole truth. Hegel speaks of the people as a "formless mass" that is "elemental, irrational, barbarous, and terrifying" (PR 303A). It is therefore unlikely that an appeal to reason alone will successfully improve such an irrational public. Furthermore, part of the education of public opinion consists in "a remedy for the self-conceit of individuals and of the mass" (PR 315). It does not appear plausible that reasoning alone will chasten the public's exaggerated self-regard. Finally, the cognitivist reading supports the common but mistaken interpretation of Hegel's tutelary or paternalistic state: that the public does not participate in the state but is passive and only learns from the state.[5]

In this chapter, I argue that this education is not just of the people's intellect but also of their sensibility. In other words, there is an aesthetic character to this political education that has not been explored thus far in the literature. In what follows, I argue that the public assembly itself possesses the features of a drama, as Hegel discusses it in his *Aesthetics* lectures—particularly in the public "collision" of government and the people (A 1159).[6] Furthermore, the assembly and Hegel's related discussions of public opinion and freedom of the press (PR 316–319) reflect the features of comedy—particularly in the "self-dissolving" character of the public gripes against the state (A 1163). Hegel does not explicitly draw this parallel between comedic drama and public opinion in the *Philosophy of Right*, but there are important structural and thematic parallels that justify this reading. In addition, this aesthetic reading can help overcome the problems I identified above with the purely cognitivist reading.

My contribution is significant for a few reasons. First, scholars have long discussed the tragic elements of modern political life in Hegel, such as his view of poverty.[7] None have thus far discussed the comic nature of modern political life, aside from the facile observation of the comic "reconciliation" of opposites effected by the modern state. Second, this specific problem in Hegel—educating public opinion—remains underexplored in the literature. Third, the political problem Hegel identifies here continues to bedevil liberal democracies, particularly the United States. In the United States, the public mistrusts government at record levels, which paves the way for populist demagogues. Political scientists have long discussed the irrational and underinformed American voter and have recently sought ways to foster trust of elites within public opinion.[8] Finally, and relatedly, this dramatic understanding of political education recasts the "democratic" nature of Hegel's state, which has been the subject of recent scholarly discussion—it challenges the overly technocratic reading of Hegel's state but resists a participatory democratic interpretation as well. This is a point I will return to in the conclusion.[9]

The Estates Assembly as Drama

In Hegel's view, the fundamental economic associations of civil society, the Estates, also serve a political function in constituting the main legislative body of the modern state. These Estates represent their members politically in the deliberative Estates Assembly, where the Estates representatives debate and discuss with government ministers the "business of the state" (PR 314). Hegel rejects the "dangerous prejudice" that the Estates are in fundamental "opposition to the government," since such essential division would mean "the state is close to destruction." Instead, the opposition is a mere "semblance" (PR 302). Hegel illustrates this semblance of opposition in the party system—the majority party in the assembly aligns with the government, while the "opposition" party stands with the "people," and a third aristocratic party mediates the two (VPR17 156A).[10] This Assembly allows for the participation of the Estates and thereby the people's will as articulated through membership in civil society.

The Estates Assembly represents the main groups structuring civil society. It does not represent the people's will, understood abstractly as a popular sovereignty preceding all political association or concretely as public opinion. "In our own times," public opinion has become a "major force," since the "principle of subjective freedom has such importance and significance" (PR 316Z). It thereby demands recognition. However, Hegel approves of Goethe's judgment that "the masses can fight respectably, but their judgments are miserable" (PR 317A). Its judgments are bad because it is an "unorganized" and undifferentiated aggregate (PR 316Z), which thereby can have little insight into complicated general problems (PR 301A). As such, the Estates Assembly must thereby be public in nature so that it has the additional beneficial function of "educating" public opinion on the complicated business of the state (PR 315). Hegel stresses the importance of this education: "When a people obtains this education . . . this provides the root of all public virtues" (VPR17 154A). At the same time, public opinion can serve as an "oversight and weighty judgment of their work," the work of the representatives of the people and the government (VPR 17 154).

The Estates Assembly demonstrates several key features of the dramatic art Hegel describes in the *Aesthetics*. Consider three in particular—the principle, aim, and mechanics of drama. First, the defining principle of drama is that it presents "collisions of circumstances, passions, and characters" that "necessitate a resolution of the conflict and discord" (A 1159). Or, in other terms, drama involves the "dissolution of the one-sidedness of these powers which are making themselves independent" (A 1163). The Estates Assembly dramatizes the "collision" between two rationally justified forces of the modern state, the subjective freedom of the people, and the rational freedom of the government. In the proceedings, there is always the temptation for the two main powers to make "themselves independent," but the deliberative institution serves to dissolve that independence, acting as a "safeguard" against the people's dominance over the state or the state tyrannizing the people (VPR17 148). Hegel distinguishes the humdrum everyday conflicts in the family from these dramatic "events in a great assembly." There, "one ingenious idea devours another" until a resolution is reached (PR 315Z). Furthermore, the drama differs from the epic in part because the former portrays individuals and their inner passions, which drama incorporates from lyric poetry. Similarly, in the Estates Assembly, the conflict is not simply an abstract one between competing ideas or powers, but it is also embodied in particular representatives. Ministers, for instance, "show their talent, skill, and presence of mind, since they are under constant attack from the assembly" (VPR17 149A).

The second key feature of drama is its aim, which, like all art, expresses the "divine and true" nature of spirit. Unlike previous forms of art, in which the divine appears "unmoved" or "blessedly sunk in themselves," the divine appears "here in its community" as the "substance and aim of human individuality, brought into existence as something concrete, summoned into action and put into movement" (A 1162). Similarly, the Estates Assembly expresses the truth of objective spirit in synthesizing the subjective freedom of the people and the rational freedom of the state. It does so in a communal assembly, that is, in an open deliberative forum with the people assembled in audience. Finally, this truth is given motion in the form of individual representatives who express these abstract truths through concrete action and discussion.

Third, Hegel enumerates a number of mechanical features of the dramatic art that align with the Estates Assembly:

Unity of place and time: In "contrast to epic," which stretches across time and place, drama must be located in an "exclusive locality" and a compressed period (A 1164–5). Similarly, the Assemblies are always located in the same place and are limited in duration.

The public as critic: Unlike other works of art or "scientific works," intended for a particular audience, dramas are written for the entire "public." The public then "has a right to bestow praise or blame" because the work was "intended to arouse a lively sympathy and give pleasure" to them (A 1175). In this way, the relationship between public and Assembly is similar to the one of public to dramatic presentation. After all, Hegel stresses that the Assembly must be public so that the people can be the assembled audience of this political drama. He stresses that the public serves to check the government and Estates representatives (VPR 17 154). In his *Aesthetics*, Hegel quickly clarifies that a dramatic artist must find the right attitude to the public, neither the French slavish catering to public opinion, nor the German "contempt for the public" (A 1175), an ambivalent attitude that reflects Hegel's view about public opinion that "deserves to be respected as well as despised" (PR 318). Just as he looks for a Schiller to find the "right note for the German people" (A 1175), so too does he call for a "great man of the age" to discern the "truth within" public opinion (PR 318Z). As such, the Estates representative or government officials should "despise public opinion as he here and there encounters it," while still attempting to find the "essence and inner content of the age" that he can express on the stage of the Assembly (PR 318Z).

Vitality of expression: Hegel criticizes the artificiality of dramatic diction and delivery. Instead, he argues that "an individual in a drama must be alive through and through in himself, whole and entire, his disposition and character being in harmony with his aim and action," an "all-pervasive individuality which collects everything together into [a] unity" (A 1177). This kind of delivery is powerful for an audience that sees embodied in the characters the self-determination of individuality that all free beings seek. In the case of the Assembly, Hegel argues that the ministers must cultivate such vitality of expression in the form of "wit and eloquence" (PR 315Z) or "talent, skill, and presence of mind" (VPR17 149A) to win over its audience. In general, the public nature of the Assembly allows "man" to "speak to man directly, heart to heart, eye to eye," such that everything "springs alive" (A 1184), in contrast to the people simply learning about the proceedings secondhand.

In sum, then, the Estates Assembly is dramatic in its nature and character. These aesthetic features of the Assembly, moreover, can ameliorate two of the problems I identified with the strictly cognitivist interpretation of the people's education. First, it seems implausible that a will Hegel characterizes as "barbaric" can be improved simply through intellectual exchange. My interpretation makes the educative process more plausible by including an education of sensibility as well. The drama of the Assembly can improve the people's sensuous grasp of the absolute by dramatizing the conflict as well as the resolution at the heart of ethical life. The people come to grasp the divine not through abstract reasoning, but through witnessing the concrete representatives with their unique traits and skills, acting in a particular place and time in an architectural edifice that expresses the ethical life of the state. The Assembly is presumably overseen by the monarch as well, whose own aesthetic majesty could be the subject of another article.

The final problem I discussed above was the passivity of the people under the cognitive interpretation. By drawing the parallel with the dramatic public's right to criticism, we can make a case for the essentially active role of the people in the state's activity. Government officials and Estate representatives, in speaking publicly to the audience of the people, are overseen by the people and thus must address the common good rather than their own particular goods. Of course, Hegel does not advocate for direct democracy or referenda, so it is still up to elite figures to discern and represent the people's will. Nevertheless, the people exercise an important role of public criticism: holding elite figures accountable for their actions.

Comic Elements of the Public Education

In Hegel's subsequent discussion of public opinion (PR 316–319), we find that the proper form of dramatic art for the aesthetic education to take is comedic in nature. Government ministers do not drone on dryly about government business but must "be armed with wit" (PR 315Z). Public opinion feigns "seriousness," but is in fact "not serious at all" (PR 317A). It even employs antigovernment "satirical songs," which are light complaints that contain their own "self-condemnation" (PR 319A). This parallel between comedy and the demos is already prefigured in Hegel's discussion of comedy in the *Phenomenology*, in which he argues that the "demos" that "knows itself as lord and ruler" is "constrained and befooled through the particularity of its actual existence, and exhibits the ludicrous contrast between its own opinion of itself and its immediate existence, between its necessity and contingency, its universality and its commonness" (PhG 745).[11]

In what follows, I shift from the dramatic features of the Estates Assembly to the comedic features of public opinion and its education. I trace the two main features of Hegelian comedic drama—the self-destruction of particularity and its cheerfulness—in *Philosophy of Right* (316–319). Finally, I will suggest that a third feature of comedy—that true comedy means "laughing with," not "laughing at"—emerges from the reciprocal lightheartedness that the people and government demonstrate toward one another.

THE SELF-DESTRUCTION OF PARTICULARITY

For Hegel, tragedy focuses on the "eternal substance of things," which emerges "victorious" out of the struggle between two conflicting ethical powers (A 1199). The epoch in which tragedy has political resonance is in the ancient world, in which the ethical powers of state and family, for instance, have not been reconciled into a rational unity. In the modern state, all such conflicts have been overcome, and the main conflict that remains is between the lone individual and the community. By contrast, in comedy, "it is subjectivity . . . which in its infinite assurance retains the upper hand" (A 1199). The comedic drama consists in the self-destruction of the "unsubstantial," or particular, features of subjectivity, and yet in the end the comic protagonist maintains his "infinite light-heartedness and confidence felt by someone raised altogether above his own inner contradiction and not bitter or miserable in it at all" (A 1200). While there were great ancient comedies—Hegel singles out Aristophanes as the apex of comedic drama—as commentators have pointed out, comedy actually does not square well with ancient ethical life.[12] Aristophanes's comedies, for instance, reveal the artificial character of ethical substance and that the gods are projections of subjectivity. Comedy unleashes subjectivity in a way ancient political life cannot contain. However, the modern state is founded on free subjectivity, a sovereign subject in the form of a monarch, and the people's subjectivity that is to "pass over" into rationality. In this way, comedy's focus on subjectivity and its redemption is particularly relevant to the modern state and our concerns here.

The first key feature of comedy is how it generates the "collision" at its dramatic heart. Comedy consists in a subject "who makes his own actions contradictory and so brings them to nothing" (A 1220). According to Hegel's typology, comedies can involve protagonists who have unsubstantial or "contradictory" aims, and "therefore they cannot accomplish anything" (A 1200); or, they can have true, substantial aims but have silly or unsubstantial means to those aims—it is "by subjective caprice, vulgar folly, and absurdity that individuals bring to nought actions which had a higher aim" (A 1221); or, their aims can be defeated by "external contingencies" that lead to a happy outcome (A 1201).[13] These protagonists can be anyone, and indeed Aristophanes lampooned the "follies of the masses, the insanity of their orators and statesmen, the absurdity of the [Peloponnesian] war" (A 1221).

Comedy works, then, by dramatizing the contrast between the universal and particular moments of subjectivity—the subject should aim at the universal ethical substance but instead gives himself over to particular vulgar desires. Public opinion is uniquely suited to comedy because it is one expression of the "principle of subjective freedom" in politics (PR 316Z), but it wavers between universal substance and particular interest (PR 317). On the one hand, public opinion involves the uninformed "particular opinions of the many," the "unorganized" expressions of the unleashed particularity and arbitrariness of modern life (PR 316). On the other hand, it contains the "eternal and substantial principles of justice" in the form of "common sense" and the "true needs and legitimate tendencies of actuality." For Hegel, the more "particular and distinctive" the opinion is, the worse it is; the more "universal" it is, the better.

Even though public opinion wavers between universal and particular, it has a powerful orientation toward the particular, making it essentially comic in nature. After all, public opinion is in large part the voice of the middle class, the "section" of the state "rooted in interests and activities which are directed towards the particular, and in which contingency, mutability, and arbitrary will have the right to express themselves" (PR 310A). Modern civil society unleashes and satisfies particular desires in a way unparalleled in previous epochs. Moreover, public opinion expresses the arbitrary will of individuals shorn of any membership in a group, in which we "pride [ourselves]" on what is "distinctive" to us (PR 317). For these reasons, Hegel, along with Aristophanes, considers the demos to be comic in nature—the "people" are full of "foolishness" (LA28, 206),[14] and the "lower social classes" are "the ones who undermine their own purposes and they are quite content in doing this, so that with this very undermining it comes to light that they are not in earnest about these purposes" (LA23 438).[15]

As such, for Hegel, public opinion has a "substantial basis" in truth, but its errors are self-created. The "people is deceived by itself" about how its universal substance "is known to it" and then how it "passes judgment on events, its own actions, etc." (PR 317A). How might this self-deception manifest itself? A comparison with Hegel's comedic genres can help flesh out this dramatic self-deception. For instance, public opinion can deceive itself by replacing its substantial end with some insubstantial end, or it can judge some insubstantial means to its substantial end. In sum, it takes seriously both its truth and its error and in this way appears comic.

In these sections, Hegel suggests that it is not primarily a paternalistic or tutelary state that educates opinion. Indeed, the thrust of Hegel's discussion of libel and sedition is that such talk should be treated with "indifference and scorn" rather than the heavy hand of censorship (PR 319A). Rather, the pride of public opinion is chastened through self-destruction. The demos, then, serves as a comic protagonist in the drama of its public education. The drama is the collision between the universal and the particular, and the comic resolution occurs through the self-destruction of the demos' subjective particularity. The end of this self-destructive process is for the demos to "realize" that "its seriousness is not serious at all" (PR 317A).

The subjective particularity of the demos defeats itself only in light of the "sound and educated insights concerning the interests of the state" expressed within the Assembly (PR 319). Public opinion is "rendered innocuous" by such insights because they leave "little of significance for others to say, and above all" they deny "them the opinion that what they have to say is of distinctive importance and effectiveness" (PR 319). That is, when the self-deceived opinions of the public are juxtaposed against the reasoned judgment of government and the assembly, the opinions of the demos appear ridiculous. In particular, they self-destruct. In his discussion of malicious libel, for instance, Hegel argues that these opinions are destroyed due to "the self-condemnation which is implicit within it" (PR 319A). For Hegel, once the demos compares such vulgar opinions that it took so seriously against the reality of rational discussion, it becomes ashamed, and its pride is defeated. Its shame undermines its self-deception, leading it to an acceptance of the absolute. The chastening of the people's pride through the comic nature of its education helps solve a basic problem with the cognitivist reading, discussed in the introduction.

CHEERFULNESS

Hegel's argument, of course, rests on the assumption that the Assembly will express well-reasoned arguments. But the more important requirement of the Assembly for our purposes is that it remains cheerful amidst the barbaric public opinion that it must recognize. This is the main lesson of Hegel's discussion of freedom of the press in *Philosophy of Right* (PR 319). In this section, Hegel urges public officials not to take the heavy hand of censorship against all forms of libel and sedition. Hegel is writing at a time in which the freedom of the press is a new and dangerous idea. The worry from elites is that slander and public criticism will undermine the legitimacy of government and the stability of the regime. Several commentators have noted the self-interested nature of Hegel's discussion here, particularly his exception of the sciences from censorship.[16] However, we can get deeper insight into Hegel's view by following the parallel to comedy.

For Hegel, the comic protagonist does not despair at the self-destruction of his particularity. Rather, he retains "an infinite light-heartedness and confidence felt by someone raised altogether above his own inner contradiction and not bitter or miserable in it at all: this is the bliss and ease of a man who, being sure of himself, can bear the frustration of his aims and achievements" (A 1200). He remains cheerful because his subjectivity persists and indeed is liberated from the confines of particular aims and foibles. As scholars have pointed out, the triumph of subjectivity in comedy explains why in Hegel's view comedy is the culmination of art.[17]

In the free-for-all that is public opinion, Hegel argues, there will be many "false judgments and public calumnies." For Hegel, "government and public figures" can be "indifferent to them" (VPR17 155). They can remain cheerful amidst their frustrations, enduring "all manner of libelous attacks on fellow citizens, officials, and rulers, and the revealing of all family secrets." Officials "deem it beneath one's notice, one rises above it" (VPR17 155A). They can do so only if the proceedings of the Assembly are public, so that "public opinion is firmly based and oriented along the right lines," and these false notions and libel self-destruct in the way described above (VPR17 155). In this way, government officials resemble the comic protagonist's cheerfulness soaring above the self-destruction of particularity. They can remain confident in the substantial character of public opinion, and the fleeting nature of its particularity.

Government officials serve to model subjectivity's self-assured cheerfulness for public opinion. They can thereby serve as an additional form of aesthetic education. They can also show the public that it need not be outraged at every slight or falsehood and that they can live up to the model of the Aristophanean protagonist who need not take his own particular failings seriously. Indeed, this parallel to comic cheerfulness explains more deeply why seriousness and the heavy hand of censorship may backfire. If officials or the public take such particular false judgments and libel too seriously, they descend to the level of particularity and threaten to make the rationality of the government into just another particular voice in the din. At this level, it is akin to wrestling Proteus (VPR 3.824). Or, in other words, it threatens a tragic outcome, dividing the rightful claim of public opinion to have its say against the rightful claim of the state to educate subjectivity to the universal.

Better in Hegel's view to adopt a comic solution, establishing publicly a deliberative institution serving as the standard for rationality and then allowing particular voices to shipwreck themselves against it.

LAUGHING-WITH

The final key element of comedy Hegel discusses is that the comic protagonist should be in on the joke; he should not be the object of derision or scorn (A 1200). Aristophanes was on this count "of most gifted mind," as he was not a "cold or malignant scoffer" but sought to join the community together in laughter at itself (A 1222). Unfortunately, modern comedies have, by and large, in Hegel's judgment, failed to live up to this promise, instead pitting one class against another, for instance (A 1235). The problem is that if comedy becomes derision, then the audience does not recognize itself as implicated in the drama. In its self-assuredness, it fails to see its own flaws and so does not overcome its particularity.

Thus far, it seems in Hegel's politics, there is more laughing-at than laughing-with. Government officials should treat with indifference the malicious irruptions of public opinion; they should "despise" public opinion (PR 318). However, Hegel's point here is rather that government and public opinion can laugh together at the terrible judgments and opinions that all modern regimes are susceptible to. They also do not laugh at those who make these terrible judgments, as if the latter are completely separable from the broader society. As is characteristic of Hegel's holism, society as a whole is responsible for all its manifestations. As such, the community's cheerfulness amounts to a laughter at itself—that it is the type of society that can give rise to such lunatic opinions.

Yet Hegel goes further, urging that there ought to be a place for the people's satire of the powerful. Indeed, as we have seen, government officials have ample opportunity to hold the people in contempt and laugh at their ignorance. For Hegel, the people, recognizing this derision, must have an outlet for their own scorn. Near the end of his discussion of freedom of the press in *Philosophy of Right* (PR 319), Hegel argues that there is a form of "nemesis" of people against government that springs from "inner impotence, when it feels oppressed by superior talents and virtues." It seeks to "reassert itself in the face of such superiority and to give renewed self-consciousness to its own nullity." His example is of "Roman soldiers" who "used to inflict a relatively harmless nemesis on their emperors by singing satirical songs during triumphal processions in order to compensate for their arduous service and obedience, and especially for the fact that their names were not included on the roll of honor; in this way, the balance was to some extent redressed" (PR 319A).

In finding a satirical outlet, the people are able to laugh back. This outlet balances derision against scorn, giving the people the opportunity to shed a spotlight on the particular foibles and corruption of elite officials. However, the people do not recognize this opportunity has in any sense real power, as this particularity gives "renewed self-consciousness to its own nullity." That is, the people have no institutionalized power to replace officials. Instead, they can only remind officials of the standards of ethical life that their particular behavior violates. In this way, Hegel scholars are wrong to insist either on a wholly elitist or democratic reading of Hegel's state. Hegel rejects any institutional, participatory role for the people but stresses the importance of an expressive, participatory role for them.

Admittedly, the people's scorn against the derision of the powerful does not seem like a good recipe for harmonious living. However, a reciprocal laughing-at is better than one that is one-sided. Indeed, Hegel hopes that the rational institution they share—the Estates Assembly—will serve as a strong enough basis to transcend their differences. Under these conditions, the reciprocal laughing-at more resembles comic banter rather than vicious, divisive scorn.

Conclusion

Scholars have discerned various ethical functions for comedy in Hegel's thought, whether in serving to reconcile individuals to the community, or to reveal subjective freedom or the theatricality of modern social life, or to critique existing institutions.[18] No one yet has explored the political-educative function of comedy, which was the task of this chapter. In recognizing such a function for comedy, Hegel appropriates and transforms Friedrich Schiller's project of aesthetic education. Indeed, Schiller himself pointed toward the theater in particular for the education of humanity. Hegel departs from Schiller, however, in institutionalizing drama into politics itself. That is, the public need not take the example of the ancient Greeks and commonly experience one piece of theater, as Schiller hoped. Modern conditions make such a return impossible. Instead, the public can commonly experience the dramatic nature of politics, and gain an aesthetic education from it. In particular, Hegel stresses comedy in contrast to Schiller's emphasis on tragedy. It is notable that Hegel is quite critical of modern comedies, perhaps because he sees in modern politics the opportunity for genuine modern comedy.

In this chapter, I have also provided a novel reading of a crucial part (PR 315–319) of *The Philosophy of Right*, which for many represents the high point of Hegel's antidemocratic, tutelary state. Accordingly, my reading sheds light on the debate about Hegel's democratic credentials. The antidemocratic interpretation of Hegel argues that the people's participation only occurs through groups—not from the people. My reading challenges this interpretation, showing that there is indeed room for a popular check on government.[19] More importantly, as I suggested above, my reading emphasizes the importance of drawing a distinction between institutional and expressive political power. Hegel is best understood as antidemocratic in institutional power in, for instance, legislation and the execution of laws. However, he encourages democracy in an expressive capacity. That is, he encourages the development and articulation of public opinion on legislation or execution, one that can hold sway by virtue of its connection to our common subjectivity, however "external" that subjectivity may be.

At the same time, Hegel insists that this expressive power be exercised responsibly. Indeed, the parallel to comedy helps demonstrate how best to exercise responsible expressive power. Currently, the United States is awash in fake news, outrageous racist language, and constant slander against the character of public officials. Unfortunately, the public also takes much of this very seriously. Many of us believe fake news, or spend hours castigating racists, or are indignant about slander. Hegel's lesson about the comic education of the public is to encourage a more disciplined expressive power, one in which the public can remain cheerful and indifferent to idiosyncratic and particular points of view but serious about the substantial matters of ethical life. Public opinion can and should leave the crazed or crazy opinions to self-destruct, rising above them. In so doing, we could heal the gulf between the people and the elites, who could laugh together about these peculiarities.

However, Hegel's view also points to a more difficult challenge for us, which is that this comic cheerfulness relies on a common public recognition of the rationality of our deliberative institutions. It is far from clear that we still possess this. Public trust of our governing institutions, particularly Congress, is at an all-time low. Without this commonly recognized rational body, we also no longer have a common standard of the substantial in ethical life. As such, we no longer have the capacity to distinguish between the particular and universal and so cannot know what to be cheerful about and what to be serious about. What is no laughing matter for one group may be insignificant for another. In this way, Hegel's view opens up a significant challenge for modern democracies. That is, they must maintain a rational deliberative body that itself is commonly recognized as rational, even while the particularity of modern societies can potentially lead to social fragmentation. They must maintain such core institutions so as to provide a basis to integrate the people's freedom with the elite's rationality.

Notes

1. PR refers to G. W. F. Hegel, *Elements of the Philosophy of Right*, ed. Allen W. Wood (Cambridge: Cambridge University Press, 1991).

2. Christopher Yeomans,"Perspectives Without Privileges: The Estates in Hegel's Political Philosophy," *Journal of the History of Philosophy* 55, no. 3 (2017): 469–90; Peter G. Stillman, "Hegel's Civil Society: A Locus of Freedom," *Polity* 12, no. 4 (1980): 622–46; Lisa Herzog, *Inventing the Market: Smith, Hegel, and Political Theory* (Oxford: Oxford University Press, 2013); Michael O. Hardimon, *Hegel's Social Philosophy: The Project of Reconciliation* (Cambridge: Cambridge University Press, 1994); and Will Dudley, "Freedom and the Need for Protection from Myself," *The Owl of Minerva* (Fall 1997), https://www.pdcnet.org//pdc/bvdb.nsf/purchase?openform&fp=owl&id=owl_1997_0029_0001_0039_0068&onlyautologin=true.

3. Paul Franco, *Hegel's Philosophy of Freedom* (New Haven, CT: Yale University Press, 2002), 328.

4. Harry Brod, "The 'Spirit' of Hegelian Politics: Public Opinion and Legislative Debate from Hegel to Habermas," in *Hegel's Philosophy of Spirit*, ed. Peter Stillman (Albany: State University of New York Press, 1987).

5. Franco, *Hegel's Philosophy of Freedom*, 328; and Dana Villa, *Teachers of the People* (Chicago: University of Chicago Press, 2017), 159–160.

6. The letter A here refers to G. W. F. Hegel, *Aesthetics: Lectures on Fine Art*, trans. T. M. Knox. 2 vols. (Oxford: Clarendon, 1975).

7. For example, Hardimon, *Hegel's Social Philosophy*.

8. Christopher H. Achen and Larry M. Bartels, *Democracy for Realists: Why Elections Do Not Produce Responsive Government* (Princeton, NJ: Princeton University Press, 2017).

9. Thom Brooks, *Hegel's Political Philosophy: A Systematic Reading of the Philosophy of Right* (Edinburgh: Edinburgh University Press).

10. VPR17 refers to G. W. F. Hegel, *Lectures on Natural Right and Political Science: the First Philosophy of Right*, trans. J. Michael Stewart and Peter C. Hodgson (Oxford: Oxford University Press, 2012).

11. PhG refers to G. W. F. Hegel, *Phenomenology of Spirit*, trans. A. V. Miller. (Oxford: Oxford University Press, 1977)

12. Mark W. Roche, "Hegel's Theory of Comedy in the Context of Hegelian and Modern Reflections on Comedy," *Revue Internationale de Philosophie* 221 (2002): 411–30; Lydia L. Moland, " 'And Why Not?' Hegel, Comedy, and the End of Art," *Verifiche: Rivista Trimestrale di Scienze Umane*, nos. 1–2 (2016): 73–104.

13. See Roche, "Hegel's Theory of Comedy" for a lengthy discussion of the genres of comedy in Hegel.

14. LA28 refers to G. W. F. Hegel, *Vorlesung zur Ästhetik*, ed. A. P. Olivier and Annemarie Gethmann-Siefert (Fink, Paderborn, 2017).

15. LA23 refers to G. W. F. Hegel, *Lectures on the Philosophy of Art*, trans. Robert F. Brown (Oxford: Oxford University Press, 2014).

16. Franco, *Hegel's Philosophy of Freedom*.

17. Moland, "Hegel, Comedy, and the End of Art"; Stephen C. Law, "Hegel and the Spirit of Comedy," in *Hegel and Aesthetics*, ed. William Maker (Albany: State University of New York Press, 2000); and Benjamin Rutter, *Hegel on the Modern Arts* (Cambridge: Cambridge University Press, 2010).

18. Rutter, *Hegel on the Modern Arts*; Moland, "Hegel, Comedy, and the End of Art"; Allen Speight, *Hegel, Literature, and the Problem of Agency* (Cambridge: Cambridge University Press 2001); and Andrew Huddleston, "Hegel on Comedy: Theodicy, Social Criticism, and the 'Supreme Task' of Art," *British Journal of Aesthetics* 54, no. 2 (2014): 227–40.

19. See, on this point, Brooks, *Hegel's Political Philosophy*, 126–27.

III
History

Chapter Eleven

Hegel's Tragic Conception of World History

Fiacha D. Heneghan

Introduction

Even sympathetic readers of Hegel are often vexed by his treatment of the philosophy of world history.[1] At best, this treatment might seem guilty of an antiquated optimism, regarding as it does history as a march toward progressively greater degrees of freedom—an outlook of which the twenty-first-century observer has been thoroughly disabused. Moreover, it seems out of place in a scientific, empiricist conception of history. It seems safe to say that the view described by Hegel in the *Philosophy of Right* § 343,[2] namely that "history [is] a superficial play of *contingent* and allegedly 'merely human' aspirations and passions" (see Remarks), has been in the ascendancy for some time now.[3]

At worst, however, Hegel's approach can be seen as a theodicean[4] apologia for world-historical atrocities. Although he admits that world-historical events, individuals, and nations do have a kind of moral valence "in the sphere of conscious actuality," world history itself "falls outside these points of view" (*PR*, § 345). It might appear, then, that the *Schlachtbank* of history is justified for the sake of the greater realization of freedom, as the moral perspective is superseded by the world-historical one.[5]

My primary goal in this chapter is not necessarily to pass final judgment on this question. However, I suggest that reading Hegel's philosophy of history in light of his aesthetics reveals structural parallels between Hegel's philosophical conception of world history and his conception of tragedy. In light of these parallels, I argue that Hegel's conception of the course of world history contains a tragic element, as Hegel might have understood the term "tragic." The upshot, I think, is that although this does not constitute a decisive deflection of the critical reception of Hegel's philosophy of history, it does at least add a layer of contextual nuance to our assessment of it.

More specifically, I begin by arguing that there are at least two conceptions of the tragic found in Hegel's thought. First, as Julia Peters argues, there is a tragic aspect to the first-personal *experience* of tragic heroes. For Hegel, this type of tragic experience consists in a sequential process of subjective alienation and (self-)recognition: the tragic hero, according to Peters, reacts with violence to what they thought was alien but was in fact a part of them—a realization that *tragically* occurs too late for reconciliation.[6] Second, there is a kind of tragic *logic* to certain aestheticized situations, initiated by the actions of tragic heroes, in which different ethical spheres conflict with one another. This is supposed to come about because tragic heroes are ethically one-sided and, as Stephen Houlgate observes, unyielding in their one-sidedness.[7]

Hegel's conception of world history exhibits these tragic elements on two levels. The first level is that of the subjective experience of the *world-historical nation* and the *world-historical individual*. The world-historical nation embodies a certain principle but becomes alienated from itself when its principle is overcome by world spirit in a higher principle, embodied by a different nation. It is too late, at this point, for that nation to reconcile itself with world spirit (PR, § 347). Similarly, world-historical individuals are those "subjectivities by which the substantial is actualized" (PR, § 348). In actualizing a substantial principle, they drive history forward but eventually become alienated from themselves when that principle is overcome. Thus, both the world-historical individual and the world-historical nation can be seen as having a kind of tragic *experience*.

The second level is that of the historical events themselves and the way in which they objectively instantiate spirit's progressive self-realization. For Hegel, it seems, the course of this history necessarily exhibits a tragic *situational* logic. The structural similarity obtains because, as is the case in tragic drama, history involves the overcoming of earlier, limited determinations of spirit in *higher* principles, which reconcile the divisions generated by the limited nature of the previous ones (PR, § 343). It becomes clear then how the tragic logic of a situation, initiated by the actions of the tragic hero, generates the hero's tragic experience, both in drama and in history. The reconciliation that obtains at the level of the polis in Greek tragedy and at the level of world history is not directly experienced by the tragic hero on the one hand or by the world-historical individual or nation on the other.

Tragic Experience

Let us begin then by determining what Hegel might mean by "tragedy." Hegel's scattered discussions support multiple conceptions of the tragic. The first is the tragic as it applies to subjective, first-personal experience.[8] In the *Phenomenology of Spirit*, this is an account of the unique kind of suffering that the hero of a tragedy undergoes. The second conception of the tragic is found primarily in Hegel's *Lectures on Aesthetics*. This conception of the tragic regards the formal structure of tragedies and articulates the underlying logic of tragic situations.

The differing emphases of these accounts would seem to reflect the respective characters of the works in which they appear. If Charles Taylor was right to claim that "the *Phenomenology* is called a 'phenomenology' because it deals with the way things appear for consciousness," then it is natural that any discussion of tragedy therein would foreground the first-personal experience of the tragic.[9] By contrast, the lectures on aesthetics—or more properly, as Hegel attests, the lectures on the philosophy of fine art—have as their concern the *beauty* of art. Consequently, Hegel emphasizes here the perspective of the audience (i.e., the structural features of tragedy as a poetic genre). Thus, the experiential content of the protagonists recedes in importance. However, nothing about the two perspectives makes them incompatible.[10]

In the account of "Reason" as "Spirit" in the *Phenomenology*, Hegel begins by noting the division of consciousness ("Spirit in its simple truth") into consciousness and substance (that is, we might say, the intentional content of consciousness) (*PhG*, ¶ 444). Substance is further divided into individualized reality and universal essence, mediated by a particular self-consciousness. Hegel says that this mediating term, "the implicit unity of itself and substance, now becomes that unity explicitly and unites universal essences and its individualized reality" (*PhG*, ¶ 444). It is in the individual *effort* to realize what is universal through this self-conscious mediation that *normativity* is generated and that the individual has the potential to act ethically (PR, § 142).

Through the division of individual and universal, Hegel says, "[the world] splits itself up into distinct ethical substances, into a human and a divine law" (*PhG*, ¶ 445). The resulting diremption constitutes the locus of action in Greek tragedy, and its unfolding directly explicates Sophocles's *Antigone*, the quintessential Hegelian tragedy.[11] Antigone seeks to give her brother, Polyneices (a traitor) a proper burial against the orders of her future father-in-law, King Creon of Thebes. In doing so, Antigone asserts the *divine* rights of family in opposition to *human* political right: burial rites are the familial deed by which the next of kin ensure that "the [deceased] individual's ultimate being . . . shall not belong solely to Nature and remain something irrational, but shall be something *done*, and the right of consciousness be asserted in it" (*PhG*, ¶ 452, emphasis in the original). Treatment of the dead represents the purely ethical moment of the family, and "[t]his last duty thus constitutes the perfect divine law, or the positive ethical action towards the individual" (*PhG*, ¶ 453).

Creon, however, is convinced of the ethical self-sufficiency of the human, political sphere from "the immortal unrecorded laws of God . . . /Operative for ever, beyond man utterly."[12] As punishment for Antigone's crime, he sentences her to be entombed alive outside of the city walls, relenting only after she has, unbeknownst to him, already taken her own life. Antigone's fiancé, Creon's son, commits suicide after raising his sword against his father, and Creon's wife follows suit. On Hegel's reading of the play, the tragic devastation that occurs to both Antigone and to Creon results from the clash of these two ethical spheres. Initially undivided in the "free and serene ethical life" of the Greek polis, the divine and the human perspective clash in a conflict of right against right (*PR*, § 356).

From a phenomenological perspective, we can say that the two tragic heroes—Antigone and Creon—exhibit both ignorance[13] and stubbornness.[14] In their unyielding commitment to their respective ethical spheres over and against the other, they fail to recognize that their perspective is part of a greater ethical whole. As Peters argues, they thus violently lash out at what they thought was something purely opposed but was in fact a part of them—in Antigone's case, the king's decree and in Creon's, the divine law. The violence they inflict not only on one another but also on themselves is born of ignorance of a higher ethical principle and is the source of their tragic *experience*: the first sense of the tragic in Hegel.

Tragic suffering is also, for Hegel, a source of learning: "[Antigone's] suffering, induced by the rejection of the citizens, makes her realize her political nature: she is a citizen of the polis, and being respected and recognized by the polis even in her death, is an essential part of her identity."[15] This is, importantly, different from the edifying effect of works of tragedy on the audience and on the broader culture. By virtue of the latter, Hegel thinks that tragedy is a means by which world history will ultimately advance beyond the "Greek Realm," by converting its unreflective ethical beauty into a reflective comprehension of the ethical whole.[16] The destruction of this form of spirit is immanently determined by the unconscious immediacy of ethical custom, which cannot be held together with "the self-conscious restless tranquillity [sic] of Spirit" (PhG, ¶ 476). Tentatively generalizing from *Antigone*, we can thus define tragic *experience* for Hegel as an educative process in which the freely acting tragic heroes severely wound themselves by believing that they are advancing an ethical cause, ignorant to the fact that their perspective is a limited one.

The Logic of Tragic Situations

According to Hegel, while the recognition that tragic experience brings about occurs too late from the hero's perspective, reconciliation is still achieved at the community level. It is in the latter that the ethical spheres rent apart by the tragic heroes are rejoined. Spirit had in fact been working through the characters and, Hegel writes in the *Lectures*, "The true content of the tragic action is provided, so far as concerns the *aims* adopted by the tragic characters, by the range of the substantive and independently justified powers that influence the human will" (VA, II, 1194). From a formal perspective, Greek tragedy is a clash of originally unified ethical spheres—each thereby justified—that destroys the individuals that identify one-sidedly with one or the other. Through their destruction, however, the ethical whole is preserved. As Houlgate puts it, "Reason and justice demand the death or ruin of the tragic individuals; and the fact that the destruction is recognized to be *rational* and ethically *just* allows the spectators to feel reconciled to it."[17] Tragedy thus serves an edifying function for the audience.

Tragedies exhibit a certain ethical *logic* that pertains to the situations of the tragic heroes. For Hegel, it is not a contradiction to say, on the one hand, that tragic heroes destroy *themselves* through their free action and, on the other, that they are caught up in a tragically unavoidable situation, as he seems at times to suggest.[18] When the tragic hero acts, she does so not on the basis of contingent impulses but according to an ethical law, either divine (substantial, familial) or human (abstract, political).[19] The tragic hero embodies an ethical principle and thus is spirit *in concreto* as it negotiates the tension between these two ethical poles. The coincidence of individuality and universality is especially acute in the Greek realm, wherein "the ultimate decision of the will is not yet assigned to the subjectivity of self-consciousness which has being for itself, but to a power which stands above and outside it" (*PR*, § 356; also see Remarks to § 279).

Nevertheless, true freedom of the will for Hegel arises when the free will wills the universal—or, more specifically, wills itself in its universal aspect (*PR*, § 21 and Remarks). It is in acting on universal principles that we act as free, rational beings. Thus, it is imperative to recognize that the tragic hero incurs guilt for their wrongdoing *tragically* precisely in doing wrong by doing right: "self-consciousness which comprehends itself as essence through thought and thereby divests itself of the contingent and the untrue constitutes the principle of right, of morality, and of all ethics" (*PR*, Remarks to § 21; see also *VA*, II, 1198).

In sum, then, a tragic situation consists in the conflict between ethical spheres, each right and justified as part of a higher ethical whole, but wrong insofar as they are taken to be complete in themselves. This conflict is immanent in spirit's need to supersede the unreflective identification with one or another ethical sphere and is enacted through the tragic hero—an aestheticized individual concretely[20] embodying a spiritual principle (*PhG*, ¶ 465). According to Houlgate, "Art, like religion and philosophy, is for Hegel a form of 'absolute spirit' in which we articulate for ourselves what we understand to be the true nature of being and of human freedom in particular."[21] Whereas Aristotle claimed that poetry arises from *mimesis*—art, in other words, imitates life—Hegel goes farther even than stating the converse. Art is not merely an imitation of life; it is, in a literal sense, a process by which spirit comes to know itself historically.[22]

Tragedy and World History

A brief overview of Hegel's treatment of world history as it appears in the *Philosophy of Right* is in order. "The *element* of the *universal spirit's* existence," Hegel begins in § 341, underscoring the claim of the previous section, "is intuition and image in art, feeling and representational thought in religion, and pure and free thought in philosophy. In *world history*, it is spiritual actuality in its entire range of inwardness and externality."²³ Hegel says in the same section that world history is a court of judgment in which particular nations and their principles appear only as ideal. World history's universality is in and for itself, which is to say that "[World history] is the exposition and the *actualization of the universal spirit*" (*PR*, § 342, emphasis in the original).

World history, in other words, is spirit actualizing *itself* as reason; spirit comes to see itself self-consciously in the progression of events leading up to that moment (*PR*, § 343). The entire history of the world is thus, for Hegel, a rational process (see *PR*, Remarks to § 343), which is meant to culminate in the reconciliation of spirit and actuality in the state, nature, and the ideal world (*PR*, § 360). This reconciliation consists in the achievement of the end of history: namely, justice as freedom, the consciousness of the necessity of which Hegel thinks is entailed by the rationality of history.²⁴ Pinkard makes this point well in saying that "the struggle over recognition is the ongoing thread in history that is the basis of justice as an infinite end in historical movement."²⁵

The progression of spirit in actuality takes place through states, nations, and individuals, which "emerge with their own *particular and determinate principle*, which has its interpretation and actuality in their *constitution* and through the whole *extent* of their *condition*" (*PR*, § 344, emphasis in the original). We should be immediately struck by what has gone before on the similarity between Hegel's presentation of these entities—world-historical nations and individuals—and dramatic (particularly tragic) characters. When considering such entities from a world-historical perspective, we abstract from their contingent features to consider only the spiritual principle that suffuses their entire condition; similarly, tragic heroes "place their consciousness into one of [the powers of the concept], find in it determinateness of character and constitute the effective activity and actuality of these powers" (*PhG*, ¶ 735).²⁶

The Tragic Experiences of World-Historical Nations and Individuals

It is consistent with this parallel between world-historical and dramatic entities that Hegel at times seems to aestheticize world-historical nations and individuals. To point to only one famous example of an individual that we can only assume Hegel regarded as world-historical, he writes in a letter to Niethammer before the French victory over Prussian forces at Jena in 1806:

> I saw the Emperor—this world-soul—riding out of the city on reconnaissance. It is indeed a wonderful sensation to see such an individual, who, concentrated here at a single point, astride a horse, reaches out over the world and masters it.[27]

To make the case, however, that there is something genuinely *tragic* in the way Hegel conceives of world-historical entities, it is necessary to look more closely at the nature of world-historical nations and individuals in the Hegelian account and highlight the similarities between their experiences and those of tragic figures.

To begin with world-historical nations, Hegel says that these nations are given a moment of spirit's development that they express as "a natural principle" and are "given the task of implementing this principle" during the course of history (PR, § 347). During the course of this principle's expression, the world-historical nation is dominant and epoch-defining, and entirely justified, argues Hegel, in being so. The world-historical nation develops this principle from latency into "free ethical self-consciousness" and is thereby, like the tragic hero who immanently expresses an ethical principle, justified in its actions thus far (PR, Remarks to § 347). In its capacity as a world-historical nation, its contingent features fall away, and only those aspects that express its essential principle count (VG, 145).

However, the destiny of world-historical nations after they have fully developed their principle is dim relative to their glory days. According to Hegel they tend to decline and fall when spirit subsequently develops into a higher principle, "which is simply the negative of [their] own" (PR, Remarks to § 347). In other words, in the process of spirit's dialectical unfolding, the principle of one world-historical nation is sublated by that of another when it can no longer reconcile its internal contradictions. These are brought to the breaking point by the "dissolving activity of thought," itself a form of the same phenomenological development of spirit as tragedy (VG, 147). In the *Phenomenology*, tragedy evolves into comedy when self-consciousness "exhibits itself as the fate of the gods" and in turn gives birth to philosophy: that is, rational thinking (PhG, ¶¶ 744–6). When spiritual self-consciousness of the world-historical nation rationally reflects on itself, it comes to recognize the limitations of its unreflective customs, which are not necessarily grounded in reason (VG, 146).

The process of reflection gives rise to the higher principle that will sublate the previous one, and once this happens, the previously world-historical nation fades in significance. Although it will absorb the new principle as other nonhistorical nations do, it will not have actively produced that principle and instead "will react to it as to an extraneous element rather than with immanent vitality and vigour" (*PR*, Remarks to § 347). When its commitment to its immanent principle betrays it, the fate that awaits might be described, colloquially, as tragic: "It will perhaps lose its independence or it may survive ... and struggle on in a contingent manner" (*PR*, Remarks to § 347). However, it can also be seen as tragic in the more specific, Hegelian sense in its similarity to the experience of the tragic hero. The world-historical nation embodies a spiritual principle—triumphantly at first, but eventually to its great detriment, as it fails to recognize a higher principle as containing its own all along.

The experience of world-historical individuals is not dissimilar (*PR*, § 348). "Since these individuals," says Hegel, "are the living expressions of the substantial deed of the world spirit and are thus immediately identical with it, they cannot themselves perceive it and it is not their object and end" (*PR*, 348). While this is a clear statement indicating that world-historical individuals, like tragic heroes, embody a spiritual principle, it also suggests a *prima facie* disanalogy between the two. World-historical individuals are unaware of the historical movement of spirit in their actions, whereas tragic heroes consciously and tenaciously (if unreflectively) cling to their ethical stance. This difficulty can be surmounted, I think, by noting that it is not the case that world-historical individuals (and nations) lack conscious ethical principles by virtue of their ignorance of the historical workings of spirit (*PR*, § 344). The historicity of the ethical principles they do embody is, as it were, of a second-order nature, and their obliviousness to it is as the obliviousness of the tragic hero to the inner contradictions of the ethical life of their nation that they expose.

When world-historical individuals have fulfilled their purpose on the world stage, their fate is similar to that of world-historical nations, although perhaps bleaker. Their existence as world-historical individual, a semiaestheticized paradigm of individuality similar to that of the tragic hero, is separate from their existence as a contingent individual. In this latter mode of existence, Hegel says, these individuals "cannot be said to have enjoyed what is commonly called happiness." (*VG*, 85). Like the world-historical nations they often lead, "[w]hen their end is attained, they fall aside like empty husks [...] they die early like Alexander, are murdered like Caesar, or deported like Napoleon." (*VG*, 85).

The Tragic Logic of the Movement of World History

It is worth noting another potential dissimilarity between the world-historical and the tragic, namely, that Hegel does not explicitly suggest that in carrying out its principle the world-historical nation or individual "does wrong by doing right," as the tragic hero does. This is a difficult interpretive point. Because world-history lies outside "the sphere of conscious actuality" in which moral and ethical claims are evaluated, it seems that, for Hegel, it is a kind of category mistake to assess *world-historical* actions in *moral* terms (PR, § 345). However, this is only part of the story. It is a mistake, Hegel thinks, to assess world-historical actions in moral terms qua world-historical (i.e., *in their world-historicity* but not as actions *simpliciter*). World history is, for Hegel, not simply the aggregate of past events; it is "a court of judgment" (PR, § 341). Like the spheres of abstract right, morality, and ethical life that came before it, world history is a "point of view" (*Gesichtpunkt*), and, specifically, one that lies outside the points of view that assess the validity of moral and ethical claims.

Like any point of view, however, it is one that we adopt as we see fit. From the point of view of world history, world-historical actions "attain . . . *absolute right*" (PR, § 345). This does not mean that we cannot assess them as actions from a different point of view (e.g., a moral one). It means simply that when considered only in their world historicity they must be seen as justified. There is, once again, a parallel here with the actions of the tragic hero. The pithy claim that the tragic hero does wrong by doing right conceals an equivocation because whether the hero's actions are considered right or wrong is dependent upon the ethical sphere under which they are considered.

Hegel identifies four "world-historical realms"—Oriental, Greek, Roman, and Germanic—each of which embodies a substantial spiritual principle that supersedes the previous one.[28] The successive realization, problematization, and sublation of each of these principles of spirit is, in other words, mediated through the rise and fall of these realms.[29] The comparison here with the logic of tragedy comes from the nature of tragedy as a situation in which ethical spheres in tension with one another come to be reconciled in a higher principle, at the cost of the protagonist (and, it should be noted, often other characters as well) (VA, II, 1194). Similarly, in the unfolding of world history, the principles that define the world-historical realms tend to eventually buckle under the weight of their incompleteness and the internal contradictions that incompleteness generates.

Thus, for example, the Oriental realm—in Hegel's interpretation defined by unknowing submergence of the individual in substantial spirit—passes into the Greek realm when this submergence hardens into brittle, ossified social structures (PR, § 355). What is required is knowledge of rather than submergence in the substantial: the defining feature of the Greek realm, which has not yet attained, however, to self-conscious knowledge (PR, §§ 353, 356). At each stage of sublation into a higher principle, much of the previous realm is lost. Although spirit achieves a level of reconciliation not previously possible at each successive stage of world history, the process of succession generates tragic experience described above for the previous agent of spirit's actualization. World-historical nations (and individuals) are thereby destroyed (often materially, always world-historically) in the unfolding of spirit's principles.

Conclusion: The Casualties of World History

To summarize this chapter, I have argued that there are two separate but closely related senses in which Hegel conceives of tragedy. One is what Peters calls Hegel's "theory of tragic experience" and consists in the first-personal experiences of tragic heroes siding wholly with one of two ethical principles that come into conflict with one another. Their devotion to their ethical principles is their undoing, as they lash out and inflict harm on what they perceive as an opposed principle, ignorant of the fact that it as well as their own have their place in a higher ethical whole. The second involves the logic of tragic situations initiated by tragic heroes: the tension between the ethical principles themselves, which must be reconciled but at the cost of the individuals actually embodying them. The destruction of these individuals is the cost of reconciliation. I have argued that both of these senses of the tragic find expression in Hegel's conception of world history: the former in the experiences of world-historical nations and individuals and the latter in the progression of spirit in world history that grounds those experiences.

What are we to make of this? I suggest two possible, divergent reactions to Hegelian philosophy of history understood as tragic—one critical, the other apologetic. First, the criticism. It might be argued that in presenting world-historical nations and individuals in terms comparable to those he uses to present tragic heroes, Hegel ultimately valorizes the fate of historical entities responsible for terrible human suffering. My discussion has framed the subjective *experiences* of world-historical individuals and world-historical nations as tragic. But to many a contemporary reader, it will seem that the colloquially tragic inflection of world-historical entities is the tragedy they *inflict* on the rest of humanity. From Achaemenid Persia to Athens, to the Roman Empire, to the colonial European powers: no nation or individual that Hegel would presumably consider world-historical has clean hands. Quite the opposite, in fact: the Hegelian world-historical entity is almost always drenched in the blood of others.

This objection or a similar one might be decisive against the appeal or viability of a Hegelian conception of world history in many people's minds, tragic or otherwise. It should also be noted that this objection is not an objection to the textual grounds for reading Hegel's conception of world history as tragic in the way it is presented here. On the contrary, it reflects yet another parallel between tragic heroes and world-historical entities: both rack up significant body counts.[30] It suggests, however, a question that could apply to tragic heroes as well as world-historical entities: When is suffering properly considered tragic? We consider Hamlet's situation to be tragic, even as we recognize the human cost of his decisions. What about the fate of Polonius, Ophelia, or Laertes? What about Rosencrantz and Guildenstern?

The apologetic response is that it is not right to describe their situations as tragic but as simply horrific. If we can grant that this characterization does not necessarily valorize Hamlet in ways we are uncomfortable with or diminish or trivialize the suffering of those around him, we might analogously defend the conception of world-historical entities as tragic. We might, in other words, be willing to accept that the subjugation of Gaul or the terrible destruction of the Napoleonic Wars were truly horrific while still maintaining that there is something distinctively tragic about the fate of the Roman Empire or the exile of Napoleon. This is because on the Hegelian conception of tragedy, the "tragic" it is not simply a synonym for suffering but a specific type. Tragedy, we might argue, is not the only kind of suffering there is in the world.

But the critic might respond again: this is simply too much to stomach. Moreover, it seems that it does not escape the very same charges with which we began, namely that Hegelian philosophy of history is at best too optimistic and at worst theodicean. We saw in the section "The Logic of Tragic Situations" that an integral dimension of Hegel's logic of tragic situations is its accessibility to and eventually pedagogic effect on the audiences of tragedies. If Hegel sees world history as edifying by way of analogy with tragedy, we might conclude that history is in some sense spirit's self-education, and consequently our own—we spectators and students of history. Would Hegel thereby be committed to an intolerably progressive view of history? The real concern here, I think, is that the tremendous human costs of this learning process are thereby justified. This potential for seeing any rationalization of historical events as a justification for them looms large for any idealistic philosophy of history that seeks to universal in the historical particular. Perhaps we ought to heed Aristotle's injunction against mixing up history and poetry:

> The distinction between historian and poet is not in the one writing prose and the other verse ... it consists really in this, that the one describes the thing that has been, and the other a kind of thing that might be. Hence poetry is something more philosophic and of graver import than history, since its statements are of the nature rather of universals, whereas those of history are singulars.[31] (*Poetics* 9, 1451^{a}39–^{b}7)

Notes

1. Among those to whom I owe gratitude for their help in making this essay what it is, I must thank first and foremost Karen Ng, whose insightful feedback on an earlier (and much inferior) draft was indispensable. Along similar lines, I would also like to thank a number of colleagues, some of whom raised important and fruitful questions at the 2018 meeting of the Hegel Society of America, including Mark Alznauer, Antón Barba-Kay, Rachel Falkenstern, Dylan Shaul, Paul Wilford, and Jason Yonover. Finally, I would like to thank Julian Wuerth for his unflagging support of my work.

2. All translations of *Philosophie des Rechts*, *Werke* VII, are taken from G. W. F. Hegel, *Elements of the Philosophy of Right or Natural Law and Political Science in Outline*, ed. Allen W. Wood, trans. H. B. Nisbet, Cambridge Texts in the History of Political Thought (Cambridge, UK: Cambridge University Press, 1991). Future references will appear in-line as PR, followed by the section (§) number. The following additional abbreviations will be used in reference to Hegel's works, along with the translations used, where not otherwise indicated:

> PhG *Phänomenologie des Geistes*, *Werke* III. Translations from G. W. F. Hegel, *Phenomenology of Spirit*, trans. A. V. Miller (Oxford, UK: Oxford University Press, 1977). Cited by paragraph (¶) number.
> VA   *Vorlesungen über die Ästhetik*. Translations from G. W. F. Hegel, *Aesthetics: Lectures on Fine Art*, trans. T. M. Knox, vol. 1, 2 vols., Oxford University Press Translations. Electronic Edition (Oxford: Clarendon, 1975). Cited by volume and page number.
> VG   *Die Vernunft in der Geschichte*. Translations from G. W. F. Hegel, *Lectures on the Philosophy of World History: Introduction*, trans. H. B. Nisbet,

Cambridge Studies in the History and Theory of Politics (Cambridge: Cambridge University Press, 1975). Cited by page number.

3. As Terry Pinkard puts it in his ambitious defense of Hegel's philosophy of history, "Was it merely a matter of blind fortune that European modernity... triumphed?... Was there a logic? From our contemporary perspective, all one has to do is state Hegel's questions to elicit what is our typical response, which is: Yes, it was contingent, and no, there was no logic." See Pinkard, *Does History Make Sense?* (Cambridge, MA: Harvard University Press, 2017), 49. In contrast to this, Hegel says, "The sole aim of philosophy is to eliminate the contingent" (*VG*, 28). Also see *PR*, Remarks to § 343: "For those who reject this thought, spirit has remained an empty word, and history has remained a superficial play of *contingent* and allegedly 'merely human' aspirations and passions" (emphasis in the original).

4. As Hegel himself attests in *VG*, 42. See Rolf Ahlers, "History and Philosophy as Theodicy," which dispels the notion that Hegel's philosophy of history affirms the status quo and Pierre Chételat's "The Historicity of Ethical Categories," which argues that the theodicy of Hegel's history does not eliminate the problem of evil. Both of these are important misconceptions to address and are, as I see it, components of a larger picture of Hegel's philosophy of history as naïvely (perhaps grotesquely) optimistic. My aim here is allied in that I try to help push back against this picture (or at least complicate it) by highlighting Hegel's sensitivity to the tragic aspects of history. See Rolf Ahlers, "History and Philosophy as Theodicy: On *World History as the World's Judgment*," *Idealistic Studies* 30, no. 3 (2000): 159–172; and Pierre Chételat, "Hegel's Philosophy of World History as Theodicy: On Evil and Freedom," in *Hegel and History*, ed. Will Dudley (Albany: State University of New York Press, 2009), 215–30.

5. And all this besides other concerns: for example, his orientalism and general Eurocentrism.

6. Julia Peters, "A Theory of Tragic Experience According to Hegel," *European Journal of Philosophy* 19, no. 1 (March 2011): 85–106.

7. Stephen Houlgate, "Hegel's Theory of Tragedy," in *Hegel and the Arts*, ed. Stephen Houlgate, Topics in Historical Philosophy (Evanston, IL: Northwestern University Press, 2007), 146–78, see especially 146, 166; and Peters, "A Theory of Tragic Experience," 85.

8. Peters is, to my knowledge, the only commentator to have explicitly identified this sense of the tragic in Hegel, and I follow much of what she says in explicating tragic experience here.

9. Charles Taylor, *Hegel* (Cambridge: Cambridge University Press, 1975), 128.

10. And further, as Peters argues, the neglect of the phenomenological perspective has led in some instances to an understanding of Hegel's conception of tragedy as inattentive to the suffering of the tragic hero. See, for example, A. C. Bradley, "Hegel's Theory of Tragedy," in *Oxford Lectures on Poetry*, ed. A. C.

Bradley (New York: St. Martin's Press, 1965), 69–95. Also see Peters, "A Theory of Tragic Experience," 86ff.

11. For example, Hegel remarks that *Antigone* "seems to me to be the most magnificent and satisfying work of art of this kind" (*VA*, II, 1218).

12. Sophocles, "Antigone," in *The Oedipus Cycle*, trans. Dudley Fitts and Robert Fitzgerald (San Diego, CA: Harcourt Brace, 1949), 186–251, see especially 208.

13. Peters, "A Theory of Tragic Experience," 90.

14. Houlgate, "Hegel's Theory of Tragedy," 166.

15. Peters, "A Theory of Tragic Experience," 91. Hegel of course misquotes *Antigone* 926: "Because we suffer we acknowledge we have erred" (*PhG*, ¶ 470).

16. "For Hegel, tragic experience thus follows the logic which underlies the experience of consciousness in general, as it is presented in the *Phenomenology*: it exemplifies a progression toward self-knowledge, of something which is initially merely in-itself becoming for-itself." See last paragraph on page 92 of Julia Peters, "A Theory of Tragic Experience According to Hegel," *European Journal of Philosophy* 19, no. 1 (March 2011): 85–106. The way in which this lines up with the progression of world history will be explicated in greater detail in the next section.

17. Houlgate, "Hegel's Theory of Tragedy," 159, emphasis in the original.

18. On the inevitability of conflicts of a tragic nature, Hegel remarks: "The substance of ethical life, as a concrete unity, is an ensemble of *different* relations and powers which only in a situation of inactivity, like that of the blessed gods, accomplish the work of the spirit in the enjoyment of an undisturbed life.... Owing to the nature of the real world, the mere *difference* of the constituents of this ensemble becomes perverted into *opposition* and collision, once individual characters seize upon them on the territory of specific circumstances." (*VA*, II, 1196).

19. For Hegel, these spheres are associated with the female and male sexes, respectively (*PhG*, ¶¶ 446–63).

20. Indeed, superlatively: "[Genuinely tragic characters] are simply the one power dominating their own specific character; for in accordance with their own individuality, they have inseparably identified themselves with some single particular aspect of those solid interests we have enumerated above, and are prepared to answer for that identification" (*VA*, II, 1194).

21. Houlgate, "Hegel's Theory of Tragedy," 146.

22. Aristotle, *Poetics* 2, $1448^{b}4$–18.

23. Emphasis in the original.

24. The more explicit statement of this claim comes from the lectures on world history: "World history is the progress of the consciousness of freedom" (*VG*, 54).

25. Pinkard, *Does History Make Sense?*, 44.

26. Translating "*Begriff*" as "concept" rather than "notion" as in Miller's translation.

27. G. W. F. Hegel, "Hegel to Niethammer [74]: Jena, October 13, 1806," in *Hegel: The Letters*, trans. Clark Butler and Christine Seiler (Bloomington: Indiana University Press, 1984), 114. What is it that gives this report its aesthetic valence? Admittedly, to avoid begging the question, an argument in defense of the claim that Hegel aestheticizes world-historical figures like Napoleon properly follows only as a corollary to the claim of this paper: that Hegel's conception of world history is tragic and, a fortiori, aesthetic. As befitting the aesthetic, however, I believe it is not entirely inappropriate to claim that we can non-discursively apprehend its presence. When Hegel writes history—in this case, as a primary source—it reads as if it were a report from inside an oil painting. I thank Antón Barba-Kay for raising this question.

28. The relationship between "world-historical nation" and "world-historical realm" is one that Hegel does not make explicitly clear. The safest thing one could likely say is that a nation serving as an exemplar of one of the world-historical realms (e.g., Athens or Sparta for the Greek realm) must also count as a world-historical nation.

29. With the exception, perhaps, of the Germanic realm, in which, according to Hegel, "spirit now grasps the *infinite positivity* of its own inwardness, the principle of the unity of divine and human nature and the reconciliation of the objective truth and freedom which have appeared within self-consciousness and subjectivity" (*PR*, § 358, emphasis in the original). It is Hegel's received view that the progressive march of spirit is meant to culminate in this, something like an end to history, in which spirit is fully reconciled with itself. This view, too, has come under critical scrutiny, however; Karin de Boer, argues, for example, that Hegel may reluctantly concede that the problems of modernity are in some way insurmountable. See Karin de Boer, "Hegel's Account of the Present," in *Hegel and History*, ed. Will Dudley (Albany: State University of New York Press, 2009). If this is the case, one might be led to wonder, then, if Hegel would have to posit a realm succeeding that of the "Germanic."

30. Antigone and Creon together cause, directly or indirectly, the deaths of three people; Hamlet, eight; Macbeth, ten.

31. Translation is Ingram Bywater's Aristotle, "Poetics," in *The Complete Works of Aristotle: The Revised Oxford Translation*, ed. Jonathan Barnes, trans. Ingram Bywater, Bollingen Series 71:2 (Princeton, NJ: Princeton University Press, 1984), 2:2316–40.

Chapter Twelve

Hegel on Tragedy and the World-Historical Individual's Right of Revolutionary Action

Jason M. Yonover

Introduction

This chapter analyzes overlooked connections between Hegel's theory of tragedy and his account of revolutionary action from a world-historical perspective.[1] Although commentators have recently noticed parallels amid Hegel's discussion of tragedy and his philosophy of action or his philosophy of history,[2] they haven't yet turned to questions concerning Hegel's thought and revolutionary action with his theory of tragedy in mind. In fact, relatively little has been said in recent years about the prospect of a right of revolutionary action in Hegel's ethical thought,[3] let alone from the perspective I take here. This may be because Hegel holds the state in rather high esteem, infamously proclaiming it "the march of God in the world" (PR 258a), and therefore unsurprisingly rejects the idea that freedom of speech could license incitement to rebellion (PR 319r). My aim in this chapter is to offer an interpretation of Hegel that affirms a right of revolutionary action, overcoming these and other barriers while responding to recent accounts in the literature.

I do so partly by acknowledging the qualified nature of this right. In short, as I clarify in this chapter, Hegel's "world-historical individuals" are, like his tragic protagonists, both guilty and innocent in certain respects insofar as they reject some present order; but in important and different ways, recognition of their paradoxical status comes belatedly. This means that the rightful revolutionary action of the world-historical individual can only be understood as rightful after the fact—and yet we shouldn't infer from this significant qualification that world-historical individuals have no right of revolutionary action. They do have such a right, and the philosophical historian will eventually see that world-historical individuals are 'on the right side of history.'

Because I understand Hegel's position on a right of revolutionary action to stand in stark contrast to Kant's, I begin in the following section by laying out Kant's strict views. Not only does Kant deny that there can be any justification from within a state for undermining that state, but he furthermore rejects the possibility that revolutionary action may be recognized as rightful on any other basis (despite some recent interpretations that I must accordingly discuss). Kant thus rules out the tragic developments that Hegel sees in history, such that clarifying Kant's position helps bring Hegel's into relief. Next, in a third section, I provide a brief overview of Hegel's theory of tragedy, in order to then formulate most vividly his position on the world-historical individual's right of revolutionary action throughout the penultimate section of the chapter. Finally, I conclude that recent work is correct to stress the limited nature of the world-historical right of revolutionary action that we find in Hegel but that we go too far if we try to defang this right altogether, as troublesome (or not) as it may be. Although Hegel's views acknowledging a right to contravene morality and ethics may be hazardous in several respects, we ought to present them as they are. We must also continue to revise our understanding of the status of Hegel's thought on this basis. Although the idea that Hegel's political thought embodies a stale, reactionary Prussian conservatism (i.e., the idea that Hegel is entirely antirevolutionary) has long since been debunked, this has only proven something like this universal affirmative's *subalternate* claim: that there are some progressive elements in Hegel. To my mind, this debunking has not shown the *contrary*: that Hegel is ultimately a revolutionary thinker. But a close look at where Hegel's political philosophy, or his philosophy of "right," transitions into his philosophy of history indicates that this contrary proposition indeed holds.

Kant's Hardline Rejection

Thus far, I have only briefly hinted at the account of Hegel's view on a right of revolutionary action that I develop in this chapter—the world-historical individual has such a right to clash with the present, but this can only be recognized after the fact. Still, even with this quick gloss, readers familiar with some recent literature on Kant and revolution might wonder whether Hegel is following Kant here. I suggest that we would be thoroughly mistaken to think so.

According to a surprisingly prevalent reading proposed, in particular, by Christine Korsgaard and also David Sussman,[4] Kant denies the right to incite rebellion but makes room for a belatedly recognized right of successful revolution. This would be very interesting if correct, since Kant is famously averse to considering the outcome of actions in determining their value (*AA* IV 394, etc.). And more important in the present context, if Korsgaard and Sussman's interpretation were accurate, Kant would prefigure Hegel in an important sense, rendering Hegel's position less original, insofar as the right of revolutionary action in Hegel is indeed retrospectively recognized.[5]

Now, of course I don't mean to say that Hegel arrives at his position ex nihilo—in fact, Hegel's view on revolution is best understood as a descendent of Spinoza's, though I don't have the space to discuss this here. Neither do I mean to say that interpreters have explored only one route to a right of revolution in Kant. Yet while the move made by Korsgaard and Sussman to uncover a belatedly recognized right of revolutionary action isn't the only one open to the commentator,[6] it's the most relevant account of Kant's stance in the context of the present chapter, and so we ought to consider it in brief.

Kant's arguments against the existence of a right to *go about staging* a revolution are clear enough; there can be no recognized right of revolution because this would destroy state sovereignty, which is held by the sovereign as representative of the general will. If one were to try to make available a space in which some people could claim a right of rebellion—and assuming that the present sovereign were not in charge of deciding the rightfulness of such a claim (as this would render the space meaningless)—one would need some third party to determine whether the people's decision to rebel is rightful. Yet, Kant thinks, to have "another head above the head of state to mediate between the latter and the people [...] is self-contradictory," for it takes away the sovereignty of the sovereign (*AA* VIII, 300, and see also *AA* VI, 319). Kant draws a harsh conclusion from such reasoning: "There can thus be no rightful resistance on the part of the people" and "it is the duty of the people to tolerate even what is apparently the most intolerable misuse of supreme power [for] it is impossible ever to conceive of their resistance to the supreme legislation as being anything other than unlawful and liable to nullify the entire legal constitution" (AA VI, 320). Yet, as clear as this conceptual argument is, one might wonder about a more complicated case. Imagine that a rebel has ignored their duties and yet has been successful in their rebellion. That rebel and their allies now hold power after the revolution. What are we to make of this?

For Kant, the successful rebel has still committed a severe wrong insofar as they *have staged* a revolution. Although they must be respected as sovereign for the same reasons that any other sovereign must be so respected,[7] they can never be redeemed with regard to their rebellious actions; they have acted (and will always have acted) without right. This matters. Remarkably, retribution is continuously owed to the revolutionary even though they are now sovereign, and if the erstwhile sovereign manages to regain power, they should give the revolutionary this "deserved punishment [*verdiente Strafe*]" (trans. mod.; AA VI, 320n). In this spirit, even after a successful rebellion, the deposed sovereign who doesn't concede retains a "right to his property [...] since the rebellion which deprived him of it was unjust" (AA VI, 323).

Of course, such consequences are only relevant if the former sovereign survives the revolution—but that may not happen, and Kant considers two further possibilities here, again putting pressure on any commentator who would hope to preserve a belatedly recognized right of revolution in Kant. The first possibility is that the sovereign is murdered extralegally or behind the scenes, so to speak, in the course of a disordered rebellion. Kant recognizes the appeal of such a move for a rebel, given that it may help secure their new state. Kant is quite clear that this act of "self-preservation" is wrong, and for all of the reasons that rebellion or murder would normally be wrong in Kant. Meanwhile, a second possibility worries Kant much more: eradicating the previous sovereign under the guise of the law. Informal assassination is bad, but really "it is the formal execution of a monarch which must arouse dread in any soul imbued with ideas of human right"; "[this] is seen as *a crime which must always remain as such* and which can never be effaced [...] and it might be likened to *that sin which the theologians maintain can never be forgiven either in this world or the next*" (emphasis mine; AA VI, 320n). Kant's emphasis on permanence in such passages shows just how austere he is in rejecting any right of revolution. Even after the fact, there's no room for justification. Success plays no role in evaluating whether or not one might have a right of rebellion. There isn't any real clash of ethical forces—we only have right and wrong forces—and there's no room for any sort of belated recognition of rightfulness to obtain; thus, there's no tragedy of the sort we will soon find in Hegel.

Commentators like Korsgaard and Sussman disagree, but they seem to overlook an important distinction between *enjoying legitimacy qua sovereign*, on the one hand, and *enjoying legitimacy qua successful rebel*, on the other. Kant clearly allows for the former regardless of how one has attained sovereignty—the revolutionary sovereign must still be obeyed (AA VI, 318– 19, 323)—but Kant also rejects the latter wholesale. Thus, even when Kant takes on what Hegel would call "a world-historical" perspective, he strongly denies the possibility of a belatedly recognized right:

> [I]t can scarcely be doubted that if the revolutions [*Empörungen*] whereby Switzerland, the United Netherlands or even Great Britain won their much admired constitutions had failed, the *readers of their history* would regard the execution of their celebrated founders as no more than the deserved judgement of great political criminals. For *the result usually affects our judgement of the rightfulness of an action, although the result is uncertain, whereas the principles of right are constant. But it is clear that these peoples have done the greatest degree of wrong in seeking their rights in this way* [...] for such procedures, if made into a maxim, make all lawful constitutions insecure and produce a state of complete lawlessness (emphasis mine; AA VIII, 301).

In this passage, Kant acknowledges the manner in which our evaluation of some actions, particularly revolutionary ones, can shift in light of their consequences. Then, he explicitly denies that we ought to authorize this shift. Kant points out that certain "readers of history" might judge rebels positively should their actions bring about something positive—and judge them negatively if they don't—but Kant makes clear that *he* will not alter his judgment just because they institute a higher ethical order. Kant doesn't think that revolution will bring about progress at any rate. Antagonism is important (without it, "all human talents would remain hidden forever in a dormant state"; AA VIII, 21), but this need only occur on a smaller scale, for instance in competition and, at most, through passive, minimal resistance.

Though Kant is an advocate of autonomy, he is strict in his view that it's best promoted under a state that holds full authority, as Rachel Zuckert has helpfully noted.[8] This is why Kant writes explicitly that "this prohibition is *absolute*" (emphasis in original; *AA* VIII, 300). Some readers feel that such a hardline rejection of revolution is abominable.[9] These readers may well be correct to harbor such feelings. But whether one likes it or not, Kant's doctrine is still Kant's doctrine,[10] and it should be appreciated as such, keeping in mind everything that's worrisome—or perhaps even appealing—about it.[11]

When faced with such difficulties, we ought to look elsewhere in the history of philosophy; and in the context of German thought, we may, for instance, consult thinkers immediately following Kant who *do* try to countenance a right of revolution, like the unduly overlooked J. B. Erhard.[12] Indeed, such a turn to neglected thinkers in the period is long overdue.[13] Meanwhile, though, our concern in this chapter is with Hegel.

Hegel's Two-Ingredient Recipe for Tragedy

Against this Kantian backdrop, we can now start to paint Hegel's complex stance on a right of revolutionary action. But doing so with full clarity requires that we now take a closer look at his account of tragedy, one of the fundamental dramatic forms he considers,[14] for Hegel's world-historical individuals that have—I argue—a right of revolutionary action also have much in common with Hegel's tragic protagonists. Although these figures must ultimately be distinguished, they share several illuminating structural similarities.

According to Hegel, particularly in his lectures on aesthetics, tragedy is first and foremost about (1) conflicts of principles. As such, tragedy is host to at least the following elements: (1.1) a principle that prescribes x and not-y; (1.2) a principle that prescribes y and not-x; and (1.3) one or more figures that wholly identify with just one of these principles for some period (*LFA* 1195). For Hegel, the definitive example of classical tragedy is Sophocles's *Antigone*, which he thinks is about: (1.1a) the principle of the family (indicating that Polyneices should, like any other kin, receive burial rites,); (1.2a) the principle of the state (indicating that Polyneices should, like any other traitor, be denied burial rites); plus (1.3a) Antigone who one-sidedly identifies for some time with the first principle and Creon who one-sidedly identifies for some time with the second. Antigone and Creon each have some right, but each understands only half of the story as they narrow-mindedly adhere to their principles (*LFA* 1217). Thus, as Stephen Houlgate puts it, for Hegel, "tragedy consists in doing wrong precisely in doing the right thing."[15]

Of course, there may be any number of ingredients on the recipe list for some given tragedy; but for Hegel this is, so to speak, the flour for the bread. So where's the water? In addition to this side of Hegel's theory of tragedy concerned with (1) collision, we may say that there is another side, epistemic in nature, according to which (2) recognition of error comes too late. Hegel formulates this aspect of his account of tragedy most clearly in the *Phenomenology of Spirit*, where his focus shifts, both because of the context of that work per se, and because of the specific transition from "Reason" to "Spirit" that takes place there. In the case of *Antigone*, at least on Hegel's reading, the epistemic lapse is (2a) the titular hero's realizing, just prior to her unglorified punishment, that her unfailing commitment to (1.1a) the ethical principle of the family only makes sense alongside a commitment to (1.2a) the ethical principle of the state, to which Creon rigorously adheres.[16] Hegel reads Antigone to concede as much in a crucial line that he forcibly translates from the Greek: "Because we suffer, we recognize that we have erred" (trans. mod.; *PhS* 469). Such recognition that comes too late is the water for Hegel's flour.[17]

Each of these two ingredients, namely (1) collision of principles and (2) belated recognition, is necessary for tragedy. Take one away, and little remains: without a real conflict, we would be left with merely idiosyncratic tensions and confusion; and without epistemic opacity in the collision—such that protagonists would then recognize themselves and their error, seeing what's needed to avoid a profound clash—resolution would be nigh, and no real conflict could obtain. Altogether, Hegel's theory provides us with a picture of a battle that's only fully understood after much of the fighting has taken place. In this clash, the figures do wrong in some respect, but only in simultaneously doing right in some other respect; and as such, they may be said to stand with right against right. This is primarily what Hegel has in mind when he notes that tragic protagonists are "just as much innocent as guilty" (*LFA* 1214). Although we should not think that holding this paradoxical status means things will go well for the tragic protagonists, it does mean we can expect some resolution, according to Hegel. "The tragic complication leads finally to no other result [. . .] but this: the two sides that are in conflict with one another preserve the justification which both have, but what each upholds is one-sided, and this one-sidedness is stripped away [such that] the inner, undisturbed harmony returns." That is, we are left with "the cancellation of conflicts as conflicts" (*LFA* 1215).

With this brief sketch of Hegel's two-ingredient recipe for tragedy, we can finally turn to his account of world-historical individuals and their right, which will lead us to several of the same themes, if with important differences that we must explore.

Hegel on a "Right of a Wholly Peculiar Kind"

In a fascinating move made within his late lectures on world history, Hegel explicitly confirms the link between tragic protagonists and "world-historical individuals" like Socrates. Socrates was ahead of his time in championing what Hegel considers to be the principle of subjectivity: turning to one's "inner life" and gathering confirmation of what is "right and good" there (PR 138a). But as important as it is, the arrival of this principle wasn't smooth. "The fate of Socrates is that of the highest tragedy," for "[o]n his own behalf he had the justification of thought; but for their part the Athenian people were completely in the right too." While Socrates was right in defending his principle, he also did so against right (i.e., in simultaneously undermining the state by encouraging doubt). According to Hegel, "the great tragic figures are those [like Socrates] who do not die innocently" (LPWH2 418).[18]

The purpose of this section is to make sense of such claims and develop my proposal that Hegel countenances, with important limitations, a right of revolutionary action. In arguing for such a proposal, with the help of reference to Hegel's account of tragedy (see the previous section of this chapter), I show that there is a great distance between Hegel and Kant on the rightfulness of such action (see the second section).

HEGEL'S PHILOSOPHY OF HISTORY

Until now, I have referred to Hegel's so-called world-historical individuals without clarifying their nature; but because this is technical terminology for Hegel, we must consider it in at least some detail, along with other aspects of his philosophy of history, in the first of three steps in this section. Hegel thinks that history is about the course of "world spirit." But as strange as it seems, and despite some misconceptions, this is no transcendent being,[19] for "spirit is only what it does" (PR 343), and "its" doing is just our doing. Although we may all have a part to play, world-historical individuals are the particularly relevant actors when it comes to advancing human freedom. As such, world-historical individuals play a decisive role in Hegel's teleological picture. But we have to say a bit more about the latter in order to understand exactly where these crucial actors come in.

For Hegel, spirit (or mind) is essentially free and comes to know itself as such. "Since spirit in and for itself is reason, and since the being-for-itself of reason in spirit is knowledge, world history is the necessary development, from the concept of the freedom of spirit alone, of the moments of reason and hence of spirit's self-consciousness and freedom" (*PR* 342). Call this (1) Hegel's *rationalism*, or a new flour—the first of two crucial ingredients in this second recipe, now for Hegel's ethical thought (insofar as it's relevant here).[20] (Note that these two ingredients or strands of Hegel's philosophy of right and history are not meant to line up in any *substantial* manner with the two aspects of Hegel's theory of tragedy discussed in the previous section.)

According to Hegel, the self-actualization of freedom takes place in history through actions of world-historical importance that correspond to particular principles: "The states, nations, and individuals involved in this business of the world spirit emerge with their own *particular* and *determinate principle*," and carry it out (*PR* 344). Such principles are decisive so long as they lead. Hegel thinks that the presently world-historical nation is truly "dominant [*herrschend*]" such that "the spirits of other nations are without right [*rechtlos*]" (*PR* 347), which shows how committed he is to the progressive development of actualized freedom, even at serious costs. But how do these entities first reach 'their' principle? Most important in the context of this chapter is what happens in transitions to arrive at—or to depart from—such a principle; and again, this is where world-historical individuals come in.

They act in the most robust sense: "At the forefront of all actions, including world-historical actions, are *individuals* [who] are the living expressions of the substantial deed of the world spirit and are thus immediately identical with it" (emphasis in original; *PR* 348). Here, too, we must be careful not to take this language to indicate that world spirit is something thoroughly beyond us. On Hegel's account, he can only speak in such a way insofar as he has recognized reason in history after extended analysis, including empirical study of the limited number of individuals who he thinks have taken world-historical revolutionary action. Similarly, when Hegel clarifies to students in the introduction to one of his courses on the philosophy of world history that history is about the progressive realization of reason and freedom, he emphasizes: "What I have said in a preliminary way and have still to say is not [...] to be regarded as a presupposition but instead as an *overview* of the whole, as the *result* of the inquiry that we have initiated—

a result that is known to me because I am already familiar with the whole" (emphasis in original; *LPWH2* 80). World-historical individuals bring about what must come, and the philosophical historian can later see how this work is in line with the self-realization of freedom. We will have to say more here, but before doing so we must dwell on the fact that the manner in which the world-historical individual moves things forward involves acting contrary to some current world-historical moment and its principle. The necessity of such transgression is a major concern within Hegel's framework, because for him what is right and good is normally tied to one's context.

Call this (2) the *contextualism* of Hegel's ethical thought, or a new water for this second recipe. Both in his *Philosophy of Right* (e.g., 153r) and in his lectures on the philosophy of history, Hegel repeatedly emphasizes the straightforward nature of ethics: being a proper citizen "consists in fulfilling the duties imposed upon one by one's social station; these can be recognized without difficulty, and their particular form will depend on the particular class to which the individual belongs" (trans. mod.; *LPWH1* 80). In short, "duty is rooted in the soil of civil life" (*LPWH1* 81). How, then, shall we treat an individual who acts contrary to the current ethical order and its principle, which one ought to follow according to Hegel's contextualism? What if an individual acts out of context in anticipating the arrival of a higher principle, which should indeed arrive according to Hegel's rationalism?

Hegel's kneading the flour and water of his ethical theory is no simple matter, and it's here that a tragic dimension begins to emerge—along with a right of revolutionary action. In one respect, history moves forward, and the means by which it does so are absolutely right; but in another respect, what's right is constantly determined at each moment by the historical moment, and so breaking off from some order will mean betrayal. According to my view, Hegel ends up combining the two major ingredients to his ethical thought summarized above in the following way. Hegel's rationalism or (1) this new flour has priority, and holds for any cases of transition (i.e., entering and exiting an ethical condition), where his contextualism or (2) this new water covers day-to-day matters. World history and its absolute right stand above all—though not so high above that we're talking about an entirely different, transcendent perspective.

With mention of this last issue, I may begin to position my interpretation between that of the two commentators that have dealt most carefully in recent years with the question of a right of revolutionary action in Hegel. Mark Alznauer has argued that Hegel draws a "principled division of labor" between the "two standpoints" of right and world history such that our responsibilities "bottom out" in a context of right.[21] Here I disagree with Alznauer and concur with Allen Wood that a true collision of rights claims, made namely by the present context and then the progress of world history, does obtain in the case of revolutionary action, such that the first aspect of tragedy that I examined in the previous section—(1) the flour to Hegel's account of tragedy—is indeed present. However, I disagree with Wood (and agree with Alznauer) that for Hegel world-historical individuals could never truly know themselves as world-historical when acting, such that the second aspect of tragedy examined in this prior section—(2) the water to Hegel's account of tragedy—likewise holds. Wood has argued that a world-historical individual could "undertake radical social change with a rational knowledge of the fact that [they] are creating a new and higher order."[22] Here I disagree with Wood and propose that he isn't faithful to opacity conditions that hold for Hegel's world-historical individual. Throughout the rest of this section, I consider the world-historical individual with each of these two aspects of tragedy in mind before concluding that Hegel affirms their right of revolutionary action—a right that Alznauer mistakenly excludes and that Wood correctly points to, albeit without sufficient qualification.

THE FLOUR TO HEGEL'S THEORY OF TRAGEDY:
WORLD-HISTORICAL INDIVIDUALS AND COLLISION

In order to clarify that there is a genuine *collision* of rights claims in the case of the world-historical individual—as in the case of the tragic protagonist—and also to specify the nature of this collision, we must first take a step back and note an important characteristic of Hegel's ethical thought: its hierarchical nature. Right or *Recht* is simply the existence of freedom for Hegel (*PR* 29).[23] Much can be said here, but in brief, such right holds at various ascending levels, each of which outdoes the other (*PR* 30r). The world-historical perspective, especially as taken in the *Philosophy of Right* (341–360), is the highest perspective of right vis-à-vis several other perspectives of right, primarily those of "abstract right" (34–104), "morality" (105–141), and "ethical life" (142–360)—though other more minor perspectives can be distinguished within these major stages.[24] Thus, while laying out the spheres of right in relation to one another in his introduction to the *Philosophy of Right*, Hegel speaks of the moment of the state, within ethical life, as "superior to [*höher als*] the other stages," mainly that of abstract right and morality; but although it's "freedom in its most concrete shape," the right of the state is still "subordinate to [*fällt unter*]" one other right: "the supreme absolute truth of world spirit" (PR 33a). "Only the right of the world spirit is absolute in an unlimited sense" (PR 30r), and thus on the other end of his *Philosophy of Right*, in the transition from international law to world history, Hegel reiterates: "it is this [world] spirit which exercises its right—which is the highest right of all—over finite spirits in *world history*" (PR 340). World history, centered on the progress of freedom, may thus involve acting in tension with a whole host of things. Hegel doesn't shy away from listing them: "Justice and virtue, wrongdoing, violence, and vice, talents and their deeds, the small passions and the great, guilt and innocence, the splendor of individual and national life, the independence, fortune, and misfortune of states and individuals" (PR 345).

Like the tragic protagonist, the world-historical individual and the principle they defend with revolutionary action can be said to collide with the principle of whatever ethical order is *ex hypothesi* on its way out. In clarifying that the ascent of a new principle can only come with the descent of another, Hegel confirms in the *Philosophy of Right* succinctly that this new principle will be "the negative" of the prior one (PR 347r). Hegel expands significantly on this point in lectures on the philosophy of history, however, claiming:

> One of the essential moments in history is the preservation of the individual nation or state and the preservation of the ordered departments of its life [...] but the second moment in history is that the further existence of the national spirit is interrupted [...] in order that world history and the world spirit may continue in their course (LPWH1 82).

Change doesn't come easy:

> It is precisely at this point that we encounter those great *collisions* between established and acknowledged duties, laws, and rights on the one hand, and new possibilities which conflict with the existing system and violate it or even destroy its very foundations and continued existence, on the other (emphasis in original; LPWH1 82).

In short, because there is a true conflict of claims of right, with world history and the world-historical individual's highest right up against the right of an existing ethical order, the world-historical individual certainly does some wrong. But this wrong is only wrong-in-some-respect—namely wrong with respect to spheres of right that have a weaker claim to existence than that of the progressive actualization of freedom. According to Hegel, the right that the world-historical individual asserts outdoes any other, such that they are justified in contravening other demands. In fact, they must do so. On this point I disagree with Houlgate, according to whom "tragedy is not an inevitability in human life."[25] Clearly, Hegel thinks that progress only comes with protest (taken in the strongest sense).[26] Thus far, the action of the world-historical individual has much in common with that of the tragic protagonist, namely as it inevitably triggers collision.

Hegel goes at least two steps further when it comes to the world-historical individual, though. Here we can mention a first crucial departure from figures such as Antigone and Creon, previously discussed; I will return to the second departure in conclusion. While on Hegel's reading each of these tragic protagonists defends one of two principles that are, in the standard case, otherwise to be synthesized (*LFA* 1197), the principle of the world-historical individual is really new, and won't be 'harmonized' with some other principle. Instead, the new successor principle will defeat this prior principle—which only emphasizes the gravity of the collision at hand. That is, while resolution in tragedy is a return to the status quo, resolution in world history is a shift to a higher ethical order. As we have seen, Hegel is explicit that arrival is departure in the case of world history: "This is accompanied by the debasement, fragmentation, and destruction of the preceding mode of reality" (*LPWH1* 82).

Again, I have until now clarified only the first structural similarity among world-historical individuals and tragic protagonists (and emphasized the important difference that the world-historical individual's principle is *novel*). In order to fully understand the world-historical individual, we must now turn to the second aspect of tragedy examined in the third main section of this chapter, or what I called there the water to Hegel's theory of tragedy, namely belated recognition.

THE WATER TO HEGEL'S THEORY OF TRAGEDY:
WORLD-HISTORICAL INDIVIDUALS AND BELATEDNESS

Not only do world-historical individuals take part in a collision, but the importance of their doing so is recognized belatedly, as proper evaluation is only possible after the fact. In the case of tragedy, according to Hegel, the protagonists with their "tragic firmness" of will (*LFA* 1203) just recognize their error once it's too late; the spectators, and perhaps the chorus, can meanwhile see where things are heading, but the tragic protagonist is blinkered. Where in the case of tragedy audience members are one or more steps ahead as they watch the protagonists make key mistakes, at real-life historical junctures *both* the world-historical "protagonists" and their contemporaneous "spectators" are rather one or more steps behind. This has consequences that press on Wood's affirmation of an absolute world-historical right in Hegel that, Wood claims, could knowingly be claimed in the present. To be fair, Wood acknowledges some of these limitations, writing that "Hegel's philosophy of history is not innocuous [and] includes a genuine amoralism, *though a restricted and conditioned one*."[27] But Wood ultimately underestimates the importance of this second tragic aspect of the world-historical individual's revolutionary action. World-historical individuals can't fully know themselves as world-historical when acting and neither can their non-world-historical peers. Although there may be reason for all of them to *hope*, this hope must remain thoroughly aspirational. Such a qualification has consequences for what the world-historical individual can reasonably claim in advancing history.

Let's first consider in greater detail the world-historical individual's *self-perception*. In one respect, world-historical individuals are oblivious: in his lectures on history, Hegel claims for instance that these figures "realize the end appropriate to the higher concept of the spirit" as "*instruments*" who are host to "a power within them which is stronger than they are" (emphasis mine; *LPWH1* 83–84). Hegel stresses such self-opacity in his *Philosophy of Right* as well: world-historical individuals are "the unconscious instruments and organs of that inner activity in which the shapes which they themselves assume pass away, while the spirit in and for itself prepares and works its way towards the transition to its next and higher stage" (*PR* 344; see also *PR* 348). With such passages in mind, Wood nearly acknowledges that anyone who wanted to invoke a world-historical right *today* would have to have a sort of futuristic knowledge;[28] but given these briefly summarized conditions, which I don't have the space to investigate further here, this special epistemic state seems unreachable.

Still, to be fair to Wood, things aren't so simple. Amid passages just cited, Hegel claims that world-historical individuals "[have] discerned what is true in their world and in their age, *and* have recognized the concept, *the next universal* [*or principle*—JMY] *to emerge*" (emphasis mine; *LPWH1* 83). On this picture, which seems to be in direct tension with the one just sketched, world-historical individuals "are the far-sighted ones" (*LPWH1* 83). However, the crucial point is that Hegel is here speaking after the fact, qua philosophical historian, for "the owl of Minerva begins its flight only with the onset of dusk" (*PR* pref. 23). The world-historical individual definitely knows how to get things done. But this doesn't mean they know with certainty if or when their purportedly higher principle will be taken up. Thus, regardless of whether or not they can tell just where things are heading and why, they sense "what is necessary and timely" (*LPWH1* 83). This is sufficient for their carrying out revolutionary action, but it's insufficient for their recognizing that this is precisely what they are up to. We can eventually see that they anticipated something, but insofar as we do so, we view things from the standpoint of the philosophical historian that retrospectively finds reason in history, which thus nearly appears as if it were carrying out its work without us all along.

We must now turn to the manner in which the world-historical individual's *contemporaries* perceive them. Hegel is more straightforward here with regard to the question of recognition—though still not perfectly clear, and so again we must be careful to remember that Hegel is looking backward, having already grasped what has happened. On the one hand, the world-historical individual's peers "flock to their standard," that is, the new principle that the world-historical individual defends, "for it is they who express what the age requires" (*LPWH1* 84). That is, there will always be some allies who perceive the gravity of this novel force that's clashing with the present one, which seems to be on its way out. But on the other hand, there's no way that the world-historical individual's contemporaries can properly evaluate what's happening.[29] As noted at the end of the previous section, no real tragedy would obtain otherwise, for resolution would immediately arrive. Everyone would throw their hands up and concede to the world-historical individual and their allies, who are clearly in the right. Unfortunately, things don't usually work this way; and instead, history is a violent affair. Hegel thus goes so far as to claim that "in history the periods of happiness are blank pages" (*LPWH1* 79).[30] Ultimately, world-historical individuals "draw their inspiration from another source, from that hidden spirit whose hour is near but which still lies beneath the surface and seeks to break out without yet having attained an existence in the present" (*LPWH1* 83). Because the next principle hasn't been actualized, as necessary as that is (Hegel's rationalism), and because non-world-historical individuals must judge the world-historical individual by contemporary standards (Hegel's contextualism), world-historical individuals are, we might say, considered guilty until proven innocent when they act in a way that fails to conform to contemporary standards. Or to be more careful: world-historical individuals will always have disobeyed some contemporary ethical order, as in Kant; but unlike in Kant, their actions are eventually understood as rightful from a higher—indeed the highest—perspective.

This is where Wood underestimates the importance of the opacity conditions on the recognition of the world-historical individual's right and where Alznauer is correct to temper Wood's account.[31] Wood muses that we could with Hegel "undertake radical social change with a *rational knowledge* of the fact that we are creating a new and higher ethical order";[32] but as attractive as this sounds, it goes too far for Hegel, given the opacity conditions mentioned throughout this section. Still, given that we are in the final analysis accountable to the course of world spirit, we shouldn't take this to mean that the demands of right "bottom out" in the status quo, as in Alznauer's view previously quoted. Joseph McCarney has similarly argued: "It seems that the judgement of history cannot legitimately be appealed to in the midst of events by any of the forms of historical spirit. It follows that there can be no alternative in practice to the authority of ethics and morality."[33] Although the premise holds, the inference is invalid. Hegel clearly thinks that there are individuals who "practice alternatives" to these lower spheres of right—and he thinks that they do so rightfully insofar as they advance things. Indeed, they have no choice: "A mighty figure tramples, as it proceeds, many an innocent flower underfoot, and must destroy many things in its path" (*LPWH1* 89). McCarney and Alznauer do help us see, however, that the world-historical individual—or the world-historical-individual-to-be—takes a great risk in their revolutionary action, as they can never really know how their actions will later be evaluated.

Conclusion

Tragically, the world-historical individual must collide with some ethical order insofar as they advance the progress of freedom—and insofar as this ethical order must put up a fight, that is no easy task. Tragically, this collision is all the more necessary insofar as ethical evaluation normally takes place with reference to the current ethical order, and the world-historical individual's revolutionary actions can only be properly understood later on.[34]

Worse still, we can note in conclusion that tragedy obtains in another more colloquial sense in the case of Hegel's world-historical individual. This is the second sense in which Hegel's world-historical individual may be understood as more tragic than his tragic protagonist. According to a simple understanding of tragedy, it's drama that ends with downfall. This simple understanding of tragedy holds for the world-historical and their revolutionary action, too, as Hegel thinks recognition comes *so* late that world-historical individuals are rarely there to enjoy it. According to Hegel, it's the "fate" of world-historical individuals that "once their [world-historical—JMY] end is attained, they fall away like empty husks" (*LPWH1* 85; see also *LPWH2* 96n44 and *PR* 348). They don't live to witness the success of their movement. Given this, and assuming downfall as something like a third ingredient for tragedy—some salt would be nice—we could say that here, too, Hegel's world-historical individuals end up even more 'tragic' than his tragic protagonists with which they have so much in common, as Hegel actually thinks that tragic drama doesn't necessarily demand the demise of the protagonists (*LFA* 1218).

In any case, it should be clear that, unlike Kant, the very different "reader of history" that is Hegel provides us with a perspective from which we can judge revolutionary action as rightful. Where Kant locks up the room in which we evaluate from the perspective of world history rather than just morality and the present order, Hegel leaves the door open, if only cracked. In particular, a tragic right of revolutionary action arises in Hegel on the basis of his mixing the two ingredients of his ethical thought. Although the flour of his ethical thought (his rationalism) has priority, this doesn't mean that the water of his ethical thought (his contextualism) is irrelevant. Notably, if the latter were irrelevant—if our evaluative position *didn't* play such an important role above, and if the world-historical individual's actions were always immediately known to be right—then the world-historical individual would simply have a *right to right* full stop, which would be far more straightforward. The implications of Hegel's contextualism (that what is rightful is normally context-dependent) are essential if there is to be any sort of tragic right of revolutionary action against right in Hegel. For Hegel, one principle holds sway so long as an ethical order remains in power. Once that world-historical order is no longer in power, following the new world-historical individual's actions that usher in the successor order's principle, this next world-historical order establishes a new context—which can, however, always be contested in the future by the progress of world history. The philosopher's work stops here, in any case, as the philosophy of history is the philosophy of what *has* happened, not what *will* happen.

A careful reading with Wood's interpretation as a reference, and informed by Alznauer's, demonstrates that there is a tragic right of revolutionary action in Hegel. While both Wood and Alznauer are on to something, I argue, their accounts end up too one-sided. I note in conclusion that the interpretation I have presented here avoids a major pitfall of prior accounts of a right of revolutionary action in Hegel, put forward by scholars like Dieter Henrich and Klaus Vieweg,[35] who attempt to ground this right in lower spheres of *Recht*, especially the moral right of necessity (*Notrecht*). With the right of necessity, one may safeguard one's life by stealing bread while starving or similar, contradicting property rights that are grounded in the most basic sphere of right (so-called abstract right). Although there isn't sufficient space to engage with the accounts of these commentators here, recall from the previous section that it's precisely Hegel's hierarchical account of right and freedom leading him to argue that world history outdoes morality and more. Only world history stands at the tip of the triangle that is right—"use sparingly"—and so only it could outdo the otherwise decisive claims of the state against which one might stage a revolution, even violently. It should therefore come as no surprise when, as Dean Moyar has recently stressed, Hegel emphasizes in handwritten notes the narrow scope of the right of necessity, clarifying that it's only valid within a "highly limited sphere" and is subordinate to the demands of ethical life.[36]

Hegel gives us reason to think that history is rife with ruthless but necessary revolutionary episodes. This may sound just as worrisome as Kant's views considered in the second section of this chapter, if from another direction—but again, such worries don't tell us anything about what views Hegel really held. And before these views appear too troubling, recall that Hegel's rationalism looms large and is, after all, part of what got us here in the first place. Hegel is committed to genuine progress as concerns the self-actualization of spirit. Thus, history isn't just a neutral proceeding: "*It is not just the power* of spirit which passes judgment in world history—i.e. it is not the abstract and irrational necessity of a blind fate" (emphasis mine; PR 342). This means that Hegel's world-historical individual must actually be moving things along and isn't just there to exercise their prominence. "It is this which gives them their power in the world, and only in so far as their ends are compatible with that of the spirit which has being in and for itself do they have absolute right on their side—although it is a right of a wholly peculiar kind" (*LPWH1* 84). Though this position may provide room for plenty of other worries, it should be clear that Hegel leaves us with a progressive, revolutionary position rather than an indifferent (let alone reactionary) one.

Among other things, one might be concerned that there could be a slippery slope from the latter to the former. Indeed, there will always be individuals who falsely claim to be advancing the progress of humanity, and we must consider them with the utmost caution. Perhaps, despite the limitations Hegel holds over us when evaluating the present, he can help us try to do that. But Hegel certainly affirms the rightfulness of the world-historical individual's revolutionary action. Recognizing as much—if belatedly—helps us to see how Hegel prefigures related and more radical theorists of social change like Marx, Douglass, Luxemburg, or Fanon. But it also demonstrates the continued relevance of Hegel's ethical thought on its own terms.[37]

Notes

1. I use the following standard abbreviations for Hegel's works: LFA=*Lectures on Fine Art*, trans. T. M. Knox (Oxford: Clarendon, 1975); PhS=*Phenomenology of Spirit*, trans. A.V. Miller (Oxford: Oxford University Press, 1977); PR=*Philosophy of Right*, trans. H. B. Nisbet, ed. A. Wood (Cambridge: Cambridge University Press, 1991). I cite the latter two works by section and not page number, with one exception; r=remark and a=addition. Because Hegel lectured on world history for many years, I have consulted several editions of the manuscripts and notes. LPWH1=*Lectures on the Philosophy of World History*, trans. H. B. Nisbet (Cambridge: Cambridge University Press, 1975); LPWH2=*Lectures on the Philosophy of World History*, trans. R. F. Brown and P. C. Hodgson, with W. G. Geuss (Oxford: Clarendon, 2011). I cite Kant's writings according to the volume numbers and pagination of the AA=*Akademie-Ausgabe* (Berlin: Reimer, later de Gruyter, 1900ff.). Translations are from Kant, *Political Writings*, trans. H. B. Nisbet, ed. H.S. Reiss (Cambridge: Cambridge University Press, 1991).

2. Christoph Menke, *Tragödie im Sittlichen* (Frankfurt am Main: Suhrkamp, 1996) discusses tragedy and Hegel's ethical thought from several perspectives. Allen Speight, *Hegel, Literature, and the Problem of Agency* (Cambridge: Cambridge University Press, 2001), chaps. 2 and 5 consider tragedy and action in particular. See also Rachel Falkenstern, "Hegel on Sophocles' Oedipus the King and Moral Accountability of Ancient Tragic Heroes," in *Hegel Bulletin* 41 (2018). Falkenstern uses resources from Hegel's philosophy of right and history to clarify issues in his aesthetics. Fiacha Henegan does something like the converse, as do I in this chapter; see Henegan, "Hegel's Tragic Conception of World History" in *Hegel, Tragedy, and Comedy: New Essays*, ed. M. Alznauer (Albany: State University of New York Press, 2021). More ambitiously, Karin de Boer, *On Hegel: The Sway of the Negative* (New York: Palgrave Macmillan, 2010) puts the Hegelian notion of tragedy front and center in order to reconsider Hegel's thought broadly, including not just his philosophy of right and history but also his logic.

3. Thom Brooks, *Hegel's Political Philosophy: A Systematic Reading of the Philosophy of Right* (Edinburgh: Edinburgh University Press, 2007) makes no

mention of the matter. Karin de Boer, "Freedom and Dissent in Hegel's *Philosophy of Right*" in *Hegel and Resistance*, ed. B. Zantvoort and R. Comay (London: Bloomsbury, 2017) primarily considers more minor cases of dissent, for which Hegel doesn't make much room. Dean Moyar, "Recht gegen Recht: Widerspruch, Kollision und Revolution" in *Ein Recht auf Widerstand gegen den Staat? Verteidigung und Kritik des Widerstandsrechts seit der europäischen Aufklärung*, ed. D. P. Schweikard, N. Mooren, and L. Siep (Tübingen: Mohr Siebeck, 2018) very helpfully contextualizes Hegel's views among those of Kant and Fichte. Finally, Klaus Vieweg tries to find a right of revolutionary action in Hegel but encounters a major obstacle that I shall return to briefly in conclusion. See Vieweg, *Das Denken der Freiheit: Hegels Grundlinien der Philosophie des Rechts* (Munich: Fink, 2012), 448–463. Vieweg follows Dieter Henrich, "Einleitung" in *Philosophie des Rechts: Die Vorlesung von 1819–20 in einer Nachschrift* (Frankfurt am Main: Suhrkamp, 1983).

4. See Christine Korsgaard, "Taking the Law into One's Own Hands" in *The Constitution of Agency* (Oxford: Oxford University Press, 2008), 259. Korsgaard concludes: "Revolution may be justified, but only if you win." David Sussman similarly claims that "a successful revolution may [. . .] be justified retrospectively should it in fact succeed, although it must always be condemned from a forward-looking perspective, where such success, even if highly probable, has yet to be made real." See Sussman, "Unforgiveable Sins? Revolution and Reconciliation in Kant" in *Kant's Anatomy of Evil*, ed. S. Anderson and P. Muchnik (Cambridge: Cambridge University Press, 2010), 225.

5. Korsgaard and Sussman both seem to have in mind retro*spectivity*, but then actually argue for retro*activity*. That is, I take them to ultimately argue the stronger view according to which Kant thinks some right obtains *in virtue of* success. I leave this issue aside for now and propose below the weaker thesis regarding Hegel, namely that his world-historical individual has a right that's retrospectively recognized, as they are fighting for major progress on behalf of some new and higher principle all the while, though this is only clear later on.

6. One ought also to consider the interpretation developed by, among others, Jan Joerden, "From Anarchy to Republic: Kant's History of State Constitutions" in *Proceedings of the Eighth International Kant Congress, Memphis*, vol. 1 (Milwaukee: Marquette University Press, 1995) as well as Arthur Ripstein, *Force and Freedom: Kant's Legal and Political Philosophy* (Cambridge, MA: Harvard University Press, 2009), chap. 11. According to Joerden, Kant's distinction between despotic and barbaric states can license rebellion-like action. His thought seems to be that where the despotic state is undesirable in many respects but still legitimate, the barbaric state deeply contradicts right and so is entirely illegitimate; and since an entirely illegitimate state isn't really a state, we can—or in fact *must*—found one on Kant's view. Now, this move merits additional discussion, but I mention two brief points in the meantime. First, on the reasonable assumption that revolution institutes only by eliminating, such a right would

better be called a founder's right. And second, for reasons that should become clear in this section, I submit that there's ultimately no room in Kant's theory for citizens to judge a state despotic or barbaric. Thus, we should remain as skeptical of this move, which seems to posit a view from nowhere, as of the one that argues for a belatedly recognized right of revolution in Kant, which I discuss in this chapter.

7. See AA VI 323: "The unlawfulness of [some state's] origin and success cannot free the subject from the obligation to accommodate themselves as good citizens to the new order of things."

8. Rachel Zuckert, "Kant, Autonomy, and Revolution" in *Humanism and Revolution: Eighteenth-Century Europe and Its Transatlantic Legacy*, ed. Uwe Steiner, Martin Vohler, and Christian Emden (Heidelberg, Germany: Winter, 2015).

9. Sussman calls it one of Kant's two "least popular" doctrines. See Sussman, "Unforgivable Sins?," 215.

10. This being said, a reader can disagree with my interpretation of Kant and still proceed to the next section without issue. I don't depend on any interpretation of Kant in putting forward my account of Hegel's position, but only use Kant as a helpful reference, given that I take his to be a historically relevant position in great tension with Hegel's.

11. I take it as obvious that we should be *worried* when there's no room whatsoever to rightfully dismantle a state we perceive to be thoroughly corrupt. But I think it's less apparent that there could be anything that *appeals* in Kant's position. I can only hint at some thoughts here but consider the consequences of Kant's strict views for the postrevolutionary state, which is in an extraordinarily sensitive condition. (Of course, revolutions will still happen, despite Kant's injunction.) The revolutionary party now has great power—they have probably used violence to attain their goal, and this will be known. Fear will thus predominate, which is likely to sour things. What the revolutionary government *should* do is immediately set to work on fixing the problems that led them to rebel in the first place. But what they may *instead* do is reap the benefits of their newfound grasp on society, even enjoying the riches of the previous sovereign. They may be tempted to exploit the fear they have cultivated, as well as the disregard for the former state that couldn't maintain power; and they may thus carry out a scapegoating campaign of persecution. Instead of fixing problems, then, the revolutionary government may distract everyone, including themselves, by focusing on the past, playing the blame game. Kant's decisive views proclaiming revolution as unrightful helpfully categorize all of this as off limits. As we have seen throughout the second section of this chapter, according to Kant the revolutionary sovereign has no right to pursue any of these diversions: they may not persecute the prior sovereign, make any claim to that former sovereign's property, etc., given that they took up their new position unrightfully. Kant thus has

the resources needed to condemn any postrevolutionary government that dwells on the past. But note that this potentially attractive side to Kant's harsh views, which deserves further attention, only becomes clear when we let Kant be Kant.

12. See Michael Nance, "Erhard on Revolutionary Action" in *Practical Philosophy from Kant to Hegel: Freedom, Right and Revolution*, ed. James Clarke and Gabriel Gottlieb (Cambridge: Cambridge University Press, 2021).

13. I have attempted to make progress on this front in Michael Nance and Jason M. Yonover, "Introduction to Salomon Maimon's 'On the First Grounds of Natural Right'" *British Journal for the History of Philosophy* (forthcoming).

14. On the essential characteristics of the three main dramatic forms Hegel distinguishes (tragedy, comedy, and the stage play or *Schauspiel*) in relation to one another, see Allegra de Laurentiis, "Substantial Ends and Choices without a Will: The Quintessence of Tragic Drama according to Hegel" in *Hegel on Tragedy and Comedy: New Essays*, ed. Mark Alznauer (Albany: State University of New York Press, 2021). On Hegel's theory of tragedy, and particularly for insightful analysis of various tragedies in Hegelian terms (which I will not be able to develop here), see the next few notes. On several interesting issues concerning Hegel's account of comedy, see Andrew Huddleston, "Hegel's Theory of Comedy: Theodicy, Social Criticism, and the 'Supreme Task' of Art," *British Journal of Aesthetics* 54 (2014).

15. Stephen Houlgate, "Hegel's Theory of Tragedy" in *Hegel and the Arts*, ed. Stephen Houlgate (Evanston, IL: Northwestern University Press, 2007), 149. Houlgate is particularly helpful on the role of collision in Hegel's account of tragedy.

16. Such an epistemic lapse is clear in the case of Creon as well, namely insofar as he comprehends, after losing various family members, that he must hold not just (1.2a) the principle of the state but also (1.1a) the principle of the family in esteem (after Creon's son Haemon, engaged to Antigone, tries to strike his father with his sword, he turns it against himself, and Creon's wife then takes her own life, too).

17. On tragedy and this more epistemic side of Hegel's theory, see especially Julia Peters, "A Theory of Tragic Experience According to Hegel," *European Journal of Philosophy* 19, no. 1 (2011): §3.

18. Without noting this passage, Ido Geiger insightfully references Antigone in a discussion of Hegel's world-historical individuals and mentions several of the issues I aim to expand on in this section. See Geiger, *The Founding Act of Modern Ethical Life: Hegel's Critique of Kant's Moral and Political Philosophy* (Stanford, CA: Stanford University Press, 2007), 132.

19. See John Searle, "Social Ontology and the Philosophy of Society" in *Analyse & Kritik* 20 (1998): 149, 157. Searle references and unnecessarily distances himself from a "kind of Hegelian *Weltgeist* that is floating around overhead, or something like that" (149). Perhaps ironically, Searle's discussion of revolution in this piece is comparable to Hegel's in at least one important sense, namely

insofar as success plays a major role: "you can do this if you can get away with it" (157). (As I will stress in conclusion, however, for Hegel world-historical revolutionary action isn't *just* about success and must truly be progressive.)

20. Here I follow Mark Alznauer, *Hegel's Theory of Responsibility* (Cambridge: Cambridge University Press, 2015), 170–71. Alznauer shows that Hegel's relevant positions—or, as he puts it, "Hegel's problems"—emerge from commitments both to the truth of progress as well as the importance of context. (I order these commitments or ingredients in Hegel's ethical thought differently than he does, however, so as to stress what I see as the priority of Hegel's interest in progress over his respect for the status quo.)

21. Alznauer, *Hegel's Theory*, 173.

22. Allen Wood, *Hegel's Ethical Thought* (Cambridge: Cambridge University Press, 1990), 233.

23. Although, for example, in PR 104, Hegel occasionally references "right" and means "abstract right" specifically—the first and lowest major sphere of right—we can safely distinguish this sense of right from the broader one that is the focus of Hegel's "philosophy of right" as a whole.

24. The careful reader will notice that the third major section of PR, namely "Ethical Life," *includes* Hegel's account of world history. But this shouldn't be taken to mean that some other normative claims of ethical life are on par with the normative claims of world history. For instance, recall that Hegel thinks the right of civil society (PR 182–256) is subordinate to the right of the state (PR 257–329), which both fall under the umbrella of ethical life. Indeed, this subordination, embodying Hegel's care to rein in the anarchic forces of the market (see already PR 33a), is one of several aspects of Hegel's philosophy of right that have guaranteed its continued relevance. See, among others, Axel Honneth, *Leiden an Unbestimmtheit: Eine Reaktualisierung der Hegelschen Rechtsphilosophie* (Stuttgart: Reclam, 2001).

25. Houlgate, "Hegel's Theory," 149; see also 169.

26. Compare Frederick Douglass, *Two Speeches by Frederick Douglass* (Rochester, NY: Dewey, 1857), 21–22: "The whole history of the progress of human liberty shows that all concessions yet made to her august claims have been born of earnest struggle [. . .] If there is no struggle there is no progress. Those who profess to favor freedom and yet deprecate agitation are men who want crops without plowing up the ground."

27. Emphasis mine; Wood, *Hegel's Ethical Thought*, 235.

28. See Wood, 231: "If, as a practical matter, you wanted to avail yourself of the absolute right of the world spirit in history, you would have to have reason to believe of your own crimes and ambitions that they promote the further actualization of spirit's freedom [in] history."

29. Compare Andreja Novakovic, "Hegel on Passion in History," *International Yearbook of German Idealism* 15 (2019): note 16: "When it comes to actions that

take place at the cusp of historical change, the social institutions needed in order to evaluate a passion's object are not yet established."

30. See also LPWH2 109: "[Spiritual] development is not just a harmless and conflict-free process of emergence"; LPWH2 421: "One must be prepared for blood and strife when one turns to world history, for they are the means by which the world spirit drives itself forward"; etc. Hegel thinks that the brutality of historical progress poses no less than the ultimate challenge to thought: "There is no arena in which [...] a reconciling knowledge is more urgently needed than in world history" (LPWH2 86). This being said, Hegel also thinks that he is up to the challenge and that the course of world history is intelligible.

31. For an earlier discussion of such opacity conditions on the world-historical individual, see also Joseph McCarney, *Hegel on History* (London: Routledge, 2000), 113–119.

32. Emphasis mine; Wood, *Hegel's Ethical Thought*, 233.

33. McCarney, *Hegel on History*, 182.

34. One might wonder whether, having worked out this philosophy of history, Hegel and the Hegelian could help us avoid such battles. According to Hegel, "statesmen, sovereigns, and generals are referred to history; but [...] history and experience teach that peoples generally have not learned from history. Each people lives in such particular circumstances that decisions must and are made with respect to them, and only a great figure [*Charakter*] knows how to find the right course in these circumstances [...] Peoples find themselves in such individual circumstances that earlier conditions never wholly correspond to later ones" (LPWH2 138).

35. See my note 3 above.

36. Cited in Moyar, "Recht gegen Recht," 84. To be clear, Moyar goes on to argue that Hegel's notion of "the good" as realized freedom *can*, however, ground a right of revolutionary action and also clarify Hegel's account of the French Revolution. I understand our proposals to be largely harmonious, though formulated in different terms.

37. I am grateful to audiences that engaged with various versions of this chapter, at a meeting of the Hegel Society of America in Boston, an MLA panel in Chicago, and a colloquium session in the German Section of the Department of Modern Languages and Literatures at Johns Hopkins University. I especially wish to thank also Mark Alznauer, Karin de Boer, Daniel Burnfin, Ido Geiger, Fiacha Henegan, Allegra de Laurentiis, Christoph Menke, Dean Moyar, Michael Nance, Katrin Pahl, Sebastian Stein, and Allen Wood for detailed comments concerning this material.

Chapter Thirteen

Philosophy, Comedy, and History

Hegel's Aristophanic Modernity

C. Allen Speight

FROM PLATO ONWARD, philosophy has always had a special relationship with the two dramatic genres: although Plato has Socrates acknowledge that the "ancient quarrel" between poetry and philosophy runs back to Homer, there is clearly an acuteness and immediacy to the rivalry that Plato saw between tragedy and comedy that animates the *Republic*'s discussion of literature.[1] But Plato's representation of the three genres as a trio in the famous conversation among Socrates, the comic poet Aristophanes and the tragic poet Agathon at the end of the *Symposium* is one that perhaps masks the even more intense rivalry between philosophy and *comedy*.[2] Although much may be said about the relationship between philosophy and tragedy, it is philosophy and comedy that are each other's most *articulate* rivals at the apex of Athenian cultural life. Of the trio still standing at the end of the *Symposium*, it is only Aristophanes and Socrates who will go on to give an *account* of each other—however misleading Aristophanes's comic portrayal of Socrates or judicially questionable Socrates's description of Aristophanes as his first accuser may be. Philosopher and comic playwright in this case are each engaged in portraying the other in a sort of rivalry that seems distanced from the celebration of Agathon's tragic prize, the putative task of the all-night party in the *Symposium*. Despite the seriousness of tragedy's challenge in both directions, philosophy and comedy are nonetheless sufficiently elastic stylistically to be the genres that offer a representation of tragedy, not the other way around, as Aristophanes's *Frogs* displays in the verve with which both Aeschylus and Euripides are sent up and the *Republic* demonstrates in casting the distracting emotional and imitative pull of tragedy on the potential young philosopher.[3]

Hegel specifically mentions this final scene of the *Symposium* in his account of Socrates in the *Lectures on the History of Philosophy*,[4] but while Plato can present an artful conversation among the great exponents of the three genres, for Hegel there is a more complicated relation in which philosophy's greater proximity to comedy is on display. Comedy is clearly said to be "that with which tragedy comes to an end" (1823, 309).[5] But comedy is said to bring to an end not merely the dramatic genre or poetry or even the artistic genres as a group but more deeply art itself—and hence usher in the importance of philosophy. "Comedy is the final form of art [*die letzte Form der Kunst*], the dissolution of art [*die Auflösung der Kunst*]," Hegel said in the final aesthetics lecture series (1828, 141). When Hegel stresses that art in its sphere "has performed the same service as philosophy" in "purifying the spirit from its thraldom," clearly comedy as the "final form" that art takes must have an important role in this task (*Enc* #562).

The organizing rubric of this exploration of comedy as *negating* or *ending* art is Hegel's remarkable claim (as expressed in Hotho) that the differentiating principle between the dramatic genres of tragedy and comedy is the *same principle* as that between ancient and modern art more broadly:

> The same principle which gave us the basis for the division of dramatic art into tragedy and comedy provides us with the essential turning-points in the history of their development. For the lines of this development can only consist in setting out and elaborating the chief features implicit in the nature of dramatic action, where in tragedy the whole treatment and execution presents what is *substantial* and fundamental in the characters and their aims and conflicts, while in comedy the central thing is the character's *inner* life and his *private* personality. (*LFA* II.1205)[6]

If Hegel means this analogy between tragedy-and-ancient and comedy-and-modern seriously, the consequences for his larger projects in art and history are significant, and it would not be surprising that Aristophanes would play a key role as the pivot to the sort of modernity that Hegel is in the process of thinking through in the Berlin lectures. In what follows, I will trace three of these consequences. In the first section, I will show how Aristophanic comedy frames the overall issue of theatricality that is both an inescapable element in the rise of modern subjectivity and something that depends on a fine-grained historical context for being understood. In the second section, I will show how the tragedy:comedy relation serves as the dramatically organizing principle for Hegel's twin narratives of art within the aesthetics lectures (a narrative that persists across the numerous versions of Hegel's engagement with aesthetics). And the final section will explore how central Aristophanes is to the placing of art and its history in the context of the larger historiographical projects of the Berlin period (in particular the lectures on the philosophy of world history and the lectures on the philosophy of religion).

Aristophanic Theatricality: Framing the Rise of Subjectivity

Among the first things Hegel says about drama as a whole and its "relation to the public" is that applause (or the withholding of it) is essential to its public nature as art. Remarkably, Hegel even uses the language of *rights and duties* in talking about the public's approval and disapproval of what it sees on the stage: dramatic works are "confronted by a specific public," and the author is "beholden" to it in a way that gives it a "right to bestow praise or blame" (Hier nämlich [mit dramatischen Produktionen] ist ein bestimmtes Publikum, für welches geschrieben sein soll, in Präsenz, und der Dichter ist ihm verpflichtet. Denn es hat das Recht zum Beifall wie zum Mißfallen" (*LFA* II.1175).[7]

Much has been made of Hegel's insistence that the Athenian audience did not have a sense of superiority over Aristophanic characters so as to view them as the "butt" of comic jokes. As Hotho puts it: "We must be very careful to distinguish whether the dramatis personae are comical themselves or only in the eyes of the audience. The former case alone"—of which, Hegel says, Aristophanes is the master—"can be counted as really comical," whereas the latter is characteristic of later comedy from Terence and Plautus to Molière (*LFA* II. 1220, 1234). Although contemporary Aristophanes scholars may disagree on whether he really turns his comic criticism on the demos itself (as opposed to the demagogues like Cleon, who are always in his sights), Hegel affirms such criticism of the audience itself as essential to Aristophanic comedy: "What Aristophanes especially loves is to expose to the ridicule of his fellow-citizens in the most comical and yet profound way the follies of the masses" in addition to specific individuals among them (*LFA* II.1221). If Hegel is right that Aristophanes does turn clear questions about the actions of the city directly toward his audience, it's worth thinking about what allows him to do this, since Hegel does seem to have (despite qualifications) a point about the difference between Old and New Comedy, as well as between Aristophanes and later figures like Molière. (For that matter, it's hard to imagine examples of contemporary late night comics in our own culture making their audience a comic target to the degree that Aristophanes does.)

Aristophanes's engagement with theatricality should, of course, be distinguished from the issue as raised by Diderot about painting and theater in the eighteenth century and by Michael Fried and Robert Pippin in discussion of nineteenth-century painters such as Courbet and Manet. Despite the crucial distinctions between period and genre, however, two aspects of the account of theatricality in authors like Fried and Pippin might be useful for thinking about Aristophanes: (1) the framing of the importance of the issue of theatricality as such within modernity (that, as Pippin suggests, there is something presentationally, not just actionally, involved in a consideration of the role of the beholder in looking at modern painting and theater) and (2) its historical conditionedness, such that a gesture that might have been in one era thoroughly theatrical (say, a subject's "facing" the spectator) can be turned in such a way as to challenge that very theatricality. As in the later painting traditions, so in Aristophanes, there is no *given* set of gestures or conditions that inherently constitutes theatricality, but it is dependent on knowing in a fine-grained way the specific artistic context in which such gestures are made.[8]

There are a number of remarkable aspects of Aristophanic comedy that thematize the issue of theatricality and that do not seem to have been part of Athenian tragedy. Schlegel and the romantics made much of Aristophanes's employment of the parabasis, in which the chorus leader speaks in the *persona* of the comic playwright himself (often to exhort the audience to vote for his work). But Aristophanic comedy seems engaged in an almost constant exploration of the conditions of theatricality, with its use of well-known characters who were present in the audience themselves, the parody of other genres and artists within one's own genre, and numerous winks at particular stage conventions. Comedy's extensive use of current settings particularly distinguished it from tragedy, since the Athenians had restricted such mentions in tragic performances following the debacle of Phrynicus's *Sack of*

Miletus (which had moved them to such grief that the author was fined for "reminding" the Athenians of their troubles and was never allowed to perform it in Athens again).

One striking element of Aristophanes's engagement with the question of theatricality is that it seems to draw on resources that are also employed by philosophy. Aristophanic comedy calls philosophy out, in other words. Nietzsche claimed that Euripides wrote for a single spectator—Socrates. But while Aristophanes is much more wide ranging in the spectators he wants to provoke, there is certainly a valid argument that Aristophanes and Socrates form a unique rivalry among all the spectators in comedy. Socrates's standing up during the *Clouds* is perhaps the most famous example of this, but there is a broader sense in which one may interpret a number of Aristophanic metatheatrical gestures as engaging with philosophically interrogative questions. Comedy in his view, in fact, seems to cast an open invitation to interpretive interaction.

Consider the following scene at the beginning of the *Peace*, an Aristophanic play that Hegel discusses a number of times in the *Aesthetics* lectures. Two servants are in the process of kneading what turns out not to be dough but rather dung—to feed a beetle that consumes it. In the midst of this bizarre scatophagous scene, Aristophanes immediately brings his audience on stage as he has one of the servants describe spectator reaction:

> But perhaps some spectator, some beardless youth [*neanias*], who thinks himself a sage [*dokēsisophos*], will say, "What is this? [*tode pragma ti*] What does the beetle mean?" And then an Ionian [*anēr Ionikos*], sitting next him, will add, "I think it's an allusion to Cleon, who so shamelessly feeds on filth all by himself."
> But now I'm going indoors to fetch the beetle a drink.[9]

The figures represented—a beardless young Athenian who only *seems* wise (*dokēsisophos*) with a key interpretive question and an Ionian philosopher with a naturalistic (but, as it turns out, false) account of an explanation—are represented as posing the sort of question that doubtless every spectator at the start of the *Peace* is asking: what exactly is going on here?[10] But what is key to understanding the theatricality of the scene is that the audience sophisticates on whom Aristophanes directs his gaze are not credited for their interrogative work but rather singled out as being *wrong*. The connection of the basic interpretive question to the broader understanding of the activity of philosophical interrogation in connection with comic spectatorship (whether pursued in the strictly naturalistic "Ionian" sense or not) is evident. And, as the play progresses, the plot turns on the rescue of the goddess Peace, who, along with two additional goddesses with the provocative names Theoria and Opora (Harvest), needs to be pulled out of a pit. Theoria's name is often translated in this context as "Holiday," but her presence signals a larger connection between dramatic spectatorship and philosophy (a point emphasized by Nightingale, who nevertheless does not connect the earlier passage with this one).[11]

From Tragedy to Comedy: Framing the Developmental Structure of Hegel's Art-Historical Project

The Aristophanic "answer" to the original interpretive question posed by the Athenian youth and the Ionian visitor in Aristophanes's *Peace* is, however, one that as it turns out requires *art*—or more precisely an understanding of the development of art in its various genres (in any case, *not* merely philosophical acumen, Ionian or otherwise)—to answer. Aristophanes makes clear that the entire genesis of his plot in this case is parasitic on a prior art form: namely, the symbolic appropriation of animal figures such as the dung beetle or scarab in the fables of Aesop. Trygaeus, the figure who has set this particular Aristophanic plot in motion, wants to make use of the dung beetle (of all conveyances) to fly to heaven and meet with Zeus about ending the war. This politically daring move has occurred to Trygaeus because "we see from Aesop's fables" that the dung beetle can indeed fly to heaven.[12] (In a typically Aristophanic moment of irreverence, Trygaeus's daughter, who has been calmly listening to her father's crazy plans up to this point, simply snaps: "Father, father, that's a tale nobody can believe!"[13])

So far we have a number of interesting Aristophanic elements—comic questioning of interpretive efforts on the part of the audience, comic political daring, and antitheological questioning. But the story for Hegel—whom this passage evidently fascinated no end—does not stop there. Aesop, after all, has a place within Hegel's history of art forms—fable as a moment of "*conscious symbolism*," an important category in the *Aesthetics*—that puts it between the pre-Greek symbolical on the one hand and the clearly classical forms on the other hand. As Hegel had evidently learned from his Heidelberg colleague Creuzer, the dung beetle or scarab was a significant symbol—Creuzer says in fact "the highest of all symbols"—in Egyptian religion, where it was a figure representing both the path of the sun and procreation, and it became a frequently represented motif in Egyptian decorative art.[14] In the lectures,

Hegel sketched the use of this symbol in a development that runs across the particular art forms, from an animal figure used in the context of (Egyptian) symbolic art to the "conscious" symbolism of the comparative art form in the (Aesopian Greek) fable to Aristophanes's comic employment of it on the Athenian stage.[15]

The longer story here is one which returns us to the striking claim of the 1823 lectures that comedy does not just bring to an end the series of artistic genres by "completing" tragedy but rather in a more general way can be seen as finishing out the larger narrative that started in the birth of the symbolic:

> Art has its end point in what is comical. We began from symbolic art. The subject makes itself objective to itself in plasticity [i.e., sculpture], setting up the individual as divine, as standing beyond particular subjectivity. The antithesis to this objectivity is the subjectivity that is satisfied with, and takes comfort in, itself and only toys with objectivity. Objectivity negates itself in this subjectivity, and in comedy it becomes the knowledge of this negation. (1823, 311)

This narrative progression is one that Hegel characterized in terms of a move from art that requires the appropriation of animal or hybrid animal/human figures as symbolic structures that are somehow separable from the meaning of the work of art itself (the characteristic of "symbolic" art and religion) to a work of art that has meaning in and of itself—the classically beautiful statues of the Greeks.

Distinctive in this move is the emergence of the *human face* as what is artistically "intelligible of itself." Hegel claims that the Greeks "understood how to achieve the particular, spiritual expression in beauty itself, so that the human countenance as such is intelligible of itself [*das menschliche Antlitz also solches für sie selbst verständlich ist*], whereas in Egypt the intelligibility is supposed to be brought about by means of animal figures" (*LPWH*, 354; *VPW*, 12.294).

This emergence of the human face—and more broadly the representation of the human figure itself—as the key transitional movement from symbolic to classical art has a corresponding moment in the later development of comedy as the last form of classical art as it begins the transition to the romantic art form. In the *Phenomenology of Spirit*, Hegel represented this moment as the "dropping" of tragic masks so that the visage of the actor behind his *persona* could now be seen and the self that now appears shown as "something actual": "The self, appearing here in its significance as something actual, plays with the mask which it once put on in order to act its part; but it as quickly breaks out again from this illusory character and stands forth in its own nakedness and ordinariness, which it shows to be not distinct from the genuine self, the actor, or from the spectator" (*PhG*, 744). In the lectures, while he does not use the metaphor of comedy's "dropping" of the mask, Hegel nonetheless emphasizes a similar conceptual development that links actor and spectator in a common recognition of selfhood: while acknowledging that Aristophanes still works within a masked tradition, what is key is the revelation of the self in the form of individual human beings (Socrates, Cleon, Nicias) who could actually be in the audience (*LFA*, II. 1188) and not merely figures known from mythic traditions.

What is striking about these two key moments within Hegel's narrative of art history—the emergence from the symbolic art form of the human face itself as the classical art form's central figure of reference, and the further revelation of the theatricality involved in the "play" of face and mask—is that Hegel is explicitly employing the analogy between the two dramatic genres in order to cast the narrative arc of this development in theatrical terms. The emergence of the human face as the decisive moment in the move from the symbolic to the classical is linked closely (beginning in the *Phenomenology of Spirit* and then apparently across the Berlin aesthetics lectures) with Oedipus's solving of the (Egyptian-symbolic) riddle of the sphinx ("human being" as the conceptual key to what Egyptian art cannot explicitly understand). And the reflexive moment in which classical art comes to terms with itself and the new notion of subjectivity that will herald romantic art is linked (again from the *Phenomenology* and in every Berlin series) with the figure of Aristophanes.

Given the dramatic shape of this narrative of art's development, the *meaning* of Aristophanic comedy as the "end" of art must be said to include, then, both the modes of art opened up by the new emphasis on the human face in the classical art form and the emergence of a self-aware form of theatricality that will involve the destruction of those plastic forms (unsurprising, then, that Hegel would represent the first by a tragic *character* and the second by an actual comic *artist*). Aristophanes's key role in this art-historical narrative needs, however, to be understood within a larger set of questions that arise when we compare this narrative to Hegel's other historiographical projects in the Berlin period.

Aristophanic History

Aristophanes is clearly a pivotal figure in the broader historiography of Hegel's Berlin period, linked with and perhaps rivaled only by Socrates, who was always for Hegel a pivotal figure in the transition from the ancient to modern worlds (1820, 271). When the historical significance we've seen Aristophanes bear for the art lectures—in opening up the issue of theatricality and revealing comedy as the art form that appropriates and negates other art forms—is placed against the role that he plays in the other historical lectures, a number of questions arise about the comic art and its persistence (or potential disappearance) in modernity.

Given what has been said about the sheer ebullience of Aristophanic comedy and the intentional cheerfulness of his characters' stances toward the inherent failure in what they undertake—if the typical Aristophanic character is indeed, as Hegel puts it, *in seinem Ernst nicht Ernst*—it may seem surprising that Hegel characterizes Aristophanes himself (especially in the context of the wider concern with his place in Athenian ethical life and history visible in the *Lectures on the Philosophy of World History*) nonetheless as *Ernst* ("in all his jokes there lies a depth of seriousness" LHP I. 427; "when Aristophanes makes merry over the Democracy, there is a deep political earnestness at heart" LHP I. 428).[16] Hegel insists that Aristophanes did not make fun of "what was truly ethical [*das wahrhaft Sittliche*] in the life of the Athenians, or of their genuine [*echte*] philosophy, true religion, faith or serious [*gediegene*] art" (*LFA* II. 1202)—but rather of sophistry, gossip, litigiousness, and other corrupting elements within their larger spiritual and cultural life, in short, what Aristophanes does put before his spectators is "the downright opposite [*Gegenteil*] of the genuine actuality of the state, religion and art" (*LFA* II. 1202; note the disappearance of "philosophy" in this second remark, however).[17]

Taking into account Aristophanes's "seriousness" and relation to Athenian ethical life raises broader questions about comedy's relation to the philosophy of history as well as its own persistence and disappearance in history. Focusing on the historically serious Aristophanes might run the risk of our missing the distinctively comic artist, however. As we have noted, Athenian comedy (but not tragedy) was focused on the contingent and the political here and now; it therefore alone allowed the kind of recounting that political history requires. In Donougho's view, this suggests an almost unsettlable

Bergsonian dialectic between comedy and the world in which comedy is seen as offering both distance from the world and an annihilation of that distance. Comedy's self-dissolution "prefigures the historical process as such" (a point Donougho finds suggested in Hayden White's employment of the comic as the mode for philosophical comprehension of history) but itself is "forever caught in the act of leaving the realm of art altogether, to become theory or social fact."[18] It may be true, as Huddleston suggests, that comedy's role as "the most actively critical of the arts" gives it unique social-critical possibilities,[19] but given the dual position of Aristophanic comedy-cum-seriousness that Hegel sees (i.e., the endorsement of the criticism of Socrates even while Athenian civic life is left behind), it is hard from this perspective not to think that the pivot point that Aristophanes represents is one of failure and disappearance (as Desmond puts it,"the modern world begins with the defeat of Aristophanes").[20]

The other side of the coin, however, is Hegel's praise for the unique achievement he finds in Aristophanes's comic art—the happy and reposeful state he characterizes as being *sauwohl* (happy as a pig). Emphasizing this aspect of Aristophanes has led to recent "reconciliationist" interpretations of Hegel's view of Aristophanic comedy as the precursor to Hegel's later appeal to objective "humor" (Hippel, Goethe in the *Divan*), something that has been heralded as a significant development in the last version of the art lectures.[21] This is an important reading and captures well the nonironist (non-Schlegelian) tendency of a Hegelian account of both ancient and modern humor. But one perplexity about such a reading of Aristophanes himself is that—despite the window Hegel gives us onto a reconciliationist view of modern humor in the last version of the art lectures—his discussion of Aristophanes in this context has a different and not always reconciliationist tone.

In the 1823 art lectures, where Hegel stresses that it is the "cheerful heart ... absolutely reconciled [*versöhnt*] within itself" (1823, 309) that provides the transition from tragedy to comedy, the discussion of Greek "reconciliation dramas" or tragedies that end with reconciliation (*Oedipus at Colonus, Philoctetes, Eumenides*) all come up for discussion in the preceding section of those lectures on tragedy. In the final lecture series of 1828–29, by contrast, there is no mention of the "reconciled" heart when Hegel discusses Aristophanes or plays like *Oedipus at Colonus* in the transitional part of the section on tragedy. The introduction of comedy is much more direct and its function more negative: *Die Komödie ist die letzte Form der Kunst, die Auflösung der Kunst, wo der Gehalt der Kunst selbst vernichtet wird* (1828, 141). Indeed the term *Versöhnung* appears nowhere in the last pages of the 1828–29 lecture transcripts on Aristophanes.

It's not clear what underlies this shift in tone from 1823 to 1828–29 (and of course the intervening lectures of 1826 are too brief on the topic of comedy to judge). It may or may not be an accidental matter in the last aesthetics lectures (time compression at the end of a lecture series could certainly be an issue), but it is at least interesting to note that the longer discussion of *Oedipus at Colonus* and Greek reconciliation plays also disappears about the same time in the Berlin series of *Lectures on the Philosophy of Religion*, as well: in both the 1824 and 1827 versions of the religion lectures, discussion of the reconciliation plays was a significant part of the account of the "religion of beauty," but in 1831 this falls out. In both the 1824 and 1827 lectures, the "religion of beauty" was considered in direct juxtaposition with the "religion of sublimity" (Judaism): in the first case Judaism precedes Greek religion, and in the second case Hegel reversed himself; however, in both cases the juxtaposition involved a discussion of reconciliation. In the reorganized 1831 lectures, Judaism went to a different part of the account, and Hegel for the first time had a direct transition of three religions—Egyptian religion (now called the "religion of ferment"), Greek religion ("religion of beauty"), and the Roman religion ("religion of expediency")—in a way that emphasized an internal artistic narrative focusing on the birth and death of images and plastic art (in this case the end is with Roman pantomime and a relapse in the circus to animal contests where the human figure is lost entirely [*LPR* 659–60]).

What could this apparent move in the last art lectures away from a "reconciliationist" Aristophanes mean? The reading suggested in this paper is one that sees Aristophanes, despite what Hegel took to be his clear significance for *ancient* comedy, as nonetheless a pivot to a modernity where an awareness of the inescapability of the theatrical and of art's own dissolutionist tendencies might give rise to postromantic and postgenre tendencies. But predictions about "future art" (whether in 2018 or in 1828) are always difficult. In addition to the question of the future of *art*, however, there is a further question less discussed among Hegelians, and that is the question of how we should view the future of the (philosophical) history of art going forward. This is a question avoided in part because of the significant disciplinary territory on which it may tread, one in which the Hegelian scholar often has to worry about forms of skepticism about whether a contemporary Hegelian must be committed to a narrative in which all past art is assigned to the symbolic, the classical, or the romantic. Even shearing away Hegel's close identification of those three art forms with specific cultures (pre-Greek, Greek, and postclassical Western), there are still residual concerns about the basic narrative being employed. But taking a stance toward modernity in which the Aristophanic issues of theatricality and art's dialectic of plastic formation and dissolution are central may give us a way to look at the surprising persistence of questions that emanate from a generally Hegelian way of considering the philosophical history of art. And many of these questions have not gone away in our own time: the perplexing appeal and enigma of early art, beauty's relation to sublimity, the distinction between terms like idol and icon, the continuing relevance of a dialectic between iconophilia and iconoclasm despite (or, in the view of some, perhaps because of) the museumification of art.[22] These are related to some of the concerns that Hegel seems to have fussed over repeatedly in the historiographical sections related to Aristophanes in his various ongoing lecture series in Berlin, and they represent questions about the relation among philosophy, comedy and history which contemporary Hegelians will likely need to continue to pursue.

I've argued that Aristophanes is cast in the pivot-position in Hegel's historiography for a number of reasons that bear on how we view the history and world-historical significance of art. I will conclude by returning to Aristophanes's play the *Peace* again: in addition to the dung beetle, there is a second key image that clearly impressed itself on Aristophanes's comic spectators, and that was Peace herself—the goddess whom all the crazy scatological preparations for flying to Mt. Olympus have been in service of, and the divine incarnation of the treaty that Athens was about to sign a couple of weeks following the play's production to end this phase of the Peloponnesian War. It's likely that Peace appeared onstage as a statue—and one, like, the commendatore in *Don Giovanni*, probably provoked wonderment in being capable of some stagecrafted movement (she turns her head when told that the demagogue Hyperbolus has now succeeded Cleon in power). Aristophanes focused his spectators' attention above all on the artistic origins of Peace: this is clear from a passage in which the Chorus expresses its joy at the return of Peace but is still unclear about where she has been:

> CHORUS (singing): Hail! hail! thou beloved divinity! thy return overwhelms us with joy. When far from thee, my ardent wish to see my fields again made me pine with regret. From thee came all blessings. Oh! much desired Peace! thou art the sole support of those who spend their lives tilling the earth. Under

thy rule we had a thousand delicious enjoyments at our beck; thou wert the husbandman's wheaten cake and his safeguard. So that our vineyards, our young fig-tree woods and all our plantations hail thee with delight and smile at thy coming.

LEADER OF THE CHORUS: But where was she then, I wonder, all the long time she spent away from us? Hermes, thou benevolent god, tell us!

HERMES: Wise husbandmen, hearken to my words, if you want to know why she was lost to you. The start of our misfortunes was the exile of Phidias; Pericles feared he might share his in-luck, he mistrusted your peevish nature and, to prevent all danger to himself, he threw out that little spark, the Megarian decree, set the city aflame, and blew up the conflagration with a hurricane of war, so that the smoke drew tears from all Greeks both here and over there. At the very outset of this fire our vines were a-crackle, our casks knocked together; it was beyond the power of any man to stop the disaster, and Peace disappeared.

TRYGAEUS: That, by Apollo is what no one ever told me; I could not think what connection there could be between Phidias and Peace.

LEADER OF THE CHORUS: Nor I, until now. This accounts for her beauty, if she is related to him. There are so many things that escape us.

The joke about where Peace was all this time ("with Phidias") concerns Phidias's exile, as alleged defrauder and friend of Pericles, but this joke won't work unless we are thinking about the relation between the embodiment of Peace and its *artistic* creator—or, as Hegel would say, between art and religion in Greece.²³ This is the "kinship" between Phidias and the goddess that Aristophanes stresses at the end of that last quoted passage, and that is perhaps what the comic poet himself has in mind in the parabasis of this play, where he speaks of having built a "palace of art" for Athens.

As Hegel made clear in placing the dung beetle across several key shapes of art (emerging from unconscious symbolic representation in Egypt to being a figure of conscious Aesopian fabulism to becoming a center of comic spectacle), comedy is above all an artistic vehicle for spectatorial and hence philosophical consideration of the role of the various arts—and by dint of that also an artistic means whereby art's influence may also dissolve in philosophical reflection. So it is with Phidias and the statue of Peace: Aristophanes's sly joke at the end reminds his Athenian audience that it is precisely the presence of artists within the polis that allows them access to divinity (this is Hegel's consistent reading of the Herodotean passage that it was Homer and Hesiod who gave the Greeks their gods—and the same claim was made, of course, about Phidias).

For all the awareness of the human artifice behind the appearance and disappearance of the goddess of Peace, the best interpretation of this Aristophanic joke in an Hegelian spirit would seem to me to be neither nihilistic nor unequivocally reconciliationist. Comedy's witty perception that it is human hands who have made both war and peace (Phidias the statue and the Athenians themselves the treaty that is shortly to be signed) does not make it the enemy of what Hegel calls "genuine philosophy, true religion, and serious art." Aristophanes, he takes it, affirms these things but sees the threat to them in falsely interpretive sophistry, scheming demagogues, and artists who don't challenge their fellow citizens. Peace is indeed a presence who should not be misused or abused, and Hegel's Aristophanes might be much like his character Trygaios, who despite the brief Olympos-eye view he has gotten of his fellow citizens' pettiness, still takes time to urge them to adore her beauty: "Friends, let us first adore the goddess, who has delivered us from crests and Gorgons; then let us hurry to our farms."

Notes

1. Plato, *Republic* 598d–608a.
2. This is a much-discussed passage with significant philosophical consequences not only for the philosophy of art but more broadly for the construal of philosophy itself: see Stephanie Nelson, "Between Being and Becoming: Comedy, Tragedy and the Symposium," in *Thinking the Greeks: A Volume in Honor of James M. Redfield*, ed. Lillian Doherty and Bruce M. King (Routledge, forthcoming).
3. Plato, *Republic* 605d–607a.
4. Hegel, *Werke: Theorie Werkausgabe*, ed. Eva Moldenhauer and Karl-Markus Michel (Frankfurt: Suhrkamp Verlag, 1969–), 18.453.
5. References to transcripts of the 1820 and 1823 lectures are to manuscript pages in G. W. F. Hegel: *Gesammelte Werke*. Bd. 28.1: *Vorlesungen über die Philosophie der Kunst*. The latter of these lectures is now in English translation as *Lectures on the Philosophy of Art: The Hotho Transcript of the 1823 Berlin Lectures*, ed. and trans. Robert F. Brown (Oxford: Clarendon, 2014). References to the Heimann manuscript of the final 1828–29 lectures are by manuscript page to *Vorlesungen über die Philosophie der Kunst Nachschriften zum Kolleg des*

Wintersemesters 1828/29, vol 28.3, *Georg Wilhelm Friedrich Hegel: Gesammelte Werke*, ed. Walter Jaeschke and Niklas Hebing (Hamburg: Meiner, 2020).

6. This and further references to the standard edition of Hegel's lectures on aesthetics as edited by his student Hotho are to the two-volume English translation (*LFA*) by T. M. Knox, *Hegel's Aesthetics: Lectures on Fine Art* (Oxford: Clarendon, 1975).

7. This passage is from Hotho, but one can find similar sections in the transcripts: see the 1828 transcript, where Hegel linked this directly to the recognitive structures underlying dramatic artwork (1828, 137).

8. See Robert Pippin, *After the Beautiful: Hegel and the Philosophy of Pictorial Modernism* (Chicago: University of Chicago, 2014) and Michael Fried, *Absorption and Theatricality: Painting and Beholder in the Age of Diderot* (Chicago: University of Chicago Press, 1988); *Courbet's Realism* (Chicago: University of Chicago Press, 1992) and *Manet's Modernism, or The Face of Painting in the 1860s* (Chicago: University of Chicago Press, 1996). The *non*-Aristophanic issue raised in these latter cases, of course, concerns the question of the possibility of negating or avoiding "theatrical" modes in painting, but that is too broad a topic in the present context. (I'm grateful to Olga Johnson for suggestions about the difficulties of this issue in interpreting Manet.)

9. Aristophanes, *Peace: The Complete Greek Drama*, ed. Whitney J. Oates and Eugene O'Neill, Jr., vol. 2 (New York: Random House, 1938) ll. 43–48.

10. Aristophanes very clearly has the Athenian youth and the Ionian visitor represented as speaking in their respective dialects (Attic and Ionian); the importance of this intercultural moment of theatrical interpretation has been differently understood. See A. W. Nightingale, *Spectacles of Truth in Classical Greek Philosophy: Theoria in its Cultural Context* (Cambridge: Cambridge University Press, 2004), 58. Nightingale stresses the "theoric" panhellenic gaze and R. M. Rosen the distinct Ionian mode of iambic poetry. See Rosen, "The Ionian at Aristophanes *Peace* 46," *Greek, Roman and Byzantine Studies* 25, no. 4 (1984): 389–96.

11. Nightingale, *Spectacles of Truth*.

12. According to the fable ("The Dung Beetle and the Eagle"), the beetle, after being brushed aside when it attempted to stand up against the eagle on behalf of the hare, gets its revenge by flying to the eagle's nest and pushing out the eggs.

13. Aristophanes, *Peace*, l. 132.

14. See Hegel, *Lectures on the Philosophy of World History* (Oxford: Oxford University Press, 1995), I. 352. On Hegel's use of Creuzer here, see Jon Stewart, *Hegel's Interpretation of the Religions of the World: The Logic of the Gods* (Oxford: Oxford University Press, 2018).

15. Hegel in fact seems to claim that Aesop already is protocomic in his treatment of the theme: in the fable "there is presented the circumstance of natural history—I leave aside the question whether this is accurate or not—that

eagles and beetles lay their eggs at different times; but there is perceptible too what is obviously the traditional importance of the scarab, which yet appears here already drawn into the sphere of the comic, as has occurred still more in Aristophanes" (*LFA* I. 386–7).

16. In the 1828–29 version of the lectures, Hegel describes Aristophanes as "*ernst, heiter, patriotisch*" (141).

17. Hegel's larger historical view of Aristophanic seriousness correlates also with his account of Socrates, who, on Hegel's view, was ultimately not comic (as in his onstage portrayal by Aristophanes) but in fact tragic—even if Aristophanes is partly correct in his diagnosis of how Socrates contributed to his fate.

18. Martin Donougho, "Hegelian Comedy," *Philosophy and Rhetoric* 49, no. 2 (2016): 196–220.

19. Andrew Huddleston, "Hegel on Comedy: Theodicy, Social Criticism and the 'Supreme Task of Art,'" *British Journal of Aesthetics* 54, no. 2 (April 2014): 227–240.

20. William Desmond, "Hegel and Aristophanes," *The Owl of Minerva* 20, no. 2 (Spring 1989): 131–149.

21. Benjamin Rutter, *Hegel on the Modern Arts* (Cambridge: Cambridge University Press, 2010); and Lydia Moland, "'And Why Not?' Hegel, Comedy, and the End of Art," *Verifiche: Riviste di Scienze Umane* 65, nos. 1–2 (2016): 73–104; and "Reconciling Laughter: Hegel on Comedy and Humor," in Moland, *All Too Human: Laughter, Humor and Comedy in Nineteeenth Century Philosophy* (Dordrecht: Springer, 2018), pp. 15-31.

22. *On the persistence of iconoclastic tendencies in modern museum culture, see, among others,* James Simpson, *Under the Hammer: Iconoclasm in the Anglo-American Tradition* (Oxford: Oxford University Press, 2010).

23. See Stephanie Nelson, *Aristophanes and His Tragic Muse: Comedy, Tragedy and the Polis in 5th Century Athens* (Leiden, The Netherlands: Brill, 2016), 221.

Contributors

MARK ALZNAUER is Associate Professor of Philosophy at Northwestern University. He is the former Vice President of the Hegel Society of America and the author of *Hegel's Theory of Responsibility* (2015).

ANTÓN BARBA-KAY is Associate Professor of Philosophy at the Catholic University of America.

JEFFREY CHURCH is Professor of Political Science at the University of Houston. He is the author of *Infinite Autonomy: the Divided Individual in the Political Thought of G.W.F. Hegel and Friedrich Nietzsche* (2012), two monographs on Nietzsche, and co-editor of the forthcoming translation of J. G. Fichte's *Contribution to the Correction of the Public's Judgments on the French Revolution*.

ALLEGRA DE LAURENTIIS, Professor of Philosophy at Stony Brook University and former President of the Hegel Society of America, is the author of *Subjects in the Ancient and Modern World: On Hegel's Theory of Subjectivity* (2005). She has co-edited the *Bloomsbury Companion to Hegel* (2013), and has edited *Hegel and Metaphysics: On Logic and Ontology in the System* (2016). She is the author of the forthcoming *Life and Psyche in Hegel›s Anthropology* (2021).

MARTIN DONOUGHO is Professor Emeritus in the Department of Philosophy at the University of South Carolina.

RACHEL FALKENSTERN is Assistant Professor of Philosophy at St Francis College, Brooklyn.

DOUGLAS FINN teaches in the Honors Program at Villanova University.

WES FURLOTTE teaches at Thompson Rivers University, where he has a cross appointment in the Department of Philosophy, History and Politics and the Department of English and Modern Languages.

FIACHA D. HENEGHAN is a Ph.D. candidate at Vanderbilt University.

ERIC V. D. LUFT earned his B.A. "magna cum laude" in philosophy and religion at Bowdoin College in 1974, his Ph.D. in philosophy at Bryn Mawr College in 1985, and his M.L.S. at Syracuse University in 1993. From 1987 to 2006, he was Curator of Historical Collections at SUNY Upstate Medical University. He has taught at Villanova University, Syracuse University, Upstate, and the College of Saint Rose. He is the author, editor, or translator of over 650 publications in philosophy, religion, librarianship, history, history of medicine, and nineteenth-century studies; owns Gegensatz Press; and is listed in "Who's Who in America."

C. ALLEN SPEIGHT is Associate Professor of Philosophy at Boston University. He is the author of *Hegel, Literature and the Problem of Agency* (2001) and *The Philosophy of Hegel* (2008); he is also the co-editor/translator (with Brady Bowman) of *Hegel's Heidelberg Writings* (2009) and editor of *Narrative, Philosophy and Life* (2015) and (with Sarah Eldridge) of *Goethe's "Wilhelm Meister's Apprenticeship" and Philosophy* (2020).

PETER WAKE is Professor of Philosophy at St. Edward's University in Austin, TX. He is the author of *Tragedy in Hegel's Early Theological Writings* (2014).

PAUL T. WILFORD is Assistant Professor of Political Science at Boston College. He is the co-editor (with Samuel A. Stoner) of *Kant and the Possibility of Progress* (2020) and co-editor (with Kate Havard) of *Athens, Arden, Jerusalem: Essays in Honor of Mera Flaumenhaft* (2017).

JASON MAURICE YONOVER is a dual PhD Candidate in philosophy and German studies at Johns Hopkins University. His current research primarily concerns Hegel and Spinoza on freedom and right. He is the author of articles on Kant, Salomon Maimon, Nietzsche, and others, and editor of *Spinoza's Moral and Political Philosophy in German Thought and Beyond* (forthcoming).

Index

Adorno, Theodor, 58
Aeschylus, 102, 105, 166, 188; Aristophanes and, 95n42, 146, 266; estrangement effect and, 105–8; Goethe on, 44; *Libation Bearers*, 95n42; *pathei mathos* in, 157–58. See also *Eumenides*
Aesop, 152n6, 270, 271, 277, 279n15
Aesthetics. See *Lectures on Aesthetics*
Ahlers, Rolf, 238n4
Alznauer, Mark, 1–11, 250–51, 256–58, 263n20
Antigone (character), 52–53; agency of, 56n13, 112; Hamlet and, 113, 119; Oedipus and, 7, 50, 52, 91–92; Socrates and, 96n59
Antigone (Sophocles), 17, 90–91; Barba-Kay on, 7, 80; divine/human law in, 46–55, 90, 228; family/polis and, 45–55, 90, 142, 228–29, 246–47; Goethe on, 6, 36n9, 45–48, 51–55; Hinrichs on, 6, 45–55; Ismene in, 48; Patricia Mills on, 52; George Steiner on, 93n2; Peter Wake on, 142–43
applause, 267
Aquinas, Thomas, 159
Ariosto, Ludovico, 151n2
Aristophanes, 8–9, 137–51, 191, 214; Aeschylus and, 95n42, 146, 266; characters of, 187; earnestness of, 273; historical significance of, 273–78; irony of, 195; modernity of, 11, 265–78; Nietzsche on, 170; nihilistic laughter of, 9, 157–72, 218–19; Nussbaum on, 154n32; personality of, 173n5; Schiller on, 191; Schlegel on, 268; Socrates and, 138–41, 145, 148–49, 157, 265–66, 269; Taine on, 179n62; theatricality of, 267–70, 273; use of parabasis by, 268, 277. See also Old Comedy
Aristophanes, works of: *Clouds*, 139–41, 145–47, 154n32, 164, 176n41, 269; *Frogs*, 150, 162, 266; *Knights*, 175n30; *Peace*, 269–70, 276–79
Aristotle, 97, 101–2, 106; biology of, 81, 101–2; on class structure, 64; on comedy, 1, 114nn7–8, 144; Hinrichs on, 44; on history versus poetry, 237; on household relationships, 96n45; on mimesis, 230; on slavery, 115n23; on tragic heroes, 144; unities of, 101–2; on virtuous training, 111
art: absolute, 160, 230; beauty of, 227; Christian, 118; "double doubling" of, 186–87; museumification of, 276; speculative theory of, 12n2; supreme task of, 153n20
"art-beauty" (*Kunstschöne*), 185–86
art-historical project, 270–73

283

"art-religion" (*Kunstreligion*), 8, 190; Wake on, 137, 141, 145, 149, 151; Wilford on, 159–60
artworks: individuality of, 191; "plasticity" of, 106; "spiritual," 141, 158; temporal features of, 99
Auerbach, Erich, 205n46
autonomōs (self-legislating manner), 111
autonomy, 60; Kant on, 26, 245–46; polis and, 96n59; "stoic," 110

"bad infinity," 182n98
Barba-Kay, Antón, 7, 79–92
Bates, Jennifer Ann, 132n24
Bauer, Bruno, 43
"beautiful soul," 52–53; Goethe on, 20–21, 23, 34; Jesus as, 6, 15–17, 32–35; Norton on, 41n116
Beck, Hamilton, 198
Beiner, Ronald, 183n101
Benjamin, Walter, 58, 71–72, 74–75
Bergson, Henri, 137, 148–51, 155n37, 155n43, 274
blasphemy, 158, 170
body politic, 64–66, 84–85. *See also* polis
bourgeoisie, 67, 215; as apolitical class, 84–85; comedies of, 188, 190, 196–97; emergence of, 65, 70
Bradley, A. C., 1, 154n29
Brandt, Bettina, 188
Brecht, Bertolt, 105, 114n13
Brod, Harry, 208
Bryson, Norman, 205n43

Carroll, Lewis, 175n18
Cervantes, Miguel de, 151n2
Chételat, Pierre, 238n4
chivalric love, 94n19
Christianity, 25–35, 125; Aristophanic comedy and, 157–72; divine comedy of, 167–69; Eucharist in, 35, 40n88, 41n111, 162; history of, 69; Lutheran, 118–19, 121; nihilism and, 182n96; as revealed religion, 137, 151, 168; Sermon on the Mount and, 26–27;

Sittlichkeit of, 15–17, 34; unhappy consciousness and, 167–72, 178n54, 179n67. *See also* Jesus
Chrysostom, Dionysius, 110
chthonic realm, 71, 85, 90, 91, 143
Church, Jeffrey, 10, 207–21
classical art, 99, 104, 114n11, 271–72
coercion, 60–62, 70
Collins, Ardis, 168
colonization, 115n18
Comay, Rebecca, 179n60
comedic exultation, 160–64
comedy, 8–10; Aristotle on, 144; as "art religion," 8, 137; Bergson on, 137, 148–51, 155n37, 155n43; bourgeois, 188, 190, 196–97; democracy and, 10, 162, 175n30, 273; detachment of, 148–49; divine, 167–69; experience of, 187; fate in, 69, 144–45, 188–89; French, 188, 192, 195, 203n29, 267; genres of, 1, 12n7, 70, 100–101, 195; German, 188, 196; Gottsched on, 188; humanity of, 150; humor versus, 153n16; hybrid form of, 12n7; laughter and, 140, 148–51; of Menander, 190–91, 196, 268; modern, 188–89, 191–200, 220; Napoleon on, 150; philosophy and, 157–58; of public opinion, 207–21; reconciliation in, 4–5, 197, 209; religious experience and, 137, 147, 150; satisfaction of, 176n42; Schlegel on, 2; self-consciousness in, 161; sentimental, 192; "serious," 195, 196; sociality of, 149–50; tragedy of, 164–67; tragedy versus, 69, 100–101, 141–46, 170, 188–89, 266. See also *Lustspiel*; Old Comedy
commedia dell'arte, 192
consciousness: comic, 141, 144–45, 148–51, 152n4, 155n46, 165–66; mythological, 107. *See also* unhappy consciousness
Cooper, John M., 110, 111
Courbet, Gustave, 268
critical social theory, 56, 59, 72, 74–75

cynicism, 152n9; ironic, 158, 175n26

Dante Alighieri, 183n99, 188–89, 202n13
de Boer, Karin, 240n29
de Laurentiis, Allegra, 7–8, 97–113
death: of God, 8–9, 151, 157–58, 166, 171–72, 173n4; of natural soul, 133n34
Deligiorgi, Katerina, 35, 42n119
democracy, 147, 209, 213, 219–21; comedy and, 10, 162, 175n30, 273; Dionysian festival and, 177n44
Descartes, René, 81, 119, 121
Desmond, William, 274
Dickey, Laurence, 39n73
Diderot, Denis, 188, 192, 195, 196, 198, 268
Dionysus, 150, 164, 177n44
diremption (*Entzweiung*), 82, 132n26, 172, 228
divine/human law, 87–91, 111; in *Antigone*, 46–55, 90, 228; in *Iphigenie auf Tauris*, 19–20, 22–24, 35; in Judaism, 25–27, 33
Donougho, Martin, 9, 185–200, 273–74; on Bergson, 155n37; on Hotho, 185–87, 191, 196, 200
"double doubling" of art, 186–87
Douglass, Frederick, 259, 263n26
douleia (servile status), 110, 115n23. See also master-slave dialectic
Doull, James, 183n101
Dover, J. K., 115n14
drama, 1–5, 12n7, 45, 195–98; elements of, 100–105; of Estates Assembly, 209–13; estrangement effect in, 105–8; "modern," 196; Plato on, 105–6, 153n13; poetry and, 3, 170; tragic, 97–113
Dutch genre paintings, 198–200
Dying Gaul (sculpture), 104–5

Eckermann, Peter, 6
Elements of the Philosophy of Right (Hegel), 72–73
Eleusinian mysteries, 162
eleutheria (political independence), 110

Empedocles, 82
Encyclopedia (Hegel), 195
"end-of-art" thesis, 195–98
Engels, Friedrich, 43
Entzweiung. See diremption
epic poetry, 141, 160
epigram (*Xenien*), 199, 205n43
Epitetus, 155n46
Erhard, J. B., 246
Estates Assembly, 207–13
estrangement effect, 105–8
"ethical health," 63
ethical life. See *Sittlichkeit*
Eucharist, 35, 40n88, 41n111, 162
Eumenides (Aeschylus), 6–7, 70–74, 85–86, 274; Athena in, 70, 77n50; as hybrid form, 12n7; *Natural Law* on, 58–59, 65, 69–71, 75
Eumenides (goddesses), 143
Euripides, 5, 17, 37n40, 105, 110–13; estrangement effect and, 105–8; Goethe on, 44; Hinrichs on, 44; *pathei mathos* in, 158; prologues of, 44; Socrates and, 269

Fackenheim, Emil, 183n101
Falkenstern, Rachel, 8, 117–29
family, 43; Estates Assembly and, 211; as "natural ethical community," 88; polis and, 45–55, 90, 142, 228–29, 246–47
family relationships, 79; Aristotle on, 96n45; ethical life and, 83; Goethe on, 48; Hinrichs on, 47–55; master-slave dialectic and, 84, 94n17; motherly love and, 48–50; reciprocal recognition in, 177n48; Schelling and, 83; Schiller on, 82; sexual difference and, 84, 89; types of, 47, 89. See also sibling relationships
Fanon, Frantz, 259
farce, 189, 193–95
fate, 18, 30; in comedy, 69, 144–45, 188–89; of the gods, 166; holiness and, 41n114; of Jesus, 32–33; Moirai as, 102; *Sittlichkeit* and, 177n52; in tragedy, 45, 69, 143–44, 188;

fate (cont'd)
    transcendent power of, 150; unconscious, 163; of world-historical individuals, 233, 235–36
Feuerbach, Ludwig, 98, 108, 115n15
Fiala, Andrew, 42n116
Fichte, Johann Gottlieb: on coercion, 60–62, 70; individualism of, 57, 62; irony of, 183n100; on natural law, 59–61, 70
Finn, Douglas, 5–6, 15–35
forgiveness. See reconciliation
Francis, Gavin, 202n19
Frankfurt School, 58, 74–75
Frede, Michael, 110, 111
free will, 108–13, 230
freedom, 32–34; of press, 209, 216, 241; progress of, 252–53; self-determination and, 100; self-realization of, 250; in Shakespeare's tragic heroes, 117–29; of spirit, 160, 249; state coercion and, 61; subjective, 117–19, 207; universal, 178n60; world history and, 225, 239n24
French Revolution, 57, 178n60, 200, 265n36
Freud, Sigmund, 131n11
Fried, Michael, 268
Furlotte, Wes, 6–7, 57–75

Galen of Pergamum, 81
Gardner, Sebastian, 112n2
Gattungswesen (essence of human species), 98, 108
Geiger, Ido, 262n18
gender roles, 7, 79–92; family relationships and, 47–50, 89–90; in *Iphigenie auf Tauris*, 37n25; "separate spheres" of, 47–48
ghosts, 193, 194; in *Hamlet*, 124–27, 132n27; in *Macbeth*, 124–26
Gibbon, Edward, 67
Goethe, Johann Wolfgang von, 5–6, 15–35, 210; on *Antigone*, 6, 36n9, 44–48, 51–55; ethics of, 16; on family relationships, 48; on *Hamlet*, 131n11;

Hinrichs and, 43–49, 51–55; *Macbeth* production by, 123–24; on *pathei mathos*, 44
Goethe, Johann Wolfgang von, works of: *Faust*, 44, 51; *Iphigenie auf Tauris*, 5–6, 12n7, 15–25, 34–35; *Die Leiden des jungen Werthers*, 51; *Morphology*, 82; *West-östlicher Divan*, 274; *Wilhelm Meisters Lehrjahre*, 34, 131n11, 197
Goldhill, Simon, 48
Gottsched, Johann Christoph, 188
Graecomania, 104

Habermas, Jürgen, 208
Hamann, Johann Georg, 81
Hamlet, 8, 236; Antigone and, 113, 119; death of, 128; ghost and, 124–27, 132n27; Goethe on, 131n11; Oedipus and, 103, 119; Schlegel on, 131n11
Harris, H. S., 150, 152n4, 154n32, 155n46
Harrison, Roger, 41n113
Hebing, Niklas, 192
Hegel, G. W. F. *See specific works*
Hegel, Karl, 98
Heidegger, Martin, 44, 172
Heimann, Adolf, 191, 195, 198
Heneghan, Fiacha D., 10–11, 225–37
Henrich, Dieter, 258
Herder, Johann Gottfried von, 81
Herodotus, 107, 113, 278
Hesiod, 98, 278
Hinrichs, Hermann Friedrich Wilhelm: on Aristotle, 44; Goethe and, 43–48; on Sophocles, 6, 45–55
Hippel, T. G., 9, 198–200, 204n38, 204n41, 274
Hirt, Aloys, 185–86
historiography, 113
History of Philosophy (Hegel), 158, 191
Hobbes, Thomas, 60, 108, 109
Hokenson, Jan, 191
Hölderlin, Friedrich, 2, 17; on *Antigone*, 93n2; on sexual difference, 7, 82
Homer, 98, 111, 166, 278; *Iliad*, 141, 179n62; Socrates's criticism of, 157
hospitality (*Gastrecht*), 24

Hotho, Heirich Gustav, 98, 114n2, 151n2, 266–67; Donougho on, 185–87, 191, 196, 200
Houlgate, Stephen, 35, 38n59, 42n121, 226; on tragedy, 229, 246, 262n15; Yonovar on, 253
hubris, 109, 166
Huddleston, Andrew, 174n7, 274
human law. *See* divine/human law
humor, 164, 274; comedy and, 153n16; of Falstaff, 154; gallows, 144; laughter versus, 153n16; "objective," 197
hypocrisy, 161, 190

Icelandic sagas, 49
Identity Philosophy, 57
individualism: abstract, 57, 62
individuality: of artworks, 191; "beautiful," 186; contingent, 190; subjective, 202n13
infinity, 182n98, 186
Iphigenia (character), 15–25, 34–35; agency of, 18, 22, 112–13; reconciliation by, 6, 16, 19, 21
Iphigenie auf Tauris (Goethe), 5–6, 12n7, 15–25, 34–35
irony, 132n18, 177n44; of Aristophanes, 195; Fichtean, 183n100; modern/romantic, 155n39; of Schlegel, 183n100; Socratic, 149, 155n39, 157, 170
Isocrates, 116n24

Jaeschke, Walter, 104, 192
James I of England, 123, 132n19
Jean Paul (Richter), 2, 198, 204n39
Jena, Battle of (1806), 231–32
Jesus, 26–27; as beautiful soul, 6, 15–17, 32–35; mocking of, 140, 153n15. *See also* Christianity
Joerden, Jan, 260n6
Judaism, 25–27, 33, 39n77, 275
Julius Caesar, 233, 236
jus civile/jus naturale, 111

Kant, Immanuel, 47, 57, 62; on autonomy, 26, 245–46; ethics of, 16, 17, 27, 32; on peace, 63; on revolutionary action, 256–58, 260nn4–6, 261n11; on sexual difference, 79, 82, 84
Kant, Immanuel, works of: *Anthropology*, 79, 84, 94n19; *Critique of Judgment*, 82; *Critique of Practical Reason*, 86; *Religion within the Boundaries of Mere Reason*, 26, 39n78
Kaufmann, Walter, 5–6, 15–17, 34–35, 36n9, 37n40
Korsgaard, Christine, 241, 245, 260nn4–5
Kottman, Paul, 130n8
Kraft, Stephan, 192, 195–96
Küng, Hans, 159

Lauer, Quentin, 176n32
laughter, 140, 171, 187, 218–19; Aquinas on, 159; Bergson on, 148–51; nihilism of, 157–72
Lectures on Aesthetics (Hegel), 3, 98; on Aristophanes, 158, 190, 191, 269, 273; on modern comedy, 192; on public education, 212; on world history, 227, 229
Lectures on Fine Art (Hegel), 11, 80, 144–48, 151n2
Lectures on Philosophy of Religion (Hegel), 171, 275
Lectures on the History of Philosophy (Hegel), 266
Lectures on the Philosophy of History (Hegel), 98
Lessing, Gotthold Ephraim, 17, 175n18, 176n43; comedies of, 188, 192, 195
love, 26–27, 83, 140; chivalric, 94n19; motherly, 48–50; unity of, 41n111
Luft, Eric von der, 5, 6, 43–55
Lustspiel (light comedy), 9–10, 188–89, 192, 195; farce and, 193; Menander and, 196
Luther, Martin, 118–19, 121
Luxemburg, Rosa, 259

MacLeod, Catriona, 93n14
Manent, Pierre, 95n29

Manet, Édouard, 268
Marcus Aurelius, 155n46
Marcuse, Herbert, 58, 74–75
marriage. *See* family relationships
Marx, Karl, 43, 259; Feuerbach and, 115n15; on private property, 68, 74–75
master-slave dialectic, 62, 65; Aristotle on, 96n45; *douleia* and, 110, 115n23; sexual difference and, 84, 90, 94n17, 94n21. *See also* slavery
McCarney, Joseph, 256
Menander, 190–91, 196, 268
Menke, Christoph, 96n62
Merleau-Ponty, Maurice, 92
Michelet, Jules, 95n44
Miller, A. V., 179n67
Mills, Patricia, 52
mimesis, 140, 148, 230
Mnemosyne, 113
Moirai, 102
Molière, 192, 195, 196, 203n29, 267
Montaigne, Michel de, 81
Montesquieu, 208
More, Thomas, 171, 182n93
Moretti, Franco, 197, 204n33
Moyar, Dean, 258, 264n36
Murillo, Bartolomé Esteban, 199–200
Murray, Gilbert, 152n9
museums, 276
mythological consciousness, 107

Naas, Michael, 152n7
Napoleon Bonaparte, 150, 231–33, 236, 240n27
natural law, 188; Fichte on, 59–61, 70
Natural Law (Hegel), 6–7, 57–60, 70–75; on Aeschylus, 58–59, 65, 69–75; Benjamin on, 71–72; on comedy, 69; Schelling and, 73–74; on sexual difference, 83–85
natural religion, 159
natural soul, 133n34
necessity, right of, 258
New Comedy, 190–91, 196, 268
Nietzsche, Friedrich, 140, 172, 179n63;

on Aristophanes, 170; *Birth of Tragedy*, 113n1; on Euripides, 269
Nightingale, A. W., 270, 279n10
nihilism, 9, 182n96; of Aristophanic comedy, 157–72, 218–19
Norton, Robert, 34; on beautiful soul, 41n116; on Pietism, 39n73
Novakovic, Andreja, 263n29
novels, 101, 197, 199, 204n34
Nussbaum, Martha, 154n32

Oedipus, 52, 53, 91–92, 153n24; agency of, 112; Antigone and, 7, 50, 52, 91–92; Hamlet and, 103, 119
Oedipus Rex (Sophocles), 51, 81, 91–92, 107, 131n14
Old Comedy, 268; Donougho on, 189–91, 195, 196; subjectivity in, 214; Wake on, 137, 146, 148, 151n2. *See also* Aristophanes
Old/Right Hegelians, 43
one-sidedness, 226, 239n20; fixity and, 118–22; Iphigenia and, 36n9
Outlines of the Philosophy of Right (Hegel), 98

Page, Carl, 172n3
painting, 268; Dutch, 198–200
Paolucci, Ann, 154n29
parabasis, 268, 277
pathei mathos, 158–59, 229
pathos, 142–43; divine, 144, 154n32
peace, 54, 67, 70–72; goddess of, 270, 276–78; "perpetual," 63
Peloponnesian War, 147, 152n9, 214, 276
penal law, 29, 38n41
Pericles, 277
Peters, Julia, 226, 235, 238n10
Phenomenology of Spirit (Hegel), 99, 151, 227, 232; Aristophanic comedy in, 8–9, 137–38, 145, 148, 158, 173n5; beautiful soul in, 34–35; on comedy, 152n4, 190; master-slave dialectic in, 62, 65, 84; *Natural Law* essay and, 58; on revealed religion, 8–9, 137, 151, 168; sexual

288 Index

difference in, 79–81, 84, 90–91; on unhappy consciousness, 9, 167–68
Phidias, 277–78
Philosophy of Nature (Hegel), 89
Philosophy of Right (Hegel), 72–73, 98, 250–52; on prepolitical stage, 106–7; on press freedom, 209, 216, 241; on public education, 207–21; on sexual difference, 81, 91; on world history, 225, 230–31, 234, 258
Philosophy of Spirit, 79, 92, 94n17
Pietism, 39n73
Pindar, 138
Pinkard, Terry, 231, 238n3
Pippin, Robert B., 130n5, 201n2, 268; on "double doubling" of art, 186–87; on unhappy consciousness, 180n70
Plato, 92, 111, 148, 179n62; on class structure, 64; on comedy, 157; on drama, 105–6, 153n13; Hinrichs on, 44; on poetry, 140, 153n13, 265; on vision, 186, 198, 201nn2–3
Plato, works of: *Phaedo*, 144, 154n27; *Phaedrus*, 138; *Philebus*, 157; *Republic*, 140, 153n13, 157, 265, 266; *Symposium*, 138, 140, 150, 157, 265–66; *Theaetetus*, 138–39
Plautus, 100, 114n7, 196, 267
pleroma, 28
Plutarch, 140, 145
poetry: drama and, 3, 170; epic, 141; Greek genres of, 141; history versus, 237; Plato on, 140, 153n13, 265
Pöggeler, Otto, 94n24
polis, 96n59; Christian, 88; family and, 45–55, 90, 142, 228–29, 246–47; in *Iliad*, 141
political parties, 210
Potts, Alexander, 205n46
prehistorical period, 98, 106, 107; sexual difference in, 80–81, 84
press freedom, 209, 216, 241
private life, 84; "universal", 66–67
private property, 58, 66–68, 71, 73
proairesis (choice), 110, 111
Protestantism, 182n96

public education, 207–21; comic elements of, 213; Estates Assembly and, 209–13

Rancière, Jacques, 200
Raupach, Ernst, 9, 192–95, 197
reconciliation (*Versöhnung*), 15–35, 75, 85, 143; in comedy, 4–5, 197, 209; in *Oedipus at Colonus*, 153n24; "instruments" of, 58; in *Iphigenie auf Tauris*, 6, 16, 19, 21; knowledge of necessity and, 68; Schiller on, 74; in tragedy, 4, 229, 274–75
religion of art. *See* "art religion"
religious experience, 176n32; comedy and, 5, 137, 141–47, 150
revealed religion, 8–9, 137, 151, 168, 181n79
revolutionary action, 11, 241–42, 246–59; governing after, 261n11; Kant on, 242–46, 256–58, 260nn4–6, 261n11; Searle of, 262n19; Spinoza on, 243
Revven, Heidi M., 56n13
Richter, Jean Paul, 2, 198, 204n39
right of necessity, 258
Roche, Mark W., 12n5, 174n7
Roman Empire, 65–68, 91, 111, 218–19
romantic art, 99, 104, 114n11, 122, 272
Romantism (German), 119, 191
Rorty, Richard, 183n100
Rousseau, Jean-Jacques, 63, 108; on second nature, 98; on sexual difference, 81; on slavery, 115n23; on state activity, 76n17
Rutter, Benjamin, 204n34

Sallis, John, 154n27
Saphir, Moritz, 192, 193
satire, 190–91, 213, 218–19
Schaeffer, Jean-Marie, 112n2
Schauspiel (stage play), 36n10, 100, 190, 262n14
Schelling, Friedrich Wilhelm Joseph von, 2, 73–74; Identity Philosophy of, 57; on peace, 63; on sexual difference, 7, 80, 82–83, 89

Schiller, Friedrich von, 8, 212; on aesthetics, 42n116, 93n14, 219–20; on Aristophanes, 191; on sexual difference, 82; tragedies of, 122

Schiller, Friedrich von, works of: *Aesthetic Letters*, 74; *Grace and Dignity*, 82; *Letters on the Aesthetic Education of Man*, 82; *Macbeth* translation by, 123–24; *Wilhelm Tell*, 132n23

Schlegel, August Wilhelm von, 132n18, 183n100; on comedy, 2; on *Hamlet*, 131n11; on novels, 204n34; on parabasis, 268

Schlegel, Friedrich von, 132n18

Science of Logic (Hegel), 102

Screech, M. A., 153n15

sculpture, 104–6, 163, 187, 271; Herder on, 81; painting and, 199

Searle, John, 262

Segal, Erich, 187

self-conscious spirit, 159–61

self-destruction: of particularity, 214–16; self-expression and, 126–28

self-determination: freedom and, 100; Protestantism and, 118–19, 121; self-reflection and, 122–26

self-estrangement, 105–8

Sermon on the Mount, 26–27

sexism: of personification, 80

sexual difference, 51, 79–92. See also gender roles

Shakespeare, William, 8, 194; Falstaff and, 154n29, 191; Molière and, 192; tragic heros of, 117–29; villains of, 133n35

Shakespeare, William, works of: *Hamlet*, 81, 124–28, 132n27, 236; *King Lear*, 120, 121, 193; *Macbeth*, 120, 122–29, 132n24; *Romeo and Juliet*, 119–20, 130n8; *The Tempest*, 119–20

Shapiro, Gary, 152n3, 154n25

sibling relationships, 4, 88–90; Aristotle on, 96n45; Hinrichs on, 47–50; in *Iphigenia in Tauris*, 19, 20, 22. See also family relationships

Siep, Ludwig, 167

simile, 118, 126–28, 133n32

Sittlichkeit (ethical life), 17, 48–49, 54, 83–87, 102; *absoluten*, 59, 62–66, 75; of Christianity, 16, 34; de Laurentiis on, 98; fate and, 177n52; religious consciousness and, 160; self and, 165, 177n45

slavery, 65–67; *douleia* and, 110, 115n23; in Roman Empire, 65–66; Rousseau on, 115n23. See also master-slave dialectic

Socrates, 97, 150, 176n41; Antigone and, 96n59; Aristophanes and, 138–41, 145, 148–49, 157, 265–66, 269; *daimon* of, 111; dialectic of, 155n32; Euripides and, 269; irony of, 149, 155n39, 157, 170; Lessing on, 176n43; on mimesis, 148; on philosophy's aim, 144; Plutarch on, 140, 145; Strauss on, 170–71

Solger, Karl, 2

sophistry, 140, 172, 273; in Aristophanes, 146, 147, 278; irony and, 183n100

Sophocles, 102, 105, 119; Aristophanes and, 146; estrangement effect and, 105–7; Hinrichs on, 6, 45–55; *pathei mathos* in, 157–58, 229

Sophocles, works of: *Oedipus at Colonus*, 153n24, 274–75; *Oedipus Rex*, 51, 81, 91–92, 107, 131n14; *Philoctetes*, 274. See also *Antigone*

speculative knowledge, 181n79

Speight, Allen, 175n24, 191, 197, 201n4; on Aristophanic modernity, 11, 265–78; on unmasking, 202n16

Spinoza, Benedict de, 68, 243

Spirit of Christianity and Its Fate (Hegel), 6, 15–17, 25–35, 125

Steiner, George, 93

Stirner, Max, 43

Stoicism, 110, 165, 176n36

Strauss, Leo, 170–71, 182nn90–93

Strong, Tracy, 172n4

subjectivity: in Aristophanic comedy,

214; doubling of, 187; finite, 133n34; framing rise of, 267–70; in Shakespearean tragedy, 117–18; substantiality and, 100–101
sublation (*Aufhebung*), 75
sublime, 34, 41n114, 91, 275–76
suicide, 128; aesthetics of, 31–32; in Euripides's *Iphigenia at Aulis*, 112–13; in Sophocles's *Antigone*, 47, 53
supersession (*Aufgehobene*), 68
Sussman, David, 241, 245, 260nn4–5
symbolic art, 99, 103–4, 114n11, 271–72
System of Ethical Life (Hegel), 83

Taine, Hippolite, 179n62
Taylor, Charles, 227
Terence, 196, 267
Thales, 138, 150, 152n6
theodicy, 11, 225, 236, 238n4
Thucydides, 113
Tieck, Ludwig, 132n18, 192, 203n24
tragedy, 5–8, 143–44, 160–61; of the absolute, 58; of comedy, 164–67; comedy versus, 69, 100–101, 144–46, 170, 188–89, 266; dramatic logic in, 45; epic poetry and, 141, 160; estrangement effect in, 105–8; of "Ethical Order," 80; on "ethical plane," 59, 65, 70, 71, 75; experience of, 226–29, 231–33, 239n16; fate in, 45, 69, 143–44, 188; genres of, 1, 7–8, 12n7, 100–101; Goethe's theory of, 44–46, 52–55; Hinrichs on, 6, 44–48; Houlgate on, 246; hybrid forms of, 12n7, 100, 114n7; logic of, 226, 229–30, 234–35; in *Natural Law*, 58–59, 65, 69–71; of recognition, 88; reconciliation in, 4, 229, 274–75; revolutionary action and, 241–42, 246–59; sexual difference and, 79–92; world history and, 225–37
tragic heroes, 109, 226; Aristotle on, 144; "sculptural" quality of, 106; in Shakespeare, 8, 117–29;

world-historical individuals and, 233–36, 246, 248
tragic poetry, 141–44
tragicomedy, 12n7, 100, 114n7
Trauerspiel. *See* tragedy

unhappy consciousness, 9, 158, 168–72, 178n54; Miller on, 179n67; Pippin on, 180n70; Strauss on, 182n91; Verene on, 182n98
unities, Aristotelian, 101–2
universal freedom, 178n60
universal law, 29
"universal private life," 66–67
utopianism, comic elements of, 150

Verene, Donald, 182n98
Vieweg, Klaus, 258
vision, Plato on, 186, 198, 201nn2–3
von Rumohr, Carl Friedrich, 199, 205n44

Wagner, Richard, 50
Wake, Peter, 8–9, 39n73, 137–51; on Eucharist, 41n111; on in-group dynamics, 42n116
Weber, Max, 166, 183n101
White, Hayden, 154n28, 274
Wilford, Paul, 9, 157–72
Williams, Robert R.., 97, 113n1, 132n25
Winckelmann, Johann, 17, 205n44
witches, 132n19; in *Macbeth*, 122–27, 132n24
Wood, Allen, 251, 254–58
world-historical individuals, 11, 106–7, 225–27, 231–36; fate of, 233, 235–36; Napoleon as, 231–33, 236, 240n27; philosophy of history and, 248–51; revolutionary actions of, 241–59; right of revolutionary action of, 241–42, 246–59; self-perception of, 254–55; tragic heroes and, 233–36, 246, 248
world history, 10–11, 91, 225–37, 264n30; casualties of, 235–37;

world history (*cont'd*)
    freedom of spirit in, 249; power of spirit in, 258; tragic experiences of, 227–29, 231–33; tragic logic of, 226, 229–30, 234–35
world-spirit (*Weltgeist*), 168
Xenien (epigram), 199, 205n43

Xenophon, 116n24

Yonover, Jason M., 11, 241–59
Young/Left Hegelians, 43

Zuckert, Rachel, 245–46

www.ingramcontent.com/pod-product-compliance
Ingram Content Group UK Ltd.
Pitfield, Milton Keynes, MK11 3LW, UK
UKHW041927140426
5217IPUK00014B/347